Advance Reviews of
Cultivating Heart and Character:

"*Cultivating Heart and Character* is one of the most comprehensive and practical guidebooks to renewing character and character-shaping institutions. No one can read this volume without concluding that the central challenge of our time is reviving the ethical foundations of freedom by encouraging the widest possible embrace of personal responsibility."

Don Eberly
Director, Civil Society Project

"*Cultivating Heart and Character* is a clear, concise, comprehensive review of what character education is, the benefits for youth and society and the resources available to teach it. It is critical reading for every school administrator who desires their graduates to succeed in life and love and contribute towards a saner, safer, more loving world."

Seth Eisenberg
President and CEO, PAIRS International, Inc.

"With an unusual a blend of East and West it comes down squarely on the side of the family and of the fundamental virtues while bringing the student through a very comprehensive overview of the themes of love, character, family and sexuality."

Patrick F. Fagan, Ph.D.
William H. G. FitzGerald Fellow in Family and Culture Issues
The Heritage Foundation

"For family educators and parents interested in values based education, *Cultivating Heart and Character* is a comprehensive, clear and articulate guide through the morass of complicated family issues facing our society."

Terry D. Hargrave, Ph.D.
West Texas A&M University
Author, *The Essential Humility of Marriage:
Honoring the Third Identity in Couple Therapy*

"Nothing is more important than character education for both personal and social good. *Cultivating Heart and Character* makes the case compellingly, with argument and statistics, and in addition offers practical guidance to parents, schools and the community. This book is an important contribution to a growing national consciousness. It should be read by everyone, for their own sake and for the love of children."

Harville Hendrix, Ph.D.
Author, *Getting the Love You Want*

"If you are a parent, educator or youth specialist concerned with character education (and you should be!), then buy this book. Filled with practical and insightful information, this book is sure to strengthen your ability to help children and youth develop the skills and knowledge they need to develop into persons of character."

Wade F. Horn, Ph.D.
President, The National Fatherhood Initiative

"*Cultivating Heart and Character* is an important contribution to the field. In addition to all its other virtues, it breaks new ground in at least three ways: It takes an international and cross-cultural perspective on character education; it places love at the center of character development, and it deepens our understanding of character development as a partnership between the home, school and community."

Howard Kirschenbaum
Frontier Professor of School, Family and Community Relations, University of Rochester

"Of all the books on character education today, this book is clearly one of the most comprehensive in its approach. Drawing upon a wide range of scholarship, the authors make the case that character education must take place not only in the schools, but also in the home and community. The insightful analysis, well-researched rationale, and comprehensive approach to character education all make this an eminently useful contribution to the field. Teachers, parents and community members alike should find *Cultivating Heart and Character* to be an indispensable source for the development of thoughtful and effective character education programs."

James S. Leming, Ph.D.
Southern Illinois University

"The book does an excellent job of delineating the foundations of good character, and then explaining how schools, parents and communities must work together to develop good character. There is a wide range of information provided—including attention paid to the current topics of conflict resolution, drug and alcohol abuse prevention, abstinence, as well as a unique look at various levels of relationships. This book provides a much-needed framework for comprehensive character development that spans a lifetime."

Lynn Lisy-Macan
Assistant Superintendent, Niskayuna Central Schools, Niskayuna, New York

"An excellent resource for parents, educators, members of the business community and anyone interested in overcoming our national crisis of character."

Sandy N. McDonnell
Chairman, The Character Education Partnership
Chairman Emeritus, McDonnell Douglas

"*Cultivating Heart and Character* is a rich compendium of state-of-the-art programs and research in abstinence education, character education, and marriage and family education; its analysis of the important interrelationship of these areas is particularly insightful.

"Healthy, loving relationships are key to happy and productive lives—and to solving many of our most devastating social problems—but historically adults have dropped the ball when it comes to teaching our youth the essential social and emotional skills. It's a whole lot easier to teach children to walk and talk, to drive a car and even to use a computer than it is to teach them how to develop strong personal ideals and to love well. But we've got to get our priorities straight. *Cultivating Heart and Character* will be a very valuable resource for families, schools and communities as we collaborate in this movement. Let's get going!"

Nancy McLaren
Co-director, The Loving Well Project

"*Cultivating Heart and Character: Educating for Life's Most Essential Goals* represents a monumental move toward whole learning based upon character development. It provides a comprehensive set of methods and strategies linking teachers, families and communities to teach children the rich value and potential of moral, ethical and intellectual character development. Devine, Seuk and Wilson are to be commended for this great work."

Thomasina M. Portis
Founder and CEO, Portis and Associates, Inc.

"This book offers a comprehensive and carefully researched diagnosis of what our problems are and what parents and teachers can do to help children forge strong characters. The authors provide a mix of sound principles, practical solutions and vivid examples. It is a very impressive book and should be widely read."

Kevin Ryan, Ph.D.
Founding Director, Center for the Advancement of Ethics and Character, Boston University
Author, *Reclaiming Our Schools*

"It made me think of the song, *MacArthur Park*: 'Someone left the cake out in the rain... and we'll never find that recipe again.' Marriage and family seem to be melting down around us, but this book gives us the recipe. It gives step-by-step instructions about what to do, how to do it and the research about why to do it. A guide for parents, teachers, kids, clergy, all of us who care, about how to rebuild trust, love, commitment, intergenerational loyalties, responsibility, character and confidence. We can remake the cake, and decorate it with renewed hope in ourselves and our institutions. A great contribution. A workhorse of a book. Beautifully written."

Diane Sollee, M.S.W.
Founder and Director, Coalition for Marriage,
Family and Couples Education

"This is a terrific resource in character education—valuable for teachers, families and individuals. It's thorough and well researched, yet practical and easy to read. It's also full of useful ideas. You'll find yourself turning to it again and again."

Hal Urban
Author, *Life's Greatest Lessons*

"*Cultivating Heart and Character* represents the best effort in presenting a comprehensive approach to character education and a well written call to action on the important role that schools, communities and families can have in positively shaping the lives of our children. It also offers a blueprint on how we as educators, community representatives and parents can begin taking the needed steps in helping children develop habits of the heart and mind. Every page is informative and perhaps best of all, appealing to our common sense. If I could recommend one book of common reading for parents, educators and youth workers, this would be it. It will remain a valuable resource for years to come."

Philip Vincent, Ph.D.
President, Character Development Group

"I give my highest endorsement to *Cultivating Heart and Character*. The authors present a well-developed comprehensive approach to character education, and provide practical examples for effective home/community/school approaches only briefly mentioned by other authors. I've put it on my shortlist of recommended readings to educators, parents and graduate students!"

Mary Williams, Ed.D.
Co-founder and Co-director, International Center for Character Education, University of San Diego

Cultivating Heart and Character

Educating for Life's Most Essential Goals

EDITORS
Tony Devine, Joon Ho Seuk
and Andrew Wilson

Character Development Publishing
Chapel Hill, North Carolina

Cover design by Jennifer Fleischmann

Library of Congress Catalog 00-108408
ISBN 1-892056-15-1

Character Development Publishing
P.O. Box 9211
Chapel Hill, NC 27515-9211

Phone (919) 967-2110
Fax (919) 967-2139
E-mail respect96@aol.com

To Our Parents

Acknowledgements

Many have contributed directly and indirectly to the development of the ideas presented in *Cultivating Heart and Character*. We are grateful both to those who provided inspirational threads as well as to those who helped us to see the vision of the greater tapestry to which they belong.

We are indebted to the many family and education experts, researchers, teachers, authors and community leaders who have guided our thinking and bolstered our ideas. Mary Aranha, Marvin Berkowitz, Pat Born, Yiyun Chen, Matt Davison, Cheryl Hogg, Howard Kirschenbaum, Lynn Lisy-Macan, Linda McKay, Tomasina Portis, Kevin Ryan and Lori Wiley graciously gave of their time to review the first draft of this text. We are particularly appreciative for the careful attention that Thomas Lickona has given to this manuscript. Diane Sollee and her colleagues in the marriage and family professions have been invaluable resources, as have Joe McIlhaney, Joshua Mann, Richard Panzer and Rich Tompkin in the field of sexuality education. There are others too numerous to name who gave of their time and wisdom. To them too we express our heartfelt gratitude.

We recognize our colleagues in the International Educational Foundation with whom we have worked closely over the years. Robert Beebe, Jack Corley, Alice Huang, Hui-chen Liu, Jacques Marion and Tom Phillips spent countless hours helping us refine the ideas and find vivid examples. Ittetsu Aoki and his associates provided practical assistance.

We are thankful to Dixon Smith and Philip Vincent of Character Development Publishing for their encouragement and to Alan Saunders for his investment. Nadine Andre, William Haines and Mark Turner made early contributions. Jennifer Fleischmann, Jonathan Gullery and Istvan Sleder gave of their talents for the graphics and layout. Humberto Avila, William Hilbert, Yuri Kaminsky, Nita McDonough, Prince Tambi and Sasha Yanitskaya facilitated this project in countless ways.

Finally, we honor our families, who supported us through long meetings and exhausting writing schedules. They, as well as our friends, neighbors and colleagues, near and far, also provided us with heartwarming anecdotes, critical reflections and personal experiences that have enriched this volume.

Contents

Foreword

"Parents want for their kids materially, but they don't give kids a purpose... something to live their lives for."
—A 17-year-old boy

"We've been doing character education for five years... where do we go from here?"
—Teacher at a character education conference

A CHAPTER IN A HIGH SCHOOL TEXT BEARS THE INTRIGUING TITLE, "The Goal of Life: Our Happiness." The chapter observes that everyone wants to be happy and asks: What is it that truly makes us happy?

The chapter goes on to tell the story of Boethius, a very learned man of the sixth century. Boethius held high rank in the government of Rome and enjoyed the confidence of the king. He was, however, falsely accused of disloyalty, condemned without a trial, imprisoned, and finally executed. During his long imprisonment, he gave a great deal of thought to how insecurely we hold the good things of this life: position, the favor of persons in high places, even the devotion of declared friends. What, he wondered, is perfect happiness—the perfect good that alone can completely and forever satisfy and quiet all our desires?

I thought of the story of Boethius when I read *Cultivating Heart and Character* because this is a book that asks the broadest and deepest questions about human existence: What makes for a meaningful and fulfilling life? What do human beings need to be happy? And how do we educate—in our homes, schools, and communities—so as to support people at all points of human development in their quest for meaning and authentic happiness?

Secular character education by definition can't teach any of the traditional religious answers to questions like these. But are there at least some answers to these basic questions about life that all persons could agree on, regardless of culture or belief? Are there some life goals whose importance for human happiness can be universally acknowledged?

Cultivating Heart and Character answers yes. It argues persuasively that there are at least three such universally valid goals of life: (1) attaining maturity of character; (2) engaging in loving relationships; and (3) contributing meaningfully to the lives of others. In reality, as the authors acknowledge, not all people make these goals a priority. But the desire to achieve them is latent in the human personality—part of our human nature. When we pursue these goals, and thereby lead a life of virtue, we are living in harmony with our deepest selves. All persons, whatever their beliefs, can recognize this core truth. We can't be happy unless we're good.

Why is it important for educators, especially character educators, to address life goals such as these? This book's authors correctly observe that without a sustaining educational philosophy that includes a vision of life, character educators may soon run out of steam. It's been wisely said, "There is nothing so practical as a good theory." If character education is to avoid becoming a superficial activity and passing trend, it needs an adequate theory of the human person, one that asks, "Why bother to develop a good character? What does it have to do with the meaning of life? With happiness?"

Questions like these, the authors point out, are especially crucial in adolescence, when the question of the meaning of life becomes a major concern. Teens need to find a purpose for their lives and to become authors of their own "life story." They need help in avoiding the seductions of a media culture that tells them the purpose of life is maximizing their pleasure, especially their sexual pleasure. Parents and teachers, by lifting up the three life goals (personal character development, loving relationships, and making a contribution) as an explicit moral framework for life, can help young people orient to what is truly fulfilling and become motivated to work toward those worthwhile goals.

This groundbreaking volume advances the theory and practice of character education in many important ways. Besides emphasizing a life-goals framework, it argues that cultivating the heart (our power to love) and conscience (the rational guide to right and wrong) are the two central tasks of character development. It helps us to see that the family is the first school of love and that a good school, one that nurtures continuing growth in character, is like a good family. It argues compellingly that the partnership of home, school, and community is the "central axis" of successful character education. All of these ideas are richly illustrated with concrete examples from schools, families, and communities, East and West. Indeed, one of the book's distinguishing contributions is its cross-cultural dimension, reflecting the many years of diligent educational work its authors have done in countries around the world.

As a logical extension of its theme that love and familial relationships are at the center of character development, *Cultivating Heart and Character* gives careful attention to educating for marriage and educating for responsible sexual love. Social historians have observed that the declining well-being of children in many nations today is directly linked to the decline of marriage and that to fail to prepare the next generation for the responsibilities and commitments of marriage and parenting is to commit cultural suicide. Similarly, historians have documented the destabilizing and destructive effects of a sexual revolution that severed the link between sex and commitment. How can we help our children to succeed in forming happy and lasting marriages and to believe that saving the ultimate intimacy for the ultimate commitment is consistent with their highest hopes and values? Drawing on reasoned argument, real-life stories, empirical studies, and illustrative curricula, the authors offer the most comprehensive case to date for making marriage education and character-based sex education an integral part of the character education enterprise.

"Our life task," the authors conclude, "is to fulfill our humanity, and our humanity is defined by our capacity to love and to live in accord with our conscience." *Cultivating Heart and Character* thus expands the scope of character education to encompass the whole of life. It tells us why the forms of love that have their origin in family remain important throughout our lives. It anchors character education in the universal desire for happiness. And it gives us tested ways to translate all these theoretical insights into effective practice. There is nothing like this far-reaching book in the character education literature. It will, I believe, be of great value to any reader, whether you come to the issue of character as a teacher, a parent, a youth worker, a policy maker, or simply someone wanting to craft a good life.

Thomas Lickona
Author, *Educating for Character*

To the Reader

IF YOU HAVE PICKED UP THIS BOOK, YOU ARE PROBABLY CONCERNED about character, youth, family life and society. So are we—that is why we wrote this book. Here you will find stories, thoughts and the shared desires of many individuals, including teachers, parents and students searching for a more integrated education that nourishes not just the intellect but the heart as well—an education that equips people to live fulfilling and useful lives. The content reflects extensive research and dialogue as well as the assistance of educators and experts from a variety of backgrounds and from all around the world. These ideas have been presented and discussed in hundreds of national and international conferences, schools, and meetings involving practitioners in education, youth development and family issues as well as community leaders and social workers.

Our views rely on three simple premises. First, the natural desire to love and be loved is a central motivating force in the development of character. Loving relationships create an optimal environment for human fulfillment. Hence, the cultivation of the heart is central to human fulfillment and a necessary part of education. An education in the ideals, norms, relational capacities and character traits required for altruistic love helps people live lives of moral integrity, spontaneity and beauty. It enables them to live a good life in community with others.

A second premise is that character development is integrally linked with the search for meaning in life. Young people learn and retain values in light of their sense of identity and purpose in life. When exhorted to be respectful, responsible, caring, etc., they ask, "Why?" We address this need for larger meaning by focusing on three life aspirations or goals: 1) individual maturity, 2) competence and satisfaction in personal relationships (especially familial ones) and 3) to make a valuable and lasting contribution beyond oneself to society. These life goals are universal and self-evident. Achieving them epitomizes a life well lived and provides great satisfaction to oneself and others.

The realization of life goals takes place in the family, school and community, and requires the continual cultivation of the heart and character as a lifelong process. Such a perspective necessitates a comprehensive approach to character development from childhood to adulthood. Therefore, this book includes chapters on marriage, family and community as well as school wide character education.

You may want to use this text to enhance a particular discipline of character and relational enrichment, or simply to broaden your own understanding. Our aim was to provide practical guidance for teachers, parents, and counselors or anyone involved in making a difference in their own lives and those of others. The spectrum of questions and issues include:

* Why does character education need to be a priority in schools and families?
* How do natural principles inform moral growth and healthy relationships?
* How is meaning in life related to character development?
* In what ways are family roles important for emotional and character development?
* How does training in relational skills and character help build and sustain a meaningful marriage?
* What are the aptitudes that make for effective parenting?
* How can schools and parents forge viable partnerships in the raising of children?
* What is the role of character development in addressing common challenges facing youth: substance abuse, sexual health and conflict resolution?
* How can various agencies and institutions in the community cooperate with parents and schools to give young people a consistent message of good character?

To encompass this range of topics, the book is divided into three parts:

Part I offers a discussion of character education, covering historical, theoretical and practical aspects. Section 1 surveys the recent history of moral education, makes a case for universal values, and defines key educational concepts such as heart, conscience and life goals.

Section 2 gives a broad description of the process of character development in the three dimensions of personal growth, relationships and civic contribution. Section 3 utilizes these three dimensions as a framework for the comprehensive integration of universal values in character education initiatives. Here are methods, anecdotes from schools and teachers, and elements of successful programs for developing individual character, a caring school ethos, and partnerships with parents and the community.

Part II sketches a portrait of moral growth through familial roles, namely, those of child, sibling, spouse and parent. The chapters in Section 4 render each role as a "sphere of love," which offers unique opportunities for the expansion of heart and conscience that remain important in adult moral development. Section 5 confronts modern culture's ubiquitous confusion about marriage and family norms by first addressing concerns about the efficacy of marriage. Next, the support that educators can give to marriage is explored through discussions of marriage preparation, marriage enrichment and parenting education. The feasibility and desirability of a lifelong marital relationship is supported with character-based insights and proven relational skills for sustaining love. Authentic narratives and strategies from marriage and parenting experts sketch the connection between character and family functioning.

Part III tackles the most urgent challenges facing young people—sexuality, drug abuse and dealing with conflict. Written with teenagers in mind but especially for the adults who guide them, Section 6 sketches a positive ethic of love and sexuality, founded upon principles of character development and fulfillment in family relationships. This same perspective underlies Section 7, which also discusses drug abuse prevention and conflict resolution. Research has shown that negative behaviors tend to be clustered where character formation is weak and protective family influences are absent. Here are valuable insights that can be incorporated into already existing character education initiatives, as well as useful guidelines for designing and implementing curricula with the cultivation of heart and character as a guiding principle. Parents, too, can find greater confidence to deepen the dialogue with their children, supporting them to successfully resist high-risk behaviors that are detours on the road to personal maturity.

Finally, this book represents a collaborative dialogue; we wrote it as a team. The cross-fertilization of ideas, research, prose and much "putting our heads together" allowed for an integration of themes and concepts across several domains. It was a challenging yet enriching experience for all of us. Through several years of arduous critique, analysis and reflection, we sought to balance individuals' intellectual integrity with group consensus. Although specific authors were responsible for sections and chapters, each of us can recognize his or her imprint on every page. Thus, in spite of vast differences in personalities, editorial opinions, academic and even cultural backgrounds, we came to speak with a common voice on the issues so close to our hearts.

Tony Devine
Josephine Hauer
June Saunders
Joon Ho Seuk
John R. Williams
Andrew Wilson

Part I

Foundations of Character Education

Section 1

Promising Directions for Character Education

ANDREW WILSON AND TONY DEVINE

THE GROWING MOVEMENT FOR CHARACTER EDUCATION SHOWS that today's educators are seeking to reclaim the moral mission of schooling. This holds an implicit promise, namely, that schools can respond effectively to the apparent moral decline in American culture.

A discussion of foundations focuses on ascertaining the universal values that undergird character education efforts. Universal values are valid for contemporary and traditional societies, and are consistent with the findings of social-scientific research as well as time-honored insights from the world's spiritual and moral traditions. Establishing such universal values is the key to teachers reclaiming their moral authority, thus ending decades of non-directive and ineffective moral teaching methods.

Several fresh perspectives are presented here. The first is that other-centered love is at the heart of moral development. Values and virtues revered by people the world over, such as courage, responsibility, caring, respect, honesty, loyalty, fidelity, forgiveness and self-sacrifice, are all about giving to others and acting with the benefit of others in mind. Thus, working towards competence in giving altruistic love is the chief objective of character development. In other words, if our life task is to fulfill our humanity, our humanity is defined by our capacity to love and to live in accord with our conscience.

The second is attention to matters of life's meaning and purpose, which turn out to be profoundly linked to character development. Notions of meaning in life need not be obscure or metaphysical. Such commonly shared life goals as personal maturity, loving relationships and family, and making a contribution to the community provide a rationale for the pursuit of virtue. They also set up a framework for understanding character development in its fullness—a life-goals approach to character education.

1

Giving Character Priority

IN A POLL CONDUCTED BY *WHO'S WHO AMONG AMERICAN TEACHERS* two years ago, teachers observed a toxic trend in their schools over the past 10 years: 81 percent reported less respect for authority, 73 percent noted a decline in ethics and morals, 65 percent observed less responsible attitudes, and 60 percent saw children as more self-centered.[1] In a June 1st, 1995 radio interview, New York City mayor Rudolph Giuliani reported that though crime that year had decreased 18 percent, crime within the school system had increased 25 percent. In late April 1999, two students at Columbine High School in Littleton, Colorado went on a murderous shoot-out, killing twelve of their fellow students and a teacher, and wounding many others. Even as America enjoys unprecedented technological and economic prosperity, it is plagued by a pervasive moral crisis. This crisis is nowhere more evident than among youth.

The once common assumption that economic prosperity would solve social problems has not proven to be true. Family breakdown, crime and social problems have increased most sharply in affluent countries and nations experiencing their greatest period of economic expansion. For example, England has enjoyed considerable economic prosperity in the decades since the 1960s. Yet the crime rate, which had been stable for a full century, nearly doubled between the late 1950s and early 1980s. It doubled again between 1985 and 1995, congruent with a huge rise in divorces.[2]

Nor has social spending made much difference in solving social problems. Former Secretary of Education William Bennett has proposed a list of "leading cultural indicators" to measure the character of a society. During the period from 1960 to 1990, America as a nation grew wealthier—the Gross Domestic Product increased 270 percent, far outstripping the population growth. Government spending on social problems increased more than five-fold, with spending on welfare for the poorest of the population increasing by 630 percent. Yet the same period saw a dramatic decline in the nation's character.[3] The billions of dollars spent on social and economic programs were of little avail in dealing with these problems, especially the problems confronting young people.

U.S. Social Trends and Cultural Indicators, 1960-1990

General Social Trends		Cultural Indicators	
U.S. Population	Up 41%	Rate of Illegitimate Births	Up 419%
Gross Domestic Product	Up 270%	Children on Welfare	Up 340%
Government Social Spending	Up 550%	Children Living with Single Parents	Up 300%
Spending on Welfare	Up 630%	Violent Crime Rate	Up 470%
Spending on Education	Up 225%	Teen Suicide Rate	Up 200%
Average TV Viewing Daily	Up to 7 hours		

Simply throwing tremendous amounts of resources at social problems has not proven effective. This raises the question of whether a more foundational approach is needed. The historian Arnold Toynbee once cautioned:

> The greater our material power, the greater our need for spiritual insight and virtue to use our power for good and not for evil.... We have never been adequate spiritually for handling our material power; and today the morality gap is... greater than it has ever been in any previous age.[4]

A good society requires effective economic programs to reduce poverty and improve living conditions, but it also requires concerted efforts to promote positive values and good character. But what are the social influences that most shape young people's values today?

The communication media and the entertainment industry often have greater impact upon young people's values formation than the great moral traditions. A Time/CNN poll found that the percentage of teenagers learning about sexual matters from television rather than from more responsible sources had doubled in the last twelve years.[5]

The American Psychological Association estimates that the typical child watches 27 hours of TV a week and witnesses 8,000 TV murders and 100,000 acts of violence by the age of twelve. The media often portray children as wiser than their hopelessly out-of-touch parents or disciplinarian schoolteachers. Young people are barraged with cultural messages teaching a perspective quite at odds with the values that caring parents, teachers and community leaders seek to transmit.[6] No wonder the Carnegie Foundation reports that "nearly half of American adolescents are at high or moderate risk of seriously damaging their life chances."[7]

A wide array of scholars, including Robert Bellah,[8] Christopher Lasch[9] and Roy Baumeister,[10] think the decline of explicit moral teachings in the last fifty to seventy-five years has left individuals with a "values gap"—no moral base on which to build a philosophy of life. Children are left to construct their own value system or even to avoid the task altogether. Without dedicated and consistent guidance, teenagers often adopt bits and pieces of values and goals from various sources, then to a large extent resort to personal satisfaction as their guiding orientation. Schools, home and the community owe it to young people to provide an explicit and consistent moral message so that popular, commercial culture and happenstance do not fill in the gap. Schools have traditionally played a key role in this socialization process, and their input is more crucial now than ever before.

Restoring Priority to Moral Education

The purpose of education concerns what sociologist Peter Berger calls "world-building."[11] The human world is a world of human achievements—of images, ideas and beliefs, of works of literature, art and music, of relationships, organizations and maxims of conduct, of skills, technologies and practical enterprises. All these are one's inheritance as a human being, and apart from them there is no humanity in a real sense. They are an inheritance that can only be grasped and possessed through learning.

Broadly speaking, human achievements have two dimensions. There is an external dimension: factual knowledge, skills, technologies, artifacts, etc. There is also an internal dimension: the wisdom of humanity concerning a good and meaningful life as embodied in its moral traditions. Literature, history, customs, religion and philosophy all convey and promote this internal side of human culture. Education is properly balanced when it encourages the pursuit of both these dimensions of life. Educator John Sloan Dickey remarked, "The end of education is to see men made whole, both in competence and in conscience. To create the power of competence without creating a corresponding direction to guide the use of that power is bad education. For apart from conscience, competence will finally disintegrate."[12]

When people focus excessively on the practical and material side of life, pursuing technology, information, wealth and status while neglecting the moral and spiritual dimension, they may find the satisfaction they derive to be empty and fleeting. A healthier life orientation balances these practical needs with a concern for the inner values of truth, meaning, goodness, beauty and love. Moral values—such as responsibility, respect, caring, honesty, courage, loyalty and compassion—help people attain the inner happiness that comes through self-respect, companionship and honor.

Of the two dimensions of human life, the moral dimension has priority. To understand why this is so, consider the relationship between a person's mind (consciousness) and body (material existence). The mind, as the source and center of moral values, is the basis for harmonious relationships with others. The mind holds purposes higher than the individual self: helping the community, going out of one's way to aid a neighbor, raising a child well. Society depends upon the mind directing people toward altruism. Meanwhile, the body urges a person toward being concerned mainly with the physical needs and pleasures of the individual self—food, clothing, shelter, sex and material comforts. When bodily urges take priority over the more altruistic urgings of the mind, then unnecessary personal, relational and social difficulties ensue.

Even by the measure of career success, the significance of character cannot be underestimated. A study at Bell Laboratories examined why among engineers of comparable intelligence and technical ability, some were more outstanding performers. It found that the top performers devoted time to cultivating good relationships with their co-workers. Hence when a technical problem arose, they could turn for help to a network of supporters and friends. Other engineers of equal intelligence, but lacking in cooperation-building skills, might wait for days to get necessary information. In the end, they did not perform as well, nor did they advance as far in their careers, as those with developed qualities of heart and character.[13]

Thus, the moral dimension has priority because it is the foundation for a worthwhile life. Good character enhances people's ability to form lasting friendships—and beyond that, strong marriages and families. People of good character can be entrusted with social responsibilities; hence they are more productive workers and citizens. From performance on the job to general satisfaction with life, the Greek philosopher Heraclitus rightly stated: "Character is destiny."

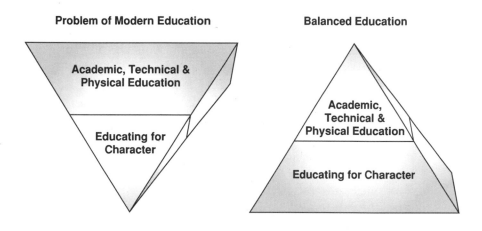

Problem of Modern Education   **Balanced Education**

Academic, Technical & Physical Education

Educating for Character

Academic, Technical & Physical Education

Educating for Character

Figure 1: Reestablishing the Priority of Educating for Character

Balanced Education

Education has a crucial role to encourage the pursuit of both dimensions of life in proper balance. What can be called conventional education—academic education, technical and vocational education, artistic and physical training—enables individuals to better pursue practical goals and objectives such as abundant wealth, a comfortable life, good health and social status. What can be called "educating for character" is about nurturing the inner side of life. Whether this endeavor is called "character education," "moral education," "civic education," "values education," "ethics" or "moralogy" (these are roughly equivalent though with some distinctive emphases[14]), it involves providing appropriate moral values and guiding students to realize them in their character.

Of the two dimensions of education, educating for character has priority. It is the broad base upon which rest all other forms of schooling: academic instruction, technical training, artistic training and physical training. A child's potential in those practical areas naturally builds upon the foundation of values fostered by attention to her character development. Indeed, the first purpose of education is not to train future technicians, journalists, scientists and businessmen, etc. It is to foster a child's humanity.

This simple insight formed the basis of classical education in ancient Greece. Here is a description by Plato:

> Education begins in the first years of childhood. As soon as the child can understand what is said, mother and father exert themselves to make the child as good as possible, at each word and action teaching and showing that this is right and that wrong, this honorable and that dishonorable.... At a later stage they send him to teachers and tell them to attend to his conduct far more than to his reading and writing. And the teachers did so...they put into his hands the works of great poets, and make him read and learn them by heart, sitting on his bench at school. These are full of instruction and of tales and praises of famous men of old, and the aim is that the boy may admire and imitate and be eager to become like them.[15]

Classical education's explicit aim was to produce a definite type of character, a definite attitude towards life. Although the acquisition of knowledge, skills and physical prowess were important goals, more important was the fostering of virtuous character. Curricula and classroom readings were selected with character formation in mind. Note that home, school and community were partners in this educational endeavor.

Today many American educators are seeking to reclaim this traditional insight. They are recognizing that the prevailing emphasis of present-day education, with its focus on intellectual knowledge and technical skills, is unbalanced. Stephen Trachtenberg, president of George Washington University, remarked that schools of higher learning must respond to the current moral decline by providing moral and ethical instruction as part of their central mission.[16] Daniel Goleman, the author of the ground-breaking book *Emotional Intelligence*, wrote, "Even though a high IQ is no guarantee of prosperity, prestige or happiness in life, our schools and our culture fixate on academic abilities, ignoring emotional intelligence, a set of traits—some might call it character—that also matters immensely for our personal destiny."[17]

Certainly, schools, parents and communities face challenges implementing effective moral education. At home, parents are tempted to push their teenage children to study hard to master a career while avoiding unpleasant moral issues. At school, conventional academic, vocational and physical education take up the majority of time and resources. The discordant values promoted in the media can lead parents to feel isolated and besieged. Yet children do best when they live in a positive moral environment formed by the cooperation and support of home, school and community. Now more than ever, educating for character remains an imperative. Here is a challenge where schools can take the lead.

There was a headmaster of a school who had survived one of Hitler's concentration camps. This man had experienced first hand how one of the most cultured, educated and scientifically advanced nations on earth descended into barbarism. He used to send every new faculty member at his school the following letter.

Dear Teacher:

My eyes saw what no man should witness: gas chambers built by learned engineers, children poisoned by learned physicians, infants killed by trained nurses, women and babies shot and burned by high school and college graduates. So, I am suspicious of education....

My request is: Help your students become human. Your efforts must never produce learned monsters, skilled psychopaths, educated Eichmanns. Reading, writing, arithmetic are important only if they serve to make our children more human.[18]

2

Recent Trends
in Moral Education

DEB BROWN IS A KINDERGARTEN TEACHER IN WEST VIRGINIA. In the most challenging class she faced in her 21-year career, 90 percent of her students came from broken homes and 40 percent had never met their birth fathers. She realized that before she could begin teaching this class academics, she had to make character education the priority. One student, Cody, talked for months about his upcoming visit to his father in prison, when he could sit on his father's lap rather than talk through a glass. His father had killed a man while trying to steal some stereo equipment. After the visit, Cody said to her, "Mrs. Brown, I just know that if my Dad had been in your class, he wouldn't have had to go to prison. He would have made better decisions in his life."[1] Deb Brown is one of a growing number of teachers who in the last decade have joined the movement for character education. It is a healthy if belated response to the moral decline in America's youth.

In recent decades, educational efforts to remedy the moral shortcomings of youth have been disappointing, even as schools excelled in imparting the skills and knowledge required for the complex tasks of the information age. This failure was not for lack of concern; polls of parents and educators show that both groups have always regarded education in sound moral behavior as an important part of education.[2] Nor can it be attributed to a by-product of prosperity; the economy had already reached a mature, affluent stage by the late 1950s. Rather, it occurred as the result of pervasive cultural changes since the 1960s and some well-intentioned yet unsuccessful attempts to reform moral education to fit within the new cultural milieu.[3].

The Decline of Moral Education and the Rise of Values Neutrality

Education in the early years of American democracy was permeated with moral lessons. The founding fathers, such as Thomas Jefferson and Benjamin Franklin, believed that a vital mission of education was to add to what they called the "moral character" of society. They understood that a people with the power to govern themselves in matters of social policy must first of all be virtuous, able to govern themselves in their personal lives. They founded great universities with a moral mission. The motivating vision of Harvard College, for example, was to train leaders who could "spell the difference between civilization and barbarism."[4] Noah Webster wrote in 1790,

> Education, in great measure, forms the moral character of men, and morals are the basis of government.... It is much easier to introduce and establish an effectual system for preserving morals than to correct by penal statutes the ill effects of a bad system.... The only practicable method to reform mankind is to begin with children.[5]

18th and 19th-century education integrated moral lessons into the school setting. School children learned to write by copying such aphorisms as: "Employment prevents vice," "Praise follows exertion," and "Justice is a common right."[6] As children copied and memorized them, these aphorisms became a part of their being.

In this regard, traditional American education was no different from traditional education in most nations around the world. In premodern China, for example, the Confucian classics that students memorized and copied were infused with moral precepts—pithy proverbs like: "Idleness when young, regrets before long," "Where there is a will, there is a way," and "Intolerance of minor insults will ruin great projects."[7]

Public education continued to maintain its moral focus through most of its period of industrialization and maturation into a wealthy market economy. It only began to depart from it in the 1960s, after widespread cultural changes and questioning of traditional values.

It is not the purpose here to analyze the complex reasons for these cultural changes, and it certainly can be argued that some traditional values deserved criticism. Americans did well to support the Civil Rights Movement's attack upon white racism and to examine the morality of the Vietnam War. However, the youth rebellion of the 1960s, despite its idealism, became infected with hedonism, narcissism and profound lack of judgment. It turned out to be the catalyst for a deep cultural shift. As the culture came to glorify youth, the moral authority of elders declined. As the culture exalted the values of freedom and equality for all, it came to tolerate and even celebrate deviant behavior. The result was mainstream acceptance of moral relativism. Many people came to believe that it was morally right to pursue personal fulfillment above social and family responsibilities, which were viewed as restricting the development of the self. An unintended result was the rise of self-centeredness.

With society questioning its moral foundations, teachers colleges and university education departments retreated from training teachers to be transmitters of moral values and instead emphasized teaching techniques, strategies, models and skills. The vision of the good teacher came to be that of the good technician—one who is effective in elevating students' scores on standardized tests of basic skills. Educational psychology, rather than philosophy and morals, took center stage in teacher training, and hence came to dominate the ethos of schools. In the opinion of many researchers in the area of character and moral development, the emphasis on technique to the exclusion of philosophy has left teachers ill-equipped to foster children's character development and often professionally indisposed to do so.[8]

Thus, in the decades following the 1960s, the most well-intentioned efforts at cultivating morals had to confront a culture pervaded by relativism and skeptical of public affirmations of traditional values. Teachers were trained to believe it was wrong to inculcate their personal moral beliefs. Many teachers and administrators came to believe that discussion of morals was entirely outside the bounds of proper curricula. Those educators who felt strongly about the importance of moral education had to find a way to do so within the constraint of a "values neutral" classroom. They gravitated to new, non-directive approaches to moral education, beginning with a movement called values clarification.

Values Clarification

When values clarification was first introduced in the 1970s, it enjoyed great popularity. *Values Clarification: A Handbook of Practical Strategies for Teachers and Students* sold over 600,000 copies, an almost unheard-of figure for a book on educational method.[9] Today, however, values clarification is regarded as a failure. The most definitive studies found it to have no significant positive impact on students' values, self-esteem, personal adjustment, interpersonal relationships or drug use, and only minimal impact on classroom behavior.[10]

Until its defects were discovered, values clarification had great appeal, particularly for educators looking for ways to promote moral learning in a values-neutral classroom environment. In certain corners of the curriculum, notably sexuality education, its basic perspective and techniques are still being practiced. Moreover, in developing countries where traditional values have been thrown into confusion by the pressures of modernization, educators are found promoting approaches that recycle its theory and methods.

To confuse matters further, sometimes the term "values clarification" is used in a broad sense to mean "clarifying the values within oneself" as one method within a moral education curriculum in which values are explicitly taught. Indeed, character education profitably utilizes many of the non-directive techniques pioneered by values clarification (see below). Yet that is far from the standard use of the term in professional circles, where it refers specifically to the values-neutral pedagogy of the '70s movement and its offshoots.

In the standard values clarification curriculum, the teacher refrains from teaching explicit values. Instead, he facilitates a process by which the student uncovers his or her own values. The method encourages inexperienced and immature young people to make their own choices about values, yet provides no moral instruction to guide them in making wise choices. Today, values clarification is widely criticized for promoting moral deviance by encouraging immature students to view themselves as arbiters of their own morality. Thomas Sowell said that a more apt name would be "values confusion," because its non-judgmental approach is at odds with any set of values that distinguish between right and wrong.[11]

Values Clarification: A Handbook of Practical Strategies declares that its purpose is to make students "aware of their own feelings, their own ideas, their own beliefs...their own value systems."[12] In its first exercise, entitled "Twenty Things You Love to Do," students are asked to identify what they like and want. They are not asked to identify moral values, what one *ought* to do, but merely to identify *wants*. Nor are they asked to consider other values that may conflict with what they value. One eighth-grade teacher who used this exercise found that the four most popular choices were "sex, drugs, drinking and skipping school."[13] Missing was any framework by which she could persuade them otherwise. Her students had clarified *their* values and could justify *their* choices. The teacher was admonished not to be judgmental.

In an exercise called "Values Voting," the teacher asks such innocuous questions as "How many of you like to go on long walks or hikes?" or "How many like yogurt?" interspersed with questions of moral content: "How many of you approve of premarital sex for boys? For girls?"[14] In this motley collection of questions, students come away with the impression that all values are a matter of personal taste, like eating yogurt. In Bennett's view, the result was to clarify wants and desires in place of values, thus undermining values.[15]

Such exercises encourage students to be "in touch with their feelings." Since "valuing" means caring about something, values certainly do entail feelings. Yet a value is, first of all, a belief or cognition about what conduct and outcomes are desirable or not.[16] A firmly held value is founded on rational arguments about what behaviors will most benefit themselves and others. Clarifying feelings does not necessarily lead to clarity about values.

The teacher's role was to be a facilitator for the students' choices. Although an immature student might make unwise choices, the teacher had to refrain from instructing the student to change his or her choice. As the seminal text of values clarification notes, "It is entirely possible that children will choose not to develop values. It is the teacher's responsibility to support that choice also."[17]

The textbooks even disparaged parents' moral guidance, thus subtly undermining parental authority: "A major influence on you has been the attitudes and behaviors of each of your parents.... Many believe that these traditional attitudes hinder growth and development of a person because they limit possibilities." "If you feel your parents are overprotective...you may feel you have to tune out their voice entirely."[18] The argument ran: parental instruction imposes the parents' values, which may not be the same as the child's values. Parents have no special claim to authority; they are just "ordinary people with faults and weaknesses and insecurities and problems just like everyone else."[19]

Yet the relationship of parent and child is no ordinary relationship. It is a unique and life-long relationship the child will never have with anyone else. Not only do parents have vastly more experience in values-formation than the child or the child's peers, they also inculcate these values out of enduring love and regard for the child's welfare.

By the early 1990s, values clarification had been largely abandoned. Merrill Harmin, a co-author of its manifesto, *Values and Teaching*, issued a retraction of sorts in 1988:

> Our emphasis on value neutrality probably did undermine traditional morality.... As I look back, it would have been better had we presented a more balanced picture.... It makes a good deal of sense to say that truthfulness is better than deception, caring is better than hurting, loyalty is better than betrayal, and sharing is better than exploitation.[20]

Howard Kirschenbaum, who co-authored the basic teacher-training manual for values clarification, has moved to an eclectic approach that combines student-centered methods with traditional inculcation of values.[21] He recently quipped, "Some administrators today would rather be accused of having asbestos in their ceilings than of using values clarification in their classrooms."[22]

Philosophical Roots of Values Clarification

Values clarification is heavily indebted to humanistic psychology. By promoting greater sensitivity to the student as an individual learner, psychology has had the salutary effect of counteracting the factory-like atmosphere in schools where education was seen as filling young minds with knowledge and where results were measured by test scores. It has promoted the notion that education is about teaching children, not just teaching subjects.

Psychologist Carl Rogers had revolutionized counseling practice by introducing "client-centered" therapy. It is a non-directive method in which the therapist refuses to give direct advice; instead, he reflects the patient's thoughts and feelings back to her as objectively as possible without instructing the patient in any way. The goal is for the patient to recognize the solution to the problem within herself by drawing out her own deepest values, desires, and goals. Such self-realizations can be effective in motivating change in the adult client, whose values are already formed. In *Freedom to Learn* and many other publications, Rogers then suggested applying his therapeutic techniques to the education of children.[23]

This begs an important question. Do children have such a strong innate tendency to develop as moral agents that they can attain personal maturity independent of learning a moral code? Abraham Maslow, proponent of a non-directive psychological method he called self-actualization, warned that these techniques may be inappropriate for children: "Self-actualization does not occur in young people.... [They have not] learned how to be patient; nor have they learned enough about evil in themselves and others...nor have they generally acquired enough courage to become unpopular, to be unashamed about being openly virtuous."[24]

A second root of values clarification is Romanticism, the philosophy founded by the French thinker Jean-Jacques Rousseau. Romanticism holds that society's conventions are artificial and corrupting. Thus, if children were only allowed to grow in a natural state, they would automatically flower to display natural virtues.

Romanticism also gives primacy to feelings over intellection. Subjective feelings are thought to be trustworthy guides, while reason is often bound to social duties and norms, imposed from without.[25] The modern cult of personal authenticity and "getting in touch with your feelings" is Romanticist at its core.[26] Values clarification shares this viewpoint, confusing personal feelings with values that can be rationally supported.

Romanticism distinguishes the individual from his social context. Yet is it not in a social context that the conscience is properly formed? Today most moral educators argue that children need to be taught the content of moral norms as well as be nurtured in their own innate virtues. Not so in values clarification, where advocating society's values is out of bounds.

The Appropriateness of Non-Directive Teaching Methods

One reason for the enthusiasm that greeted values clarification was that it introduced new non-directive teaching methods that are sometimes more effective in promoting learning than traditional didactic lectures. While traditional lectures can result in students merely parroting the teacher, the teacher who uses a non-directive method refuses to give a pat answer. Her purpose is to set the students on the path of self-discovery. The resulting disequilibrium in the students can be productive of personal growth. It challenges students to draw upon their knowledge and life experience. It spurs their reasoning process and forces them to reflect deeply. Students become active participants in an engaging journey of learning.

Although education traditionally favored the methods of didactic lectures and rote memorization, non-directive methods are as old as Socrates and Confucius. Socrates invented the Socratic dialogue, a method of questioning designed to draw out his students' values. Confucius constantly questioned his disciples and encouraged them to state their own views. He remarked, "Only one who bursts with eagerness do I instruct.... If I hold up one corner and a man cannot come back to me with the other three, I do not continue the lesson."[27] However, a critical step in Confucius' non-directive method was evaluation—rational discussion of the students' answers and comparison against the moral standard. Socrates would not employ his dialogical method with students under 30 years old.

Today non-directive methods are being successfully employed in the context of positive moral instruction. For example, within the context of a lesson on friendship, it is good pedagogy to ask students to explain how they personally would treat their friends in a given circumstance. However, to complete the moral lesson, there follows an evaluation step where explicit moral discourse takes over. The previous cautions concerning values clarification are not a critique of all non-directive methods, but rather warn against using such methods *from a morally neutral stance* and *in the absence of moral reasoning*.

Raising Self-Esteem—A Moral End?

Another influence of the therapeutic perspective is the educational goal of raising self-esteem. Few doubt that valuing and respecting oneself is part of a healthy personality. Very low self-esteem is a character flaw that can lead to delinquency or even suicide. The question, however, is whether promoting self-esteem as an end in itself is consistent with character development.

"A dozen years ago, research was showing heavily positive things about high self-esteem," says Roy Baumeister of Case Western Reserve University. "Since then, questions have been raised about the size of effects, the direction of effects, and whether in fact it's a mixed blessing even to have high self esteem."[28] After all, people find self-esteem in things that have little to do with morality—high grades, popularity with peers, winning schoolyard fights, sexual conquests and bullying.

Traditional education was suspicious of self-esteem, valuing humility and self-denial as a better guide to life. A healthy sense of guilt and shame can steer one away from deeds that violate the conscience. When these negative emotions have the effect of reinforcing proper behavior, they promote a solid basis for self-worth.

Teachers concerned with educating for character would rather foster a healthy sense of self-respect that stems from being a person of integrity, kindness, loyalty, etc.—the aspects of good character. Following Aristotle's teaching that character is built through surmounting challenges, effective character education programs challenge students to strive for high goals and real accomplishments.

Focus on self esteem, particularly in programs aimed at poor and underprivileged students, can become a kind of crutch to justify and even reinforce low achievement, according to Richard Elmore, a professor of education at Harvard University. "For most teachers, self-esteem is a theory they invent to cover the fact that they have low expectations for kids."[29] Sooner or later the students are disillusioned and deflated, realizing that their self-esteem has no basis in objective fact. Spurred by these findings, educators today are returning to more traditional achievement-based programs. Honest criticism and fair evaluation can actually accomplish more for young people's self-esteem by giving them the knowledge and skills necessary for accomplishing their life goals.

The Moral Reasoning Approach

As values clarification lost its appeal, many moral educators turned to the moral reasoning approach pioneered by Lawrence Kohlberg. Following the work of developmental psychologist Jean Piaget, Kohlberg found that moral reasoning develops in distinct stages from infancy to adulthood.[30] His mapping of the process of cognitive moral development and his practical methods for measuring it were valuable contributions to moral psychology, and are his lasting legacy. The application to moral education, however, was less successful. Only a few of the "Just Community schools" established to practice his pedagogy remain open.[31]

At the heart of the moral reasoning pedagogy are discussions of moral dilemmas, in which the students are asked to discern the best course of action among several plausible alternatives. They can be phrased for any grade level, like this middle school example:

> Sharon and Jill were best friends. One day they went shopping together. Jill tried on a sweater and then, to Sharon's surprise, walked out of the store wearing the sweater under her coat. A moment later, the store's security guard stopped Sharon and demanded that she tell him the name of the girl who had walked out. He said that he'd seen the two girls together and was sure the one who left had been shoplifting. He warns Sharon, "Come on now, tell me. You could get in serious trouble if you don't give us your friend's name." Should Sharon tell on her friend? Why or why not?[32]

These moral dilemmas are not provided with a right or a wrong answer. Instead, they stimulate the moral reasoning process itself, making the student more aware of the choices at stake. In this example, Sharon could decide to tell out of fear of punishment, or deny all for fear her friend would spurn her. She could protect her friend because she owes her a favor, or turn her in because of remembered slights. Any number of reasons could be given for either course of action. The logic by which students arrive at their choices is more significant than the choice itself. It was assumed that presenting students with moral dilemmas and discussing their answers together would stimulate development of their moral reasoning towards higher stages.

Kohlberg's Stages of Moral Reasoning—illustrated by Sharon's dilemma[33]

Stage 1: Avoidance of Punishment: "Will I get in trouble?"

Sharon should tell, otherwise she will be in big trouble.

Sharon shouldn't tell. Otherwise Jill will be angry and make her life miserable.

Stage 2: Tit-for-tat Fairness: "What's in it for me?"

Why should Sharon have to take the rap for Jill? Jill looks out for herself, so Sharon should do likewise.

It depends on whether she owes Jill a favor, or wants Jill to cover for her sometime.

Stage 3: Interpersonal Loyalty: "What will people think of me?"

What kind of friend would turn in her best friend? Everyone will think she's a fink.

If she doesn't tell, she's an accomplice in a crime. Her reputation will suffer.

Stage 4: Concern for Larger Consequences: "What if everybody did it?"

Sharon should tell, even though it would be hard to do. It's not fair for people to go around stealing. If you don't obey laws, society will fall apart.

Moral reasoning pedagogy is helpful because it allows a teacher to get inside the students' heads to understand how they think about moral issues.[34] This is essential if she is to meet the students' cognitive level and engage them in their moral development. Second, the method encourages students to "hear" their own way of thinking and to reflect critically upon it. They can listen to others' reasoning and think about which kind of reasoning will best guide them to become the people they really want to be. Third, it fits the common experience that moral-ity is not always black and white, but requires choosing between com-peting goods. Fourth, since moral reasoning is grounded in rational principles, teachers can guide a discussion comparing and evaluating the various judgments.

Moral reasoning is non-relativistic—it assumes some moral values are superior to others. Thus, it is superior to values clarification. Still, its methodology resembles values clarification in requiring open discus-sions in which students offer various answers. Does this mean that the teacher lets go of the opportunity to give positive moral teaching? A teacher cannot simply declare, "This is wrong!" or she will short-cir-cuit the students' reasoning process. Yet if she merely clarifies and appreciates all students' reasoning, she would fall into the role of a facilitator in the way of values clarification. The teacher's role is to wisely guide the discussion, allowing students to critically reflect on each other's reasoning, to raise the level of moral discourse.

Unfortunately, in the culture of values-neutrality that still pervades many classrooms, teachers find this difficult to do. One remarked, "I often discuss cheating this way, but I always get defeated because they will argue that cheating is alright. After you accept the idea that kids have the right to build a position with logical arguments, you have to accept what they come up with."[35] Many teachers, particularly at the high school level, shy away from open-ended moral discussions for fear that they will degenerate into arguments for undesirable values.

Proper implementation of moral reasoning, therefore, requires a great deal of the teacher. A teacher cannot prevail with this approach without strong moral convictions and considerable training. Herein lies its practical weakness as a pedagogical method.

A theoretical weakness of moral reasoning is that it only deals with the intellectual aspect of the moral self. Educating for character involves training the emotions and will as well as the intellect. As character edu-cator Thomas Lickona states it, "Good character consists of knowing the good, desiring the good, and doing the good—habits of mind, habits of the heart, and habits of action."[36] Knowing what is right does not necessar-ily mean choosing to do what is right. A one-sided reliance on intellect may also lead to sophistry. Critics of moral reasoning often cite the unin-tended consequence that students come away from class believing that morality is complicated and that, as Richard Baer put it, "almost everything in ethics is either vague or controversial."[37]

More commonly, people know the better choice but lack the courage to do it. A student may suddenly face a question of an embarrassing nature and be tempted to lie, all in an instant, to avoid humiliation in a social situation: "Yeah, I've done that (taken drugs, cheated, driven at high speed)." This is an experience more in keeping with a student's day-to-day life. While the student may *believe* in being truthful, the emotional pain of being left out may be a stronger prompt to action than an intellectual belief. Indeed, research on morally exemplary adults and adolescents shows that sustained moral commitment and a strong sense of personal responsibility do not always correlate with one's level of moral judgment according to Kohlberg's measure.[38]

Today's character educators have not abandoned moral reasoning. But they have turned away from a stand-alone moral reasoning pedagogy in favor of integrating it within a comprehensive character education curriculum. (See Chapter 10) Because character education explicitly teaches universal values, it sets a classroom context and tone that does not permit values-neutrality. The values-oriented classroom gives the teacher a platform upon which to utilize discussion of a moral dilemma as a constructive lesson.[39] Character educators also contextualize moral reasoning within a more complete theory of the moral person. Thus, while moral reasoning stimulates moral knowing, it complements other features of the curriculum, including good literature, a sound discipline policy and a caring classroom atmosphere, all of which stimulate moral feeling and moral action as well as moral reasoning.

The Character Education Movement

The declining morals and the rise of negative behaviors among young people reached crisis proportions in the 1990s. In the words of the National Commission on Excellence in Education in 1993, "if an unfriendly foreign power had done this to us, we would have deemed it an act of war."[40] Parents began to harshly criticize the public school system, many even removing their children and placing them in expensive private schools where moral education is traditional and content-driven. Other parents resorted to home schooling. Among public educators there was a growing desperation that something needed to be done, and done quickly.

Moreover, as a society, Americans began to give more importance to character and personal integrity. Stephen Covey, the author of the widely-read *The Seven Habits of Highly Effective People*, claims that people are shifting paradigms, from a concern for personality to a concern for character. They have grown dissatisfied with the mere social savvy of "winning friends and influencing people," and are recognizing the personal need for the bedrock values that give stability to life.[41]

Growth of Character Education in the United States

A new movement for moral education in the public schools has emerged under the rubric of character education. Character education has been defined as "the deliberate effort to develop good character, by inculcating core virtues that are good for the individual and good for society."[42] Fundamentally, the character education movement rejects the notion that educators must avoid advocating particular values. Christina Sommers states, "In teaching ethics, one thing should be made clear and prominent: Right and wrong do exist. This should be laid down as uncontroversial lest one leaves an altogether false impression that everything is up for grabs."[43]

The character education movement is gaining widespread support. While in 1990 intentional character education programs were a rarity, today 5 to 10 percent of public schools have them.[44] There is rapid development in the quality and comprehensiveness of curricula and methods. (See Section Three) Endorsements by public officials have encouraged the movement. Since 1994 the White House has held annual conferences supporting character education, and the President specifically endorsed it as an educational goal in the 1997 State of the Union Address. Currently, ten states have legislation mandating some form of character education in public schools and six more have pending legislation. Federal grants have been offered to help states implement character-based education programs since 1995.[45] Congress has declared October 16-22 as "National Character Counts Week."[46]

Several character education organizations have played a seminal role, acting as resource centers for the character education initiatives being implemented in schools throughout the country. They act as advocates for character education and organize conferences for teachers and principals. The Character Education Partnership, chaired by Sanford N. McDonnell, is a nonpartisan nationwide coalition of organizations and individuals based in Washington, D.C. The Character Plus (formerly PREP) program in St. Louis, through the efforts of Linda McKay, pioneered overcoming the presumption of the values-neutral schooling by building consensus among teachers, parents and administrators around teachable values. The Center for the Advancement of Ethics and Character at Boston University, founded by Kevin Ryan, focuses on teacher competence. Thomas Lickona heads the Center for the 4th and 5th Rs at SUNY Cortland in New York. On the West Coast, the International Center for Character Education (ICCE), co-directed by Mary Williams and Ed DeRoche at the University of San Diego, organizes an annual international conference and offers extensive teacher training, including a Certificate program and the first Master's degree program in character education.

There is also an emerging trend to include character education training in the curriculum of teacher education programs. This is not a simple matter, as it confronts teachers college faculties with challenging questions. The teacher education programs that are reporting success are those whose faculties are aware of the need for character education; have given careful thought to the moral goals of schooling; and have made character education foundational for their own programs, infusing its ethos into staff and students alike, in order to create a model.[47]

Assessments of Effectiveness

Although national statistics do not yet exist because the character movement is so new, early assessments attest to the effectiveness of character education programs. The Child Development Project (CDP), a comprehensive whole school elementary character education program that as of 1998 had been implemented in 46 schools in four states, was evaluated in three different studies. The results demonstrate that students have consistently shown positive changes in a broad range of attitudes, inclinations, feelings and behaviors. These include: conflict resolution skills, concern for others, trust in and respect for teachers, prosocial motivation, altruistic behavior and positive interpersonal behavior.[48]

A study of the Mound Fort Middle School of Ogden, Utah, shows that incidents of cheating, vandalism, violence and other behavior problems declined significantly after character education was implemented. The school used to see students fighting daily; now it sees one or two fights a month.[49] At Atlantis Elementary School in Cocoa, Florida, scores on a statewide writing test for fourth graders rose substantially, due in part to a decline in disciplinary problems.

At Marion Intermediate School in Marion, South Carolina, in one of the poorest communities in the state, a 5-year character education initiative was responsible for reducing office referrals for discipline problems by 50 percent. Meanwhile, staff absences of 10 or more days declined from 68 percent to under 20 percent, while school-business partnerships leaped from 25 to 75.

At the Kennedy Middle School in Eugene, Oregon, office referrals for discipline dropped from 100 per month to 35. Academic performance on state exams rose 15 percent in one year. Teacher morale also improved. One teacher who had resisted the character education initiative admitted, "Students are more respectful and caring. I didn't think it could happen in this day and age."[50] These and other empirical assessments are placing character education on a scientific footing.[51]

Towards a Comprehensive Framework for Character Education

Character education shows every sign of being adopted by the mainstream educators. The trend to implement programs that deliberately foster universal moral values is likely to accelerate in the years ahead. Parents support such explicit moral instruction. When asked what they want from schools, they consistently emphasize two things: first, to teach children how to speak, write, read, think and count correctly; and second, help them to develop reliable standards of right and wrong that will guide them through life.[52]

Nevertheless, many educational leaders wonder whether character education will last, or be just another passing fashion in the continually changing face of education. They question whether it is adequate to the task of reversing the moral decline among youth.

James Leming contends that at present the character education movement lacks a comprehensive theoretical base, with the current research consisting of disparate pieces of sociology, philosophy, psychology, and program evaluations.[53] Ivor Pritchard of the U.S. Department of Education wrote, "the formulation of an adequate philosophical psychology is the primary condition for significant improvement in educational theory and is the source of root conflicts between traditional and progressive schools of educational thought."[54] Leming calls for the development of a "grand theory" of character education as the next crucial step.[55] Without developing an adequate theoretical foundation for values, the promise of character education may be only ephemeral.

Such a theoretical framework must tackle an array of philosophical and educational issues. It will address moral issues throughout the life span, not shirking controversial topics such as love and sexuality and their relationship to character. It will of necessity give consideration to the role of the family in character formation. It will address questions of meaning: why ought a student to develop good character? At the very least, it will give firm grounding to the values taught by character educators, demonstrating beyond a shadow of a doubt that they are universal values that transcend religions, cultures, politics and ideologies, the diversity of which is often used as an argument for moral relativism.

3

Ascertaining Universal Values

I know that some people say... different civilizations and different ages have had quite different moralities. But this is not true.... If anyone will take the trouble to compare the moral teaching of, say, the ancient Egyptians, Babylonians, Hindus, Chinese, Greeks and Romans, what will really strike him will be how very like they are to each other and to our own....

Think what a totally different morality would mean. Think of a country where people were admired for running away in battle, or where a man felt proud of double-crossing all the people who had been kindest to him. You might just as well try to imagine a country where 2 plus 2 equals 5. Men have differed as regards what people you ought to be unselfish to—whether it was only your own family, or your fellow countrymen, or everyone. But they have always agreed that you ought not to put yourself first. —C. S. Lewis[1]

THIS COMMENT BY BRITISH WRITER C. S. LEWIS SETS OUT THE fundamental premise behind character education: Certain moral values are in fact universal. Yet how do educators establish that universal moral values in fact exist? How can universal values be distinguished from other sorts of values that may not be universal? This question is preliminary to the character education enterprise.

Whose Values Do You Teach?

With the rise of moral relativism in the 1960s, whenever moral education was ventured critics immediately posed the question, "Whose values do you teach?" The common presumption of that era—that values were the product of culture—meant that any attempt to teach values was in reality only fostering cultural hegemony. This so disoriented that generation of educators that they retreated to values neutrality. Those who wished to pursue moral education eschewed teaching values and instead focused on non-directive methodologies such as values clarification that encouraged students to arrive at their own values—as defective as they might be.

Moreover, educators were caught in confusion over whether teaching values was a subtle way of promoting religion. Religion has traditionally been an important—but not the sole—foundation for morality and ethics. Since Supreme Court decisions in 1962 and 1963 banned school-sponsored prayers and devotional readings from public schools, educational authorities have scrupulously avoided even the appearance of religious instruction. These court decisions may certainly be justified on Constitutional grounds that the state is not permitted to establish or favor one religion over another, or even religion over atheism. However, fear of religious indoctrination in the schools had the negative effect of contributing to the neglect or outright rejection of any deliberate teaching of moral values.

How times have changed! Today, educational leaders critique the value-free atmosphere that still lingers at many schools and call for deliberate ethical instruction. Derek Bok, former president of Harvard University, has stated, "There are fundamental working principles of ethical behavior which are important, and we're not indoctrinating our students by making a conscious effort to make them understand, appreciate, and live by those principles."[2] Kieran Egan asserts that education should be explicit in its moral goals: "to believe that you can educate in a value-free environment is to believe that you can love non-emotionally."[3]

Character educators are no longer reticent about affirming the universality of moral values. Being universal means they transcend any particular culture or creed. They are cherished by people everywhere: East and West, North and South. They are valid today, they were valid in the past, and they will be valid in the future. They apply to the whole person, linking material welfare and spiritual well-being.

An example of a universal moral value, one that appears in each of the major ethical systems of the world, is the precept: "Treat others as you would have them treat you." Most people's common sense tells them that this is a reasonable and right way to behave. No conscientious parent would object to having their child taught this precept; nor would they object to a school that upholds and teaches the virtues of honesty, honor, respect and courage. Nevertheless, it is still helpful to elucidate the theoretical foundations of universal values.

Values as Beliefs, Virtues and Norms

A teacher in southern California tells of an Asian student named Ming who always addressed her as "Teacher." The other students, who called her "Mrs. Morrison," teased Ming for the funny way he spoke. Tim spoke up in class, saying he thought Ming was being disrespectful. Later, Ming explained to his teacher, "In my country, to say 'Teacher' shows respect. I don't want to address you disrespectfully merely as 'Mrs. Morrison.'"

This incident points out the important distinction between universal moral values and the manners and customs rooted in culture. Ming and Tim both understood that the question of their cultural differences was not a serious issue, but the matter of showing respect— a universal value—was. This problem lurks in the shadows of character education. Perhaps some of the social conventions Americans take for granted are not universal values. How does one distinguish between universal values and values that are culture-bound?

Another pitfall character educators learn to avoid is to allow discussions of values to become politicized. These days, politicians and interest groups wave the flags of human rights, freedom, and other universal values to justify controversial positions and policies. Sometimes these issues can generate informative class discussions that an experienced teacher can guide into lessons of moral insight. Nevertheless, more often than not, they become arid intellectual debates having no impact on the students' lives. This is a reason to keep the classroom focus on personal virtue and character. The learning experience is directed into the more fruitful avenues of self-reflection and cultivating personal responsibility.

Defining Values

To better grasp these issues, it helps to first clarify the catch-all term "values." Ethicists distinguish between several different types of values. In the most general sense, *values* are what people judge worth having (e.g., wealth, wisdom), worth doing (e.g., helping others, a rewarding career, gardening) or worth being (e.g., honest, happy, successful).

Moral values carry within them an obligation to others or to some greater whole. They may be intrinsically right (e.g., do not murder) or socially right (e.g., do not shout in a library). In either case to violate them does harm.[4] As the example of the Asian student demonstrates, these two domains overlap and are intimately connected.

A few ethicists distinguish such values as perseverance, empathy and self-discipline as a distinct group of "meta-moral characteristics." They are not intrinsically moral—for example, one can persevere in doing evil or use empathy to con someone—and yet they aid in proper moral functioning.[5] However, for anyone with a moral orientation, these values become obligatory for the full flowering of moral personhood. Thus, they are moral values that no character educator can afford to ignore.

Finally, non-moral or *personal values* are things people want or desire but are non-obligatory (e.g., exercise, reading). They are matters of personal preference or taste.

Character educators are more properly interested in moral values. Moral values appear in three forms: *beliefs, virtues* and *norms.* Universal moral values are beliefs, virtues and norms that are true—helping people thrive—regardless of place and time. Let's begin by surveying the meaning of these terms.

Values as Beliefs

A standard definition of value is "an enduring belief that a specific mode of conduct or end-state of existence is personally or socially preferable."[6] As a belief, a value includes a strong emotional component, since "valuing" also means caring. Still, values have a rational basis and cannot be reduced to mere wants. They can be rationally defended and critiqued. As such, universal moral values can be said to exist objectively regardless of whether people believe them or live by them.

Values Embodied as Virtues

Something is "valuable" because it has qualities that make it desirable to people. An expensive diamond has value because people esteem its flawless beauty, color and sparkle. Likewise, a person has value if other people like her, respect her, and want to be her companions. Everyone in a company values the diligent, helpful employee. Like a diamond, she is desirable because she embodies valuable qualities. From this perspective, moral values are to be embodied. Socrates once said, "Make yourself the kind of person that you want people to think you are."

A lived moral value is called a *virtue*. A virtue is attained when its value is practiced consistently and continually. A person of good character embodies many virtues. These days, many character educators have replaced the language of values with the language of virtues, especially as a way to distinguish their enterprise from the older and discredited method of values clarification. [7]

Values as Norms

Values also occur as norms, or the expected standards of proper behavior in relationships with others. The function of norms is to serve as guidelines for showing respect and facilitating harmony.

Some norms are rules that cut to the heart of the moral life, for example, the expectation of fidelity in marriage. Other norms are more superficial, e.g., manners and customs of appropriate dress and speech. With social norms especially, some people draw a sharp distinction between universal "moral" values and relative "cultural" values. Nevertheless, Emily Post, the classic expositor of manners, insisted that good manners in any society are rooted in morality and are rarely a matter of mere social graces. For example, consider the brainy political activist who refuses to wash up or comb his hair before he speaks at government hearings; to him, it's a matter of principle. Yet he complains that the officials don't want to listen to him. They interpret his "style" as indicating a lack of respect for them—and it does.[8] His violation of the expected social norm indicates his lack of moral sensibility.

A courteous person will be recognized worldwide even if he or she makes a cultural faux pas or two. When a professor from Chicago who travels extensively in Europe was asked how to navigate successfully in other countries, he replied, "Be humble. Humility is appreciated everywhere."

The limitation of not addressing social norms in certain character education efforts is illustrated by a breakout session entitled "The Self-Esteem Scene," presented at a recent character education conference in Connecticut.[9] Conference-goers viewed several student-authored morality skits that posed moral dilemmas and then suggested their resolution.

Four fifth-graders, two boys and two girls, performed one skit that was well received by the educators. The girls played best friends. As the boys walked by, the first girl told the second how much she wanted to date one of those boys. The second girl replied that the boy had already asked her to go on a date to the mall. Now that she knew that her friend liked the boy, the second girl has to make a choice. The performers stopped the scene and asked the audience. "What should the girl do? Accept the date or give the date to her friend?" The audience replied that she should give the date to her friend.

The skit's lesson was clear enough: be loyal to your friends. Yet it sidestepped a larger issue—in this case, the norms expected by the fifth-graders' parents. Would their parents approve of exclusive dating at such a young age? And even if they did, is such dating in the children's best interests? Loyalty to a friend may be a virtue, but it could be more than offset by the larger concerns of disobeying parents and engaging in premature dating. Without attention to familial and social norms, such well-intentioned efforts to teach good character may send unintended, contradictory messages.

Integrating Individual Virtue Ethics and Normative Social Ethics

The moral philosopher who gave the most thought to integrating individual virtues and social norms was Confucius. Rightly understood and modernized, his ethics speaks to the universal human condition. In his view, individuals realize their full humanity precisely through fulfilling their obligations within familial and social contexts. Consider this passage from *The Doctrine of the Mean*:

> The gentleman conforms himself to his life circumstances; he does not long for anything beyond his situation. Finding himself in a position of wealth and honor he acts as required of a man living in a position of wealth and honor. Finding himself in a position of poverty and humble circumstances, he acts as required of a man living in a position of poverty and

humble circumstances.... In a word, the gentleman can find himself in no situation in life in which he is not master of himself.[10]

Excepting the antiquated notion that there should be different norms for rich and poor, this text makes a relevant point. People everywhere find themselves thrown into particular social roles, sometimes of their own choosing and sometimes not—as a husband, a wife, a father, a mother, a child, an employee, a boss, a student, a teacher, etc. Keeping to the norm required by a given social position affords the opportunity for character development; indeed, a person's success in keeping to the norm is a good measure of his or her character.[11] There are lessons here for a society where people sometimes make light of social norms as they pursue self-fulfillment.

Character education often focuses on cultivating individual virtues, a tendency that may have its philosophical basis in Aristotle. Many of the widely used concepts in character education derive from this philosopher. And with good reason: Aristotle propounded undoubtedly the most profound and complete moral philosophy in the Western tradition. At the heart of Aristotle's ethical teachings was the moral cultivation of the individual. Developmental psychology, a second root of modern moral education, is likewise individual-centered.

Nevertheless, the task of solving present-day moral problems—those that revolve around issues of family life, for example—requires linking individual virtue ethics and normative social ethics, as Confucius sought to do. They can be linked ontologically: Just as virtues are universal by way of people's common humanity as individual beings, so certain norms are universal by way of their common humanity as social beings. They can also be linked functionally and relationally: It takes virtuous individuals to properly keep the norms that make for just and loving relationships, and conversely, personal virtue is properly cultivated through fulfilling familial and social norms.[12]

Five Criteria for the Universality of Values

Having discussed what things—beliefs, virtues and norms—might be called universal values, it is useful to establish some criteria for establishing universal moral values. Five criteria or warrants for establishing the universality of moral values are identified, drawing on Eastern as well as Western thought. They are: democratic consensus, philosophical examination, evidence from comparative cultures, basis in human nature, and basis in natural law.

Democratic Consensus

Advocates of character education have learned that before beginning a program, it is frequently necessary to establish a community consensus among teachers, parents, administrators and civic leaders. The effort expended in surveys and committee meetings helps overcome people's hesitations about teaching a particular set of values and results in strong community support. Even participants coming from different political or religious persuasions soon realize that they can agree on a set of common values.

Consensus can form on the level of a single school, a community, district or state. Character Plus pioneered consensus building at the community level. It was started as the Personal Responsibility Education Process (PREP) in 1988 by a concerned group of parents, educators and business leaders in St. Louis who determined that something had to be done about the deterioration of basic values. A crucial early step was for the group to invest themselves in a consensus-building process to decide upon the core values they wanted reinforced by the schools.[13] This process has been employed to set up character education programs in over thirty public school districts involving over 400 schools.

There have been several attempts to arrive at a universal list of values or virtues through democratic consensus. The Josephson Institute assembled a diverse committee of experts in 1992 to generate a list of universal values. They announced a universal list of "Six Pillars of Character": trustworthiness, respect, responsibility, fairness, caring and citizenship. Rushworth Kidder of the Institute for Global Ethics surveyed international leadership cohorts from many cultures and found seven values that were overwhelmingly selected as most important: truth, responsibility, compassion, reverence for life, freedom, self-respect and fairness.[14]

The consensus approach has the benefits of keeping education near to the people and building community support. It can be viewed as a good starting point and a guideline. However, to be deemed universal, a value should be able to withstand certain philosophical tests.[15]

Philosophical Tests of Universality

There are four widely recognized philosophical criteria for determining whether a particular moral choice or value is universal.

- *It is reversible*: If I do something to you, how would I feel if it were done to me? Respecting another person's property and not taking what does not belong to one meets this test.

- *It is generalizable*: Would it be good if everyone did it? If everyone in the world had compassion, for instance, then surely this would be a better world.

- *It produces good consequences*: It yields objective benefits over the long term to both the individual and the whole society.

- *It is compelling to the conscience*: It rings true to the intuition as well as to reason. Even young children understand values when they cry out for justice in the schoolyard: "He hit me first!" Instinctively, they know that the provocateur is considered the guiltier party.

In fact, the moral values that are arrived at by democratic consensus, such as respect, responsibility, caring, justice, integrity, etc., almost always pass these tests, attesting to their universality.

Comparative Cultures

As the world grows smaller and people become educated about other cultures, it becomes more apparent that among the earth's peoples there is not only wide diversity but also much common ground, particularly in the area of values. A heroic act of self-sacrifice, such as risking one's life to save a drowning child, is honored everywhere, from industrialized societies to aboriginal tribes. Evidence for this can be found by studying the traditional wisdom of cultures around the world.[16]

For example, the principle of reciprocity was stated by Confucius, "Do not do to others what you would not have them do to you," in the Bible, "Whatever you wish that men would do to you, do so to them," and in the Indian epic the *Mahabharata*, "One should not behave towards others in a way which is disagreeable to oneself." It is echoed in an African proverb, "One going to take a pointed stick to pinch a baby bird should first try it on himself to feel how it hurts."[17] Indeed, this ethic is affirmed in all cultures.

"Repay Evil with Good"

A particularly good example of a universal moral principle, because it is quite challenging to practice, is to repay evil with good. Consider the following quotations:

"Love your enemies and pray for those who persecute you." —Jesus[18]

"The good deed and the evil deed are not alike. Repel the evil deed with one that is better, then lo, he between whom and you there was enmity shall become as though he were a bosom friend." —Muhammad[19]

"Conquer anger by love. Conquer evil by good. Conquer the stingy by giving. Conquer the liar by truth." —Buddha[20]

"I treat those who are good with goodness, and I also treat those who are not good with goodness. Thus goodness is attained." —Lao Tzu[21]

"Hate cannot drive out hate; only love can do that." —Martin Luther King, Jr.

Every culture in the world condemns murder, adultery, theft and the character flaws of arrogance, lust and greed. Every culture in the world encourages self-cultivation in the ways of self-control, moderation, purity of heart, sincerity of intention, vigilance over one's actions, and endurance in adversity. Every culture without exception teaches kindness, honesty, service to others, charity for the poor, and fulfilling one's duties to family and community. These are only a few of the great array of values that are universally shared among cultures.

Human Nature

Human beings are a single species, and as such share common biological and psychological characteristics and functions. It stands to reason that people also possess common moral faculties. Traditionally, human nature was studied in the field of moral philosophy; today it is fashionable to look to psychology. Both fields have worthwhile insights.

There is a broad consensus among philosophers that human beings have an innate and irreducible moral sense. The human moral essence is essentially rational, according to Immanuel Kant who defined its core as the "categorical imperative." Other philosophers have described it with such terms as reason, conscience and moral cognition.

On the other hand, Jean-Jacques Rousseau spoke of man's natural goodness being cultivated through the sentiments, and Martin Heidegger described the human essence using the language of emotion—terms like "care" and "attunement."[22] In the East, Mencius taught that the core of human nature is the heart of compassion, saying, "no man is devoid of a heart sensitive to the suffering of others."[23]

Developmental psychology comprises the theoretical foundation for much of educational theory and practice. Among educational psychologists, Kohlberg employed a Kantian perspective. His research plumbed the rational-cognitive aspect of the moral self. He described the development of a child's sense of obligation as a succession of stages: from external concern about rewards and punishments, to a self-interested "tit-for-tat" ethic, to a concern for the valuation of peers, and so on. (See Chapter 2) Cross-cultural research with children in China, Japan and the Middle East shows that the path of cognitive moral development is the same everywhere.[24]

Carol Gilligan criticized Kohlberg's work by raising the issue of gender. She argued that women voice a morality of care that puts priority on affective relationships. They are more concerned about the welfare of the persons they care for, about preserving and enhancing relationships with them, than they are about rational considerations of justice and principles of right and wrong.[25] Recent research suggests that both men and women show moral development along both the rational-cognitive and emotional-relational dimensions.[26]

These diverse lines of inquiry affirm that human beings have an innate moral nature with both emotional and rational aspects. The two roots of the moral self may be called *heart* and *conscience*. The heart is the emotional and intuitive root of the moral self; the conscience is its rational root. The affective desire springing from the heart is what motivates a person to seek joy in loving relationships with others. Therefore, the heart motivates caring and altruistic behavior. The conscience is a moral compass that consistently points toward goodness and warns against potentially destructive behavior. It asserts the priority of obligations and duties over the self's egoistic desires. These moral faculties are discussed in the next chapter.

Natural Law

Philosophers East and West have analyzed human existence as manifesting the principles of the natural order. They studied human beings and the natural world, seeking to deduce the principles of their operation. They sought for the way of life by which people could be true to nature—and their own nature. In this way, they sought to deduce rational, ethical principles for living.

The Stoics of ancient Greece were the first to articulate the philosophical concept of natural law. They held that nature is designed according to a rational principle (*logos*), the very same rational principle by which humans can control their passions and create an ordered society. The rational principles that guide the movements of the stars, the growth of a seed, and the harmony of music will, when properly understood, also teach humans how to live their lives. Natural law philosophy, though sometimes disputed, has been a guiding philosophical idea in the West.

In the East, Confucianism also affirms natural law. It teaches that the way to self-cultivation begins with rational knowledge of moral truth, which is discovered through "the investigation of things" in the natural world. [27] A well-known maxim directly affirms the correspondence between the laws of the universe and the moral laws in human life:

> "The hawk soars to the heavens above, fishes dive to the depths below." That is to say, there is no place in the highest heavens above or in the deepest waters below where the moral law is not to be found. The moral man finds the moral law beginning in the relation between man and woman; but ending in the vast reaches of the universe. [28]

This correspondence cannot be a simplistic equation. Human beings are not of the same order of existence as birds or fish. The key distinction, of course, is that humans possess reason to understand moral choices and the freedom to make them. Decisions between right and wrong do not present themselves to animals, who act instinctively according to their given nature. Human life proceeds by conscious intention, decisions are made amidst knowledge of moral responsibility. Nevertheless, human beings are not alien to nature. In biology and in behavior, humans share much with the natural world. They exist within nature and are subject to its laws. Therefore, it stands to reason that human life is enhanced when lived in harmony with nature and its principles.

The import of the last sentence of the above passage is that love and the norms of the family—"the relation between man and woman"— is the beginning of the moral law. The centrality of the family as the natural school of morality and ethics is a continuing theme of this book.

Some scientists regard the human imperatives to grasp universal values and to know the principles of the natural world as fundamentally connected. Human beings, who have the intelligence to apprehend the meaning of existence, emerged through natural processes; they are the universe's way of becoming conscious of itself and completing itself. Humans prize the values of truth, beauty and goodness because these are inherent in the universe's structure. Nobel prizewinning biologist Christian de Duve writes:

> I opt in favor of a meaningful universe against a meaningless one—not because I want it to be so, but because that is how I read the available scientific evidence.... For me, this meaning is to be found in the structure of the universe, which happens to be such as to produce thought by way of life and mind. Thought, in turn, is a faculty whereby the universe can reflect upon itself, discover its own structure, and apprehend such immanent entities as truth, beauty, goodness, and love.[29]

Taken separately, any one of these five warrants for affirming universal values can be criticized, but together they make a strong argument. Moreover, given the pitfalls of considering one criteria such as "consensus" exclusively and leaving other criteria unexamined, multiple warrants for values provides for a richer, more comprehensive understanding of what makes values universal.

Survival of the Fittest?

One common objection to natural law theory is the view that, as nature is governed by natural selection and "the survival of the fittest," morality in the human world must be utterly unlike nature's "law of the jungle." However, modern evolutionary biology understands the law of survival of the fittest to be far more subtle. Biologists recognize that animals employ cooperation, altruism and even self-sacrifice as effective strategies to survive, attract mates, and raise offspring. Likewise, human nature is highly adapted, through millions of years of evolution, to participating in a social order, because people living in social groups are better able to survive and reproduce. People enjoy associating and working with others and are highly attuned to others' opinions, and influences and praise, because it is most often in their self-interest to cooperate. According to evolutionary psychology, moral impulses are motivated at the psychological level because they are ultimately conducive to reproductive success.

Biologist E. O. Wilson writes, "The evidence shows that because of [biology's] influence, people can readily be educated to only a narrow range of ethical precepts. They flourish in certain belief systems and wither in others."[30] In other words, the moral values and virtues that human beings universally prize—respect, altruism, courage, responsibility, honesty, etc.—are wired into human biology.

In an age when the hard "facts" of material existence often relegate the concern for values to the sidelines, and the emphasis on science, economics and technological subjects to the exclusion of values has left many students morally impoverished, such a case for universal values is necessary. It establishes the foundation for restoring balance in education and giving character its due priority.

Universal values integrate the best of Western and Eastern cultures, insights from modern science and traditional philosophy. They pertain to an individual's personal character and social relationships. They affect people's material success as well as their emotional well-being. Grounding them on a wider foundation of philosophy, psychology and world cultures validates them even as it provides rich resources and a more profound direction for character education.

4

The Heart of
Moral Education

ETHICAL CONDUCT IS NOT MERELY A MATTER OF KNOWING right from wrong. An interviewer once asked John Dean, who was sent to jail for his role in the Watergate scandal, whether he would have acted differently had his law school education focused on matters of professional responsibility. He replied, "No, I don't think so. I must say that I knew the things I was doing were wrong; one learns the difference between right and wrong long before entering law school. A course in legal ethics wouldn't have changed anything."[1]

Far more important than knowing what is right is *desiring* to do right and *caring* about what is right. An investigation into the core of a person's moral behavior thus leads to the emotions, and an examination of emotion leads inevitably to the issue of love. The capacity to love—to care about and for a person or thing and live for their sake—is the quintessence of character. What one loves determines what one does; how one loves determines how one does it.

True Love: The Essential Moral Value

There are several different kinds of human love: the love of children for their parents, love between siblings or between friends, love of parents for children, romantic love, love between spouses, and love of things (e.g., a pet, a garden, an automobile). To a greater or lesser degree, each of these kinds of love builds upon physical and instinctual desires: maternal, filial, or sexual. Yet while physical desires are certainly present in human love, they are relatively low on the list of the necessary factors. Far more important is the moral quality of love; for this reason people seek a love that is true. *True love* refers to the ideal of ethical love.

There is an essential link between love and ethics, one that is not always recognized. There is no argument that the love of parents is essential for the moral formation of children and therefore has ethical content and implications. Devotion among friends grows as they practice the values of respect, loyalty, honesty and self-sacrifice. Conversely, the ethical content of love may surface when it is violated. A mundane and taken-for-granted sense of camaraderie among close friends may hide powerful passions that come to the surface when the friendship is betrayed. The emotional pain—the rage, hurt and self-doubt—manifests in reverse the deep affective content of the ethic of loyalty.

True love is a moral ideal, and it has the following characteristics:

1. True love is for the best interests of the other. It is by nature unselfish; the other's welfare is the primary concern. For example, parents live to benefit their children, doing whatever they can to help their children realize their fullest potential. True friends enjoy helping each other with little thought to "what's in it for me."

2. True love is unconditional. It does not demand anything in return—no repayment or appreciation. The other person's welfare is reward enough. Yet the unconditional nature of true love should not be confused with blind love that is excessively indulgent; in its trueness there is wisdom about what sort of caring is actually helpful.

3. True love is serving and sacrificial. "Love... whether sexual, parental or fraternal, is essentially sacrificial," said philosopher George Santayana. People give everything for the sake of the ones they love, not counting the cost. A father dismisses a day's exhaustion and heads out to a second job to earn extra money for his son's college education. Yet he is not depleted by such sacrifices. Love has the peculiar property that the more it is given, the more the giver is filled—and the more joy returns.

4. True love is constant and everlasting. It endures because it is not negated by the whims of feelings, convenience or circumstance. A good

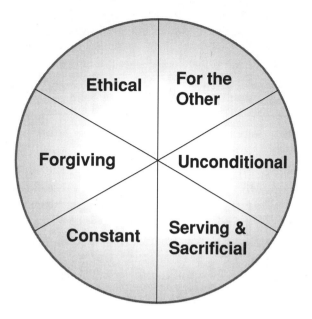

Figure 2: Qualities of True Love

friend stays at his pal's side in good times and bad. Devoted sons and daughters care for their elderly parents when they can no longer look after themselves, remembering with gratitude all the nurture they received when they were young.

5. True love is forgiving. Out of true love, brothers forgive each other after fighting, all grudges forgotten. Good friends tolerate each other's faults and character flaws; they forgive each other's mistakes and angry outbursts. Ideally, a person of true love has compassion even on his enemies, knowing that they are people just like him, only as yet unable to overcome their insecurities, ignorance and fears.

6. True love is ethical. The adjective "true" placed before the noun "love" qualifies its meaning. Harmonious and enduring relationships are possible only when they are conducted according to ethical principles.

Since true love places the benefit of others above the needs of the self, it follows that mastery over the self is a prerequisite for loving another. To become capable of true love, a person cultivates self-control and other virtues of good character. The ability to freely give and fully receive true love is attained through years of moral training, just as ability in painting or sports requires years of practice.

The Ideal of True Love: The Core of Universal Values

Character education begins with the universal values that are affirmed by all people. Everywhere in the world people revere such values and virtues as courage, responsibility, caring, respect, honesty, loyalty, fidelity, forgiveness and self-sacrifice. What do these values all have in common? They are altruistic. They are about giving to others and acting for their welfare. At the same time, they require self-denial, placing others' needs ahead of one's own. Therefore, the core principle behind all these virtues is true, unselfish love. Love is, in the words of Harvard sociologist Pitirim Sorokin, "the supreme value around which all moral values can be integrated into one ethical system valid for the whole of humanity."[2]

On the other hand, consider a list of vices: greed, cruelty, lust, dishonesty and exploitation. They characterize using others for one's own benefit. Even minor vices such as laziness and rudeness are rooted in a self-centered orientation that is lacking in regard for the needs or feelings of others. These vices manifest misdirected love, or love of self at others' expense.

True love is the root of universal values because it is linked to moral motivation. It pursues acts that are totally genuine, spontaneous, arising out of the core of being. A mother reaches for her newborn in tears of inexpressible gratitude after a harrowing delivery. A little boy nestles an injured sparrow tenderly in his hands and brings it home to care for. True love is patient, spurring a student to wait another hour in the rain hoping his friend might be on the next bus. True love breeds courage, leading a passer-by to rush to the aid of a woman who is being assaulted. Its power stirs people to acts of extreme bravery and self-sacrifice, where reasons of the heart prevail over calculations of the head.

The Inheritance of Love

People in every role and in all stages of growth can display the moral qualities of true love. Spouses demonstrate true love when they sacrifice for each other and persevere with each other through stormy times in their relationship. Children cultivate true love through experiences of giving to their siblings. Neighbors practice it in their communities when they come to each other's aid.

The devotion of fathers and mothers to their children particularly exemplifies the ideal nature of true love. Even parents who are in other respects morally deficient are moved to unselfishness for the sake of their needy offspring. Most parents try their best to care for their children with unconditional, constant, sacrificial and ethical love. They work long hours only to return home to do housework, make dinner, help José with his homework and read Maria a bedtime story—all without condition or complaint.

Children first experience the altruistic and sacrificial quality of true love as their fathers and mothers model it. In a good home, they experience parental care as generous, steadfast, and entirely for their sake—and internalize that experience as pointing to the kind of love they want. Therefore, it is natural that such young people have an ideal of love—true love—and hope to attain it.

In their study of rescuers of Jews in Nazi Europe, Samuel and Pearl Oliner found that rescuers were motivated by strong values of care and inclusiveness. These were in large part transmitted to them through the bond with their parents in early childhood, which became the "prototype for all subsequent relationships."[3]

The reality of home life, however, is not always nurturing and enriching. Parents have their own difficulties: moments of self-absorption and outbursts of temper. Try as they might, their expressions of caring still involve a mixture of altruistic and egocentric motives. Consequently, the children inherit their parents' mixed quality of love.

Regardless, young people have opportunities to overcome even a difficult home life. This depends on the choices they make every day in relating with siblings, friends, relatives and teachers. They can let matters take the path of least resistance or choose the more challenging and yet rewarding path of living for others. Where effective parents are lacking, a grandparent, aunt, cousin or teacher may step into the breach and offer children the care, modeling and discipline they require as the foundation for moral development.

Teachers supplement parents by continuing to work on raising the level of children's moral sense, especially their moral emotions—the cultivation of the heart. They impart wisdom about the nature of love and training in the standards of proper conduct. They also provide role models by their own example of generous service for the sake of their students. Such intentional character education efforts help to properly nurture the young generation. It brings dividends in the future when these students grow to adulthood and have greater internal resources to bequeath to their children. Thus moral civilization is sustained and renewed.

Heart—The Core of Character

True love is the core of moral motivation and the ideal of moral striving; accordingly, there are innate human faculties for its expression. These are the heart and the conscience. The heart is love's emotional source, and the conscience is its guide. Formation of good character that is capable of giving true, altruistic love is centrally concerned with cultivating these faculties.

The motivational center of character is the "heart." It signifies the energy source for moral striving. The heart has been called "the core-force of personality...the locus of personal authenticity, the holistic force that is the shape of what we really are."[4] It is the core of human nature and the innermost center of character.

The heart is the seat of intention, because the deepest of human intentions are rooted in the affections. This is why the heart is so often depicted by emotional language. A person's heart may be aflame with passion, or cold, or broken. Lovers' hearts are said to "beat as one"; a whole community united in spirit "acts with one heart." Although the heart is first a faculty of feeling, it also has its rational aspect—people speak of someone having "an understanding heart." The heart has a volitional aspect as well: a person may be "faint-hearted" or "stout-hearted"; a boxer who fights gamely against a superior opponent is said to "have heart."[5]

Impulse for Relatedness

The heart's fundamental impulse is towards relatedness. It is the root of the emotional need for love. The affective desire springing from the heart is what motivates a person to yearn for the joy of loving and being loved, the satisfaction of valuing and being valued. Love and relatedness are human needs as strong as those for food or shelter; indeed, people have forsaken both for the sake of love. As psychologist Erich Fromm once stated, "The desire for interpersonal fusion is the most powerful striving in man. It is the most fundamental passion, it is the force which keeps the human race together, the clan, the family, society."

By driving the self to relate with others, the heart motivates moral behavior. Ethicist James Q. Wilson, author of *The Moral Sense*, states, "The mechanism underlying human moral conduct is the desire for attachment or affiliation."[6] As a person's heart reaches towards love, he tries to act for the benefit of his object of love. His heart draws him to manifest virtue.

In Chinese ethical thought, the heart is the root of a person's humanity. The philosopher Mencius gave the example of a child who is about to fall into a well. Anyone who passes by, regardless of his relation to the child's family, cannot but be moved by anxiety for the child's safety and rush to save her. This is because all people have such a heart that "when they see another person suffer, they suffer, too." Mencius claims that not to feel such compassion would not be human.[7]

An actual incident of this sort happened in Midland, Texas, in 1987 when two-year-old Jessica McClure fell down an abandoned well and was trapped for 58 hours. During the anxious hours rescue crews worked to save her, the entire world watched the drama on the news. Strangers from all over the country showered the child's family with gifts, letters and money. When the child was rescued unharmed, the whole nation breathed a sigh of relief.

In people with poorly formed character, their heart's original direction may be powerless against the pull of self-centered desires, and therefore it remains undercultivated. Nevertheless, even the most depraved people have a heart and thus are capable of reform. Gangsters love their wives and children and want a better life for them. The presence of heart in every person means that no criminal is immune to rehabilitation. Russian writer Alexander Solzhenitsyn wrote movingly of this realization as he lay in prison:

> In the intoxication of youthful successes I had felt myself to be infallible, and I was therefore cruel.... It was only when I lay there on rotting prison straw that I sensed within myself the first stirrings of good. Gradually it was disclosed to me that the line separating good and evil passes not through states, nor between classes, nor between political parties either—but right through every human heart—and through all human hearts. This line shifts. Inside us, it oscillates with the years. And even within hearts overwhelmed by evil, one small bridgehead of good is retained.[8]

Assessing the Heart

In this discussion, "heart" is not simply a neutral term for passions and feelings. Rather, situated at the core of the self, heart is inherently moral, just as the term "character" by itself denotes a positive, healthy state of moral integrity. As the motivating and integrating center of character, the heart's promptings are generally productive of positive character development. Psychologists can recognize the functioning of the heart in the following measures:

a. Empathy
b. Sense of meaning and purpose
c. Self-ideality (sense of one's own integrity)
d. Moral reaction (when presented with scenes of good and evil)
e. Moral passion (zeal for justice)
f. Emotional intelligence

Cultivation of the Heart

Moral educators in both the East and West have emphasized the cultivation of the heart as the foundation for education. The 19th-century Swiss educator Johann Pestalozzi conceived the task of education to foster students' innate abilities, and viewed it as having three components: education of the mind, education of the hand, and education of the heart. Cultivating the heart lies at the core of education because the moral sentiment to love is the power that can unite these three realms of human ability. In this regard, Pestalozzi pointed to the educational process of a mother with her young child. Drawn to the mother's affection, the child tries to please, and in so doing his heart is naturally trained and molded by her moral instruction.

Mencius taught the doctrine of the "four foundations" of ethical behavior, all centered in the heart. Humane behavior arises from a heart that sympathizes with pain, he declared. Right action arises from a heart that is repelled by vice. Respectful behavior arises from a heart that is willing to defer. Receptivity to education is rooted in a heart that loves truth. Building up these four foundations means fostering a strong moral sensibility through cultivating the heart that lies at their root. When this cultivation is neglected, the people become morally incompetent: "Leave [the four foundations] unfilled, and it will be impossible for a man to take care of his parents."[9]

Modern educators also affirm the centrality of heart in moral education. They understand that the quality of motivation is a primary factor in determining whether students develop quickly, slowly or veer off the path of optimal character development. They recognize that the motivational dimension often dominates the way people use reason and logic in solving moral challenges.[10] Advocating cultivation of the heart, Boston College psychologist William Kilpatrick states, "In education for virtue, the heart is trained as well as the mind. The virtuous person learns not only to distinguish between good and evil but to love one and hate the other."[11]

Experiences of Love

Among the ways the heart is cultivated, of first importance are experiences of loving and being loved in the family. Family experiences are foundational in moral development. A mother's care and concern naturally induces feelings of gratitude and filial respect in her children, along with a natural attitude of obedience. Following the example of their parents' love for them, they practice loving their siblings and peers and honoring their elders. Furthermore, the warm affection they have for their mother and father gives children an abiding sense of self-worth and the inner confidence to reach out to others and form lasting friendships.

Julie was a shy girl from Milwaukee who faced a difficult adjustment when she first attended college in California. It was her first time away from home. She felt awkward in social situations, lonely and homesick. But she discovered that the best "medicine" to her heartsickness was her weekly phone call to Mom on Sunday mornings. Those nurturing phone conversations reminded Julie that she had people who loved her. They gave her the confidence to come out of her shell and make new friends.

Teachers do well to be aware of these profound moral influences on their students. As Kieran Egan says, "What children know best when they come to school are love, hate, joy, fear, good and evil. That is, they know best the most profound human emotions and the bases for morality."[12] Teachers supplement the care and nurturing received in families and can also serve a remedial function when such experiences are lacking. When surveyed, most teachers agree with the statement, "I hope that I can have a lasting effect on the students whom I teach, not just by making them better students, but by making them better people."[13] Teachers have profound impact on their students not only by their values, but also by showing positive love in the form of personal attention and encouragement.

Role Models

Children's hearts are also cultivated through imitating moral examples. Social learning theory recognizes that parents and teachers play the most meaningful roles in modeling behavior.[14] The primary role models are parents and grandparents; adolescents look to them far more than to pop stars, politicians, sports figures or religious leaders, according to a German study.[15] Likewise, students are drawn to a teacher who genuinely displays the warmth and care of a good parent or wise aunt or uncle. Such a teacher forms a connection of heart that is both motivating and convincing.

A large part of moral teaching in the classroom is through example. Students resistant to a teacher's spoken instructions may be quicker to model his behavior. One teacher in an inner-city school recounts that shortly after he first began teaching, a kid wrote him a poem:

Oh, how I loved to watch you when you teach.
Oh, how I hated it when you preached.

Realizing that it was true, the teacher began to model what he believed in. He describes his method, "When I am giving 'morning lectures' about how messy the room is and we go to pick things up, I am picking up too. I'll say, 'If I can pick it up, you can pick it up, too.' They take to it very well."[16]

Conscience—The Moral Compass

Although the heart is ever prompting people to ethical behavior in the service of love, by itself this emotional faculty functions rather poorly as a guide to love. People's self-centered desires, felt as personal needs—and sometimes family needs—make a noisy claim on their consciousness, often drowning out the moral impulses of the heart. The love that flows between two people can easily be derailed unless the relationship is guided by moral truth. When people behave ethically towards one another, their love is strengthened and affirmed. Discerning right from wrong is necessary to properly guide the heart's impulse into constructive behavior. The conscience is the faculty that does this.

Psychologists distinguish two modalities of the conscience. The first positively regulates behavior based on internal values.[17] This "active conscience" consistently points toward goodness and warns against potentially destructive behavior. It urges people to live for the benefit of others rather than for themselves. The second modality creates emotional discomfort subsequent to a transgression—guilt, remorse, and empathy for the victim—the "pangs" of conscience.

Active Conscience

Brian, a ninth-grade student in Poughkeepsie, New York, needed money desperately because he owed a friend. When he saw the cassette player sitting on a table in his Global Studies classroom, he was tempted to steal it. The room was empty; it would be easy to put the cassette player in his bag. The chances of being caught were minimal. Yet a voice in Brian's mind told him not to do it. "Why can't I just steal this cassette recorder?" he thought, as he kept walking down the corridor. "I know many other people who would snatch it without hesitation. Why am I different?" Brian is not "different"; his active conscience was strongly at work. By facing his conscience sooner rather than later, he would not have to suffer the pangs of conscience that a light-fingered classmate would inevitably face.

Humorist Mark Twain did not doubt the existence or power of the conscience; in fact, he considered its constant prodding toward goodness something of a nuisance. He wrote a humorous fantasy to that effect in which his conscience appeared personified as a leprechaun-like creature. Here, he wrote, was the source of his constant moral discomfort with smoking, cursing and all his other vices! In the story, Twain rose up and killed his conscience. Finally free to do as he pleased, he went on a crime spree, even burning down a neighbor's house that obstructed his view. The humor of this piece comes from the reader's recognition of himself (and his conscience) in it.[18]

A strong, active conscience is an effective guide to moral behavior. In a person of mature character, the directives of the conscience and moral impulses of the heart act in unison as the center of an integrated *moral identity*. A person with a strong moral identity identifies her self-interest in moral terms. In other words, she regards herself as a good person and strives to act accordingly.

Weak Conscience

On the other hand, when the conscience is weak, it is always a poor second to the self. People with a weak conscience form an egocentric identity that places self-interest above the needs of others. Their life is mainly occupied with gratifying the desires of the moment. The voice of the protesting conscience grows faint in this poorly formed self.[19]

Stacy remembered the first time she stole a candy bar. Dozens of people were swarming around the candy display. She was so nervous, her pulse raced and her hands sweated. And afterwards she felt really terrible. She thought about it for a long time: "What if everybody else did it?" A week later, Stacy found herself in the same store stealing again. It didn't feel so bad, and besides, the lady at the checkout line was in a foul mood. Three of her friends were waiting outside. First she told Erica about stealing the candy, and she was upset. But then she told Joanne, who thought Stacy must be pretty brave and even dared her to try to steal four candy bars at one time. Now it was simply a challenge, and Stacy knew she could do it.

Stacy has found rationalizations and excuses to justify her continued larceny. The poor manners of the checkout lady and the desire to win a friend's dare easily overpowered her conscience, which had bothered her the first time she stole. She also found peer support. Perhaps Stacy will feel pangs of conscience later, after her stealing gets her into trouble. But for now, her weak conscience is easily defeated. She is on her way to creating a badly formed moral self.

Educating the Conscience

Moral training establishes an integrated moral identity by strengthening the conscience and subordinating self-centered desires. The unhappy experience of educators in recent years with values clarification and other non-directive approaches has served to reaffirm the traditional wisdom that properly directive moral education is needed to educate and strengthen the conscience. Today, character educators inculcate positive moral values to fortify a young person's conscience with a firm knowledge of right and wrong.

Conscience is innate; its directives are felt even in young children. Although they are not yet able to completely articulate a rational justification, in exercises in which they are presented with simple moral dilemmas of right and wrong, they can usually choose between the two. Michael, a four-year-old, was playing at a neighbor's house. In a fit of anger, he smashed his playmate's plastic toy truck. There was a moment of silence, and then he broke into tears, knowing that something was wrong. However, for every Michael with a sensitive conscience there are many children whose anger against their playmate would blind them to any thought that they had done wrong.

With the conscience's intrinsic sense of truth as a foundation, moral education adds strength and confidence. Only through education do most peoples' consciences grow powerful enough to overcome the competing egoistic desires of the self. The conscience sometimes also needs correction, as it can be distorted by mistaken social beliefs and implicit negative messages in the culture.

Conflicting Moral Obligations

Sometimes there is a felt tension between conflicting moral claims, for example between love of neighbor and care of one's family. Judy, a young mother, was walking to school to pick up her children when approached by an elderly neighbor using a cane. The neighbor asked her to walk her home, saying that her nurse was sick for the day. Judy was torn by the request, because she was already a few minutes late to get her children. What if something happened to her children during her delay? Still, she knew she ought to serve her neighbor. Despite her fears and annoyance, she helped the woman. Later, with the children safely home, Judy's heart flooded with feelings of lightness and pride. Her choice to serve her neighbor was in accord with her conscience, which gives priority to the greater purpose. She felt its reward as a deep inner satisfaction.

Generally, the duties of citizenship and neighborliness are considered to have greater moral pull than the needs of family and self. A healthy society, after all, provides the context for family and self to thrive. (See Chapter 9) Yet mature moral judgment affirms the need to strike a balance between familial and social duties.[20] There is also something unhealthy about extreme selflessness that suggests low self-esteem and can invite exploitation. Ethicist Steve Post warns, "Love requires the acceptance of a self-sacrifice justly limited by reasonable degrees of self-concern, lest love become oppressive and destructive of the agent."[21] People with a healthy sense of dignity and value are able to balance their own emotional and physical needs with those of others to whom they are obligated.[22] The intuitive messages of the heart can be a check upon an overly rigid and demanding conscience.

Character and Love

Character and love are inextricably connected. It should not be astonishing that a person of mature character with an integrated moral identity is far better able to form joyful, loving relationships than a person of immature character who is conflicted between his conscience and the lower desires of the self. Joshua, a young father in San Antonio, Texas, was out of work and short of money. When his 3-year-old daughter Trish wasted a roll of gold wrapping paper while decorating a box to put under the Christmas tree, he was furious and spanked her. The next morning, Trish brought the gift-wrapped box to him and said, "This is for you, Daddy." Joshua was embarrassed by his earlier overreaction, but his anger flared again when he found that the box was empty. "Don't you know that when you give someone a present, there's supposed to be something inside of it?" he yelled. Trish looked up at him and said, "Oh Daddy, it's not empty. I blew kisses into the box. All for you." The crestfallen father was humbled. Recognizing how his character limitations had led him to hurt his daughter, he saw a glimpse of himself he didn't like and resolved to change.[23]

A caring heart and a righteous conscience enable altruistic love. They are the primary faculties of good character development. Therefore, cultivation of the heart—the source of love and affection—is at the center of character development from an early age: so are moral training and self-discipline to establish the primacy of the conscience. These elements form the core of moral education. They provide the basis that young people need for personal growth and emotional and moral development in the school years and beyond.

5

Life Goals and Character Development

MOST CHARACTER EDUCATION SCHOOLS SHOWCASE A VIRTUE of the week or of the month. Each has an operating list of 6 to 12-plus virtues, which was arrived at after a process of consensus building. Other virtues among the many that have been identified are often attached as adjuncts to the core virtues on the list. The question can be posed: among the lists of virtues used in various schools across the country, which list is superior? Which virtues are the most important or fundamental to teach? More importantly, how can the practice of virtue be demonstrated as being relevant to a young person's life?

The end toward which virtues are practiced is as important as the virtues themselves. Simply practicing a set of virtues does not necessarily make for a person of character. For example, the members of the Mafia practice virtues every day. They value the virtues of honesty, trust and loyalty so highly that they commit to them with their lives. They love and care for their families. They are responsible and persevering in their work. Yet does this mean that Mafiosi are virtuous people? The more fundamental question is, what purpose and goals are the virtues serving?

Making a case for universal moral values relates to large questions of meaning and purpose. Alisdaire MacIntyre, a prominent contemporary ethicist, places instruction in virtues within the fundamental human need to have a meaningful life story. He states, "To adopt a stance on the virtues is to adopt a stance on the narrative of human life... Belief in the virtues being of a certain kind and belief in human life exhibiting a certain narrative order are internally connected."[1] In other words, the way people conceive of virtues and vices depends upon their overall view of their life's path. When young people make a personal connection between values and their own life's purposes, they are more inclined in the end to act in valuable, prosocial ways.[2] Thus, a vision of the moral life as learning about love appeals to individuals' moral as well as romantic imagination. All in all, adopting a view of life's meaning affords a valuable perspective for understanding the elements of character development and fortifying the character education process.

A Framework for a Meaningful Life— The Three Basic Life Goals

Are there certain goals for life, which people universally desire and pursue? The universal longing for a happy and prosperous life is innate in human nature. All people seek the material goods that make for happiness—adequate food, shelter, material comfort, good health and long life. Likewise, people strive to attain spiritual and moral goals that are needed for lasting happiness. These may be broadly classified as follows:

(1) Personal maturity
(2) Loving relationships and family
(3) Contribution to society

For simplicity, these can be referred to as the Three Basic Life Goals. Achieving personal maturity, engaging in loving and satisfying relationships and contributing meaningfully to society are important priorities for achieving a fulfilling and balanced life.

These three purposes are found throughout the spectrum of moral thought. They are found in a foundational Confucian text that begins, "The Great Learning teaches: to manifest shining virtue, to love people, and to rest in the highest good." Covey expressed these goals as "to live, to love, to learn, to leave a legacy," and considers them fundamental to human life.[3] "To live" and "to learn" are aspects of the first life goal of personal maturity. "To love" encompasses the second life goal of loving relationships and family, and "to leave a legacy" describes the third life goal of making a contribution to society. Longer lists of life's priorities can readily be classified accordingly.[4]

The purpose of education in the broadest sense is to produce decent, competent human beings who will form strong families and be assets to society. These three educational goals were identified by British educator Richard Livingstone as: 1) to achieve personal maturity and integrity; 2) to find happiness in love through having a family and friends; and 3) to be successful in one's chosen career and so to contribute to society.[5] Likewise, Brentwood High School in St. Louis County, Missouri arrived at a framework for their character education curriculum that affirms three fundamental moral domains:

- Personal goals (first life goal): accountability, honesty, perseverance, and respect for self.

- Social goals (second life goal): abstinence from drugs, alcohol and sex; caring about others; commitment to family; positive work ethic; respect for others and service.

- Civic goals (third life goal): equality, freedom, justice, respect for authority and respect for property.[6]

One parent expressed her expectations for her son as, "I want my son to be a decent human being first, someone who can win the respect of others, love his wife and children and make a difference in the world."

Psychological research into the meaning-dimension of personhood broadly supports the three basic life goals. Conner and Chamberlain's study of the dimensions of meaning at mid-life[7] found that the most common sources of meaning in the participant's lives correlated with:

- *Personal development* (first life goal). Abraham Maslow wrote of life as a process of "self-actualization." The theme of responsibility for self is found to be a common source of meaning in many studies.[8]

- *Relationships with people* (second life goal). This is consistently reported as the most frequent source of meaning across the life span.[9]

- *Creativity & relating with nature* (third life goal). Psychologists Victor Frankl and Irvin Yalom emphasize creativity as an important source of meaning.[10]

In reality, many people do not make these goals a priority. Even while they pursue them, they don't necessarily achieve them. Yet the desire to attain them is latent in the human personality. When parents and schools lift up these goals as an explicit moral framework for life, young people can orient themselves to what is most meaningful and identify those values and tasks that may bring the greatest fulfillment.

Life Goals and Universal Moral Values

Establishing life's priorities brings added clarity to the Why of universal values. Virtues such as honesty, respect, responsibility, caring, etc., are "values" because people find them "valuable" in journeying towards fulfilling their life goals. As such, the perspective of basic life goals answers the question, "*Why* should I be honest, respectful, responsible, caring?"

The path to attaining a fulfilling life requires people to learn and practice what Peter Bertocci, a personalist philosopher, called a "symphony of values."[11] Values are like the instruments of the orchestra that play together to create the music of a worthwhile life. The full spectrum of values forms a unity in a person of character, concurs William Kilpatrick.[12] Likewise, in Chinese moral philosophy, the purpose of following moral precepts is to train people who are fully human. Ethics is about "person-making," not "rule-following." Rules and values are but the means to the end of self-realization as a moral person who can fully participate in civilized life.[13]

Internally and relationally oriented goals of personhood comprehend the fact that virtues are expressed differently and developmentally throughout life. Values are elastic, in that they appear appropriately different in age-appropriate phases. For example, obeying rules and fulfilling tasks such as returning toys to their proper place may exhibit responsibility for kindergartners. For a middle school student, responsibility expands to include personal accountability for one's work and actions. For teenagers, responsibility may include a broader context of seeing the impact of one's own behavior on the group and society. These changing and developing values are readily subsumed by the unchanging life goals of personal maturity, loving relationships, and contributing to society. These goals set a distant horizon, an inner ideal that pulls human development in a healthy direction.

Establishing life goals is particularly important for adolescents. Unless they develop a clear moral identity and find a sense of meaning in life, they are likely to struggle with feelings of hopelessness, lack of purpose and anomie. This leads to antisocial behavior. Many studies have confirmed that both exemplary and antisocial behavior can be predicted by the manner in which adolescents integrate moral concerns into their theories and descriptions of self.[14]

Long past the point where simple appeals to responsibility, caring and honesty are effective, the life goals beckon teenagers and young adults to stretch themselves to embody virtues in new ways in each phase of development. This holds promise to not only engage reluctant teenagers in the character education classroom, but also to keep them mindful of character and moral purpose later in their adult lives.

The failure of the educational system to contend with the anchoring question of life's purpose and meaning has resulted in considerable confusion. Kevin Ryan asserts that the absence of discussions of life's meaning and purpose puts character education at great peril, and that ignoring it is "miseducative."[15] Yet many schools have difficulty handling these questions, for fear of ranging into territory usually considered to belong to religion, a highly contested and divisive issue.[16] However, questions of meaning and purpose are appropriately—even profoundly—addressed under the rubric of the three basic life goals. Their universality may be intuitively affirmed.

A Holistic Outline of Character Development

Viewing character development through the prism of the three basic life goals suggests a dynamic and multi-dimensional process. One may examine character development as the flowering of innate and learned personal virtues, as a social process nourished by family relationships, and as acquiring the virtues and attitudes that make for good citizenship. In fact, these three aspects are integrated in the development of moral persons. Examining them both separately and as interrelated in the makeup of whole persons provides a rich fabric for understanding what is centrally important in life.

A life goals perspective informs and supports current methods in the domain of character education: teaching values through the curriculum, moral reasoning, conflict resolution, cooperative learning, service learning, or a focus on a particular virtue for an entire week or month. (See Chapters 10-13) It is helpful in illuminating theoretical connections among existing frameworks, such as the eleven principles of the Character Education Partnership.[17] Furthermore, sometimes character educators after their initial efforts find themselves running out of steam. "We've been doing this for five years," said one teacher at a character education conference. "We're wondering now: where do we go from here?" A larger rationale grounded in clearly articulated philosophy and research, with a clear goal orientation based on meaning-centered, relational themes, can help refresh the conviction and renew the creative inspiration needed to continue.

As various components of the life goals perspective will be referred to again and again throughout the book, it is worthwhile sketching it out in brief.

The Individual: Cultivation of Heart and Conscience (First Life Goal)

The starting-point for character development is the individual as a being of heart and conscience. The heart, as the innate impulse to love and be loved, is the emotional and motivational center of the moral self. It provides the impetus to altruistic love, caring, and ethical action. The conscience, as the cognitive center, distinguishes between right and wrong and steers the self accordingly. It stands in tension with self-centered desires; its proper function therefore depends upon taming these desires and channeling them towards moral ends. Cultivating the heart and conscience are the central tasks of character development.

Through this process, the individual acquires a good balance among the primary moral faculties: moral feeling, moral knowing and moral action. [18] Moral feeling involves empathy for others and a zeal for righteousness; moral knowing includes wisdom, honesty and prudence; and moral action includes courage, integrity and self-control. When these work together in harmony, the desires of the heart and the wisdom of the conscience bear fruit in moral behavior and upright character.

Family: The School of Love and Relationships (Second Life Goal)

Next, growth of character is molded through the familial and social relationships experienced on the journey from child to adult. The good family is primarily a school of love. Its lessons begin for the child in the context of the relationship with his parents. There are more lessons for the older child as he relates with siblings, friends and other peers. Learning about love and training in character continue on life's journey into marriage and parenthood. The lessons of love and character learned in the family also facilitate forming good relationships with superiors, peers and subordinates in any social group. Recognizing the value of the caring community of the home leads by extension to efforts at building caring communities in schools, neighborhoods and at work.

The school of love that is the family has four progressive stages, or spheres: child's love, sibling's love, spouse's love and parent's love. These are called the Four Spheres of Love. (See Chapter 14) When a child practices generosity in relating with his parents, it broadens and deepens his capacity for unselfish giving later in life. A teenager who makes loyal and affirming friendships with siblings and peers is more likely to have an enduring marriage. Conjugal love forms a sphere unique to itself, deepening the heart through new experiences of intimacy, commitment and sharing. Parents' love deepens still more through the many sacrifices needed to raise the next generation.

However, to be successful in each successive sphere of love, the pace of inner character growth should match the challenges and opportunities afforded by the roles and relationships specific to the sphere.

Social Contribution: The Fruition of Character (Third Life Goal)

On the basis of life lessons learned in the family, people attain the maturity to take on civic responsibilities. The harvest of mature adulthood is to become a good parent, teacher and leader. Society functions at its best when its teachers, leaders and managers are capable of empathy and altruistic concern for those who look to them for leadership and instruction. Likewise, workers who practice an attitude of ethical caring are more productive. They take pride in providing attractive products and superior service; they have the relationship skills to get along well with their colleagues and bosses. Indeed, regardless of social position, people who possess mature character and live to be of service to others will have a positive impact on their communities.

An Integrated Dynamic

The personal, familial and social aspects of life are deeply intertwined with one another. A person's capacity for love, and hence her ability to build a strong family, is predicated on the content of her individual character—her depth of heart, clarity of conscience, and balanced functioning of moral feeling, moral knowing and moral action. Conversely, the atmosphere of love and caring in her family fosters the cultivation of heart and conscience; the habit of living for others practiced at home and with friends molds her good character. Character development and competence in the succession of life's relationships go hand in hand.

Individual character and its expression in a family context are foundational for the ability to function as a responsible citizen and take on leadership roles in society. Conversely, a family that practices good citizenship and cares about the welfare of its neighbors naturally deepens the love and respect at home and provides a more directive environment for the growth of individual character. Parents who serve their community naturally set an example for their children to do the same.

True Love: The Inner Dimension

Finally, the inner dimension of this rich dynamic of character development is the expanding scope of love. True love is both the motivating force behind the growth of character and the ideal of its expression. Efforts to achieve personal maturity, to make a loving family, and to contribute to society are fundamentally motivated by the heart's desire for affiliation—to experience belonging and affection, to feel value and find meaning. Moreover, each of these three life goals can best be realized by practicing true love, which takes the form of living for the sake of others.

Out of love, a child internalizes the moral demands of his parents in his budding conscience. He learns the norms of behavior that bring acceptance and positive regard by peers. His character is shaped and formed in the matrix of loving relationships—notably with parents, then siblings and peers, spouse and sons and daughters. His love for community and country becomes the impetus to civic participation. At each stage on his journey toward achieving the three life goals, his capacity to love and be loved deepens and expands accordingly.

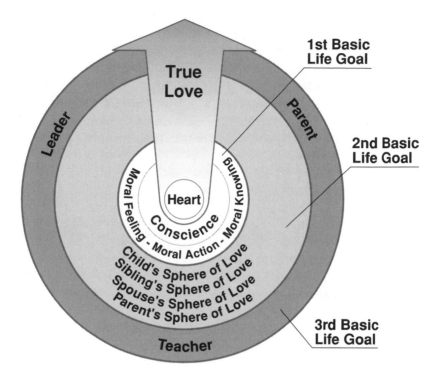

Figure 3: Character Development through
the Pursuit of the Three Life Goals

The dynamic process of character development according to the framework of the three basic life goals is illustrated in Figure 3.

The central area represents the individual's moral faculties and the dynamic among them. At its core is the heart, the root of moral motivation and source of true love. The first ring depicts the balance between conscience and individual desires. The second ring represents the outward manifestation of individual character through the interplay of moral feeling, moral knowing and moral action. This is the domain for realizing the first basic life goal—personal maturity.

The middle area with its four concentric circles represents the Four Spheres of Love, the primary family-based relationships through which the individual grows in love and develops his or her character. This is the domain for realizing the second basic life goal—loving relationships and family.

The outermost ring represents the fruition of character in the context of society, as manifest in the civic responsibilities of parent, teacher and leader. This is the domain for realizing the third basic life goal—contribution to society.

The large, broad arrow represents the force of true love, which emanates from the heart outward. It signifies its ever-expanding momentum and nature, permeating life's various relational and familial contexts and extending to social responsibilities and beyond.

Section 2

Principles for a Meaningful Life

ANDREW WILSON

CHARACTER IS NOT A SKILL ONE LEARNS, NOT A BEHAVIOR ONE chooses to do in a particular situation, but is an aspect of one's very self. Built up through experience, education and self-authorship, character only grows to the extent that a person lives out his or her values and ideals. It is linked to a sense of personal meaning and purpose—which in this context can be summarized as three basic life goals: personal maturity, loving relationships and family, and contribution to society.

At the same time, the fruitful pursuit of these goals is not arbitrary. While human beings are to a large extent the architects of their own character and destiny, attaining mature character and a satisfying, productive life requires conscious effort tempered by wisdom. One aspect of wisdom is understanding the universal principles operative at the root of human existence as individuals and as social beings. Disregard for them leads to frustration and isolation. Respecting them leads to fulfillment, personal integrity and a positive outlook on life.

Likewise, satisfying and lasting relationships do not happen automatically. Wisdom about the principles of good relationships can guide people in general, and especially parents and educators who are responsible to raise young people to find happiness in their relationships with others. The capacity for caring and the competencies to get along well with others are cultivated in the family, which is called the "school of love," as well as in the larger worlds of school, work and community. By the same token, the life objective of making a social contribution requires understanding ethical norms; these can make the difference between a genuine contribution and mere self-seeking.

Adherence to universal principles is not to be confused with simple rule-following. Having focused on love as the core motivating force of moral development, it is understood that principles function mainly as guidelines for the realization of an individual's fullest potential as a moral person, a loving person, and a productive member of society.

6

Universal Principles

The laws governing human behavior are not invented by us or by society; they are the laws of the universe that pertain to human relationships and human organizations.... These principles are woven into the fabric of every civilized society and constitute the roots of every family and institution that has endured and prospered.

—Stephen Covey[1]

IN HIS BOOK *PRINCIPLE-CENTERED LEADERSHIP*, STEPHEN COVEY examines the moral principles that undergird every successful and enduring human institution. He criticizes the modern fashion of re-inventing society based on the "improved" values advocated by the latest social theory. Such social engineering inevitably fails, he believes, because it ignores the fact that human life is grounded in unchangeable principles; principles as inexorable as the laws of nature.[2] A baby's need for love and affection from her parents is as unchangeable a reality of life as the law of gravity.

Natural law—the idea that the principles governing nature trace out the way for people to live in accordance with their own inherent nature—has guided philosophers and thinkers East and West. (See Chapter 3) The neo-Confucian philosopher Chu Hsi wrote, "If we wish to carry our knowledge [of how to cultivate the self] to the utmost, we must investigate the principles of all things we encounter, for there is not a single thing that lacks an inherent principle."[3]

Humans, as rational beings, are not strictly determined by the laws of matter. They are not impelled by brute instinct, as animals are when they feed and mate. Humans have free will. Speaking of love, for example, psychologist M. Scott Peck said, "True love is not a feeling by which we are overwhelmed. It is a committed, thoughtful decision."[4]

Nevertheless, nature and its governing principles provide the background and context for human decisions. For example, the human body is constituted by nature to need protection from the cold. Someone may choose to work outdoors on a frigid winter day without wearing an overcoat, but as a consequence he is likely to become sick. A healthy lifestyle is not instinctive; mothers teach their children about the habits of good health.

By the same token, there are natural and universal principles governing a person's pursuit of a meaningful and moral life and satisfying relationships with others. These principles lie at the root of human existence as individuals and as social beings. Disregard for them leads to frustration and isolation. Respecting them leads to personal fulfillment and lasting love. As natural as these principles are, understanding and applying them does not come naturally to people. Education helps people exercise their uniquely human freedom and responsibility to do so.

Seven Universal Principles
and Their Application to the Human Condition

(These are discussed at length in the following chapters.)

Growth

Natural Principle

Entities develop in stages from a seed to their mature form. With favorable conditions—ample sunshine, water and good soil—a seed, which contains the plant's genetic blueprint, sprouts into a seedling and grows into a fruit-bearing plant. The grown plant manifests the full potential latent in the seed.

Application

There are predictable stages in the growth of character and in the development of a person's capacity to love. With love and the proper education, a child's innate potential for goodness can blossom into mature character.

Complementarity

Natural Principle

All entities in nature exist as a paired structure, and each attracts its complement to form paired relationships. Examples include anions and cations, male and female, stamen and pistil. Nature is replete with complementary opposites—hot and cold, light and darkness, high and low, etc. Things also are composed of external and internal dimensions, as an animal and its instinct, a computer and its program, an atom and its quantum state.

Application

The complementarity between male and female is evident in the universal human tendency to form families. Moreover, individual human existence deals with two dimensions—mind (consciousness) and body (material existence)—that generally reflect one another.

Interaction

Natural Principle

Two entities form a relationship and solidify it through giving and receiving elements of themselves. Through interaction, the entities unite and produce the forces needed to exist and act. In physics, electromagnetic forces are produced through the interaction of photons.

Application

The Golden Rule, "Treat others as you would wish others to treat you," is a moral principle underlying lasting and harmonious relationships. Training in reflective listening and other communication skills that facilitate good giving and receiving improves relationships of all kinds. Economies thrive through the fair exchanges of goods and services.

Distinct Roles

Natural Principle

Relative and distinct positions are established in the course of any interaction. Animal communities establish distinct roles: the queen bee, drones and worker bees; the alpha male in the wolf pack and subordinate males, to give two examples. Conflict is avoided as long as each animal keeps its position.

Application

Negotiating roles and keeping to them is a critical, if under-appreciated, factor in maintaining harmonious relationships. Good etiquette recognizes the role of each person in a relationship. Effective managers clarify the responsibility of each member of an organization and respect those positions.

Situatedness in Time and Space

Natural Principle

A being is situated in three dimensions—horizontally among other entities on its own plane, and vertically with respect to time and the succession of cause and effect. A tree, for example, is situated within a forest that is in a centuries-long process of succession from scrubland to mature forest. At the same time, each year the tree provides nesting-sites and shade for the fauna and flora of the forest community.

Application

The norms of a "vertical" relationship between parent and child are different from those of a "horizontal" relationship between friends the same age. Moreover, each person exists not only as an individual within a society of his peers but also as a link in a historical lineage extending from the distant past to the future.

Purpose

Natural Principle

Entities manifest purpose, and their interactions are founded upon a common purpose. Most animal behavior is purposeful: for survival and propagation of the species. Only in human beings does purpose become a conscious choice.

Application

A moral life is strengthened by a sense of meaning and purpose. One factor in the strength of relationships, such as a family, is the depth of a shared purpose.

Hierarchy

Natural Principle

Individual beings uphold interdependent hierarchies of existence and are sustained within them. Examples include the hierarchy of cells, tissues and organs in the human body, and the hierarchy of living things, from soil microorganisms to dominant predators in an ecosystem.

Application

Humans are members of a social hierarchy. Participation in the social order adds a greater dimension of meaning and value to life. The values of patriotism and charity are rooted in a benevolent social order. So is the value of work well done.

7

The Path to Personal Maturity

GLORIA WORKED AS A WAITRESS IN A COFFEE SHOP IN RALEIGH, North Carolina. On the surface of it, hers was a nondescript, unremarkable life. She had not even finished high school. But when she died suddenly, over two hundred people attended her funeral. Her stepdaughter gave the eulogy, recalling how her mother had accepted and nurtured her when she was a rebellious teenager and had changed her life. The mailman spoke up, remembering the cookies she had baked for him. The people who turned out for Gloria's funeral in such numbers were all people whose lives had been touched by this simple woman with a generous heart, who was ever reaching out to make life better for others.

Kevin Ryan uses the metaphor that character is engraved on the self, like a sculptor shaping and polishing a stone to reveal its innate beauty and create a fine statue.[1] A person's very life becomes a work of art as he or she consciously practices good habits that deepen the mind and beautify the heart. Gloria had cultivated her character through thousands of small acts of giving and helping, until giving and helping became an ingrained habit. In the same vein, Abraham Maslow spoke of life as a process of "self-actualization." Confucius termed it "self-cultivation."

Aristotle defined good character as the inner disposition conducive to right conduct. This definition is particularly cogent, because it defines character as an inner property of personhood. This means that character is not a skill one learns, not a behavior one chooses to do in a particular situation, but is an aspect of one's very self. Character begins with innate capacities and is built up through experience and training. It grows to the extent that a person lives out his or her professed values. Character is self-embodied knowledge. A good or integrated character—in which the person's subconscious habits and conscious ideals are somehow aligned—may bring wisdom and a deep sense of personal meaning and purpose.

Character and Personality

There is a significant distinction between "character" and "personality." Personality is unique. It varies from person to person, as do talents, gifts and abilities. Character, on the other hand, refers specifically to moral qualities, and these are universal. All people can embody the virtues to the extent that they make effort to practice them.

Ethicist Steven Tigner illustrates this distinction using the Seven Dwarfs in the Disney movie *Snow White* as an example. Each dwarf illustrated a distinct personality type. In the old-fashioned language of the four "humors," Grumpy is choleric, Happy is sanguine, Sleepy is phlegmatic and Bashful is melancholic. Doc is gifted, Dopey is mentally slow and Sneezy is constantly sick. Yet despite their different personalities, all seven dwarfs were unified in character. They were hardworking, reliable, loyal, cooperative, tolerant, compassionate and brave. They sang together, worked together, and fought together to protect the special guest whom they graciously welcomed into their house.[2]

People of limited moral development tend to select their friends on the basis of personality. A morally aware person prefers friends of good character.

Pathways of Character Development

The human body forms as an embryo in the womb, grows through the childhood years and eventually matures physically into an adult. As with animals and plants generally, the body's growth is automatic.

A seed germinates and becomes a sprout, a growing sapling, and finally becomes a mature tree yielding fruit. The design of the mature tree lies latent within the seed. As long as the proper nutrients are supplied—sunlight, water, clean air and rich soil—growth follows according to the seed's innate design and the laws of nature. Animals likewise grow to maturity and bear offspring according to the innate pattern written into their genes and unfolding in their instinctive drives.

The inner aspect of a human being—character—also possesses innate tendencies that guide its development. The love of parents and the guidance of good teachers are input for the growth of the young person internally, just as food, water and air nourish the body externally. As he or she grows, the response to this input becomes more and more a matter of choice and will. Therefore, unlike the body, character does not grow automatically. Observing the great disparity in people's character, it is evident that moral development is not obtained except by making conscious effort and investment.

Psychology describes an optimal developmental pathway for moral development through a sequence of stages.[3] Yet how far a person progresses on this pathway is variable, depending on upbringing, education, and the person's own efforts. Every person is endowed with a heart and conscience, providing a natural orientation towards morality and goodness. When the heart is nurtured in its aspiration for genuine love, and the conscience is supported by good choices in daily life, these moral faculties grow into the organizing center of a confident moral self with a strong sense of life's responsibilities. Psychologists Anne Colby and William Damon describe this process as the "progressive formation of a sense of self around a moral center."[4] On the other hand, without proper rearing and upright living, a person's moral development may take one of the many "sub-optimal paths" which lead to stagnation.[5]

Tom, a well-educated and respected businessman and father of twin boys six-year-old, would fly into a rage every time the boys would not listen to him. Scared for their children's welfare, Tom's wife insisted he go for help. Through time and effort, Tom was able to change and learn how to process his anger and frustration in healthier ways. In therapy, Tom realized that his behavior had always been like this from childhood. When he could not get his way, he would act irrationally because as a child that was the only way he could get attention from his parents. Although Tom had received two college degrees and was very successful financially, this aspect of character remained "stuck" at an immature stage.

Examples abound of adults like Tom whose character has not grown past that of a child. Therapists routinely find that patients deal with unresolved conflicts that are a direct result of difficulties experienced in childhood. They are held back by immature emotional needs that were never outgrown, even though their bodies reached adulthood. (See Chapters 14 and 17)

Much of character development is about people expanding their awareness of others' needs. It involves enlarging their sense of self from a limited bodily sphere to encompass family, friends and others in society. This process begins in early childhood. Babies are inherently self-centered. Their world revolves around their bodily needs. As they grow, so does their consciousness of the world around them. They begin to have relationships with others, and in so doing they learn responsibilities and codes of behavior. They learn to respect others. They learn to share.

The importance of parental values and nurturing early in life for later character development cannot be overstated. When parents and teachers cultivate the hearts of their children and students by their warm care and nurture, they enhance their capacity for caring and compassion. The child's conscience develops first through following parental rules; later these rules become internalized as a personal moral code. Over time, the child identifies her personal goals with moral ones and expands her sphere of concerns and relationships.

Responsibility and Character

In adolescence and in adulthood, character development focuses more and more upon fulfilling responsibility. Indeed, responsibility is the key distinction between the growth of the body and the growth of character. Responsibility is as inexorable and immutable as any law of nature. Jean Paul Sartre once said, "Man is responsible for everything except his responsibility."

Responsibility is defined as being answerable for one's actions. To whom is a person answerable? There are obligations to parents, spouse, children, friends and neighbors, and to self. To encourage teenagers to realize that their every action and even their attitudes have consequences for the lives of others, one character education text offers the following exercise:

> Look at any situation you're in as if it were a stage play, with you as one of the actors. Every one of your actions and attitudes helps write the script for that play, whether you see it or not and whether you like it or not. If what you contribute to the script is anger, blame, cynicism, fear or hopelessness, then you push the final act of the play in that direction. On the other hand, if the behavior and attitudes you bring to that situation are caring, courageous and hopeful, you'll influence events in that direction.[6]

An individual's ability to fulfill responsibilities depends upon preparation and training. Even highly motivated and naturally gifted people cannot fully express their talents without rigorous training and practice. A musician is responsible to himself, his audience and his art to allow sufficient time for practice and prepare himself mentally before each performance. Likewise, Aristotle compared learning moral uprightness to learning a skill. "We learn by doing, e.g., men become builders by building and lyre-players by playing the lyre; so too we become just by doing just acts, temperate by doing temperate acts, brave by doing brave acts." He points out that people can equally well learn bad habits by repeatedly doing acts that are unjust, cowardly, ill-tempered or self-indulgent. He concludes, "Whether we form habits of one kind or another from our very youth... makes a very great difference, or rather all the difference."[7]

Purpose of Responsibility

What is the purpose of responsibility? Raymond is exercising responsibility in order to complete a job. So is Carmen when she is resolving a personal problem or caring for another person. In either case, the exercise of responsibility enables the person to demonstrate his or her intrinsic value.

Indeed, responsibility is a special privilege of human beings. Animals are driven by instinct; only humans are faced with moral choices. Human beings are unique among all of nature in that they exercise responsibility in the course of their development. In so doing, they become the architects of their own character. Thus, responsibility is essential to the full flowering of a person's humanity.

Responsibility is also a qualification for enjoying rights and privileges. Doctors, for example, earn the right to practice medicine only after they have fulfilled their responsibility to gain a medical degree and professional license. Wealthy parents who want to leave a sizeable inheritance to their children look for evidence of responsible character lest the fruits of their hard work be squandered or mishandled.[8] Thus, fulfilling responsibility is the means to gain authority, rights, privileges and the freedoms that go with them.

Freedom: Opportunity for Responsibility

Indeed, freedom and responsibility are tightly interconnected. Just as responsibility earns freedom, so freedom is a prerequisite for responsibility. In law, a judgment of responsibility assumes freedom as a moral agent; thus Francesca is not legally responsible for hurting her neighbor if she is pushed and knocked into him. Likewise in moral development, freedom is the context for practicing responsibility.

A child's moral development requires a measured amount of freedom to provide opportunities for responsibility. Young people need freedom to practice what they have been taught, to test boundaries and learn from experience. An effective math teacher welcomes wrong answers and employs them in lessons to encourage creative problem solving. An ineffective teacher, on the other hand, might inspire fear in students that would inhibit them from suggesting an incorrect answer. These students may turn in accurate work in terms of content but may not understand the implications and applicability of math in real life. They have not learned creative and independent thinking. From this standpoint, it can be said that without freedom, a young person's potential—moral and otherwise—cannot be realized.

However, with too much freedom, a child may fail to learn responsibility and stray into destructive pursuits.[9] It is useful to distinguish genuine freedom from irresponsible freedom or license. It is obvious that if people took the license to ignore traffic laws, fatal accidents would become commonplace. In the same way, indulging the young can lead to bad habits, exploitative relationships and high-risk behaviors.

The great challenge parents and teachers face is to give young people sufficient freedom within proper boundaries. Thus, they welcome their children's use of the wide-ranging, educational explorations possible on the Internet, but at the same time they would like to block out pornographic and violent websites. It is the right balance of obligations and opportunities that is most conducive to responsible choices and sound character development.

Setting Priorities

The proper exercising of responsibility demands not only discerning right from wrong but also the better of two rights. In other words, deciding priorities is a perennial challenge. Practical necessities and emergencies—making dinner, repairing the car, tending a sick child—tend to make a dominant claim on an individual's sense of responsibility. However, these are what personal development coaches like Anthony Robbins call "urgent but not important." The secret to ultimately fulfilling life's responsibilities is to attend to those matters that are "important but not urgent," what Covey calls "sharpening the saw."[10] This includes such things as regular exercise, time set aside for reflection, and thoughtful gestures towards spouse, family and friends. These activities maintain the personal and relational resources needed to realize cherished long-term goals as well as to better deal with problems as they develop. People pressed by the urgent affairs of the day may put these matters off, only to find weeks or months later that they are faced with serious health problems, relationship difficulties or other crises of major proportions.

Rafael, a middle-aged technician, had not seen what happened; he awoke in a hospital bed Saturday afternoon. The nurse told him of the accident—a car had run the red light as he crossed the street. He would need to spend weeks in bed. Rafael suddenly thought of his aging mother who lived with him. Who brought her food last night? What about his cat? The deadline at work? When he found the strength he called his house. The neighbor downstairs answered his phone. After updating her about his prognosis, he asked about his mother. "Oh, don't worry, Rafael. I'm visiting with her right now, after I heard what happened. I'll check in with her every day and make sure she is fed, and the cat, too.

I'm just returning the favor you did for me when I had to stay three extra weeks in Brazil two years ago, remember? Don't worry." At work his co-workers were willing to cover for him; he had done it for them many times. Rafael was a proactive person. He took care of the "important but not urgent" moments when other people needed him, and thus prepared forces to come to his aid when he faced his own "important and urgent" dilemma. Likewise, it takes daily diligence and self-discipline to resist the seemingly expedient and to give matters of character and love the priority they deserve.

Self-Control

A fundamental responsibility and essential element in the development of mature character is self-control. The moral will to delay gratification, resist unhealthy attractions, and suppress the body's impulses is crucial to optimal life development.[11]

In a revealing study, preschoolers were given a choice of eating one marshmallow right away or holding out for fifteen minutes in order to get two marshmallows. Some youngsters ate the treat right away. Others distracted themselves—looked away, buried their heads on their desks or counted fingers—to control their bodies from grabbing the treat. They were duly rewarded with two marshmallows. A follow-up study when the children graduated from high school found that those who delayed gratification grew up to be more confident, persevering, trustworthy, and had better social competencies; while the grabbers were more troubled, resentful, jealous, anxious and easily upset.[12]

People with a developed moral sense tend to follow their conscience and endeavor to act in the interests of others and for the sake of causes beyond themselves. In the process, they place long-term goals ahead of immediate gratification and channel their impulses toward constructive ends. Conversely, those with weak character favor selfish needs ahead of obligations to others. With conscience weakened from lack of use, they may develop a negative belief system that rationalizes this behavior. As one 14-year-old juvenile delinquent said, "I was born with the idea that I'd do what I wanted. I always felt that rules and regulations were not for me."[13]

Most people fall somewhere between these two poles. Sometimes they are generous and kind; at other times they are self-absorbed and uncaring. A mother who cares the world for her children may suddenly erupt in anger at the slightest provocation after a long day. Under the stress of losing a key account, a usually kind and friendly boss may take out his frustration on his employees.

The human experience is that people do many things they know they should not do and immediately regret them. In the deepest part of themselves they wish to take the long view and seek what is truthful and just, but this innate good sense can be overwhelmed by negative passions and desires. James Q. Wilson remarks,

> Our selfish desires and moral capacities are at war with one another, and often the former triumphs over the latter. However great this war may be and no matter how often we submerge our better instincts in favor of our baser ones, we are almost always able, in our calm and disinterested moments, to feel the tug of our better nature.[14]

To win this inner war requires the habit of self-discipline. The power of the conscience is strengthened through education to a greater vision of the self; its muscle is exercised through continual practice of good deeds. At the same time, self-centered desires are curbed and controlled. William Bennett writes, "In self-discipline one makes a 'disciple' of oneself. One is one's own teacher, trainer, coach and 'disciplinarian.'"[15] Extensive research reveals that adolescents who have learned self-discipline enjoy increased self-confidence, affording them greater resistance to the appeal of negative peer groups. These teenagers are less likely to cut classes or abuse drugs or alcohol. They have less anxiety and depression and perform better in school.[16] A positive attitude toward discipline leads to respect for legitimate social institutions and civil laws.

The Mind-Body Dynamic

The source of this struggle lies in the dynamic relationship between a person's mind and body through which character is forged. The body is an integral part of the self; it has legitimate needs and desires. Still, it plays a supportive role to the human mind, which guides it in purposeful activity. The challenge of character development is to set up the appropriate order between mind and body, so that both can function optimally.

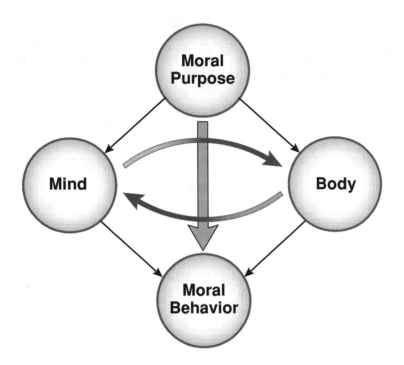

Figure 4: The Mind-Body Dynamic

In a person of mature character, the inner self—the heart and conscience—directs the outer person—the body and its behavior. They work in partnership, inner and outer, the mind seeking value and the body realizing value. The focus of their partnership is the higher purpose toward which they move.

Attaining that mature state requires training in self-control in order to establish the correct relationship between these two dimensions of the self. Particularly in adolescence, the body's impulses can rage out of control. They can be overpowering to a young and impulsive mind that does not have a sense of higher purpose or vision of life's goals. This is one reason why young people need activities that can focus and channel their bodies' overflowing energy towards worthy goals, whether they be sports, academic achievement, putting on musical or dramatic performances, community service projects or entrepreneurial enterprises.

Inner and Outer Self

The mind-body dynamic in human beings is an instance of a more general duality of inner and outer natures that characterizes all beings. Aristotle termed these two dimensions *eidos* (idea) and *hylê* (matter). Indian philosophy calls them *purusha* (spirit) and *prakriti* (matter-energy). The inner nature of a being endows it with purpose and direction and commands its outer form. Animals move their bodies in a purposive manner as directed by their instinctive mind. Plants likewise exhibit sensitivity and responsiveness to their environment by virtue of the invisible life within them.

Inner and outer natures are not incommensurate substances; each contains an aspect of the other. Otherwise, they could not interact.[17] The body has emotion and volition just as the mind does, only at a lower level. The mind possesses inner sight and intuition that complement the body's five senses. The Chinese yin–yang symbol pictures this duality well: within the yin is a spot of yang, and within the yang is a spot of yin, showing that they inhere in each other.

The mental and physical aspects of animals are in natural harmony, with the mind's instinctive impulses directing the body's behavior towards purposeful action. Humans ideally exhibit this same dynamic; but unlike animals, it is not obtained automatically. People need to practice self-control to achieve a beautifully ordered mind-body dynamic.

Worthwhile and achievable goals provide the motivation needed to maintain a healthy mind-body dynamic. Consider Florence Chadwick, who in 1952 attempted to be the first woman to swim from Catalina Island to the California coast. She had been swimming for sixteen hours in a fog so dense she could hardly see her support boats. She struggled on, hour after hour, against the frigid grip of the sea. Alongside her in one of the boats her mother and trainer offered encouragement, telling her that land wasn't far off. But all she could see was fog. With only a half mile to go, she asked to be pulled out.

Still thawing out her chilled body several hours later, Florence told a reporter, "Look, I'm not excusing myself, but if I could have seen land I might have made it." It was not fatigue or the cold water that defeated her, but her inability to see her goal. Two months later, she tried again. This time, despite the same dense fog, she swam with her goal clearly pictured in her mind. This time she succeeded, beating the men's record by two hours.[18] People can mobilize tremendous powers of self-discipline when they can sustain the vision of reaching a meaningful goal.

Meaning and Maturity

As the example of the swimmer illustrates, possessing a clear goal and meaningful purpose supports the development of self-control. In fact, purpose and meaning are important factors in their own right for character development. Psychologist Erik Erikson taught that attaining maturity required satisfying the self's natural proclivity for meaning.[19] Empirical research confirms this.[20] A strong sense of meaning in life has been found to correlate positively with self-esteem and self-control,[21] extraversion,[22] and general psychological well-being.[23] A study of unusually altruistic adults found that they stood out from the general population in seeing a greater meaning for their lives than personal happiness, achievement or gain.[24]

Many people are by nature task-oriented and achieve little in life without setting goals and making priorities. Educator Deb Brown believes that people who set down their goals in writing achieve 50 to 100 times more than those without goals do.[25] Goals and motivation are closely related,[26] especially in academic and personal matters. Studies show the clearer the goal, the greater the motivation for achievement.[27] Many people set tangible goals in terms of career development and financial security and then labor hard to achieve them. However, when they accomplish these things, they may recognize that their ladder of success is "leaning up against the wrong wall."[28]

A clear sense of meaning and purpose is a constant guide on life's path. It can motivate praiseworthy and even heroic behavior, or impart the inner strength needed to overcome adversity.[29] Victor Frankl, a psychologist who spent years in a Nazi concentration camp, reported, "Whether the inmate had the courage to live or became sick and tired of life always depended just upon whether the person could see meaning in his personal life...meaning had to be deep enough to embrace not only life but suffering and even death."[30]

In adolescence, the question of meaning in life becomes a major concern. The activity of making meaning can become an idealistic quest for truth and principles of justice, or a choice to live for mundane ends like the pursuit of wealth. Effective parents and teachers recognize this search for meaning and channel it in positive directions, towards significant life goals. They can ask teenagers to look around at people they know and ask, "Are they leading meaningful lives?" John Graham, director of the Giraffe Project, believes that this question is important for adolescents to consider because, "We want to be able to look at ourselves in the mirror and know that who we are and what we're doing matters, that we're not just marking time. We want to feel a purpose for our lives that fulfills our yearning for meaning and makes us feel totally alive."[31]

Balanced Character

Mature character is balanced character. According to Thomas Lickona, character has three primary components: moral feeling, moral knowing, and moral action.[32] In a person of mature character, these three moral faculties are well developed and balanced. Moral feeling, moral knowing and moral action operate together in the expression of altruistic love. An individual's ability to act with genuine caring is only as strong as the weakest trait among these three components.

Consider the scene that confronted 39-year-old Brent Burkett as he was out driving with his family. Two teenagers were frantically waving from the roadside, pointing to a rubber raft caught under a concrete bridge and yelling that a woman was trapped beneath it. Burkett stopped his car and assessed the situation; then he borrowed a hunting knife and swam out into the cold water. "Don't drop the knife, don't drop the knife," he told himself as he slashed underwater to puncture the raft and liberate its occupant. For his heroism he received a medal, and he made a friend for life.[33]

Brent's heart mind, and will worked together to effect the rescue. Consider what might have happened if he had lacked in one of these three faculties. If he had little empathy for others, then most likely he would have driven on, considering it someone else's problem. What if he had the heart to help, but lacked the will to drive himself into the cold water? What if he rushed to the rescue but could not keep his head enough to procure the all-important knife? If any of these factors had been missing, the woman would not have survived. Therefore, on the path to maturity, consideration is given to developing and honing each of these three faculties.

Moral Feeling

Moral feeling means moral emotional sensibility. At the core of emotional awareness is empathy: the ability to feel another's heart, understand another's situation, and care about another's welfare.

Empathy is one of the fundamental moral emotions;[34] it is basic to the definition of being human. A person with empathy takes the reality of other persons seriously, their inner lives and emotions as well as their external circumstances. Empathy is necessarily linked with compassion, caring and altruism.[35] It generates fellowship and sharing. A person with empathy sees in his neighbor another person like himself.

In the aftermath of the devastating 1995 earthquake in Kobe, Japan, an American reporter met a local woman who had set up a makeshift store out of boxes and was selling flashlights and batteries. The reporter asked why she wasn't selling these essential items for more than the regular price. The woman answered, "Why would I want to profit from someone else's suffering?"[36]

A second aspect of moral feeling is an innate sense of righteousness: loving the good and rejecting the bad. This moral sense produces a visceral reaction to injustice as one would react to a foul odor or a repugnant sight. This quality of moral feeling is often poorly developed, however. A high school teacher in Bristol, Connecticut asked his class whether cheating is right or wrong, and everyone agreed, "It is wrong." But when he polled them, "How many of you have cheated in the last four years?" the majority raised their hands. Although they believed that cheating is wrong, it seemed that they didn't feel its wrongfulness deep inside. They lacked a strong love of goodness—or indignation at its absence. Developed moral feeling fuels the motivation to act morally—with heartfelt concern, sincerity and zeal.

Moral Knowing

Moral knowing refers to the use of the intellect for moral discernment. It encompasses the virtues of wisdom, honesty, prudence and self-reflection. On the simplest level, moral knowing is the ability to discern right from wrong. More developed, it includes honesty to face oneself and others squarely, in order to make an accurate assessment of one's inner and outer situation. Aristotle wrote, "Anyone can get angry—that is easy—or to give or spend money; but to do this to the right person, to the right extent, at the right time, with the right aim, and in the right way, that is not for every one, nor is it easy."[37] This life wisdom is quite different from the type of intelligence measured by IQ tests.

Part of moral knowing is prudence in dealing with others. For example, moral knowing aids Kevin, age 10, who had just moved into a new neighborhood, to discern who might be a good friend. Tex invited Kevin to join in playing a prank on the biology teacher. Kevin began to fidget as he listened to the plan to soap up the teacher's new car. "Well, it's just soap," he thought, "It's not like it's slashing tires or breaking glass." But then he remembered how proud his Dad was when he bought his new car and imagined how upset he would have been to find it smeared with soap. Dad was always talking about respecting others' property, too. Tex and his friends seemed to accept Kevin into the group, and Kevin knew that he would risk their friendship if he backed out of the prank. "Uh...my Dad would ground me for a month if he found out about this, and besides I have something else to do." Kevin left and walked slowly home, telling himself that there are other ways to make friends.

Moral Action

Moral action means the moral directing of the will. It is the capacity to pursue goodness even under difficult circumstances. Its virtues include integrity, self-control, courage and endurance. Courage is "a settled disposition to stand one's ground, to advance or retreat as wisdom dictates...facing fears and taking stands."[38]

In order to find and maintain courage to do what is right, a person can remind himself of the meaning of the event. Keeping focused on the goal can enable a person to face his fears. Brent Burkett clearly demonstrated courage when he risked his own life to save the woman trapped under the raft in the flooded river. Another kind of courage involves taking social risks—losing face with peers, for example—to maintain a principled stand. Kevin showed that kind of courage when he walked away from Tex and his gang.

Moral fiber, like muscle fiber, is built up by daily habit, by the constant small choices to do the right thing despite fear, pain or fatigue. In this regard, wise parents and educators give their children challenges and allow them to encounter adversity as occasions to toughen their moral fiber and develop inner strength of will. (See Chapters 11 and 22)

Personal Maturity — The First Basic Life Goal

Attaining a mature and admirable character requires conscious, informed effort. This is a human being's unique responsibility—to be the architect of his or her own destiny. The inner thrust toward attaining personal maturity is such that it may be called one of life's basic goals. Why is it a goal worth striving for?

First, achieving personal maturity satisfies an innate drive—the drive for meaning, wholeness, poise and self-worth. Lingering feelings of anxiety, dissatisfaction and meaninglessness can plague those who fail to achieve it. Thus, it is deeply rewarding in itself.

But there is an even better reason to strive for personal maturity: it is the best foundation for success in all areas of life. People who have cultivated integrity and the habit of responsibility in their personal affairs are well equipped to deal with family issues and social responsibilities. Neither wealth nor power nor technical skill can replace the essential personal asset of good character. Stephen Covey remarks:

> Creating the unity necessary to run an effective business or a family or a marriage requires great personal strength and courage. No amount of technical administrative skill in laboring for the masses can make up for lack of nobility or personal character.... It is at a very essential, one-on-one level that we live the primary laws of love and life. A sense of purpose, empathy, self-control, courage and other assets of mature character are needed to master the[se] challenges.[39]

8

Dynamics of Loving Relationships

How far you go in life depends on you being tender with the young, compassionate with the aged, sympathetic with the striving and tolerant of the weak and the strong. Because someday in life you will have been all of these.

—George Washington Carver

LOVING AND BEING LOVED IS A BASIC HUMAN NEED. PEOPLE THRIVE on the joy that comes from loving relationships of all kinds: the warm concern of a mother's love, the camaraderie of siblings, close friends who can share their deepest secrets, and the special intimacy of conjugal love in marriage. Loving relationships are a basic life goal; they are essential to realizing our value and true humanity. Take away love, and life's journey loses vitality. Yet satisfying and lasting relationships do not happen automatically.

It was mentioned that the family is the primary school of love, where the capacity for warmth, caring and commitment is cultivated. Parents are in a position to nurture the seeds of goodness in their children by giving them affirmation, support, protection and encouragement. With warm affection balanced with moral discipline, they impart the values and habits that make for success in forming good relationships. (See Chapter 22)

Schools can helpfully supplement parents' efforts through a comprehensive character education program that creates a caring home-like atmosphere in the classroom and throughout the school. (See Chapter 12) Family connectedness—a feeling of closeness to parents and of being loved—and school connectedness—a school with a family ethos—are two factors shown to be protective of teens becoming involved in high-risk behaviors.[1] Young people who experience a caring and loving environment at home and at school accumulate valuable character assets for forming healthy relationships throughout life.

In addition, there are objective rules that can be applied to forming good relationships. As Eric Fromm says, there is an art to loving. Making and maintaining loving relationships requires the skillful practice of ethical principles.

Relationships Build upon Ethics

Most people understand that love is the key to good relationships; nevertheless, the word "love" is frequently misunderstood. It is commonly equated with the passionate feelings of romance. Pursuing "love" is thought to mean acting as prompted by the affections. Yet on further reflection, it is evident that lasting love cannot result from passions that blow hot and cold or emotions that rise and fall. To impart a coherent understanding of love necessitates dispelling the common misconceptions promulgated by music, television and movies. "True love" defines an ideal that can focus the discussion of relationships on their ethical foundations.

True love is firstly a moral ideal. (See Chapter 4) Its practice lies in living to be of service to the other. It is an attitude of the heart accompanied by altruistic acts that engender trust, respect, intimacy and harmony.

Love in this sense is not solely or primarily experienced in romantic liaisons. It has many forms and varied expressions. Love includes the attachment of children to parents, the loyalty and solidarity among friends, the sacrificial investment by parents to provide a brighter future for their children, the caring that is characteristic of the helping professions, and more.

Such relationships where love blossoms and thrives are cultivated with effort, care and investment. Success in forming and keeping them requires observing certain norms—such as fulfilling obligations, living up to commitments, and observing proper manners.

At the same time, people hope that their siblings, friends and spouses will not only be loyal and dependable, but also interesting and fun. Ethical principles are like the skeleton upon which warm-hearted relationships grow. In turn, a rewarding friendship takes on a life of its own and becomes the natural inducement to fairness: "I wouldn't lie to him; he's my friend!" Yet take away ethics, and even the closest friendship would be strained.

It can be concluded that the very purpose of ethics is to foster love and harmony between people. It begins with the norms of family life and extends to relationships of all kinds. All loving relationships display certain basic characteristics. The qualities that make for a vibrant and lasting relationship are not arbitrary; they are grounded in universal principles.

To Be of Service to Others

A loving relationship begins with the attitudes the two people bring to it. At the most basic level, loving relationships are about living to be of service to others. This means each person approaches the other with an attitude of respect and care, recognizing how they need one another and how deeply intertwined the benefit of one is with the other.

Although people have varying abilities and talents, in a loving relationship they complement and offset one another's strengths and weaknesses. Elder siblings use their superior strength and maturity to protect younger siblings, while younger siblings' vulnerability nurtures the elder's sense of compassion. A father who at work is a no-nonsense manager transforms into a jovial playmate in front of his growing toddler. Love creates balance between high and low, strong and weak.

This balance characteristic of loving relationships has its basis in nature. It is an expression of *complementarity*—a principle running throughout all existence. Eastern philosophy explains that the universe is replete with complementary dualities: male and female, high and low, large and small, hard and soft, light and dark. The harmony of opposites fills the universe with energy, structure, life, beauty and joy. Male and female eagles join claws and turn cartwheels in the sky. The peacock carries around his heavy tail feathers to make the colorful display that will attract a peahen, who will in turn bear his young. Frosty mountain peaks overlook green, verdant valleys. A large, muscular lioness picks up her tiny cub gently between sharp teeth that previously tore at the side of a zebra. An electron weighs less than a thousandth of a proton, yet in an atom they precisely balance. The harmony and balance among complementary opposites occurs because the elements exist for one another. Paleontologist Teilhard de Chardin observed in nature an internal "propensity to unite, even at a prodigiously rudimentary level—indeed in the molecule itself."[2] Even a corpuscle, he maintained, "can only be defined by virtue of its influence on all around it."[3] In other words, things in nature exist in symbiotic relationships as a matter of course: they exist for one another.

Humans, too, feel incomplete without a counterpart. Man yearns for woman and woman yearns for man. Children need their parents, and parents find joy in their children. It is natural for people to seek one another out, form relationships and support one another; loneliness and isolation are known to be unhealthy. When people make "living to be of service to others" a priority, their relationships exhibit the qualities of caring, respect and commitment and reflect the harmony and balance of nature itself.

Caring

Healthy relationships involve caring. Good friends are attentive to each other's feelings, moods and needs. They do not take each other for granted. If one is troubled, the other will come to his aid.

Jackie Robinson made history as the first black major league baseball player when he joined the Brooklyn Dodgers. Branch Rickey, owner of the Dodgers at that time, told Robinson, "It'll be tough. You're going to take abuse you never dreamed of. But if you're willing to try, I'll back you all the way." Sure enough, Robinson endured constant taunts and racial slurs from the crowd, from opponents, and even from members of his own team.

One day Robinson was struggling, unable to get on base, and the crowd was booing loudly. Then Pee Wee Reese, the team captain and Dodger shortstop, walked onto the field and put his arm around him as a gesture of friendship and solidarity. "That may have saved my career," Robinson reflected later. "Pee Wee made me feel that I belonged."[4] Pee Wee didn't mind that he might take some flak for his gesture in a time of tense race relations. He only saw his friend in trouble, and he cared enough to help him.

Respect

Respect is about valuing one another. In loving relationships, people encourage each other to be the best that they can be. Parents are proud if their children even surpass them. A loving husband is supportive of his wife, valuing her as his "better half"—and vice-versa. Respecting and edifying one another, a family advances together.

The rule and courtesy of respect is maintained when family members temper their criticism with acknowledgement of each other's good points. Making a habit of recalling the good points in a spouse can be a great marriage-saver. (See Chapter 21) Sometimes what looks like a weak point may from another perspective be a strength. "I used to be annoyed by my wife Nadia's constant yakking on the phone, talking with all the neighbors," said Martin, of Toronto. "But when our son got really sick and needed lots of blood donors, it wasn't me who was able to drum up 30 volunteers. My wife did, because she had kept up with so many friends." Likewise, praising a teenager for chores well done or a good grade on a test can go a long way towards maintaining respectful and smooth communication during a phase of life when scolding and tussles over privileges are all too common. By respecting each other as unique individuals, family members give each other room to change and yet maintain their closeness.

Commitment

Commitment denotes constancy and security of loving relationships. It means to be constant and loyal in difficult times as well as in good times. Committed love is not satisfied with halfway measures, nor can it be at one's convenience. For example, when Violeta from the Bronx was teaching her five-year-old son to ride a bicycle, she was determined to see it through, no matter how long it might take. "I got hot and tired and I wondered if and when he would ever get it. But he wanted so much to learn, I determined that I'd run up and down the block a thousand times if I had to. The funny thing was, as soon as I made that determination, he took off on the bike all on his own! I was so thrilled!"

Family relationships, being permanent, are the primary context for exercising commitment. Good parents never stop feeling responsible to help their children, nor do children ever stop caring for their parents. People may change their friends, but they cannot change their parents or children or brothers or sisters. For this reason, family relationships are the model for understanding commitments of all kinds.

Principles of Good Interaction

In establishing and maintaining loving human relationships, good interaction is essential. Many of the strategies for character education, effective parenting and building strong marriages that are discussed in subsequent chapters are basically about improving the quality of interaction.

Traditional maxims encourage people to promote fair and harmonious interactions in their social relationships. This is the function of the Golden Rule, "Treat others as you would wish to be treated yourself,"[5] as well as maxims like: "As a man sows, so shall he reap,"[6] and "Those who act kindly in the world will have kindness."[7]

Interaction is a universal phenomenon in nature; it is the process by which any two entities form a relationship and solidify it through giving and receiving elements of themselves. Interaction produces the energy that powers nature, from the nuclear reactions in the heart of the sun to the biochemical reactions in the living cell. Interaction is the source of power to unite, act, grow and multiply. It is what invigorates a friendship and animates a classroom lesson. It is the pulse of the city and the lifeblood of an economy.

As productive interaction includes giving and receiving, five characteristics stand out: 1)truthfulness, 2)giving first, 3)receiving well, 4)giving continually, and 5) observing norms and roles. These characteristics apply to all kinds of relationships—among friends, in business and in school.

Truthfulness

A constructive interaction is truthful in two ways. First, it is honest and without guile. The interaction is not conducted with an ulterior motive, to manipulate for some personal advantage. Second, it is grounded in universal principles.

Kant's famous Categorical Imperative states that one should treat all persons not as "means" to their own ends but as "ends" in themselves. This means to respect them as people—their views, their values, their personalities and their desires. In most situations, this dictum is a sound guide to truthful relationships. Nevertheless, the truth stands higher than individual desires and values. For example, if a fellow student is routinely stealing the work of other students and presenting it as his own, the right course of action is to stop him, even though it does not seem to respect his purposes and desires. In this case, the cheater has already violated the moral law by treating other students as a means, and so has forfeited his right to be respected as an end. Thwarting the cheating maintains the moral order—a higher truth—even while denying the will of the cheater. At the same time, it can be argued that this action represents a deeper respect for the more honorable potential of the cheating student.[8]

To always have authentic and honest interactions, of course, is not easy. Some people hesitate out of shyness or timidity; some are afraid of hurting others' feelings; some are not skilled in making appropriate statements. Being truthful may sometimes cost a friendship. Yet more often than not, truthful sharing in a respectful and sensitive manner works to enhance a relationship.

Laurie, a 28-year-old mother of two, was concerned that her children watched scary videos at their friend's house. She did not want to seem like a prude, but she was troubled that some of the videos were R-rated for violence. Hannah, the mother of the children's friend, sensed how evasive Laurie was about the children getting together at her home. When she asked Laurie what was wrong, Laurie plunged ahead and truthfully shared her feelings about scary, violent movies and children. Hannah was surprised but relieved at Laurie's honesty. "I didn't know all that," she said, when Laurie cited statistics about media and real life violence. The two had a long, fruitful discussion about standards and values. Laurie agreed that her children could continue to visit sometimes, with the proviso that there be no scary videos. The truthfulness of this interaction between these mothers, based on concern for the quality of their children's friendship, deepened the bond between them and engendered greater trust.

Giving First

The second principle of productive interactions is to give first. Human relationships flourish when there is a generous attitude and practice of initiating service—when participants are more interested in what they can give to each other than what they will receive. Jonica enjoys compiling funny stories to send to her friend; Desmond delights in surprising his son with baseball cards for his collection.

Educators have come up with creative ways to teach this principle. Mr. Mastriano, an eighth-grade teacher in New Jersey, noticed a wide deviation in the test scores of his students. He created a buddy system, whereby the students who were doing well were paired off with those who were doing poorly. He told the students that from now on they were responsible for their buddy's grades as well as their own, and instructed students with higher grades to tutor and help those with lower grades. At first it was a bit awkward, because the better students felt they alone earned their grades, but in a short time there was a miraculous transition. The students who were doing well became so involved in helping their buddies improve that their own grades shot up. Their partners' grades also improved in a short period of time through their mentors' help. In the end, the whole class learned a lesson about how helping their fellow student also meant helping themselves. In other words, giving leads to receiving.9

A giving attitude is a key to business success. Winning companies stand out by going "the extra mile" to serve customers' needs—the furniture store with the supervised playground so parents can shop in a relaxed way, the shopkeeper who lets his shoppers buy food on credit between paychecks, the department store offering wheelchairs for the disabled. Customers then buy often and recommend their products and services to others. Stanley and Danko's study of American millionaires found that most of them made their fortunes through offering their customers a genuine service and quality products. It debunked the vulgar notion that success in business requires taking advantage of people or cheating them.[10]

Receiving Well

The other side of the interaction is receptivity. Being able to receive well—gracefully and appreciatively—inspires the giver to want to give again. At the same time, it renews the recipient's capacity to be able to give in return. Receiving well does not mean always looking to receive, so as to become indebted to others. Nevertheless, sometimes people who are great at giving have difficulty receiving. Gladys, widowed at 45, had thrown herself into community service, running a food program for house-bound seniors and working at the local homeless shelter. Then she contracted an illness that weakened her for months. It was her turn to receive from others. "I don't need charity! I can take care of myself," she grumbled. She was not used to seeing herself so needy, and was uncomfortable with all the attention. "How can I let them see me like that?" she thought through her fear and loneliness. Gladys found herself avoiding others, seeking solace on a park bench.

One evening Francis, a frequent visitor to the homeless shelter, noticed her sitting there. "Why don't you just tell me what's on your mind?" she said. "You know, folks care about you whether you're doin' for us or not." Gladys looked up at Francis; at that moment she understood: letting those she had cared for take care of her gave them dignity, and she could open herself to experience the joy of receiving.[11]

Continuing to Give

At the outset of any relationship, giving is fairly easy and there is a ready supply of good will. The initial excitement and pleasure of a new relationship lend impetus to striving to please the other person in creative and relationship-enhancing ways. As time goes by, however, people tend to take one another for granted and get lazy about continuing to invest in the relationship. Relationships can atrophy and even turn sour as each wonders why the other is not giving anymore.

Good relationships require that the people involved be committed to continual investment in one another and in the relationship. This means going beyond a "tit for tat" mentality: "I did this for you, so you do this for me." Indeed, it is impossible and counter-productive to "keep score" in relationships. Relationships flourish when the parties decide to give without keeping a tab and without expecting anything in return except the pleasure and benefit of the other. In this way they are able to turn a blind eye to the times when the giving is uneven. Even if one party is giving considerably more than the other, continuing to give without expectation of return can spark consciousness in the other to do likewise.

The ethic of giving continually can overcome the inevitable complaints and slights that plague all relationships from time to time. "I don't even know what prompted me to pick up the phone," Zoë recalls, of her contacting her former best friend. They had become estranged when her friend had not repaid a sizeable loan. "I was thinking of her and I dialed her number before I could talk myself out of it. She was so happy to hear from me and she had wanted to call me and apologize but just couldn't. Honestly, I was surprised how much I missed her voice. I felt so relieved to have that old connection back."

Principles of Interaction

- Truthful relationship
- Giving precedes receiving
- Norms and roles
- Shared purpose

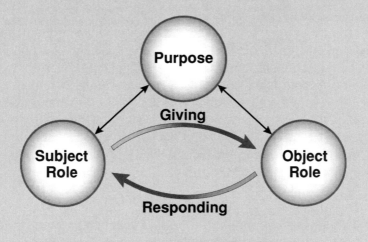

Figure 5: Interaction with Order and Purpose

Norms and Roles

The art of fostering harmonious relationships with others includes observing etiquette and manners, using appropriate language, and knowing what is expected of oneself and others. These are collectively called norms.

Norms are not ends in themselves; rather, they exist for the sake of facilitating congenial relationships and civil peace. Just as travel by automobile can be safe and rapid only when people obey the rules of the road, so social relationships are harmonious and loving when rules and manners are understood and observed. Rules direct the interaction into fruitful channels, promoting cooperation and good will. A person well educated in norms can relate well even with people who are difficult to like.

Today there is a growing dissatisfaction with the anything-goes casualness that has become commonplace in our culture. School administrators are re-instituting school uniforms and policies to curb unruly behavior and offensive language. Companies nervous about how their salesmen will behave when meeting a client at a business lunch are sending them to etiquette classes.[12] There is renewed appreciation of the advantages of practicing good manners.

One purpose of the rules of etiquette is to establish clear roles. At a party, for instance, it is proper for the host to introduce the guests to one another, and it is expected that a guest will ask the host's permission to use the telephone or take food from the refrigerator. If the host neglects to introduce a guest, or if a guest forgets to thank the host, the social flow is interrupted and everyone feels vaguely uncomfortable. When people practice good manners, they honor roles and set up a structure that facilitates warm feelings and prevents anxiety and uncertainty.

Traditional ethics upholds distinctions between different roles and teaches people to honor these roles. The idea is that where there is order, it is possible for harmony to come; where there is harmonious interaction, care and concern will flow. Therefore, as with norms, the purpose of respecting different roles is to facilitate the flow of love. The value of roles and structure in interaction is an important but often poorly understood aspect of relationships.

Distinctions of Roles

In any relationship there are two essential roles: one initiates and the other responds; one sets a direction and the other enlarges upon it. Using terminology from grammar, these two roles in their most general sense may be distinguished as the *subject role* and the *object role*.[13] At the party mentioned above, the host has the subject role; she sets the tone of the party and welcomes the guests, who are in the object role. The host is responsible to put on the party, while the guests provide its sparkle and fun. The party would not be a success without both. Thus, subject and object roles have equal value. (These roles are *relative* positions that will be different for each relationship; thus among the guests at the party are those who have subject and object roles within their own circles.)

Subject and object roles are ubiquitous in nature. The sun and planets in the solar system are in subject and object roles, respectively; so are the nucleus and cytoplasm in a cell, the brain and limbs in an animal, the nucleus and electrons in an atom. In addition to these permanent roles, there are countless temporary and alternating subject-object relationships: between bees and flowers, flexor and extensor muscles, cations and anions, xylem and phloem.

In human interactions, as in nature, the roles of subject and object can be either permanent or changing. In a classroom, the teacher has the permanent subject role, being the responsible center of the classroom in terms of conveying knowledge and establishing discipline. Yet from time to time for the sake of facilitating learning, a teacher may adopt a changing subject and object role by letting students report or even teach, and by setting up small groups where they can collaborate.[14] A common example of an interaction with changing subject and object roles is a conversation. At any moment, one person is talking and the other is listening; but at the next moment the roles switch. Whether permanent or changing, subject and object roles constitute a partnership in which each side is essential to the other. A teacher cannot teach without students. Students do not learn without a teacher. A speaker has no purpose in talking if no one is listening.

Respecting the roles of subject and object makes for fruitful interaction. That is why in polite conversation one does not interrupt the speaker and talk out of turn. In the classroom, most teachers have experienced trying to teach a wise-guy student who always insists on his ideas and thinks he knows more than the teacher. He sets himself up in the role of a subject in opposition to the teacher. Just as two positive charges repel each other, two subjects cannot generate effective interaction. In such a case, little interaction or learning takes place.

Roles Facilitate Communication and Harmony

In any relationship, it helps if people are aware of whether they are in the subject role or the object role. Observing these roles clarifies the terms of the relationship, thus facilitating communication and interaction. People in the subject role may provide leadership or impart knowledge. Those in the object role may offer support or receive instruction. At the same time, those who are most effective in the subject role are good listeners who are concerned about issues raised by their subordinates. Likewise, a valued person in the object role aims to stimulate the one in the subject role with helpful ideas and initiatives. On the foundation of mutual respect, these roles establish mutual obligations: leadership and obedience, protection and loyalty, benevolence and gratitude.

In Asia, the distinction between elder and younger is codified in the norms of culture and impressed upon the young from an early age. Alice and Rory invited the family of a co-worker, David Vinh Deng, to dinner at their house one Saturday night. The Vinh Dengs were originally from Viet Nam, a country with a tradition of well-demarcated elder-younger relations. When dinner was ready, Alice said to Lisa, the Vinh Deng's twelve-year-old daughter who was helping her serve, "We have two big pans full of chicken. The children are going to eat here in the kitchen, so why don't you pick out what piece you want for your plate." The girl hesitated and then said softly, "I would prefer it if the elders chose their food first." Lisa respectfully helped Alice serve the food and then took her place with the younger children for dinner, apart from the adults. Throughout the dinner, she could be heard gently admonishing her younger brother, "Don't be so noisy," or "Don't bang your plate with your fork." Yet Lisa also joined in merrily as the children joked and teased one another, giving herself over completely to the joys of being a child. This young Asian girl knew that as a child she should defer to her elders, and as the eldest child she should guide her juniors. Her understanding of what behavior each role called for made the evening go more pleasantly for everyone.

It cannot be overemphasized that the purpose of observing subject and object roles is to facilitate good interaction, not to establish rank or status for its own sake. In the safety training of airline pilots, the cautionary tale of Melburn McBroom is told as a way of letting pilot trainees know the importance of open communication between captain and crew. McBroom was a competent but irascible pilot, given to outbursts of temper. One day in 1978, he was about to land in Portland, Oregon when a problem developed with the landing gear. He put the plane into a holding pattern while he struggled to correct the problem. So absorbed was he, he did not notice that the plane's fuel was almost depleted. His copilot noticed, but was afraid to say anything for fear of one of his pilot's famous outbursts. The plane crashed, claiming ten lives. Although McBroom had all the skills of a pilot, there was a fatal defect in his character—unwillingness to accept advice from his crew. The copilot, who lacked the courage to "take the heat" of McBroom's anger, was likewise at fault.[15]

Unfortunately, there have always been people who abuse their position to dominate others, suppressing their individuality. Thus misused, traditional roles can become strictures preventing people from blossoming to their full potential. They can poison communication, as in the above example, or even engender rebellion. Hence, the modern trend is to do away with distinctions of order and position in the name of absolute equality.

The lowered expectations and relaxed collegiality of peer relations has its appeal and it no doubt drives some of the contemporary tendency to level relationships. Nevertheless, there is much wisdom in the norms of traditional societies the world over, which honor the natural distinctions among roles. Having a sense of automatic respect and support for those in the senior position as well as a heart of concern to help those in the junior position promote tolerance and patience in human relations.

In fact, these distinctions among roles become a cause for complaint only when genuine love is lacking. Love is the great equalizer and harmonizer. When there is care and respect, there is no sense of diminution or deprivation. People in every position are satisfied. Parents' downward benevolence and affection for their children induces obedience and genuine respect in return, and encourages them to be more caring towards one another as well. The star athlete on a baseball team tutors and encourages the rookies, creating solidarity and team spirit among all the players. When these roles are fulfilled with a loving heart, they facilitate harmony among people in every position.

The Dimensions of Order

Broadly speaking, the order of roles in the family has three dimensions. There is a *vertical order* from elder to younger, a *horizontal order* among peers, and an *individual order* by which individuals govern themselves. In the family, vertical order refers to relations between generations: between children and their parents, grandparents and great grandparents. Horizontal order refers to relations between people of the same generation: brothers and sisters, cousins, husband and wife. Individual order, by analogy, refers to the priorities and values by which a person organizes his or her life.

The richness and beauty of family life arises from the integration of these dimensions of order. Parents and children form a vertical relationship. Brothers and sisters form horizontal relationships—though there can be a vertical dimension, as among younger and elder siblings. The dynamic of these relationships differs accordingly.

For example, in a family with small children, the vertical love between mother and child stabilizes, nurtures and harmonizes the developing horizontal relations between the child and his siblings and peers. On a rainy Saturday afternoon, Erica's 8-year-old son Tim and a friend were playing with Lego blocks. Tim was rambunctious with pent-up energy, and in a dispute over a coveted piece he tore apart his friend's construction. Erica realized that her child needed to calm down, but just telling him to do so would not help. Instead, she took him aside and spent a few minutes alone with him. The rowdiness and aggression then ceased. Tim needed that connection to the soothing steadfastness of his mother's heart.

An apt metaphor for these types of order is the arrangement of the planets in the solar system. The Sun is at the center of the solar system, the Earth revolves around the Sun, and the Moon revolves around the earth. Furthermore, the whole solar system revolves around the center of the galaxy. This hierarchical relationship among the centers of revolution—the Moon, the Earth, the Sun, and the galactic center—comprises a vertical order. Horizontal order refers to the mutual relationship among those entities that relate to the same vertical center. In the solar system, the planets Mercury, Venus, Earth, Mars, Jupiter, etc., revolve around the same center, the Sun. Their "peer" relationship to one another is an instance of horizontal order. At the same time, each planet rotates on its own axis to establish its individual order. The Earth's rotation on its axis establishes a far-reaching order within itself: the 24-

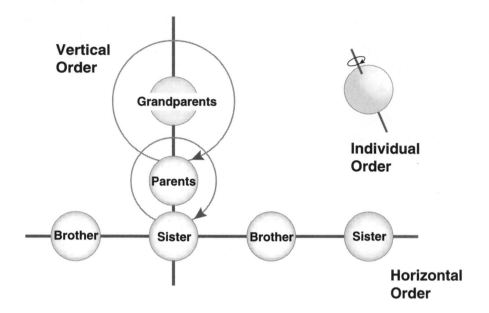

Figure 6: Types of Order and Position in the Family

hour cycle of day and night, the ebb and flow of the tides, the direction of the prevailing winds, and all the activities of nature that depend upon this daily rhythm.

The natural order of the solar system is only a metaphor for human life, which is lived in freedom. Being free to set up their own order, people are responsible to rationally regulate their lives in a manner that is consistent within the order of the universe. The rewards of doing so are families and societies functioning as harmoniously as the movement of the spheres. Describing a healthy family, psychologist John Rosemond said, "The marriage was the nucleus of the family, the children were satellites that revolved around the nucleus like planets to a sun."[16]

When people neglect to maintain ordered relationships, their family life can become chaotic. Imagine what would happen to life on Earth if the planet changed its axis from day to day—some days north-south, some days east-west, or if it suddenly changed its center of revolution from the Sun to Jupiter! In the same way, a person who frequently changes his values, disregards his parents or betrays his friends would naturally find his life in disarray.

Expressions of Order in the East and West

Eastern cultures tend to emphasize vertical order, while people in the West pay more attention to horizontal order. Thus, Confucian ethics stresses obedience to one's parents and loyalty to legitimate authority. It ascribes levels of respect even in horizontal relationships among siblings, based on age.

When Asians greet each other, the junior bows to the senior, connoting vertical respect. Far beyond "sir" and "ma'am," the Japanese and Korean languages have elaborate distinctions among the forms of address to be used with people of different ages, even in intimate speech. When meeting a stranger, a Korean frequently asks about his age. Though it may seem impolite to Westerners, he is seeking to know whether it is proper to address him as an elder or a younger. In the Asian way of thinking, establishing vertical order is the prerequisite for social harmony.

On the other hand, the Western way of greeting—a handshake—connotes equality. At school and at work, superiors and subordinates often address each by their first names as a sign of camaraderie and solidarity. Western families usually make little distinction between the first-born son and his younger siblings. In the spirit of democracy, equality is the norm.

Both Eastern and Western culture beautifully express a different aspect of the natural order. Each has its insights and is incomplete without the other. The West offers lessons on equality and freedom that are correctives to the abuses of the rigid hierarchical systems of the past. The Asian sensibility for vertical order helps avoid the chaos and excessive competition so prevalent in Western society. In fact, Eastern and Western ways of thinking are complementary. When each culture inherits the strength of the other, a more complete picture of healthy human relationships emerges.

Orienting Towards Meaning and Purpose

It is a natural trait of human beings that they strive for truth, beauty, goodness and love—in short, to find meaning in life. The pursuit of meaning leads beyond the self to relationships and the greater sense of value that they can provide. Thus, when two people engage in a relationship, a new intention comes to the fore beyond that of the individuals involved: the purposes they share in common. Shared values and mutual interests create the enduring foundation for a relationship to thrive.

Aristotle recognized "sharing a common conception and pursuit of a good" as one of the two central features of friendship—or any relationship. Emotional attachments and feelings of mutual satisfaction are quite secondary, in his understanding, to this crucial basis of relationship. Sharing a common purpose for the good, friends want good things for each another and act for one another's benefit. The satisfying feelings that people sometimes take to be the defining feature of friendship are rather a byproduct of this more fundamental bond.[17]

In marriage, too, a shared commitment, a shared history, and a shared sense of what is worthwhile in life are crucial pillars for a lasting love.[18] A shared sense of purpose keeps Margaret and Tom's family together, even though they are often hundreds of miles apart. Tom drives trucks cross-country for a living and is on the road for weeks at a time. When they first married he had a regular desk job in Wichita, and just hated it. Having grown up on a farm, he longed for open spaces. When Tom saw an opening to become a truck driver, Margaret didn't hesitate to support him, knowing full well that caring for her three young children for weeks by herself would require quite an adjustment. She reminded herself that the purpose of their relationship was to create a happy family. That goal, she knew, required a husband who was at least content at what he did for a living. When Tom is home, he cares for the children and gives his wife a break from the daily routine. He also stays in regular contact while on the road. Margaret remarks, "I think it works because we want the same thing: a family that cares for each other and is flexible about who does what. We share tasks and are equally responsible for making the family system work for all involved."

Equality under a Common Purpose

In a harmonious and lasting relationship, the purpose is impartial, not favoring one person over the other, but guiding both towards a larger vision and objective. Since shared purpose and meaning encompasses the interests of both parties, it is a natural starting point for cooperation and synergy.

In organizations, generally speaking, the CEO and management craft the vision and establish the general direction for the company in order to effectively compete, while hopefully the employees are motivated to execute that vision. Subordinates submit to a leader because their common mission or cause is greater than all of them. They cooperate in the roles of subject and object because they know this enables them to accomplish more. The apparent inequality of positions conceals a more fundamental equality that bonds people together to realize a shared purpose.

A wise leader knows not to exploit his position for personal gain. He knows that skewing the purpose to make it favor himself would only cause resentment and spoil organizational unity. Instead, he willingly sacrifices more, takes on greater responsibilities and works harder than his subordinates do. He maintains his leadership because he acts to benefit the greater purpose of the group. "Every time I wanted to get mad at my coach because of the insane practice schedule," recalls Barry of his high school basketball days, "I realized he was there longer than I was and he really cared about us winning the championship. He was doing it for me, the team, the school. What could I say?"

Noble Purpose

Purpose is the invisible center of any relationship, and good relationships are established around good purposes. A noble purpose, higher than the personal interests of the parties, calls them to a greater vision of themselves. As in Tom and Margaret's family, it can call forth sacrifice. A higher goal has the power to transform a relationship, setting it within an unlimited universe of potential for growth and affection.

The higher the shared objective, potentially the deeper the bonds. Drinking partners can't expect much resilience in their relationship. Conversely, war buddies who once protected each other from death on the battlefield while fighting for their country share a bond that may last forever. "I belong to them and they to me; we all share the same fear and the same life, we are nearer than lovers, in a simpler, harder way"— these are the sentiments of a soldier for his comrades.[19] From love of country to love of the environment, public-spirited concern inspires all manner of close and rewarding relationships with like-minded people.

Family counselor Ross Campbell states that all the strong and happy families he has met have some sort of moral or spiritual ideal that binds them together.[20] In any case, all families revolve around some value or purpose. If it is a lesser purpose such as money, social status or leisure activities, the family may find that it is not truly satisfied, even if it achieves and enjoys these ends. The happiest families are those that cherish and practice altruistic love.

Joe and Judy moved from Atlanta to an economically depressed area in Alabama. Although they had little money, they wanted to do something for their new community. As both had experience in the theater, they decided to initiate a community play. They couldn't afford to buy costumes, so they showed their children how to make them from scraps. Judy coached local people in their parts, while Joe organized others to make the sets. The play was a great success. In no time, their family went from strangers to respected members of the community. Joe was elected to several civic boards. The whole family felt pride and a sense of belonging.

Model of a Purposeful, Harmonious Family

The family is the primary locus of loving relationships and the starting-point for gaining competencies in relationships of all kinds. The relational principles discussed above suggest a model of family that can be helpful for understanding relationships and organizations in general.

A loving family is an integrated unit, harmonious and purposeful. The parent-child and husband-wife relationships support each other synergistically, invigorated by the love flowing through them. This can be diagrammed as a dynamically interacting structure with four positions.

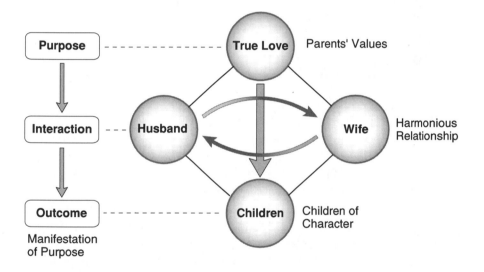

Figure 7: Dynamics of a Purposeful, Harmonious Family

Thus, when a husband and wife relate to each other based on a noble purpose and commitment to true love, they create a whole that is greater than both of them together. This outcome includes the enhanced quality of affection between them and children who feel loved and cared for. It can extend to neighbors and the community that is enriched by the family's presence.

Older parents and grandparents who embody the wisdom and traditions of the past are usually the primary source of the couple's values. Their marriage is a model for the couple's marriage; their way of parenting likewise is a model for the couple's parenting. Children are the fruits of a marriage; as they grow in character they come to reflect their parents' values. Family values are thus passed on vertically from generation to generation. (See Section Four)

On the horizontal axis is the interaction itself. Naturally, every husband and wife wants to enjoy a pleasurable and congenial relationship with each other and with their children. Therefore, each makes effort to invest in the relationship, guided by a vision of true love and shared values. Their interaction generates the commitment and affection that animates the family. Their relationship is further strengthened when they practice the principles of good interaction described above.

Family—The Center of Ethics

If the purpose of ethics is ultimately to realize true love, then the family is the primary standard and measure of ethics. While the growth of individual character remains an essential moral goal, it is nevertheless shortsighted to regard individuals as autonomous units, abstracted from the matrix of family. Personal character development is a relational enterprise that is cultivated through the affectionate bonds of child and parent and culminates in the ability of a mature adult to give altruistic, other-centered love. Participation in family life is thus a minimum condition for a person to realize his or her full humanity.

The proposition that the fundamental unit of ethics is the family—not the individual or the society—is not self-evident in the present culture. In the last century there were attempts to eliminate the family unit altogether, replacing it with communal or collective living arrangements. These largely failed. Still, the diversity of contemporary living arrangements makes the notion of the traditional two-parent family seem almost antique.

A contemporary trend is to replace the ethic of binding marriage—the traditional linchpin of stable families—with an individualistic ethic that regards all relationships, even marriage, as contracts between autonomous individuals. Yet relations in the family are established by love and strengthened through years of caring and living for each other.

To pretend that family members are autonomous individuals who can break cleanly with a divorce is to ignore the ensuing emotional devastation for the adults and especially the children involved.

Reaffirming the centrality of the family requires an updated understanding of its meaning, purpose and function. Social theorist Amitai Etzioni admits that the traditional family deserved criticism; yet he argues, "The trouble is that no new concept of the family—of responsibility to children, of intimacy and of commitment to one another— has emerged to replace the traditional form.... It is time to reconstruct, in the full sense of the term—not to return to the traditional, but to return to a moral affirmation, reconstructed but firmly held."[21]

Therefore, when reaffirming the importance of the family, it is important to examine the values upon which it is based. The strongest families are those imbued with sound moral values, higher purpose and a vision of true love. They feature healthy interactions and a clear distinction of roles. Such families have vitality and freshness; their love is ever growing; they have the strength to weather any storm.

The family is the primary school of loving relationships of all kinds. Since family bonds are permanent, they require special care and continued investment to maintain. Then, on the foundation of these primary relationships in the family, people can get along well at work, at school and in the community by engaging in temporary and less demanding relationships with peers, superiors and juniors. James Q. Wilson states, "We learn to cope with the people of this world because we learn to cope with the members of our family."[22]

There are many other rewarding relationships—with teachers and caregivers, employers, co-workers and friends—wherein people also learn the ways of effective interactions and catch glimpses of the ideal of true love. They also provide needed moral and psychological assets for surmounting life's challenges—and even bettering their families. The ability to form good relationships is an essential quality and an important life skill, one that benefits a person when learned from an early age.

9

Making a Meaningful Contribution

LOIS GIBBS' CHILDREN WERE SICK, AS WERE MANY OF THE OTHER children in her Love Canal neighborhood in Niagara Falls, New York. She found out why: her neighborhood was built on a toxic waste dump. When she first set out to notify her neighbors, she was unsure of herself; but remembering that lives were at stake, she started knocking on doors. People ridiculed her, calling her "that hysterical housewife." Experts told her that she was unqualified. Still she pressed on, convincing others not to yield to the government officials who claimed nothing was wrong. Eventually, the effort she started got all 900 families in Love Canal relocated.

Gibbs understood that to safeguard her own family, she had to work to protect other families, too. She went to Congress and pushed for the creation of the Superfund Law to clean up these toxic dumping grounds. She founded the Citizen's Clearinghouse for Hazardous Wastes, which helps polluted communities all over America. This formerly shy homemaker became a national leader on an issue of vital importance.[1] She found meaning in life through helping people avoid the illnesses caused by chemical poisons.

Helping others is a fundamental human need; it brings its own inner sense of satisfaction. In general, a person's sense of value is derived not only from a sense of personal integrity and the affection of loved ones, but also from having "objective worth," a value that comes from benefiting the public good.[2] As Eleanor Roosevelt once said of citizenship, "When you cease to make a contribution, you begin to die."

Most often, people give to society through their work. Employing their labor, intelligence and artistry, they produce products and provide services that benefit the communities in which they live. Their industry and creativity both enriches them and adds to the general prosperity. Individuals also make meaningful social contributions through hobbies and interests outside of their employment: leading a scouting troop, organizing a community picnic, planting flowers in the park, helping a destitute stranger, or just being a good neighbor. Simply cleaning up a trash-strewn yard is the sort of small effort, multiplied many times over, that helps care for the environment and improves the appearance of a neighborhood.

Education has long been concerned about providing the requisite skills to prepare students for work and participation in a democratic society. Character education adds an emphasis on the inherent moral component in these activities. There are ethical norms involved that can make the difference between a genuine contribution and mere self-seeking. These norms are often discussed in terms of business ethics, professional ethics, medical ethics, etc. First, however, there are foundational issues to be considered, such as: Why should a person want to contribute to society? What constitutes a social contribution? What are the principles for achieving this life goal?

Serving the Greater Good

Just as the essence of true love is living to be of service to others, the core of social ethics is to benefit the greater good. Mature moral consciousness in adults requires self-transcendence. A person who grows in the capacity for altruistic love is able to go beyond conventional obligations to relate to progressively greater frames of reference—to his or her family, community, country and world. This capacity redounds to the person's own worth and meaning—as one who makes a difference. Character education teaches that it is in a student's enlightened self-interest to contribute to these greater goods.

Learning to Contribute

Children first learn the ethic of making a contribution concretely through respecting and obeying parents, teachers and elders. Parents' wishes are usually not arbitrary or self-serving; they have the maturity and perspective to put the family's welfare first. Therefore, by respecting and obeying their parents, children naturally are placing the benefit of the family above their own personal interests. Regular chores around the house engender a sense of participating in the family and teach basic lessons about giving priority to public duties.

A family is not an island to itself; it participates in the life of the community. Therefore, wise parents also raise their children to think beyond the family's well being and to want to give social service. As children grow, they learn to extend the ethic of making a contribution to the classroom, the football team—any greater good. Thus, the ethic of serving the greater good that begins with respect and obedience to parents extends to every level: citizens serving the community, patriots serving the nation, and humanitarians serving the world.

Schools reinforce this lesson. Lisa, a student in Grace Tahana's elementary school class on Long Island, was frightened when her father was called to go to the Middle East to fight in the Gulf War, for what would be a four-month absence. The teacher involved her class and eventually the whole school in supporting Lisa. The students wrote letters to Lisa's father and the other soldiers and sent them food and gifts. They composed stories about love and courage. They discussed the meaning of serving and protecting one's country. This teacher had turned a difficult experience into a teaching opportunity about caring, courage and patriotism.[3]

Everyday Heroism

When people think of heroism, they usually think of soldiers, generals and patriots whose exploits are praised in history books. Yet just as great are the countless small and unrecognized things that ordinary people do for the sake of others. The poet Wordsworth wrote:

The best portion of a good man's life,
His little nameless, unremembered acts
Of kindness and love.

A social worker related the story of Tommy, a young man who suffered from a disability and struggled to talk and walk. Yet he was always doing something for someone else. Tommy found out that a group home for retarded men was ignored at Christmas time. With his faltering gait and halting speech, he personally went door to door to every business in town and collected donations. Then he spent days on end putting together the best Christmas they could ever imagine.[4] Such small acts of caring and service by everyday citizens are the glue that binds society together and builds its moral strength.

The Flow of the Social Order

At the root of the ethic of social contribution lies a natural principle. Human beings are situated within a social hierarchy, a ladder that begins with the individual and extends to the family, community, nation and world. A social hierarchy is but a special case of the hierarchical structure of nature generally. From the organization of cells and organs in the human body to the ecological web of life, there is a natural circulation of energy through these interdependent hierarchies, from bottom to top and then back down to the bottom.

Recall that in relationships generally, the interacting participants take on a subject role and an object role. (See Chapter 8) There is a distinction among roles, yet the roles are of equal value, as one cannot function without the other. A mother cannot be a mother without her child; a teacher cannot teach without students. Likewise, in any hierarchy, the higher and lower positions are interdependent. An individual finds value in contributing to a larger social unit. The larger social unit depends upon the individuals that support it; therefore, it in turn protects and enriches them and provides them with opportunities to enrich themselves. This fundamental synergy is behind all systems that thrive.

Complementary Public and Private Purposes

People thus have individual goals and social goals, complementary purposes that should be in balance. The innate desire to find value through contributing to a greater good is called the *whole purpose*, and the desire to maintain and benefit the self is called the *individual purpose*. Families, communities, nations, and indeed all beings likewise have dual purposes: to contribute to a larger whole and to benefit themselves. The ethical issue is the balance between them.

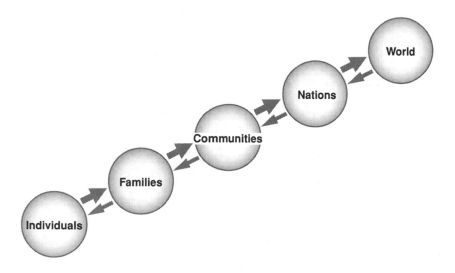

Figre 8: Interdependent Social Hierarchy

The human body provides a ready illustration of the complementarity of public and private purposes. Cells, organs and systems form an interdependent hierarchy with ascending purposes. Cells work to establish the function of organs. An organ, the stomach, supports the functioning of the digestive system, and the digestive system provides nourishment for the entire body. At the same time, the body cannot be healthy unless all its cells and organs function well and manage their own needs. Thus, whole purpose and individual purpose are synergistic. When the whole body is healthy, the individual cells and organs are nourished and protected. Conversely, the individual cells and organs maintain themselves for the sake of the whole body.

Cancer is a disease in which the tumor cells cease to honor the greater purpose of the body. Cancer cells stop responding to the signals coming from their organ system. Instead, they divide uncontrollably. The tumor is parasitic, feeding on the body for the sake of its own growth. Eventually the cancer saps the body of its vitality, and the body dies. This is analogous to what happens in a society when greedy individuals pursue private gain while disregarding the public good.

Amitai Etzioni said, "To take and not to give is an amoral, self-centered predisposition that ultimately no society can tolerate."[5] Like a cancer, excessive selfishness can sap a society of its strength and cohesion.

A Healthy Social Order

A social hierarchy functions like a human body. In a healthy society, people give priority to the collective purpose and receive support for their particular contributions. Workers who are diligent about their craft aim to produce quality products for consumers, products that will sell well and make profits for their industry. Retailers who are honest and provide good service build customer loyalty. This give-and-take builds and sustains a thriving and civilized social order. Henry Ford once remarked, "No society of nations, no people within a nation, no family can benefit through mutual aid...unless we all see and act as though the other person's welfare determines our own welfare."[6]

The synergy within the social order benefits everyone. Workers labor for their company, and the company rewards workers in the form of higher wages, bonuses and stock options. Citizens give of themselves for the sake of their country's development, creating the capital that eventually results in a higher standard of living. Thus, the whole supports the welfare of the individual, and prosperous individuals are better able to contribute to the whole—a virtuous cycle in which both are winners.

Enlightened businesses find that they can facilitate their employees' natural desire to make a contribution to the whole by helping them better meet their individual needs. When Baxter International, a manufacturer of medical supplies, found that conflicts between work and home were affecting morale, it began offering flexible work schedules, allowing employees to work at home or fulfill their hours in four days instead of five. Harry is one of the more than 2,000 employees who take advantage of this program. He can be home by 4 p.m. to practice baseball with his children; then after 10 p.m. he takes care of business with e-mail and voice mail. The company seems to have profited from this investment in its workers' welfare, with increased productivity and sales volume doubling in the last six years.[7]

Relating to Authority and Being in Authority

Structures of authority are pervasive in human life. Beginning with the family and school, children learn to deal with people in positions of authority. These lessons are the key to developing good professional relationships in the workplace later in life.

Character education can help foster healthy attitudes towards authority. Virtues such as respect, obedience, patience, empathy, tolerance and self-respect are valuable assets when dealing with a difficult boss or a capricious manager. Instead of being quick to criticize and complain, a wise subordinate maintains respect. She works diligently and takes care of matters her boss may have overlooked. At the right time and place, she offers constructive advice. She helps to build a trusting and respectful atmosphere among all the members of the organization. Eventually, by winning everyone's respect, a subordinate with such a mature attitude may gain an unspoken, informal authority of her own.

Likewise, all people at one time or another find themselves in a position of authority over others. They may be parents or elder siblings, or mentors to younger classmates. They may be teachers or coaches or camp counselors. They may be a government official who oversees a county or a businessman who runs a company with a hundred employees. They are ordinary people with no official position who take the responsibility to do a tough job when no one else will.

A person may fulfill multiple roles of authority, perhaps as a parent, a teacher and a leader at the same time. Indeed, the self-same individual may be both in a position of authority and subject to authority; this is the case for the vast majority of people. For example, Fred works as an assistant production manager in a Connecticut aerospace company. He is the father of three children. He spends his Saturdays as a Boy Scout troop leader, teaching a group of boys about camping, teamwork and character. One of the children in the troop happens to be his boss' son. When this boy was having difficulties, the father, Fred's boss, came to Fred for help and advice.

Positions of authority are little more than roles to be assumed or relinquished as the situation requires. Thus, it is a mistake to judge the value of a person mainly by his or her social role—or to evaluate oneself in that way. The real worth of a person is internal—a matter of character. That worth shines forth in how well he fulfills the responsibilities that his position entails. Not dependent on recognition, wealth or status, the virtuous person "finds himself in no situation in life in which he is not master of himself."[8]

Ethics of Legitimate Authority

People are grateful for good parents, good teachers and good leaders. How can those who find themselves in positions of authority fulfill their roles well, meeting the challenges of public responsibility? In general, it depends on developing mature character and cultivating the capacity to give love.

Lacking these inner qualities, even the best performers in subordinate roles may be challenged beyond their capacity when given a leadership responsibility. Doug was the star running back on his high-school football team when his coach took sick and asked him to fill in and lead the team in the biggest game of the season. Doug was well liked and respected by his teammates, and many were his friends. But as a coach, he favored his friends over the other players, giving them more playing time. The others began to grumble, and they did not play their best. As the team fell behind and the pressure mounted, he began cursing and berating his players. The game did not turn out well. Although Doug had the athletic ability to be a good player and the social skills to be a good friend, he had not yet acquired the necessary qualities of character to meet the challenge of bearing authority.

The Good Parent

The inner qualities that come with personal maturity and genuine love are apparent in outstanding parents, teachers and leaders. Good parents nurture their children with a deep, abiding love. They are always available to give them guidance and support. They enforce rules and discipline with the children's character and growth potential foremost in mind. They are known for their compassion, fairness and generosity. In these and other ways, they inspire respect and devotion on the part of their children. They become exemplary authority figures to them.

Indeed, among all the types of authority the role of parent is primary and archetypical. This is because the heart that a parent brings to raising his or her own children extends naturally to the approach of a caring teacher and an effective leader. (See Chapter 18) A parent's heart is naturally oriented to investing for the sake of the children. Teachers who bring a parental heart into the classroom give their students the personal attention that can spark learning. Their experiences raising children give them better insights into the challenges their students may be facing. Likewise, leaders who bring a parental heart and a parent's experience to the task of managing people have a more mature perspective on life and more versatility in dealing with their subordinates' diverse situations. Celeste became a successful CEO of a large food company after returning to work in her late 40s. When asked how she was able to do it, she replied, "Raising five kids taught me the basics: listen to people and make them feel appreciated, encourage and reward them a lot and rein them in when necessary." For those who are not parents, practicing parental-type roles as an elder sibling, uncle, mentor or coach is also good preparation for leadership.

The Good Teacher

An effective teacher guides her students to bring out their personal best. She cares for each student individually. The scope of the education she gives is not only the specific subject matter but encompasses the whole human being. Many people cherish the memory of a good teacher they had, one who cared about them and regarded nothing as more important than developing in them wisdom, compassion and self-confidence.

One teacher who brings a parental heart to her teaching is "Mama Hawk" Hawkins, who works with difficult inner-city children in Chicago. She teaches them in a room she has furnished herself as a home-like setting. She sews clothes for them, haunts bargain stores for them and raises donations for school supplies. She doesn't hesitate to hug and affirm them. Her philosophy is that "Every child is gifted," no matter how buried those gifts may seem. One of her young boys was often seen dealing drugs; his addicted mother left him alone for days at a time. School personnel had labeled him a future criminal, and he fit the profile. But Mama Hawk believed in him. Noticing that he was good at talking his way in and out of situations, Mama Hawk encouraged him to use this gift in a useful way. He eventually earned a scholarship to a Midwestern university to study law, a profession where today he uses his rhetorical gifts to help others. He still helps Mama Hawk in his spare time by tutoring her students.[9]

The Good Leader

A good leader takes responsibility for the organization's overall mission while leading his people to be successful in their individual tasks. He sets the example by investing more and working harder than anyone else. He motivates his workers and staff to great efforts for the sake of the organization's purpose, while caring for their personal welfare. He treats them with respect and kindness and, ever mindful of morale, fosters a spirit of cooperation.

As president of Sony's Online Entertainment unit, Lisa Simpson has to find ways to motivate her talented and highly paid staff. Internet businesses must deal with some sensitive staff issues: an increasingly blurred line between work and home, a hectic work schedule, and creative young people who don't take well to being bossed around. Simpson finds that one of her most valuable skills is to know how to listen. "There's a certain finesse to maintaining authority but doing it in a way where people can openly challenge your thinking," she says. With her attentive attitude, "people aren't afraid to tell me that they don't know how to do something, or don't know enough to make something happen. They don't think that I will punish them or take away their assignment if they raise a red flag."[10]

Unequal power relations are ubiquitous and inevitable in social organizations, from families on up. Problems arise, however, when there is disharmony between the leader and those below him. A leader may be arrogant, or simply fail to understand the needs and desires of his subordinates. Yet each person, regardless of his or her position, has the same value. A leader who treats his employees with care and respect affirms their dignity and humanity. In the long run, an organization prospers when all its members feel needed and valued.

Work and Wealth

Work is the way most people make a contribution to the public good. Society advances on the shoulders of working people: farmers, artists, scientists and engineers, laborers, teachers, business people and civil servants. Their labors, large and small, affect the lives of others and bring innumerable benefits to society.

People measure the value of their employment not only by the size of their paychecks, but also by the inner satisfaction they derive from having helped others or from creating something of utility or beauty. The assembly-line worker who builds cars, the mechanic who repairs cars, and the dealer who sells cars are each helping many people have the satisfaction of owning and driving quality automobiles. The wage they are paid is in some sense a measure of how much other people value the work they do. Work well done is thus a source of dignity and self-worth.

Most people are concerned about the meaning of their work. Job satisfaction rises considerably when an employee is able to see how his or her effort contributes to overall productivity and a greater social good. William Bennett remarks, "The most satisfying work involves directing our efforts towards achieving ends that we ourselves endorse as worthy expressions of our talent and character."[11]

The Work Ethic

The values that make for productive workers, sometimes called the "work ethic," are rooted in and inseparable from moral values. These values include perseverance, diligence, thrift, initiative, resourcefulness, cooperation, teamwork and pride in one's craft. General Colin Powell once said, "Success is the result of perfection, hard work, learning from failure, loyalty and persistence." There are many aphorisms, traditional and new, that support the work ethic. Schools have many avenues for inculcating the work ethic, including ample homework and high academic standards.

In a study of America's millionaires, Thomas Stanley and William Danko found, surprisingly, that these wealthy men often have less education and poorer mastery of their chosen occupation than do many of the people who work for them. Yet typically they are hardworking, frugal, sacrificial and self-disciplined. They are moral in both their private lives and their business dealings. They do not make their money through dishonest means; they do not spend their money on high profile luxuries but save it for their children and their children's children. Most of them have been married to the same woman for more than 20 years. In short, they are honest people who excel in the work ethic.[12]

A cardinal virtue of the work ethic is service. Successful businesses live by the motto, "The customer is king." They make it their aim to anticipate and meet the needs of the buying public. The case of the American auto industry in the 1980s is instructive. Up until the

1970s, Detroit took the consumer for granted. Operating under the doctrine of planned obsolescence, they produced mediocre vehicles and made frequent model changes so the public would be enticed to buy a new car every few years. The workmanship was shoddy; the corporate culture was lazy. Moreover, American cars guzzled gasoline at a time when the price of oil was increasing dramatically. Meanwhile, Japanese automobile companies concentrated on quality. They schooled their workers to take pride in their workmanship. The American consumer liked a superior automobile, so while Detroit was sleeping, Japanese companies grabbed one-third of the American market.

The Pursuit of Wealth

Today there is a gold rush to the Internet and e-commerce. All around the world, people with opportunity and privilege are scrambling to accumulate riches. Certainly wealth creation is a vital part of economic development. Yet whether this abundance adds to the public welfare depends on how it is used and distributed.

There is a danger that excessive wealth may have negative effects on the wealthy individuals themselves. The old adage, "Money cannot buy happiness," is confirmed by numerous studies. Psychologists Richard Ryan and Tim Kasser have concluded independently that people for whom affluence is the number one priority in life tend to experience an unusual degree of anxiety and depression as well as a lower overall level of well being. "Americans are encouraged to try to strike it rich," says Ryan, but "the more we seek satisfactions in material goods, the less we find them there. The satisfaction has a short half-life; it's very fleeting." Kasser and his associates collected data from 13 countries, including Germany, Russia and India. They found that in every culture they studied, pursuing wealth is psychologically unhelpful and often destructive. Pursuing goals that reflect genuine human needs—such as fostering caring relationships and helping others—turns out to promote more of a sense of well-being than trying to impress others or accumulating trendy clothes, cars, gadgets and the money needed to buy them.[13]

Philanthropy

People with means testify that they find more lasting satisfaction from using their wealth for socially beneficial purposes. Hospitality to guests, helping needy relatives, kindness to strangers, volunteering for charitable community work, philanthropy—these are activities that make constructive use of affluence. When people with means practice charity to help those who are less fortunate, they facilitate the circulation of wealth throughout society.

An under-appreciated secret of America's broad-based economic prosperity is its tradition of public responsibility and philanthropy among its wealthiest businessmen. Steel tycoon Andrew Carnegie established the first charitable foundation in 1911, with an initial donation of $135 million; it funded hundreds of libraries and concert halls throughout the country. Carnegie wrote in *The Gospel of Wealth* that any riches above and beyond what people need for their family should be regarded as a public trust, to be managed and then expended to benefit the ordinary citizen. Philanthropy has been the social norm among America's wealthy class ever since, as the generosity of many CEOs of today's largest companies attests.

Making a Difference with Money

Henry Ford, the father of the American automobile industry, shocked the business world in 1914 when he began paying his workers five dollars a day—nearly double the average wage. Ford detested handouts, but he believed people needed opportunities for work to maintain their self-respect and be productive. He funded educational programs for his workers, and hired blind, deaf and crippled men that other companies refused. By paying his workers above-subsistence wages, he enabled them to become consumers who could buy his mass-produced Model-T automobiles. His generosity laid the foundations of America's consumer-driven economy, while at the same time opening up a huge market for his cars.

Ford showed that it could be good business to invest in one's employees, affording them benefits and paying them more than the prevailing wage. Bill Ford, a descendant of Henry Ford and the current chairman of the company, continues this tradition. He recently initiated a program to empower his employees by providing all of them with a computer, printer and Internet usage at home for a nominal fee. Sometimes the human factor can be as decisive as the financial side for determining business success.

The ethical issues around the use of wealth become more pressing as social prosperity increases. Business owners must decide how much of their profits to plow back into building their business and how much to distribute to their employees in the form of higher wages. People who have money confront choices about how to use it: whether to spend it on personal luxuries, invest it in their family's future, or give it away to charities that help the less fortunate. These economic choices are also moral decisions that bring greater or lesser benefit to society, as well as to the individuals concerned.

Environmental Conservation

Making a social contribution includes caring for and preserving the natural environment. Although wealth may be acquired by harvesting the elements of nature, exploiting nature and extracting its resources faster than they are regenerated is in effect stealing from the future. The environment is a fragile resource.

According to the United Nations Environmental Program, "A new ethic, embracing plants and animals as well as people, is required for human societies to live in harmony with the natural world on which they depend for survival and well-being."[14] What might be a family-based environmental ethic? If people regard the planet Earth as the great Mother who provides all the elements that nourish their bodies and keep them alive, they will care for her with gratitude, just as children show gratitude to their elderly parents.

The natural world forms a wider "society" that is responsive to human beings and deserving of their care. People sense their kinship with other living creatures, feel empathy towards them, and want to protect them. Even mechanical things, like automobiles, are tinged with a mysterious sensibility, seeming to respond to their owner's care. Computers have been known to go haywire when their users are frustrated or furious. A well-kept house will sparkle with warmth and comfort if it is cared for with love.

Nature has a natural balance; it is marvelously harmonious and fecund. When nature is exploited, the resulting devastation—poisoned air, filthy water and littered land—is only too obvious. Thus, the condition of the environment is a transparent indicator of human moral standards. For this reason, environmental education is a helpful complement to character education.

Environmental education helps integrate the various areas of human awareness on the way to becoming a complete human being. It combines the folklore and wisdom of native peoples with the latest findings of science. It serves to reunite the facts of the scientific world-view with the spiritual and moral values that guide humans in their responsibility to be caretakers of the natural world. Moreover, the same sensitivity and care that is required to establish a balanced relationship with the earth is desirable for building well-balanced relationships with one another.[15]

For example, Catherine Sneed, a counselor at the San Francisco County Jail, created an organic garden on land adjoining the jail for use in the rehabilitation of inmates. Gardening teaches life lessons. Prisoners with drug problems see how well the plants grow without chemicals. Many of them had lived on junk food; now they discover the natural taste of fresh vegetables as they enjoy the garden's bounty. They see that harvests cannot be cheated on or rushed; they receive based only on what they give. Small farm animals give them experience in nurturing; planning the garden shows the benefits of long-term thinking. But the most powerful lesson is that mistakes in life, like those in the garden, can be corrected. The recidivism rate of the gardeners is only one-fourth that of other inmates.[16]

Whether in regards to leadership, work, money or the environment, the governing ethical principles of contributing to society are simple: live for the benefit of others, serve the greater good, and care for others with a parental heart. An enlightened restaurant owner handles all his patrons as if they were kin and offers them a relaxing and satisfying time. An auto worker who takes pride in his work puts care into every weld and rivet, wanting his product to carry a family with safety and reliability. A conscientious veterinarian treats all the animals she tends to with the same care and concern as if they were her own pets. True love is the motive for service and giving. It is the essential quality for leadership in any field.

All social ethics, then, whether applied to business, law, medicine or the environment, is founded upon an altruistic heart, mature personal character and the norms of family life. As Confucius wrote in *The Great Learning*:

> When the heart is set right, the personal life will be cultivated; when the personal life is cultivated, the family will be regulated; when the family is regulated, the nation will be in order; and when the nation is in order, there will be peace in the world.[17]

Section 3

Life Goals as a Framework for Character Education

TONY DEVINE AND JOSEPHINE HAUER

THE CONCEPT OF LIFE GOALS PROVIDES A LARGER PERSPECTIVE for conceptualizing character education. It provides a theoretical scaffolding that encompasses the diverse aims and methods of character education and shows their inter relatedness. Appealing to youth's imagination with attractive images of growth, relationships and creativity, a life goals framework allows teachers to fully articulate the "why" of good behavior. Moral ideals and goals point youth toward activities inherently worthy and rewarding. They provide long-range, meaningful motivation for character educators and students alike.

Chapter 10 discusses and illustrates the central axis of character education—the partnership between schools, parents and the community—and relates this to the three life goals of personal maturity, loving relationships and family and making a contribution. Character education that recognizes the importance of this three-way partnership is naturally compatible with a life goals orientation, as its efforts include the personal, interpersonal and public dimensions of life.

Chapters 11 to 13 consider current classroom and school methods in their supportive role to the development of character as a lifelong process. Teachers and educators are continuing and supplementing a process that preferably begins in the home; yet their efforts may at times provide ethical inspiration that has impact over a lifetime.

10

Life Goals and the Partnership of Home, School and Community

Through all the daily transactions of family, school and neighborhood, young people [should] encounter a unified consensus of core values.

—William Damon

THE HOME, SCHOOL AND COMMUNITY ARE CENTRAL FORCES for the cultivation of heart and character. Together, they form a powerful partnership. The perspective of three life goals—1) personal maturity, 2) loving relationships and family, and 3) contribution to society—speaks to the nature of this partnership and how it fosters the education of the whole person. When schools implement a life goals approach, they are naturally strengthening the relationship between these three strong influences and helping them to send a consistent moral message.

The first life goal is supported by schools' commitment to character development. The second life goal is cultivated by recognition of and facilitation of parental involvement in character and academic objectives. The third life goal is modeled by community service activities and creative school projects in conjunction with business, government, the media and community agencies. Thus, the three life goals framework pulls together the three crucial elements of comprehensive character education—the home, school and community.

Toward the First Life Goal: School-Wide Character Education

School-wide character education means to intentionally provide opportunities for character development as an integral aspect of school life. When all members of the school community—faculty, staff, and students—share the commitment to character education, it leads to the creation of an ethos conducive to respectful and caring actions. For example, how respectfully and politely the students line up and take their food in the cafeteria, how they clean up after themselves, how they show respect for the cafeteria workers and how the cafeteria workers show respect for the students are all opportunities for training in character. In such ways, students have a consistent experience of moral concern throughout the school day, in and out of class.

Fostering the First Life Goal— School-Wide Character Ethos

- Planning and leadership for the character education initiative

- Public commitment to character

- Observable standards

- Balance between character goals and academic performance

- School-wide culture of character

- Time for moral learning

Planning and Leadership for the Character Education Initiative

School-wide character education begins with the process of planning where all stakeholders—including parents and representatives of the community—are involved and their concerns addressed. Sanford McDonnell and Esther Schaeffer, chairman and executive director of the Character Education Partnership, sent out a letter in early 2000 to all state governors and legislators across the country, offering suggestions on ways to ensure that character education is both effective and comprehensive. Among other guidelines, these character leaders emphasized influencing both school culture and academic curriculum. They also affirmed that planning should address "transformations of the school environment and classroom culture, revised curriculum, new teaching strategies, discipline, school procedures and evaluation of all grade levels."[1]

Leadership, professionalism, staff training, clear program expectations, communication and assessment are commonly affirmed as hallmarks of an effective character education initiative. David Wangaard, Director of the School for Ethical Education in Bridgeport, Connecticut, helps schools to begin the character education process, encouraging school leaders to consider a five-component model:[2]

1. *Partnership Mission Statement and Role Modeling*: Develop a mission statement that clearly states goals for all those involved in moral education and keeps the ultimate outcome constantly in focus. It may include specific behavioral and/or attitudinal goals for students.

2. *Teacher and Staff Training*: Schedule time for teacher and staff training in character education methodologies and techniques. Teachers also need a basic grounding in the moral developmental needs of children and training in cooperative learning and behavior management skills.

3. *Curriculum and Project Activities*: Provide students with consistent exposure and opportunities to learn, reflect upon and practice ethical values.

4. *Assessment*: Include assessment in regard to implementation as well as its impact on students and faculty. Character education efforts are best designed with evaluation and assessment in mind. Assessment may include both formal and informal activities—review of the school's baseline statistics, parent meetings, questionnaires, impromptu meetings, general observations, community service activities, and empirically based evaluations.

5. *Principal Leadership*: Leadership from the school principal is essential. Supportive principals publicly demonstrate commitment to the school's character efforts and recognize worthy efforts of faculty, parents and community helpers.

Public Commitment to Character

Many educators agree that a school's commitment to character should be intentional and public. This may take the form of a mission statement posted in the classrooms, hallways, and in printed materials. One reason for this is to counteract the negative effects of the "hidden curriculum." Daphne Paxton, principal of Cross Roads School from Georgia warns: "In many southern communities, the school is thought to exist so the inhabitants have athletic teams to support on Friday nights. The hidden curriculum then becomes one that produces winning teams. Character and academic development often get lost in the compelling pursuit of getting a winning team."[3] Every school has some sort of ethos, for better or for worse. Public commitment to character allows educators to gain control of this ethos and direct it to educative purposes.

In a growing number of schools throughout the country, character traits are posted in classrooms, on bulletin boards in the hallways, and in the cafeteria. Elementary schools have incentive plans to recognize students displaying model behavior: posting their pictures in the cafeteria, treating them to lunch at a local restaurant, or having students read the morning announcements over the intercom. Motivational speakers reinforce the importance of good character. Brookside Elementary School in Binghamton, New York, has monthly assemblies promoting a particular virtue. The principal may read a story; students present skits, join in cheers or recite a pledge. "My kids are always talking about the assemblies," says one parent.[4]

Buck Lodge Middle School of Prince George's County, Maryland, offers a daily closed-circuit television broadcast featuring "Dr. Character," who tends to the ethical questions common to adolescents. Questions are posed to the puppet character who becomes a focal point for peer discussions about a multitude of behavioral and attitudinal issues. Situations that arise when applying virtues are dealt with in a compelling way that gets the students talking and gives the teachers a point of reference to discuss virtue throughout the day.[5]

Observable Standards

When values are expressed in terms of concrete behavior, the entire school is more likely to be held accountable. Telling students and faculty to show respect means little if it is not explained in terms of actions. Explaining precisely to students how to greet elders or school administrators overcomes the ambiguity and variety of interpretations that can accompany and even obfuscate the norm of respect. When good character is modeled, it can be learned.

At the front door of Douglass Academy in Harlem, rules are laid down the instant students step inside. In the alcove are nine mirrors and several benches where students adjust ties, skirts and shirts and change from street sneakers into regulation black dress shoes. "At the front door, you set the tone for the entire school day," says Principal Hodge, who makes no apologies for his role as fashion cop. Appearance, he believes, means self-respect.[6]

The Character Plus program in St. Louis uses consensus building to identify good traits and behaviors. Parents, teachers, administrators, bus drivers, custodians, librarians, etc. come together for a series of meetings to decide on a manageable number of character traits, to prioritize them, define them and clarify the behaviors that exhibit them. Then they incorporate these into the mission statement and policies of the school and guidelines for each grade level.[7] The Traut Core Knowledge School, an alternative public school in Fort Collins, Colorado, uses a "Door to Door Handbook of Character Education" to describe for adults what student embodiment of the core values looks like, from the time of leaving home in the morning to arriving back in the afternoon.[8]

Character Balanced with Performance

Academic achievement is a primary means of character building. The Camden, New York, Middle School instituted an "I Can" program in which students set a goal to improve their grades in one or more courses and sign a pledge that is co-signed by a parent. In addition to the academic benefits, the experience of setting a goal and accomplishing it is a valuable character lesson.

Nevertheless, assessment, tracking and other aspects of academic evaluation need review in light of the ethos they support. Are effort and improvement recognized, or only the number of correct answers? Is constructive risk-taking rewarded or punished? Are good grades trumpeted more than good character? A balance in emphasis can go a long way towards discouraging cheating and cutthroat competitiveness.

To make this character emphasis, the school leaders have to be careful to avoid an excessive focus on external achievements such as test scores. This is no easy task when teachers too often feel their main job is to get the students to pass the next round of state examinations. The subtle pressures for teachers to "teach for results" on standardized achievement tests often undermines the more important character and social development of students in the classroom. Yet a character focus can improve academic results. "We get more done because we have fewer disciplinary problems," says Camden Middle School principal Vicki Mace.[9]

School-Wide Culture of Character

A teacher can best foster character growth in her classroom by promoting a caring environment and at the same time requiring that her students be morally accountable. This principle applies throughout the school. Any disparity between the warm feeling of a favored teacher's classroom and coldness or downright hostility in the rest of the building is not lost on students, especially adolescents. The young readily revert to selfishness when the environment seems to demand it. This is a special challenge in large institutions, which tend to be impersonal.

Consistency of standards applies throughout the whole school community. "The character of the adult community" is the third of three pillars of the character education Responsive Classroom™ project of the Northeast Foundation for Children, after curriculum and the school climate. Co-founder Chip Wood describes the challenge: "This issue is probably the crux of the matter. As in most professions, we in education have been focused largely on a 'client-centered' approach... We have done all this without really looking closely in the mirror. What is it like in the teachers' room?"[10]

In families, the relationship between parents greatly influences the spirit of the home. In the same way, the most confronting reality for administration and faculty is not what the students do, but how the adults treat each other. Educator Roland Barth remarks, "Four years of public schooling... and ten years as a principal... convince me that the nature of the relationships among adults who inhabit a school has more to do with a school's quality and character, with the professionalism of its teachers, than any other factor." Barth noticed that when staff improved their interaction, they tended to be more caring toward students. He found that after establishing a character initiative, staff no longer left office equipment broken without reporting it. Even staff members who did not like each other began to treat each other with respect.[11]

Creating a consistent, school-wide culture of character requires attention to the typically unsupervised and unstructured areas where the worst demonstrations of anti-social behavior are too often the norm. These areas include the school bus, hallways, study halls, bathrooms, playground and cafeteria. When standards of propriety are brought into these outside-the-classroom areas, they enhance a positive school ethos that is supportive of character. The fundamental objective is to cultivate within students the essence of Lord Macaulay's comment that "the measure of a man's real character is what he would do if he knew he would never be found out." Otherwise, these areas often become negative pockets of fear and abuse. A classroom reminder that "The pen is mightier than the sword" can be neutralized by a lunch table experience that asserts that "Might makes right."

In Tonawanda, New York, the bus drivers in the district formed a committee to implement a values education program. They posted signs on the buses stating that these were "positive buses," and some of the drivers began teaching bus safety and conduct in the primary classrooms. Mindful of the need to recognize all members of the school community, the bus drivers organized a "Caring Day." They gave out pieces of green ribbon to all the students and asked them to give the ribbon to an adult in the building who showed them care and concern. Students gave the ribbons to secretaries, cafeteria workers, guidance counselors and teachers, who wore them proudly.[12]

Time Dedicated to Character

Weaving moral discussion into daily life is an invaluable part of character education. Yet there is also merit in devoting some time for exclusive exploration into morality, ethics and meaning. In the realm of formal education, besides that which arises in religion classes at parochial schools, some schools choose to dedicate periods of time or specific courses to character education.

The Kimberley Academy in Montclair, New Jersey, has a general morality and ethics course in each grade. Students learn about ethical traditions and are coached in moral reasoning skills. Allotting time for such courses is more common in China, Russia and other countries where what once were ideological political indoctrination classes on all grade levels are now yearlong character education classes, and new character education curricula have been developed for them.

Many schools allow a short time daily for reflection, often at the start of the day. It is commonly focused on a specific theme or character trait. Principal, teachers, and students may address the entire school through the public announcement system. In this way, the Buck Lodge Middle School introduces a virtue on Mondays and explores positive and negative experiences related to the virtue on Tuesdays. A community guest comes in to discuss its practical application on Wednesdays, while Thursdays bring narrations about historical role models. On Fridays, students present projects showing an understanding and application of the virtue.

Toward the Second Life Goal: Home and School Partnership

The school and the home are natural partners in character education, since these contexts dominate a young person's most formative years. Attitudes and discipline gained in the home affect success at school, while the demands of school influence home life. Over 90 percent of Americans believe that public schools should share with families in the responsibility of teaching universally held values such as respect and responsibility.[13] When teachers are asked what single most important improvement could be made in education, they invariably cite greater parental involvement and cooperation.[14] The National Association of Elementary School Principals NAESP "strongly urges the formation of 'home-school partnership programs.'"

Researcher Michael Rutter found that good schools resemble good homes.[15] In particular, a comprehensive character-building environment in a school holds some similar features to a home with a strong moral ethos. (See Chapter 12) In those cases where the home is not working well, the school ethos provides a measure of compensation, showing what a positive and caring atmosphere looks like.

Fostering the Second Life Goal—Home and School Partnership

- Respectful and frequent communication between teachers and parents

- Parent collaboration in the school's character education program

- Parent engagement in character lessons in school and at home

- Cooperation against destructive influences

- Family activities at schools

- Parent cohort groups

- Parenting education seminars at schools

Communication

Respectful and frequent communication between teachers and parents helps to foster mutual trust and good will. Some teachers take the time to call parents in early September, thus starting the year positively. Susan Pelis of Greenfield Center School in Greenfield, Massachusetts, engages parents at the start of the year with "book bags." These bags hold the student's storybook that is read in class by day and is finished with the parent at night. This simple device strengthens the bond between school and home.[16] Teachers in School No. 2 in Kamenka, Russia, pass along information through a notebook, which includes comments and scores on behavior, attitude and grades. If a disciplinary problem arises, the teacher has a greater chance of winning the sympathy of parents if a dialogue as already been established.

The Internet is providing new ways for families and teachers to communicate with one another. America Online's Family Education Network is a service that allows teachers and students to create their own secure websites. Through this medium, teachers involve parents in the daily life of their class by posting homework assignments, class activities, academic goals and even student grades. Teachers and parents exchange comments and ideas daily by e-mail.

One of the most striking examples of home and school cooperation is the Jefferson Junior High School in Washington, D.C., located in a district beset with teenage pregnancy, violence crime and drugs. It was able to turn things around with an award-winning character education initiative, the key to which was setting high expectations for parents. Parents are required to come to school for Back-to-School Night and to parent-teacher conferences during the year. Parents are also asked to volunteer twenty hours of service to the school each year.

Collaboration in Planning and Implementation of School Programs

Schools can encourage direct parental involvement in the planning and implementation of character efforts. The Character Plus program brings parents into the planning process from the very beginning—to meet, reflect, develop goals, define desirable character traits, and develop school policies. This process typically takes a year or more, but the wide consensus it builds makes it worthwhile.

"It is not top-down management, but truly a collaborative process. As a result, teachers, parents and neighbors of the school feel like stakeholders; they have ownership," said B.R. Rhoads, Principal of Bristol Elementary School in Connecticut. "We learned that it has a lot to do with compromise. Our communities include right-wing groups, liberals and people who find themselves somewhere on the continuum between these two poles."[17]

The Benjamin Franklin Charter School in Franklin, Massachusetts, has parental involvement as one of its four pillars.[18] A parents' committee actively helps plan and troubleshoot their character education efforts. In addition, teachers send home a curriculum description for all grades with suggestions as to where parents may be helpful, such as teaching a section, providing background information or sharing experiences from different cultures. The school also sends home Family Readings Suggestions, a list of books to complement that month's character focus, as well as Family Service Suggestions—ideas for the practice of virtue at home and in the neighborhood.[19]

One of the benefits of a solid character building effort is the greater willingness of parents to volunteer at school. At Kennedy Middle School in Eugene, Oregon, parents were reluctant to volunteer for lunchroom monitoring or much of anything else due to serious student discipline problems. After three years of a character focus, parent participation became so high that one parent serves almost as a fulltime volunteer to coordinate it all.[20]

Parental Engagement in Character Lessons

A character education program can increase parental involvement through engaging them in their children's lessons. English teachers might assign students to ask their parents what person has had the greatest impact on their lives and why. Students may write a short essay on a parent's hero, or ask a parent to share about a challenge they faced and overcame. This idea is popular with parents, as it facilitates meaningful conversation and offers occasions for passing on important values to their children. In homes where a parent asserting his values only provokes emotionally charged conflicts, it provides a neutral context in which children can learn their parents' point of view and engage in reasoned reflection.[21]

When Jeff's ninth-grade economics teacher assigned the class to interview their grandparents about life during the Great Depression, Jeff discovered that his grandparents, who now owned a mansion and a golf-range on their extensive property, had suffered greatly, sometimes going without food. This was quite a surprise for the teenager. When he interviewed his grandmother, she could barely speak about it without sobbing. "Hard times. Hard times," she said, and went on to describe daily life. Now a graduate student, Jeff recalls this assignment as one of his most memorable ones.[22]

An innovative approach in School No. 10 in Novotalitsa, Russia, invites parents into classrooms to observe and participate in moral lessons.[23] Larisa Schmakova, a seventh-grade teacher, asked both the students and their parents to write down the names of each family member and list things that they were learning from and teaching to that person. When parents and children compared their lists, it generated both humor and insight. Parents were surprised by the youngsters' views and experiences. Students learned something new by hearing their parents' images of responsibility. The exercise promoted perspective taking and generated meaningful conversations between students and parents.

Cooperation against Destructive Influences

Parental guidance regarding use of alcohol, tobacco and other substances is one of the critical factors in helping youth avoid destructive habits. School counselors provide invaluable support by coaching parents in how to discuss sensitive topics with their children.

Parents often appreciate school support in controlling and limiting television viewing. Some schools have participated in a national "Turn It Off" or "Pull the Plug" week where families voluntarily give up television for a week. In general, the response is positive. One mother said that during that week without television her son developed a lasting interest in reading. Another mother commented that without the anesthetizing effect of television, her children fought more, but they fought more fairly. Some families reported not missing television at all and became busy with other interests. Many families reported a heightened awareness of how television watching had taken an excessive toll on their family life.

Family Activities at School

Schools also might sponsor appealing parent and family initiatives. Brookside Elementary School invites families to come to the school for PTA-planned games and crafts once a month.[24] On a recent Valentine's Day the school sponsored a father-daughter dance night. This was one of its most popular events, where fathers and daughters had an unusual opportunity to connect in a positive way.

Hazelwood Elementary School of Louisville, Kentucky, sponsors evenings that bring families together to participate in enjoyable, interactive activities. On Family Science night, parents do hands-on science activities with their children. On Family Reading night, parents and children read together in small groups, and on Family Arts and Crafts Night, parents and children work together on a craft. [25]

At Kennedy Middle School, parents are encouraged to stop in and have lunch with their children whenever possible. "One father arranged his work schedule so he could eat lunch here every Thursday," says Kay Mehas, director of school services. She emphasizes to parents that their presence is needed in middle school even more than when the children were younger. "Students are figuring out where they fit into society. When they see you at school, it sends them a message about your priorities."[26]

Many schools have designated a Grandparents Day, which is an opportunity for older family and community members to share their wisdom and to experience the school and community's respect and appreciation.[27] "Grandparents and Books" is a national program that brings seniors to children in the library. Don and Rosemarie Sparling are among the many senior volunteers who host young visitors to the school library after school, sitting and reading a book together. "Most of these children have no money, they have no place to be after school and they need to know that someone really cares about them," says Rosemarie. "I feel like she's really my grandma," says Sean Cortez, 7.[28]

Parent Peer Groups and Parenting Education

Certain schools have formed parent peer groups which meet periodically either in the school or in parents' homes. This is a response to the reality that many parents find little time to socialize with other parents and may have never met the parents of their children's friends. When they meet in organized peer groups, they often compare notes with each other and determine mutual standards on such matters as bedtimes, permissible movies and television programs, and dating. Parents work together to plan events for the school and community, and support each other by reinforcing their commitment to good values.[29] The schools participating in the Child Development Project in California have parent groups that help families implement the same character goals affirmed in the classroom.[30]

Some schools offer parenting programs to help parents improve their discipline and communication skills. Others offer workshops about the parents' role in building up their child's character. The Los Angeles Parent Institute for Quality Education offers a nine-week course, taught in both the morning and evening to accommodate working parents.[31] The Easterling Primary School in Marion, South Carolina, provides a variety of workshops for parents on topics ranging from discipline to the content and methodology of their character education program.[32] The school has a parent resource center with books and tapes on child development and character education that is open to all families. The school also makes house calls that strengthen the home-school liaison.

The Mt. Lebanon School District in Pittsburgh, Pennsylvania developed the Parent Education Action Plan. In the fall, they present a six-part series devoted to several elements of character education, such as the stages of moral development, and skills and strategies for helping children recognize and adopt core values. They also dispense parenting advice. During the spring term, a series of single topics extend the subjects introduced earlier. These include the father's role in moral development, media literacy, the acquisition of virtues and discipline.[33]

Through such education, parents can gain valuable insights and skills. They become aware of their strengths and weaknesses, and as a result strive to better themselves for their own sake as well as that of their child. They can also learn to have higher ethical expectations of their children. Hearing teachers tell about how fifth grade children gave up a Saturday to clean out a trash-laden river, or that a group of high school students are volunteering to tutor the learning disabled encourages parents to believe in their child's moral potential.

Toward the Third Life Goal: Community Partnership

Aristotle taught that people become virtuous by participating in the life of a moral community. Likewise, communities become moral through the cultivation of virtuous individuals. Schools and communities nurture each other's moral ethos in a variety of ways. Schools fulfill their primary obligation to society through supporting student's individual moral growth into worthy citizens. Likewise, schools can harness community involvement in support of its moral education goals. Drug abuse prevention and community health experts,[34] social workers, family therapists[35] and character educators[36]all agree that promoting prosocial behavior among the young requires community modeling and multifaceted learning opportunities in the community.

Schools enhance the promotion of character when they recruit the help of local community groups—businesses, youth organizations, service organizations, social organizations, local government, and the media.[37] Likewise, the community supports character efforts of the school by promoting service opportunities, values in the workplace, civics and environmental conservation.

Fostering the Third Life Goal—Community Partnership

- Partnership between school and business
- Media involvement
- Local government participation

Partnership between School and Business

In 1994, Walter Segaloff of Newport News, Virginia, decided that businesspeople needed to help the schools, government and churches with the job of education. He established the award-winning An Achievable Dream Academy, a public school for at-risk children, which partners with businesses and non-profit organizations in a program called "job shadowing."[38] For two weeks in the summer, seventh and eighth-grade students volunteer to help in local workplaces. The work connects the youngsters—most of whom have only one parent or guardian—to mentors in local hospitals, colleges and universities, in law firms and science laboratories. Though the practical benefits are apparent, "the primary purpose of this program is to develop the relationship between students and mentors," says Richard Coleman, principal.[39]

Business representatives perform a helpful service when they speak in schools about how ethical practices pay off in greater productivity and personal advancement at work. This is regular feature at the James E. McDade Classical School in Chicago, which emphasizes using real life to reinforce good values.[40] Easterling Primary School invites business leaders to serve as role models and tutors to their students.

Media Involvement

Schools have recruited local news media to publicize its core values and promote examples of character in daily life. In collaboration with St. Louis's citywide character education effort, the local CBS affiliate television station produces a Saturday morning program on storytelling for young children, emphasizing good character traits. In that same city, the local newspaper in conjunction with the local police department joined with Character Plus in a project called "Do the Right Thing." This program recognizes young children who are setting an example of service in their community.

The local newspaper in Binghamton, New York, features a "Character Corner" that highlights the Brookside Elementary School's designated virtue of the month. Senior citizens look forward to the feature and express their support. Once a week a community television station airs a student-written "Character Minute" on the evening news.[41]

Local Government Participation

The Utah Project, a statewide character education initiative, gives children practice in participating in public forums. They learn the rules of decorum and respectful debate and gain practice in good citizenship. This initiative has also fostered partnerships between schools and local governments.[42]

At the An Achievable Dream Academy, soldiers from nearby Fort Eustis actively mentor youngsters. After leading the 90-minute morning ceremonies for third through fifth graders, the soldiers spend time in classrooms helping with teaching, disciplining or simply listening and offering advice.[43] The Yu Ying Middle School in Beijing, China partners with the army in a preventative approach to discipline that helps set the tone for courteous relations among teachers and peers. During the first week of the academic year, seventh and tenth-grade students train and drill with the soldiers. They learn proper bearing and manners. In the process, they come to appreciate and make friends with their mentors in uniform, who also perform many functions in the community. Parents attend the event at the end of the week for a report and celebration.

"We are a community of character" is emblazoned on the police cars of Lombard, Illinois, reflecting the training officers have received.[44] Reflecting the character education initiative in local schools, a police department in Wake County, North Carolina, developed a program that employed police and community members as role models for youth. The result was a halving of the juvenile court referrals after just two years. The county park and recreation department integrated virtues into their summer program so that all 5000 youngsters participating received similar messages, ones that echoed what they heard in schools.[45]

In these and myriad other ways, the basic human aspirations for personal maturity, thriving families and a healthy society are served when young people's characters are formed through the concerted efforts of home, school and community. Yet these three life goals also frame a variety of educational methodologies employed in the character-building classroom and school-wide efforts. The following chapters demonstrate how methods of character education can be understood as fostering one or another of these basic life purposes.

11

Fostering Character in the Classroom

COMPREHENSIVE CHARACTER EDUCATION EMPLOYS DIVERSE methods to cultivate moral maturity in each student. Most character educators support eclectic approaches for reaching the whole person. When teachers create a moral ecosystem within their own classroom, replete with explicit and implicit moral reasoning, stories, problem solving strategies, self-evaluation and rewards for mastery, they equip students to fulfill the first life goal of personal maturity.

A mature person will, without supervision, intrinsically desire, decide to do, and come to embody what is right, true and good. Therefore, fostering personal maturity involves cultivating the student's inner *telos* toward "a higher self," integrity, or a moral identity. When students see themselves in relation to the moral ideal of personhood, it facilitates gaining mastery over academic as well as personal challenges.

Methods that Foster Personal Maturity

- · Utilizing the entire curriculum

- · Lifting up unifying character themes

- · Lessons through stories

- · Accountability

- · Encouraging self-discipline

- · Setting high and consistent expectations

- · Joint rule-making

- · Opportunities for moral reasoning and moral imagination

- · Socratic questioning

- · Skills for solving interpersonal problems

- · Self-evaluation

- · Constructing a moral identity

- · Facing physical challenges

Utilizing the Entire Curriculum

How can today's curricula, filled to the bursting-point with information, properly guide students to live exemplary and noble lives, leading them to realize the importance of aspiring to mature character? Educators Kevin Ryan and Karen Bohlin have observed:

> There is a danger of churning out students who are rapid processors of information but may not necessarily be more reflective, thoughtful, and able to give sustained consideration to the information that matters most. When students

aren't engaged by the curriculum in school, they are more likely to be seduced by the culture of easy pleasure and instant gratification.[1]

Often curriculum itself is an excellent opportunity for a thoughtful teacher to illustrate life's moral lessons in compelling ways. Teaching values through the curriculum entails highlighting the moral issues and values within class subjects.

History offers endless opportunities to highlight heroes and villains, the moral choices they faced, and the consequences of their choices. The social studies class might explore the centrality of personal responsibility in the functioning of democracy. Jack Lapolla, the director of Social Studies at Wilton High School in Connecticut, encourages students to identify the clash of values behind many of the turning points of American history, "so that students don't get the idea that Lincoln's primary motivation was economic."[2] A talk by a real-life war veteran teaches children that their country did not come cheaply, engendering the virtue of gratitude. Current events provide opportunities for class discussions on ethical issues such as how personal morality relates to public service.[3]

Science students in Buck Lodge Middle School draw parallels between the interactions among organisms necessary to maintain a viable ecosystem and those of responsible people in a caring community.[4] A math teacher at Hazelwood Elementary School poses ethical problems: "What would you do with the extra money if you received $9.75 from a $20 bill for an $11.25 purchase?"[5] A business course may include a discussion with local businesspersons about practical issues involved in doing business honestly and making ethical decisions in their professions.

At Mountain Pointe High School, Phoenix, Arizona, students in Evan Anderson's writing class write reflective essays on a subject of character. Atlantis Elementary School in Cocoa, Florida, does the same with younger students. "We read a character quote every morning and that often becomes a writing prompt," says principal Linda Mace. The children also analyze literature based on the highlighted virtues. "The kids start these discussions. They start looking for the pillars in stories."[6]

Character education infused into the curriculum also has the advantage of avoiding the appearance of repetition, says Art Dillon, principal of the Traut Core Knowledge School. Students may encounter the same core virtues each year, but they experience them in a fresh way since they are embedded in different content each time.[7]

Lifting Up Unifying Character Themes

Ethical themes transcend individual subjects; hence they are usefully employed across the entire curriculum.[8] For example, the theme of interdependence that is studied in biology in relation to the web of life, and in global studies through an examination of the world economy, can also be lifted up in English class through a novel that views the complex interaction between lives. It is a theme that naturally brings up issues of empathy, responsibility for others and respect for nature.

Another approach is to prominently feature one virtue throughout the various disciplines. If self-mastery is the virtue of choice, classes in science, mathematics, art and music can draw attention to great figures in their field and the self-mastery they needed to become proficient. Physical education and health classes can stress how self-mastery is necessary to keep a fit and healthy body. History teachers can point out great examples of this virtue in the past. English classes can find similar examples in literature, and students can write about their successes and experiences in making that virtue a reality in their own lives.[9]

Lessons through Stories

Stories from good literature and historical narratives are emotionally compelling and appeal to children's natural interest in exploring the dramatic possibilities of life. Even reluctant readers begin to devour well-written stories, becoming lively participants in discussions about topics that spark their imaginations.

In the area of children's education, psychologist Bruno Bettleheim praised the value of fairy tales and stories of heroes. They teach that, "a struggle against severe difficulties in life is unavoidable...if one does not shy away, but steadfastly meets unexpected and often unjust hardships, one masters all obstacles and at the end emerges victorious."[10] On the primary level, *The Little Engine That Could* demonstrates the values of perseverance, courage and caring for others, while *Aesop's Fables* teaches the values of prudence, moderation and hard work. At the middle school level, *King Arthur and the Knights of the Round Table* demonstrates the values of courage and courtesy, Anne Frank's *Diary of a Young Girl* inculcates an unforgettable lesson in compassion, and *The*

Odyssey teaches courage, dedication and commitment to family.

Stories can be encounters with real-life heroes, too. The Giraffe Project's "storybank" is a resource for teachers containing over 800 stories of ordinary people who became heroes. These are people whose courage and compassion made a difference to others. Among them are Sarah Swagart, who decided it was wrong for young skateboarders to be treated unfairly with fines as high as $500 for skating in parking lots and sidewalks. She spearheaded efforts to get the town to build a skateboarding park. Another is Hazel Wolf, who started working in 1911 to gain equality for women before moving on to fight for civil rights and fair work laws. She was still publishing an environmental newspaper and fundraising for environmental causes until shortly before she died at age 101.[11]

Young people naturally want to identify with heroic and successful people. Tales from good literature and history are storehouses of role models to emulate—and villains to be repelled by—that are remembered as they encounter difficulties in their own lives. They thus help them to make better choices. Great literature is true to the human condition. Thus, it speaks to the human heart with the voice of truth beyond time and place.

Moral Discipline for Self-Authorship

Moral discipline involves utilizing rules, limits and accountability procedures as an impetus to practicing good habits and experiencing the satisfaction of self-authored moral growth. Ultimately it is not merely a means of enforcing order in the home or classroom. Discipline is best employed to aid people in designing their character toward a self-defined moral ideal. This approach implies going beyond external motivators such as prizes or awards towards ultimately instilling in children self-discipline and a personal commitment to respecting rules, defending the rights of others, and loyalty to home, school and community.

Moreover, discipline that promotes the youngster's inner growth as well as control of behavior improves the quality of the teacher-student relationship by imposing a structure and direction on the relationship. When authority is exercised with the proper combination of firmness and warm-heartedness, people feel cared for. They tend to give admiration in return. They are more likely to believe that the rules have value for them, obey them willingly, and internalize them. This is a basic principle of effective parenting. (See Chapter 22)

Accountability

Fundamental to this process is holding youth accountable for their words and behavior, conveying that actions have consequences and promises mean something. Effective teachers set up and enforce consequences in a manner that lets students understand why unacceptable behavior violates the standard of integrity and respect. Moral psychologists know that children respond better to correction when adults point out how breaking a rule hurts someone.[12] It helps children develop empathy and realize that rules exist to protect people.

High-school teacher and author Hal Urban invites a student who has broken a rule during class to sit at a certain table to write out how he or she may have violated the principle of treating others as one would like to be treated. Thus, the student dialogues with him or herself to prod the conscience and help sharpen moral reasoning. The Marion Intermediate School has young students write out a Responsibility Plan to help correct misbehavior and avoid punishment. "We want to keep the focus on good behavior rather than coercing them into behaving," says principal Rick Menzer.

High and Consistent Expectations

Setting high expectations conveys to young people their value and potential for becoming good citizens. Lax discipline that accommodates poor behavior sells them short, implying that society does not expect much from them. The children with special emotional, mental and physical needs at Atlantis Elementary used to be the toughest group to discipline. But then, says principal Linda Mace, "the more I bragged about these kids, the more their behavior started to drastically change.... They are the pride and joy of the building instead of the 'most difficult.'"[13]

A policy of setting consistent expectations throughout the school reinforces the efforts of individual teachers. Chip Wood remarks, "Consistency around rules and discipline provides all the children with a sense of safety and security when behavior becomes an issue.... Consistency in discipline procedures helps teachers to know exactly what the 'fall-back' position is for them and the precise steps to take when they find themselves in a power struggle with a student. Consistency on the part of all adults in the building...enhances the spirit and cooperative engagement of the adult community in carrying out its mission to teach and care for the children in the school."[14]

Joint Rule-Making

An effective strategy to promote moral discipline is to have students set some of the rules for the classroom themselves. Young people have a strong intuitive grasp of the need for rules, and by making rules they gain a sense of ownership over the rules and their own moral choices. They often come up with innovative and effective rules—sometimes more strict than what adults would do on their own.

Patty Brody, a second-grade teacher in Syracuse, New York, became frustrated at the end of each day as the children rushed to the coat closet as a chaotic herd—pushing, shoving, jumping over each other and exchanging angry words as they tried to find their coats and mittens. She posed a question at a class meeting, "How can we, working together, solve this problem?" After brainstorming possible solutions, the class decided to assign everyone a hook, which they would use to put their things. Brody then questioned how they would make sure that everyone did this. One girl suggested that if someone did not put their things where they belonged, they would have to keep them at their desk during the next day. Brody then drew up a class agreement, had each of her thirty-four children sign it, and posted it next to the coat closet. After adopting this plan, the trip to the coat closet was an orderly and cordial one.[15]

When students help make the rules—under the guidance of the teacher—and agree to a certain consequence if the rule is broken, they are less likely to resent the teacher for enforcing that consequence and more inclined to assume responsibility. Here is an opportunity for lessons in citizenship, linking class rules with the laws of the community.

Moral Reflection

Moral reflection is the area of character development that involves encouraging the capacity for right thinking about moral issues. It includes being morally aware: knowing the virtues and what they require of people in concrete situations. It involves being able to reason morally—to understand why some actions are ethically better than others. Moral reflection also encompasses being able to make thoughtful moral decisions, to use the moral imagination to consider alternatives, consequences and the values at stake. It requires being able to take the perspective of others—the cognitive side of empathy—and recognize their strengths and vulnerabilities.[16] It also includes self-knowledge and the capacity for self-criticism.

Opportunities for Moral Reasoning and Moral Imagination

Moral reasoning is encouraged when students encounter moral issues in daily life, current events and historical situations. Exercises that afford opportunities for dialogue and role-playing encourage students to consider different perspectives, note their consequences, and craft their own position.

Games and group exercises can be employed to bring out students' moral imagination. At a teacher-training seminar in Ivanova, Russia, teachers divide into groups and spend an hour preparing skits, poems and stories about love, responsibility, good and evil, marriage, friendship, etc.—themes found in the moral education texts. They perform them at the evening's program. Teachers new to these methods begin to experience for themselves the value of encouraging creativity and creating an atmosphere of genuine caring in a moral education classroom.

Class discussions and debates can develop moral reasoning. Mrs. Paulson's sixth-grade class at Dundee Middle School debated the heroism or cowardice of the adolescent character in *The Red Badge of Courage* who runs from his first battle, pretends he is wounded to be reinstated into his company, and goes on to become a seasoned soldier. One side of the class had to maintain that he was not a true hero; the other side had to maintain that he was. The debate reached fever pitch, with emotions running high. At the peak of the conflict, the teacher suddenly shouted, "Switch sides!" The students had to physically shift their desks to the opposite side of the room and rethink their positions from the opposite point of view. They gained new tolerance and respect for the opinions of others as they struggled to come up with reasons to support the side they had initially opposed.

Moral reasoning methods are effective even for elementary school children. When asked to figure out what a storybook character should do when faced with a tough choice, their responses will range from noble and altruistic to selfish and calculating. But when asked what's the *right* thing to do, children usually know what's right; they simply need the confidence and the encouragement to reason it out and to act on it.

Teachers at the Atlantis Elementary School cultivate youngsters' moral reasoning through the use of a reminder list:

"Before you make a choice, ask yourself:

· What does my conscience say about it?
· Could it hurt anyone, including me?
· Is it fair?
· Would it violate the Golden Rule?
· Have I been told it is wrong?
· Deep down, how do I feel about this decision?"[17]

Socratic Questioning

The Socratic method of questioning is a time-honored method to stimulate higher reasoning. A simple inquiry about what would happen if a movie character chose an alternative course or why a particular action of a figure in the news is good or bad enlightens the moral imagination.

David Elkind, who produces a series of videos that stimulate Socratic dialogue, cautions that in issues involving right and wrong it is important to guide students to the right conclusion rather than allowing them to think that whatever they conclude is acceptable. Anybody can give a simple, unsupported answer, but asking a student to justify an answer forces reflection and analysis—which often results in the student modifying his or her initial position. Questions that stimulate thoughtful responses include, "What would you think of a character in a movie who made the same choice?" "How would you feel if someone else acted that way toward you?" and "Why or why not?"[18]

Owning Values through Peer Dialogue

The EQUIP program[19] is a peer-helping approach to moral development used effectively for youth at risk in detention centers such as Teylengerind, a prison for young male adolescents in Holland. EQUIP utilizes a group setting where participants learn first to make "I" statements, think about consequences of behavior, identify negative thought patterns—such as the victim syndrome—and begin to think of the pain their antisocial behavior has caused others. The final stage of the program is for the group to learn to make fair social decisions through discussing real-life moral dilemmas that they face. The goal is to come to a morally mature unanimous decision on what *ought* to be done. For example:

Alonzo is walking along a side street with his friend Rodney. Rodney stops in front of a beautiful new sports car. Rodney looks inside and then exclaims, "Look, the keys are still in this thing! Let's see what it can do! Come on, let's go!"

What should Alonzo say or do?

Should Alonzo try to persuade Rodney not to steal the car?

What if Rodney says to Alonzo that anyone who is that careless to leave the keys in the car deserves to be ripped off! Should Alonzo try to persuade Rodney not to steal the car?

Jan van Westerlaak, an EQUIP trainer finds that most of the time the majority of the group comes up with the more mature answer, although many viewpoints are discussed. The majority then is encouraged to convince the minority through discussion and argumentation. The goal of these meetings is to make a fair decision that a majority can agree with. By establishing peer helping as a foundation for cognitively based character education, the EQUIP meetings seek both to motivate and to teach young people how to help one another think and act responsibly.

Skills for Solving Interpersonal Problems

Many schools have incorporated programs dealing with violence prevention, conflict resolution, peer mediation and interpersonal problem solving to help resolve situations that invoke intense feelings of anger, frustration and alienation among students. These programs empower students and teachers with skills and techniques that keep tensions from escalating into unmanageable crises. They are also preventative measures against future troubles as communication and understanding among disputing parties often improves.

"I Can Problem Solve" is an interpersonal problem-solving model that teaches students how to think before problems occur in relationships.[20] It provides short twenty-minute lessons, incorporating games, stories, puppets and role-play. Teachers guide students through the problem-solving practice sessions in elementary classrooms. The "Second Step Violence Prevention Curriculum" targets pre-K through middle school students and uses a lesson format that addresses empathy, impulse control, and anger management.[21] These models teach preparatory techniques for problem solving as well as problem-solving strategies.

Researcher Gordon Vessels maintains that emotional readiness and the multi-step process of interpersonal problem solving are best taught within the context of a comprehensive character education program emphasizing self control, an awareness of others' feelings and social skills training in the early grades. Formal peer mediation introduced in the fourth grade can be based on the lessons learned through teacher-led practice sessions in earlier grades. These kinds of programs, Vessels concludes, fulfill their potential as part of a character education initiative, and not as isolated "add-on" lessons.[22]

Self-Evaluation

Coaching in moral reflection includes helping youth observe and evaluate themselves. Jack was running for a class position sponsored by the student newspaper at Highland Park Middle School. He was also editor of the paper, and thus was in charge of counting the votes. He had voted for the other candidate, thinking it would be immodest to vote for himself. Nevertheless, when he counted the votes, he found he was tied for the position. Remembering his parents saying that political candidates always voted for themselves, Jack then decided to change his vote. He voted for himself and won the election. Later, however, he felt conscience-stricken. A teacher helped him walk through the reasons why what he did was wrong. He came up with, "I had the opportunity to change my vote, but the other students didn't have the same chance. If they'd had, maybe they would have changed their votes too, and I wouldn't have won." Painful as it was, Jack decided to rescind his position.[23]

Through learning how to evaluate their own thinking process, young people are empowered to anticipate and resist temptations as well as avoid tempting others. When teasing started to become hurtful in a kindergarten class in Montclair Kimberley Academy, the teacher read a poem, "Teasing," that helped her students reflect on their experience. They realized that the person doing the teasing easily forgets about it, but the hurt person stays wounded a long time. The class then all agreed to be more careful about teasing in the future.[24]

Students at the Benjamin Franklin Classical Charter School are encouraged to better internalize and make a commitment to virtues through reflections in their character education journals. The focus of their writing is on three reflective questions: "What have I done today to put this virtue into practice?" "How have I failed to practice this virtue?" and "What can I do better tomorrow?" In the same vein, Youth Opportunities Unlimited, a public school for teenagers in trouble with the law in San Diego, California, uses a racetrack as the metaphor for a constructive direction. When students create a disciplinary problem—go "off track"—they reflect in writing about where they went wrong, how they could have avoided it, and what undesirable consequences might result from their misstep. Then they list three things they can do to stay on track next time.[25] Such exercises coach young minds to think about their behavior and its consequences. They teach the valuable skill of revisiting a provocative situation and thinking out alternative and more constructive courses of action.

Constructing a Moral Identity

Teenagers are particularly prone to challenge the parent or teacher with, "Why should I be honest?"—or good, generous, or any other virtue. Younger children are easily motivated to please adults; older children need to find deeper motivation to fully realize their moral potential. "We've got everything in our lives, but no purpose behind them," says

Bill Saul, age 18. "A kid will be willing to go all out for a purpose he is needed for, if it is big enough." Teenagers are naturally attracted to themes of personal development, friendships and marriage, and career. They are also innately idealistic and oriented toward romanticism, exhibiting a desire to participate in a heroic story. They want and need to see morality and ethics in light of these concerns.

Constructing a moral "life story" for oneself is perhaps one of the most potent forces in forming character over a lifespan.[26] Italian educator Pablo Paolicchi reminds teachers that students are simultaneously "characters that have lived their own stories" as well as "authors of their stories" that "influence their further development."[27] Classroom reflection on ethics provides perspective for students as they construct their personal narratives and endow them with meaning. Developing an ethical perspective on their life's journey encourages youth not to simply follow someone else's morality, but to practice living out of a consciously constructed moral narrative framework.

In addition, a wholesome self-image and a goal-orientation toward life can be mutually supportive in defining and developing character.[28] Researchers find motivation to achieve concrete goals increases when teenagers are behaving in ways that reflect or fulfill the needs of their self-image.[29] The inner recognition that "I am a reliable, hard-working student" provides impetus toward activities that reflects these inner qualities.[30]

Overcoming Physical Hardships

Man versus nature is one of the most common themes behind thrilling adventures in compelling short stories and novels. Dealing with trials presented by an environment that cannot be fully tamed has always been a character-building exercise. Nature is powerful, unpredictable and offers innumerable physical and mental challenges.

Adventure learning is the name given to supervised experiences in nature designed to foster character growth. The adventure might be an elaborate exercise through an obstacle course for a group of teenagers supervised by skilled staff, as in the Outward Bound program, or a simple weekend canoe trip in the wilderness. The key element of adventure learning is facing uncertainty and real or perceived danger, usually in a group setting. Through adventure, the participants face their deepest fears, discover what it means to need and be needed by others, and even confront the meaning of their lives.[31]

Experiences of physical challenge foster ruggedness and resourcefulness, countering the softness and complacency that accompany city life where there are few natural hardships. Ironically, the experience can also promote appreciation for modern comforts. "I've noticed my 16-year-old Jonathan complains a lot less since he spent a few weeks in Haiti on a service project last year," observes Roger, an accountant in the Northeast. "He'll even eat vegetables more often now."

One adventure-learning program, called Ropes Adventure, works with adolescents detained for minor felonies and misdemeanors. The staff guides participants through a series of games, low-rope initiatives, and high-rope challenge activities. By evoking and then taming fear, they learn the power of personal accomplishment, trust and cooperation. Reviewing the dynamics of the ropes program, Lori Holyfield affirms that to engage in the building of character via adventure is to take an emotional journey inward, to face difficult feelings and learn how to express them in an appropriate way. With the hunger for excitement guided constructively, individuals become less inclined to act upon destructive impulses.[32]

Experiences of uncertainty and deprivation come in many forms, and not all of them require going out of doors. Commitment to the care of fish in hallway aquariums posed quite a challenge to elementary school children in Ivanova, Russia in the winter of 1999. The principal had agreed to allow the aquariums as long as students were completely responsible for feeding and caring for them. In the middle of winter, the temperatures in the hallways dropped because of a lack of fuel. Schools in town were closed, but the students took turns twice a day to pour warm water in the tanks so that the fish would survive.

In schools with a commitment to character education, teachers utilize a wide range of methods to support students' achievement of moral maturity. The school's commitment to the students' character development is evident in classrooms where moral standards are inculcated throughout the curriculum, where discipline is used to promote self-discipline and responsibility, and where students learn the skills of moral reasoning and reflection, problem solving and self-authorship. Thus, they become confident citizens with a core moral identity. However, character development is not only a personal journey; it takes place in community. The school's commitment to individual moral maturity is usefully complemented by attention to the social world of the classroom, where character education is fostered by creating a "caring community." Such relationship issues are also vital to healthy character development, as they concern the second life goal.

12

Creating a
Caring Community

CHARACTER GROWTH AND MORAL VITALITY ARE FOSTERED AS MUCH from interpersonal interactions as from individual efforts. Indeed, the fundamental energy for character development comes from the context of social relationships. Heart expands and grows with feelings of satisfaction and self-confidence through fulfilling ethical obligations, norms and duties to others. Learning how to successfully interact with others is a constant but essential challenge. A deficit in these skills leaves children at a distinct disadvantage.[1] Research suggests that social and emotional learning is one of the missing pieces of educational reform.[2]

The second life goal—loving relationships and family—highlights the relational nature of character development. Learning to relate well, as a younger to an elder and as peers, is the foundation for success in marriage, adult friendships and professional settings. The primary training ground for the life skills of good relationships is the family. For this reason, many of the most promising character-education practices focus on creating a family-like atmosphere in school, thus reinforcing in a school setting the competencies that should naturally be fostered in a good home.

Methods for a Caring Community in the Classroom

- Teacher as moral exemplar
- Establishing caring rapport
- Developing teacher competencies as moral educators
- Building a sense of belonging
- Sharing student biographies
- Cohort groups among students
- Intervention in peer harassment
- Buddy activities
- Attention to manners
- Sports teach teamwork, leadership and fairness
- Cooperative learning
- Class and group meetings

Teachers as Moral Examples and Mentors

A survey of teachers on the subject of being an agent for the moral development of children led to this response by a teacher who understood that her main responsibility was to model it in herself:

> You should live a life the students can learn from.... For example, if you're going to advocate temperance to the student, then you've got to practice it yourself. You can't live for parties and drinking. In that case you'd just undermine the bulk of what you are standing there teaching. Children can learn a lot indirectly by observing the life you lead as a teacher.[3]

Numerous studies point to the power of teacher modeling in influencing children's social-moral learning.[4] Much of human behavior is acquired through observation and imitation rather than through direct instruction. When the teacher fulfills his role as the center of ethical concern for students, this sets the moral foundation for the entire educational experience. His moral position becomes comparable to a parent in the home, with similar authority and responsibility. To be that parent-like figure, moral example and mentor is no small responsibility.

A teacher's character seldom escapes students' notice. Students in an accelerated math course in a Cook County, Illinois, high school were horrified to find their brilliant teacher pulling the wings off flies at his desk during break time. Janet, a student sensitive to the plight of animals, remarked that she never attended math class after that without a feeling of horror toward the man who entertained himself so cruelly: "It made you wonder what he'd do to you if he got you alone and powerless. It definitely eroded trust. No wonder I hated math."

So critical is the moral example of faculty and others at school that some school administrators spend the first several years of the character-education initiative focusing on just one goal: enlisting the agreement of the teachers and all adults in the school to be proper role models of care, respect and self-discipline. Moreover, a teacher's behavior and attitude set the classroom atmosphere, another factor influencing students' moral growth.[5]

Establishing Caring Rapport

The parent-like role of teachers begins with the caring, investment and moral guidance they offer students. Though no teachers are free of character defects, when students feel their earnest commitment to personal integrity and moral growth, the learning atmosphere of the classroom is enriched. On one hand, a teacher need not be afraid to assert his or her legitimate moral authority and declare what is acceptable and unacceptable in the classroom environment. Strong guidance and coaching in proper attitudes and behavior demonstrate the more assertive side of love. On the other hand, a caring heart toward the students, more than other aspects of good character, is a mark of genuine maturity and depth. The heart of a teacher who invests continually in students' well-being is remembered over a lifetime.

Students need individual attention, and the teacher who demonstrates personal caring can make a lasting impact on a child. Hal Urban demonstrates moral mentorship by coming in to class fifteen minutes early and waiting at the door to personally shake each student's hand as he or she enters the classroom. Through this simple act, he welcomes his students as an uncle might welcome his nephews and nieces. He demonstrates his respect for them as whole persons, letting them feel valued. Urban finds that this kind of personalized affirmation by a teacher transforms the classroom. On a final exam, when he asks students what they think they'll remember about the course ten years from now, many write they will remember the way he started each class.[6]

Teacher Competencies as a Moral Educator

Besides establishing a warm and caring rapport with students, teachers also require training to be able to integrate character content into their subject areas. Without skill and practice at developing imaginative lessons, a teacher's effectiveness as a moral mentor may remain underdeveloped.[7] Teachers engaged in moral education vary widely in their practices and understanding of the activity.[8] Many studies highlight the need for teachers to learn how to craft activities that help students internalize the moral dialogue of the classroom. Gordon Vessels found that even teachers with enthusiastic attitudes require support, extensive feedback, visits to model classrooms and training in classroom management techniques in order to create a warm and caring classroom atmosphere.[9]

Teachers who view themselves as moral educators naturally want to share their inner richness and reach out to students in a warm and helpful manner.[10] Experienced teachers give priority to building an ethos supportive of a caring and moral classroom. Some attitudes, practices and objectives germane to building this ethos include:

- Teach an ethic of interdependence;
- Foster empathy;
- Encourage the class to own each class member's problems;
- Help students to know one another well;
- Engage students in the process of making others feel important;

- Help students express appreciation to each other;
- Actively discourage selfishness and cruelty through swift intervention;
- View discipline problems as character-development opportunities;
- Allow students to participate in decision-making.

It comes as no surprise that most of these practices foster caring relationships within the classroom. A relationship focus affords many teaching opportunities for building character.

A Caring Community

The Child Development Project considers that learning takes place most effectively in a school setting of a caring community.[11] A caring community in the school that begins with faculty and staff development bears fruit by helping students know each other, care about each other, and feel a sense of belonging and responsibility towards each other. Where positive school spirit is lacking, students can be quite cruel to each other, even when they esteem the teacher. Such a climate is not only antithetical to character development, it also has a negative effect on academic performance, since students are inhibited by fear of ridicule and abuse by their peers. An atmosphere of rapport and positive regard among classmates, on the other hand, is naturally conducive to best efforts and helps prevent many behavior problems.

Building a Sense of Belonging

St. Rita's Catholic Elementary School in Dayton, Ohio, groups students in "family teams" of nine, consisting of one member from each grade, K to 8. A seventh and eighth grade boy and girl serve as the parent figures and are called the group's "mom" and "dad" by younger members. The older members look out for younger students and help them solve problems. At the start of the school year, these groups spend much of the first three days together in games and other activities that build emotional bonds. During the rest of the year, these family groups come together for regular events such as assemblies. Principal Maryann Eismann remarks, "There is no craziness in our school, just a peaceful, loving atmosphere. We think that much of this is due to our family groupings."[12] This is an illustration of one imaginative way that schools of character build a caring community that can foster social intelligence and relational skills.

At East Side High in Paterson, New Jersey, Principal Joe Brown required that students be able to sing the school song upon request. Most schools have such a song, but few students know it, or else they dissolve into fits of derision when singing or listening to the song. East Side students thought the school song was so hopelessly out-dated that they re-vamped it into a more modern, upbeat and catchy version. The new school song provided yet another way for students to feel good about themselves and their school as a caring, spirited community.

Fostering Caring among Peers

Regularly changing seat neighbors, pairing different students up for projects, and creating opportunities for students to talk about themselves assists students in getting to know and be concerned about each other. Some teachers have students interview each other for biographical information. This can consist of asking the derivation of their name, their dreams, their heroes or heroines, etc.[13]

Hal Urban asks his students through partner interviews to explore questions such as: "What's something good that has happened to you recently?" "Is there someone in the class right now you could say something positive about?" "What is something you are thankful for?"[14] Debbie Wilcox fosters respect and kindness among her fifth grade students in Johnson City, New York, by gathering them in a circle three times a week and inviting them to express something appreciative about what a classmate did.[15] Efforts like these encourage a positive peer culture, which has a powerful influence on student conduct, as well as promoting character competency in relationship building.

Fostering a moral community means intervening when students harass each other. It is promoted by showing tolerance of and fostering empathy for students who are different from each other. The teacher models this by discouraging disparaging discourse among students and valuing each student's unique contribution to the classroom and school community.[16]

Buddy Activities

A buddies program is an intentional community-building activity at school where older children are paired with younger children. In these teacher-organized buddy activities, children are given real opportunities to practice mentoring others. Older children can read to younger ones and tutor them in various class subjects. These activities give older children a sense of responsibility and foster friendships across grades. They realize they are setting an example, so they are more mindful of their behavior. By helping their younger peers in learning, they benefit by extending their own learning as well. Younger students no longer feel intimidated by their older peers but look to them as friends.

Students make connections on the playground, in the hallways, lunchroom and on the bus. These unsupervised areas are the places where the worst behavior is often exhibited, and transforming them is one objective of the buddy program. Rebecca Harmon, the principal of Frayser Elementary School in Louisville, Kentucky, comments on its results: "Bus referrals have decreased. Older students now know the younger students and realize that they are the models for them. They see one another in a different perspective as a result of being buddies."[17]

Relationships are built not only with students but also between buddy teachers, who collaborate on teaching and discipline. As a result, schools become more than a collection of separate classrooms. They become caring communities where both faculty and students feel a sense of belonging. The school becomes a structured environment where students feel safe and empowered to develop caring relationships, thus furthering their aspiration toward the second basic life goal.

Etiquette and Manners

Social skills training includes the art of good manners. A centerpiece of the character-building program at the Fairfield Country Day School in Fairfield, Connecticut, is the daily formal lunch that teachers and students share. Seated in groups with one teacher per table, students dine with linen napkins and water glasses. A "manners coach" instructs and reminds diners on how to place napkins on laps, conversational tone, and the proper way to request food. Beginning in the fourth grade, students may become "lunchroom servers" and bring food to the table. This is a coveted position, eclipsed only by the third grade position of "table cleaners" who get to sponge clean each table after the meal is finished. Headmaster Robert Vitalo remarks that the lunch-room ritual provides a central place for the transmission of the school's norms: "We are modeling old fashioned manners."

The Power of Sports

The value of physical education and sports in fostering relation-ship-building competencies deserves special consideration. Sports are a time-honored way to socialize young people in culturally specific ways of living with others. Team sports, games and physical challenges are ready metaphors for the challenges that lie ahead in adult life. Further, because they are fun, sports are a uniquely engaging vehicle for character growth. Sports provide opportunities to explore what it feels like to win magnanimously or arrogantly, to lose gracefully or resent-fully, to cheat and to be cheated, to struggle or to give up, to cooperate or not cooperate, to have a respectful or bossy leader, to be a good or bad teammate, etc. These are enriching contexts for self-reflection and moral development that cannot be as readily learned in the classroom.

Lessons of Leadership, Authority and Teamwork

Sports encourage virtues such as self-discipline, but more impor-tantly, they train in cooperation and teamwork. They implicitly and explicitly teach about authority. Team sports give participants experi-ences of leading and following, and they learn the reciprocal nature of these roles. A student thrust into the role of captain learns leadership skills—how to motivate others. Other players on the team learn that they need to support each other even if they do not like each other. How individual team members work together largely determines their success. Coach Vince Lombardi remarked, "Individual commitment to a group effort—that is what makes a team work, a company work, a society work, a civilization work."

Sports also demonstrate the relativity of winning and losing. When boys and girls find themselves on top one day and on the bottom the next, they learn humility and compassion. Indeed, they discover that treating the defeated well pays off when the tables turn and they are in the winners' position on another occasion.

Citizenship Training

Child development theorist Jean Piaget asserted that games teach children the necessity and value of conducting themselves according to rules. Thus, they teach how to function in a rule-governed environment such as a market economy. Piaget observed that the players learn that rules should be enforced impartially to protect all participants and ensure that "victory be honorable."[18] A team or player who cheats or is unnecessarily aggressive may win more often to start with, but will end up with a bad reputation and not be regarded as the true winner.[19] Students have the opportunity to observe how maintaining personal integrity is ultimately more important than outcome.

In School District 44 in Lombard, Illinois, the Friday night football game becomes an occasion for reminders about character for both players and spectators. The high school band plays Aretha Franklin's song, "Respect." Student speakers reflect on sportsmanship during half time. The audience is encouraged to be courteous in their role as fans.[20] A character-minded parent, teacher or coach utilizes the lessons of the gymnasium and athletic field to socialize good character, multiplying the effectiveness of classroom efforts.

Class Meetings

Class meetings build a moral community by giving students the experience of talking and listening to each other respectfully in a group. In this way it teaches how to participate in a democratic process. The teacher may simply facilitate the discussion, but more often she takes a parental role, setting the moral tone and mediating disputes. Just as the parent's valuing of each child models how siblings should respect each other, so the teacher's example in the class meeting demonstrates what valuing each member in a group looks like.

A class meeting can be a few minutes or a half-hour long, conducted daily or periodically. The teacher, or a student under the teacher's direction, leads the meeting. The topic can range from the academic—planning a project, discussing values, hearing and discussing a student presentation, reflecting on a lesson—to the interpersonal—affirming each other, sharing feelings, problem-solving, resolving a conflict, making rules, or improving class procedures. At the initial meeting on the first day of school, the teacher explains the purpose and rules of such meetings. Students consider individual and class goals for learning, conditions supportive of such learning, and suggest ways to create a good learning environment in their classroom.[21]

Shoreham-Wading River Middle School in Shoreham, New York has built an advisory system of student teams that emphasizes support and advocacy for each adolescent. This is designed to give teachers a context in which they can effectively guide the seven to twelve students that make up each team, and students are provided with a supportive peer group. The group meets for twelve minutes each morning and for fifteen minutes during lunch. They discuss school concerns; share what has been happening to individuals within the group, solve problems and discuss important issues. The teacher advisors keep parents informed on both good and bad news regarding their children. Following implementation of this system, the school has found that discipline problems declined, staff moral improved, and parental involvement increased.

Cooperative Learning

Cooperative learning is a method that structures learning around collaborative tasks. Extensive research has found that in addition to increased academic learning, students engaged in cooperative learning activities develop more positive social attitudes and behavior.[22] This form of learning fosters interdependence, trust, respect, tolerance of diversity, and it reduces interpersonal conflict. It tends to break down cliques and encourage more interactions between competent and less competent students.[23] In addition, working together to achieve a common goal teaches attentive listening, responsibility to a team, taking the viewpoint of others, communicating effectively and solving conflicts.[24] These are invaluable competencies for building and sustaining good relationships throughout life.

In schools that have adopted the Child Development Project, many of the literature units make extensive use of a format called "think-pair-share." After reading or listening to a story, students work in pairs to discuss plot, themes, characters and vocabulary, which are shared with the whole class.[25] Small cooperative teams can research a big topic such as a period of history by delegating, for example, areas like politics, culture and economics to different team members. These "specialists" do the research and report to fellow members. Everyone must do his or her part or no one will be able to complete the assignment as a whole. This strategy encourages low achievers to make more effort. Having a student specialize and be needed by the partner or team builds self-confidence and demonstrates how each person has something essential to offer.

A teacher provides guidelines and structure to facilitate effective cooperative learning.[26] She emphasizes that cooperation itself is an important classroom goal. She helps students understand how rules are for the sake of facilitating cooperation, and may possibly assign roles to group members. She instructs in the specific skills needed to cooperate, such as listening, taking careful notes, and communicating regularly. She provides an opportunity for students to reflect and discuss how well their groups are functioning and how they can improve their working relationships in the group.[27]

These are some of the methods by which schools pursue the character education mission by building a caring community. A school that functions as a caring community fosters young people's moral development in the second life goal of loving relationships and family. The effective teacher recognizes his quasi-parental role towards his students, and hence seeks to act as a moral exemplar and mentor. His emotional and social investment fosters a caring environment and feeling of family in the classroom. Good peer relationships are encouraged and guided through coaching in social skills and strategies that build a sense of interdependence and shared responsibility, as well as teamwork, moral community, and cooperative learning. These elements provide a wholesome relational ecosystem out of which altruistic attitudes and good character may more readily emerge.

13

Learning to Serve

TWELVE-YEAR-OLD CRAIG KIELBURGER OF TORONTO, CANADA, felt horrified after reading about a boy who was killed after speaking out against child labor in Pakistan's carpet weaving industry. He formed an organization called Free the Children, dedicated to ending child exploitation throughout the world. Within two years, Free the Children not only created an education and rehabilitation center for Pakistani youngsters to keep them out of the child labor system, it stirred an international ban on products produced with child labor. "I'd like to make a difference here," says Craig, "and I see that what's needed to solve this problem is for everyone to get involved and relay the message that we want this to change."[1]

The task of educating youth to follow Craig's example and make a positive difference in the world involves several components, including inculcating high work standards, service-learning projects, and programs to educate about consumer and environmental issues. They further the innate aspiration to realize the third basic life goal—making a contribution to society.

Learning to Make a Contribution

- Academic excellence
- Service learning in the community
- Helping the elderly
- Classroom chores and school service
- Environmental education
- Gardening
- Animal care
- Conscientious consumption
- Media literacy
- Discussing and practicing charitable giving

Academic Excellence

Most schools set high academic expectations. High standards impart the virtues of self-discipline, diligence and perseverance, since good work requires small sacrifices on a daily basis. Further, insisting on academic excellence signals adult trust in the ability of each child and teenager, which in itself boosts a sense of pride and self-worth. High work standards thus offer intrinsic as well as extrinsic rewards. The ultimate goal is to help students adopt ambitious standards for themselves in order to gain a sense of pride in their craft that will become a foundation for success in the world of work.

Engaging students' interest in their studies and helping them want to invest in learning is a time-honored method of promoting academic excellence. Students are further motivated to strive for high standards when they gain real expertise in a particular area. When a child receives recognition for her depth of understanding about the pyramids of Egypt, for example, she will tend to incorporate competence into her self-image and aim for expertise in other areas as well.

Julie, a West Coast ninth grader, maintained a C average in science. Despite her loathing of the subject, she determined to bring her grade up and pushed herself to study long hours. Eventually she not only mastered the material—achieving As—but became genuinely interested in it as well. Now a promising pre-med student, she's learned that hard work and diligence will bring her mastery of any subject. "I did it then—I can do it now" is part of her self-talk.

Promoting good study habits, especially as regards homework, also builds character competencies for the life goal of contributing to society. When managed properly by teachers and parents, homework fosters a spectrum of values collectively known as the work ethic. These include responsibility, autonomy, perseverance, time management, initiative, self-reliance and resourcefulness. "Homework can and should be a character-building experience," says John Rosemond, a teacher at the Camden Middle School.[2]

Service Learning

Structured experiences of service learning provide students with rewarding experiences of making a contribution that can inspire a life-long orientation toward helping others. There are numerous opportunities for young people to invest themselves in service. Ruth Charney voices the deliberateness of doing this: "We need to teach children to give care as well as to receive care. We must help them learn to contribute, to want to contribute."[3] "No one who desires to become good will become good unless he does good things," wrote Aristotle. Service learning activities such as working in soup kitchens, roadside cleanup or helping out in specialized institutions challenge students to develop their awareness of the needs of others, the desire to help others, and the skills and habits of helping. It expands their level of moral knowing, moral feeling and moral action and connection to the community.[4]

More and more schools are requiring community service as part of their character education program. Research in the U.S. shows about 60 percent of adolescents twelve to seventeen years of age volunteer at least three hours weekly in service. The helping response is especially strong when they are directly asked to be of assistance.[5] Many high schools have mandatory service hours that students are required to complete in order to graduate. Typical is the Camden Middle School, where all eighth graders are required to perform a minimum of three hours of community service during the school year as part of their social studies program. Students can receive credit for up to 15 hours. The service must be unpaid, be outside of regular school hours, help others outside of the student's immediate family, and be documented in writing by an adult.

Igniting intrinsic motivation within students can help overcome the common complaint that they are being asked to do service involuntarily. The Giraffe Heroes Program recommends asking students to choose a concern that they share and to develop a response to that concern.[6]

Chuck Wall, who teaches human relations in Bakersfield College, California, was listening to the radio news when he heard the newscaster say, "We have another act of senseless violence to report." When he walked into his class of eighteen students, he gave them an assignment to commit "one random act of senseless kindness" during the next week. At the class's next meeting, all had stories to report. Shane bought blankets from the Salvation Army and distributed them to a group of homeless people. Lisa rescued a ragged stray collie, bathed and fed it, then put up posters that reunited the dog with its owner. The assignment had such impact that the students were inspired to continue their campaign for kindness on their own. They had bumper stickers printed up; the Kern County sheriff ordered 150 for his patrol cars.

School Service

The school itself is a natural locus for diverse service activities. A simple one is peer tutoring, where adept students coach classmates having a difficult time with a subject. Peers may also befriend and help disabled students. In an intriguing twist, a Canadian project has 9 to 12-year-old learning-disabled students reading to kindergartners, thus boosting the older students' academic performance.[7]

Assigning class chores encourages service in the classroom, fostering citizenship from the early grades. At a kindergarten class at Sacred Heart School in Lyndhurst, New Jersey, one child is designated the "table manager" who makes sure the baskets of scissors, glue and construction paper are filled. Another child is the "folder person" who puts notices from the school into the children's take-home folders. Melissa, 6, boasts of her assignment to make sure all the closet doors are closed after use.

Litter Critters is a program suggested by the Child Development Project in which a student club or an entire grade helps regularly to clean the school inside and out, and sometimes helps with a clean-up project in the community.[8] Schools in Asia typically apportion chores through a team system. In Beijing's Yu Ying Middle School, each class in divided into six groups, which take turns each day to stay late and clean the classroom. An entire class from each grade takes responsibility to clean the school each week. These students do not view it simply as an obligation; they take pride in helping provide a clean and safe environment.

Schools have had great success conducting food or clothing drives for disadvantaged people in the surrounding communities. The Mound Fort Middle School involves the entire school in making quilts for the needy. After school, students can be found sewing and tying quilts. This one project has unified the once-violent urban school and transformed its atmosphere dramatically. "Often students come to school with a 'What's in it for me?' attitude," says the Mound Fort principal, Tim Smith. However, in service they come to "discover a joy they never knew before." They feel needed and more connected to their community.[9]

Serving the Elderly

Activities involving the elderly link students to the community and its living history, and they provide particularly enriching experiences of service. Newsome Park Elementary encourages cooperation of children and seniors through a program called "Joining Old and Young." Kindergarten and first grade students visit a plant nursery and work together with seniors to build a greenhouse when studying living things. When technology is the focus, the elderly share about past days without modern conveniences while their young partners take them to the school's computer room. Despite their knowledge of computers and the Internet, the kids soon realize that their elderly friends possess the more important and profound insights about life. Also, children in the fourth and fifth grades serve elderly patients at a local veterans hospital, reading to them, assisting them, and becoming their friends.[10]

Reflection and Integration

For service learning to be effective, it should include time to reflect upon and learn from the experience, later that day or the next. This is what distinguishes service learning from volunteerism and traditional service projects. This moral reflection is a conscious and intentional activity of thinking about and connecting the service activity to character lessons and integrating the experience into one's own value system.

Adolescents thrive on discussion and reflection with peers in order to understand the meaning of moral commitment and action. This is an opportunity to teach the value of making an investment in society. In Atlanta, Georgia, students manage a food closet for local residents. Through peer dialogue and essay reflection, they consider how to solve the issues of homelessness and poverty. Awareness of the complexity of social issues grows and students realize that there are no simple answers to society's problems. More importantly, many students begin to recognize the power of compassion in action for healing wounds and imparting a sense of value and dignity.[11]

Reflection is conducted in a variety of ways. Journal writing is a common practice, as is voluntary sharing of thoughts in class. By hearing about the experiences of others, students amplify and deepen their own interpretation of the activity's meaning. Other forms of reflection include writing poetry and stories and performances of music and drama.

Research that compared the strengths and weaknesses of ten different service learning projects at six high schools in one urban school district concluded that students had greater benefit in programs that rated highly on four criteria: duration, location, amount of personal contact with beneficiaries, and focus of the project.[12] To have a meaningful influence on students, service-learning projects strive for a delicate balance between the service and learning components. Projects with a clear emphasis on service fare better than those with service as an adjunct feature. The learning component is optimized when carefully incorporated into the service component.

Rewards of Service Learning

Service learning offers an abundance of rewards. It has been shown to boost interpersonal and human relations skills and to enhance academic learning.[13] A teacher from the environmental service project of the East Peoria, Illinois, school district exclaimed, "Service learning works! The students were working cooperatively, developing their academic skills, and learning that they are an important resource to the community. They felt a sense of ownership of their community's resources and a sense of stewardship."[14] Kathy Winings of the International Relief Friendship Foundation explains, "Those who become involved in service learning are able to witness up close that the real truth of our world is found in the quality of our human relations and in the concept of family. A teenager helping in a homeless shelter in lower Manhattan as part of the Youth Service Opportunity Project comes to see a human face on what previously may have been an abstract concept— homelessness."[15] One student who visited handicapped children at a local hospital in a class project of the Shoreham-Wading Middle School commented on the transforming power of these face-to-face relationships: "When I used to see retarded kids, I was afraid of them, Now the retarded have become people to me, with needs and wants."[16]

Service learning turns the ethic of making a contribution into a compelling human experience. When students are able to witness the beneficial impact of their actions on others, their sense of meaning and pride is enriched. This becomes the most potent incentive to want to repeat that experience and reach out to help again.

Environmental Education

Caring for the environment is not only an indispensable part of character education, it is a valuable vehicle for it. In East Peoria, Illinois, students centered their service learning on the local river and reservoir. In an application of cooperative learning, one class took responsibility to evaluate the drinking water on a daily basis. Another measured the rate of evaporation and replacement, and yet another class studied the immediate area for environmental factors that would affect the quality of the water supply. The issues of water pollution, usage and conservation were raised. Some students spoke in school convocations to help the other students become more aware of water issues. Others mounted a public water conservation and proper usage campaign to heighten the community's awareness of the issues. As a result, the students gained a deeper appreciation of the community's water supply and how many living things rely upon it. They also realized how much water they waste on a daily basis and what actions they could take to conserve water.[17]

A community garden is a highly visible and satisfying school project.[18] Few things spark a greater sense of wonder and connection to the earth than a simple experience of planting, cultivating and finally enjoying fresh tomatoes right out of the garden. Gardening teaches a plethora of lessons, from natural science to perseverance and patience. Abandoned lots or school property can be utilized. At the Atlantis Elementary School, students fashioned a butterfly garden and tend an ongoing compost pile for their "Kinder Garden."[19] Bruce Laberee, the art teacher, introduced the techniques of pruning and training juniper bonsai trees. These activities offered a new way to view trees—as a work to be sculpted with meditative clarity and beauty.

Young people's natural affinity for animals can be utilized to teach character lessons in compassion and responsibility. At the East Harlem Maritime School, teacher Joe Binenbaum operates a small zoo of snakes, birds, lizards and small mammals adopted from pet owners and the local ASPCA. The ninth-grade students care for them, even raising money for their feed by holding bake sales and other fundraising events. They visit their pets daily even when school is out. Some students who had previously been truant returned to school to work with the animals.[20]

Concern for animals led a group of second graders in Vidya Elementary School in Petalume, California, to environmental action. Moved by the plight of endangered elephants, these youngsters organized the Friends of Wild Life Club to make efforts on the elephants' behalf, raising money for research and lobbying for their protection. The notable elephant researcher, Oria Douglas-Hamilton, testified that while living in Africa, her greatest morale boost to fight for the international ivory ban came from this group of American schoolchildren.[21]

Environmentalism and Culture

Every community has effective environmental teachers that may go unnoticed: gardeners, carpenters, canoeists, cycling instructors and others who show youngsters different aspects of how a culture and its people live in an ecologically sustainable manner. Valuable too are elders who carry the wisdom of forbearers who lived closer to the natural rhythms of the land. Farmers, fishermen and naturalists have stories and insights to share that they gained by observation and intuition through living intimately and respectfully with nature.[22] The art of indigenous people serves in a similar way.

Learning to respect and care for their natural environment affords many benefits for developing good character. In *Connect*, a Rhode Island newsletter for K through 8 teachers, educator Loraine Keeney reports these efforts "are proving that environment projects not only lead to solid scientific learning but also dispel attitudes of hopelessness and despair about the environment, develop citizenship skills, and instill self-esteem."[23] In turn, people who have learned to value themselves and other people through an edifying human environment are "more likely to pick up litter, avoid stepping on plants or destroying animals' homes, conserve energy, and generally care for the earth and its creatures."[24]

Conscientious Consumption and Charitable Giving

Material comforts and financial security are prized, yet affluence presents its own challenges, some of them moral. Excessive materialism often blinds people to life's priorities, while wealth wisely used brings personal rewards and benefits society.

"Conscientious consumerism" is the term used by Albert Conquest in his eighth grade class in Albion Elementary, Albion, Connecticut, to describe enjoyment of available material comforts with a mind towards conserving the earth's resources. It links the inculcation of ecological awareness and the shunning of waste to an ethic of mindful and conscientious consumption.

Training in media literacy means teaching youth to be perceptive consumers and acquire a critical stance on commercially driven media and advertising. They learn to question whether they really need a certain product and whether it will deliver on its claims and promises. This is an important aspect of moral citizenship in an information-driven society.

America's tradition of charitable giving exemplifies another time-honored way to make a social contribution. An activity in which students decide where to donate accumulated money integrates lesson objectives in civic, economic and social areas. Students might do research projects on great philanthropists or how foundations decide on which projects to support. At the Rawlings School, three students took on the task of deciding where to donate the $100 they raised through two car washes. Debating the merits of various charities, they finally decided on an overseas program for needy children. "They discussed whether it was better to give locally or internationally, to an organization or a family. Next year it will be even more interesting!" said Clarissa Evans, the fifth grade teacher.

Intentional character education provides a variety of opportunities for students to experience the joy and energy stemming from being active social agents. "Nothing bigger can come from a human being than to love a great cause more than love itself and to have the privilege of working for it," wrote the British-born physician and reformer, Anna Howard Shaw. From the virtues engendered by good study habits to service learning and environmental education, character-building schools equip youth with the competencies to become productive citizens who contribute to their community.

Part II

The Family as a School of Love

Section 4

The Four Spheres of Love

JUNE SAUNDERS

THE FAMILY IS THE CRUCIBLE OF CHARACTER, IMPLICITLY "TEACHING" about virtues of honesty, loyalty, trust, self-sacrifice, personal responsibility, and respect for others. More fundamentally, it is the school of love and relationships, where the foundational capacity to invest love and the associated relational skills are optimally acquired. Embodied in the family is a natural moral and relational growth dynamic: the familial roles of child, sibling, spouse and parent. Each role may be conceived of as a "sphere of love," bringing its unique challenges and rewards, its distinctive norms and objectives. The early spheres of child and sibling's love present the first opportunities for the development of heart and conscience; these become foundational for adult moral functioning. The spouse and parent's spheres provide specific settings and challenges for character and relational growth to realize complete fulfillment. Yet, as an individual can be simultaneously a child, a sibling, a spouse and a parent, all the spheres remain important throughout life. Moreover, the Four Spheres of Love, as a family-based paradigm, is the basis for all successful social relationships.

14

Family Roles and Moral Growth

As far back as our knowledge takes us, human beings have lived in families. We know of no period where this was not so. We know of no people who have succeeded for long in dissolving the family or displacing it.... Again and again, in spite of proposals for change and actual experiments, human societies have reaffirmed their dependence on the family as the basic unit of human living—the family of father, mother and children.

—Margaret Mead[1]

FAMILY RELATIONSHIPS ARE ESSENTIAL FOR REALIZING KEY moral aspirations. The family is "the institution which most effectively teaches the civic virtues of honesty, loyalty, trust, self-sacrifice, personal responsibility, and respect for others," concluded a diverse board of experts.[2] Sociologist Brigitte Berger says that the stable family is "the culture-creating institution par excellence."[3] This is why efforts to shore up and support the family are well worth society's investment—in fact, they are crucial to society's long-term well being.

Schools are an important part of that effort. Effective character educators respect the powerful influence of the family and are concerned with issues relating to marriage and family. They encourage parental participation and model their schools and classrooms after good homes. They help students gain the skills necessary for developing healthy marriages and families. Such education counteracts and prevents a host of social problems, fostering productive citizens who have a greater chance for personal success and happiness.

The Family: Crucible of Character

By the time they come to school, children are already well on their way in their moral education. As Berger notes, family life has already exposed them directly or indirectly to the most elementary emotions of human nature—love, hate, longing, anger, sacrifice, selfishness, loneliness, honor, etc.[4] Their moral foundations have largely been formed. The family will continue to be a lasting and deeply felt influence throughout their lives. Effective educators and community leaders seek to facilitate the healthy aspects of this influence.

Family interaction invariably teaches moral lessons that have repercussions in growing children's futures. The seemingly minor incidents of family life accumulate over the years of growing up to affect the way family members relate to others for the rest of their lives. People's view of themselves and the way that they relate to their spouses and children, authority figures, subordinates and friends are all influenced by the moral and emotional subtexts coursing through everyday events in their families of origin. Indeed, the family is a veritable melting pot of emotional and moral learning—the crucible of character.

Universal Pattern

People find themselves in all sorts of families, and all families, like all individual human beings, deserve to be treated with respect. Yet single parents know that children need a mother and a father and often feel called upon to try to play both roles. They intuit that the family has a standard form, a structure that is grounded in nature. (See Chapter 8)

Dutch historian Jan Romein termed the family "the common human pattern."[5] Even when people reject or bypass the traditional configuration of father, mother and their children, people tend to follow its patterns anyway, as if the family were a groove from which humanity cannot escape. A young man at Woodstock in 1992 said that he was there, among strangers, because of his yearning for a family. Homeless youngsters often form bands in which they take care of each other as well as they can on the street, calling themselves little families.

Gang formation is another illustration of the natural, irrepressible yearning to be part of a family. Young people often join gangs because they get familial feelings of solidarity, strength and protection from the gang.[6] In fact, the emblems of gangs, their unique modes of dress and speech, their codes of behavior and initiation rites are all strongly binding forces similar to those of kinship tribes.[7] Gangs do not set out to build a familial identity. They follow their instincts, which direct them to bind themselves to one another with ties that resemble those of blood. Cody Scott, the convicted criminal leader of the notorious L.A. Crips, said in an interview on *60 Minutes* that if he had had a proper family he would never have turned to the streets.[8] A reformed juvenile delinquent told a counselor, "No one understood that all my rough stuff and drug stuff was because I needed a dad."[9]

The Four Spheres of Love

The roles people play in the family of origin as well as in the family they create—those of son or daughter, brother or sister, husband or wife, father or mother—are life's most fundamental ones. These reflect four distinct types of love: child's love, sibling's love, spouse's love and parent's love. Each type of love forms a world of experiences and responsibilities that is a matrix for the growth of heart and conscience. This world of dynamics, sentiments, perspectives and lessons characteristic of each type of love may be called a "sphere of love." The concept of spheres captures the potentially all-encompassing dimensions and infinite possibilities of these realms of concern and investment.

The four spheres of love form a global, inter-related dynamic of experience. Taken as a whole, they create an emotional reservoir from which the maturing person may draw to lead a life of integrity and value. The four spheres of love is a helpful model for understanding the dynamics of character growth and relational skills acquired in family life, and for describing how the capacity to love develops through family roles. As educator Gabriel Moran observes, the family "teaches by its form."[10]

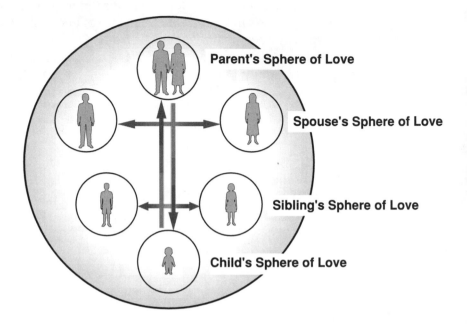

Figure 9: The Four Spheres of Love

Worlds of Experiences and Responsibilities

Each sphere of love is defined by a certain set of partnership relations—the interplay of complementary roles between particular significant others. The son or daughter interacts with the parents, the sister
with the brother, the husband with the wife, the father or mother with
the child.[11] Each sphere opens access to receiving care and wisdom
from the complementary partner; thus the parent-child relationship has
immense influence on the children's character and social development.[12] Each sphere also provides lessons in how to give to the other.
One study suggests that young siblings through their cooperative play
help each other grasp relational concepts that help them in later life to
discern deception and make moral decisions.[13] Thus each sphere of
love sets up a structure to foster an individual's maturity of heart and
conscience.[14] As psychiatrist Frank Pittman quipped, "Never forget the
end product of child raising is not the child...but the parent."[15]

The four spheres—the child's sphere of love, the sibling's sphere of love, the spouse's sphere of love and the parent's sphere of love—build one upon another, like expanding concentric circles, as the heart grows throughout life. The later ones call for more developed character and relational skills than the earlier ones. Each sphere includes the ones before, and facility in previous ones aids in mastery of those upcoming. Research that looks at the impact of family relations as "internal working models" reinforces the idea that the quality of early relationships with parents or caregivers has broad implications in character and social development across one's life,[16] impacting romantic relationships,[17] mental and emotional health,[18] and resiliency and hardiness,[19] thus underscoring the foundational nature of this earliest sphere.

Though some roles are entered into simultaneously—an infant can be born both a son and a brother; a young woman may become a wife and soon after an expectant mother—from a developmental standpoint, each sphere has its "season" that unfolds in a sequence. The season of a particular sphere is the time when it is the developmental focus in life. Prior to puberty, for example, the youngster is preoccupied with the child's sphere, and this sphere is central to his development. His primary complementary partners are his parents. The sibling's sphere comes into prominence on the heels of the child's, when siblings and then peers become the absorbing focal point of affection and moral influence.

In late adolescence or young adulthood, romantic attraction exerts its pull to move the individual towards the world of the spouse's sphere, which begins with marriage. The star attraction and impetus for character growth at that stage of life then becomes the husband or wife. The experience of parenting sons and daughters becomes the focus of moral growth through much of adulthood in the parent's sphere of love. Thus, the spheres of love can be seen as representing relational—and moral—milestones in the human life span.

Yet passing into the next sphere of love does not mean the prior one no longer develops. The spheres impact each other in a dynamic way. Significant developments in one sphere—a sibling's wedding or a parent's funeral, for example—can deepen and refresh the other spheres. Thus, after a year of marriage, 23-year-old Francine finds herself with a broader perspective on life that helps her to empathize with both her mother and her married sister in a new way. Experience in the spouse's sphere has enriched her participation in the child and sib-

Figure 10:
Each Sphere
Builds on the
Previous One

ling's spheres. Indeed, the scope of growth of heart and wisdom in all of the spheres is endless.

Ethical Implications of the Spheres

A sphere of love includes both a role and a norm. These norms consist of the implicit responsibilities and rewards—attitudes, etiquette, competencies and virtues—associated with the role at the center of each sphere. When the individual commits to a given role and embraces the ethical norm implicit in it, then he or she can be said to be fulfilling the moral challenges of the sphere. Culture specifies the ideal norm for these roles: the perfect wife, the model son, and the exemplary father. Details may differ among cultures, yet beneath this diversity lies a common denominator of caring. For example, in Asia an adult child is expected to move his aging parents into his home, while in the West he may choose to live nearby to help his parents fulfill their wish to live independently as long as possible. In either case, however, the son who is devoted to helping his parents is prized.

On the other hand, the man who renounces his parents or the woman who cuts off her brother and only sibling has effectively put participation in the child's and sibling's sphere—and the enjoyment of its bounty—on hold. In the same vein, the mere fact of giving birth or fathering a child does not denote growth in the parent's sphere. Growth only occurs when the father or mother—biological or adoptive—is actually nurturing the child through taking responsibility and making the investment of love. Similarly, the rewards of the spouse's sphere are available only when the couple commits to each other as husband and wife. This sets up the conditions that bring about the growth and enrichment characteristic of that sphere. As psychotherapist Harville Hendrix asserts in regard to the conjugal sphere, "All the ingredients necessary for full growth and healing... are possible only in marriage... [not] open-ended, precarious relationships."[20] (See Chapter 19)

It still must be acknowledged that the act of conceiving a child or giving birth, even if the child miscarries or the baby is put up for adoption, certainly leaves an indelible imprint on the mother and often on the father. Even without becoming parents they register some of the feelings and sense some of the responsibilities, even unconsciously, comprising the parental sphere. Likewise, the intense emotional bonding of an insecure sexual relationship can bring some of the psychological impact associated with the spouse's sphere. Still, without making a lifelong commitment to each other, the couple ends up with many of the expectations of the conjugal sphere—consciously or not—yet without all of its advantages. This is similar to eating a fruit that is not yet ripe.

Ecology of Love

In their hearts, people desire the fullness of the four spheres experience, either in actuality or by proxy. This is why the only child latches onto her cousin as her "older sister," the widower joins a dance club, the infertile couple adopts a son, and the "empty nest" seniors find themselves welcoming neighborhood children into their home and acting as substitute grandparents.

The ideal conditions for inner growth require participation in all four spheres throughout one's lifetime. Researcher Willard Hartup classifies sibling and peer relationships as "symmetrically or horizontally structured" in contrast to adult-child relationships, which are "asymmetrically or vertically structured."[21] These vertical and horizontal relationships taken together create a greater ecological system that encompasses all four spheres. They surround the individual with the support and stimulation he or she needs to internally grow. When this ecology has an imbalance—when one or more relational direction is empty—individuals are left vulnerable and often try to fill the need in a way that is ultimately false and unhealthy.

Family Ecology

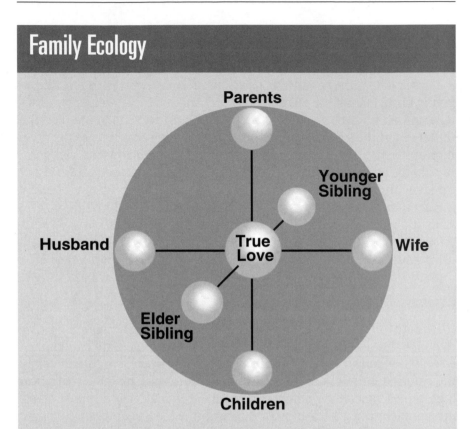

Figure 11: Six Directions of Family Relationships

When the vertical and horizontal relationships of the four spheres of love are depicted in three dimensions, the family system can be characterized as having six directions: up and down, right and left, and front and rear. Above are parents and grandparents; below are children and grandchildren. On the left and right are husband and wife respectively. In front are elder siblings and cousins; to the rear are younger siblings and cousins. Ideally, what flows through and binds the system together is a commitment to true love, to serve and care for one another.

Which spheres comprise this ecosystem depend upon the age of the individual and his or her stage of life. For example, 14-year-old Elena is in the child's and sibling's spheres. When she has a good number of complementary partners for these spheres—parents, grandparents and other elders on the one hand, and brothers, sisters and perhaps cousins on the other—she enjoys a wealth of possibilities in terms of receiving and giving love and developing her character. These are growth-enhancing relationships for Elena's stage of life. Jon, 27, is likely to have different relational needs. He may be more fulfilled and challenged to grow by being fully involved in the spouse and parent's spheres. He would thrive by having a good mate and a child or children as reciprocal partners. This would be in addition to the parents and siblings with whom he continues to have a relationship. Thus Jon's ecology of love includes all four spheres, and the absence of any of them—especially the conjugal sphere—may be felt as emptiness in his life.

Social Extensions of the Spheres

Since children and adolescents thrive when they have many seniors above them and juniors below them to interact with, as well as those on their same level, the family ecosystem is supplemented by the relationships outside the family that replicate the basic pattern. Seniors can include anyone from their grandparents to a student tutor from the next higher grade, and juniors can range from their infant siblings to the new co-worker at their after-school job.

These wider social relationships are simply extensions of these prototypical family loves.[22] Being in the subordinate, follower or student role has similarities to occupying the son and daughter sphere, just as acting in the role of the superior, leader or teacher corresponds to the parental sphere. The social extension of the sphere of siblings is the world of peer relationships—between friends, colleagues and co-workers. However, the spouse's sphere has no social counterpart. The intimacy between husband and wife is so encompassing and exclusive that it is unlike any other relationship.[23]

Skills and qualities of heart and conscience gained within these family spheres of love spell greater facility in their social extensions. This works the other way around as well. The young soccer coach is cultivating traits that will prove useful when he becomes a father. The girl who lifeguards with a male colleague all summer may gain insights that translate into a better relationship with her brother.

Helping Character Growth Keep Up

If every sphere of love has its season of focus, each season also has its basic developmental tasks to master—ideally before moving on to the next one. A youngster does well to learn certain lessons, acquire certain virtues, and gain certain skills in her relationship with her parents and other elders that will enhance her ability to better relate to her older sister and friends when they come into center stage. Likewise, accomplishing a satisfactory degree of success with her siblings and peers would serve her well before moving on to an exclusive relationship with a future mate. Finally, it follows that she achieves a certain foundation of harmony in her relationship with her husband before going on to enter the absorbing world of parenting a child.

Real life, of course, is often far from ideal. The imperative of physical maturation brings many individuals into the fraternal and especially the conjugal and parental spheres while their inner maturity and the necessary competencies are still wanting. This causes many difficulties: the mother who prefers to be her daughter's best friend rather than her parent, the husband who feels more comfortable treating his wife like a kid sister instead of a spouse, the adult daughter who wants to be her aging dad's little girl rather than a caregiver. Even if they are responsible and are doing all the "right" things, they may find themselves lacking in the heart's resources of genuine concern and compassion, the kind that animate growth in relationships and arise only from experiences of giving and receiving unselfish love. They may lack the ability to make themselves emotionally vulnerable, as relationships in the more advanced spheres of love call for. This is the guilt-driven wife and mother who demands perfection in herself and everyone around her. This is a father working 16-hour days for his wife and sons who nevertheless cannot emotionally connect with them.

Unless someone or something intervenes, the pattern of relationally immature people relating to relationally immature people tends to multiply, causing unnecessary heartbreak and moral difficulty. Families tend to perpetuate negative patterns of relationship if they are not in the process of consciously constructing positive ones.

Education can help. The character education movement is one response to youths' needs in the child's and sibling's spheres, helping to support parental efforts to inculcate respect and responsibility. Marriage enrichment and education are productive as well. Groups such as Marriage Encounter, Marriage Savers and Relationship Enhancement, among many others, allow couples to repair and correct their shortcomings from the earlier spheres of love and thus bring greater wisdom and compassion to the marital relationship. The growing men's movement, represented by groups such as the ManKind Project, holds programs that bring deep self-renewal to men whose scars from early lives have hindered them from being responsible and loving husbands and fathers.

Ethicist James Q. Wilson makes the point that the family "is a continuous locus of reciprocal obligations that constitutes an unending school for moral instruction."[24] Through family roles in the spheres of love, the individual expands his or her heart and conscience. Each sphere is a potential gold mine of inner enrichment. Understanding of the four spheres of love and the life tasks intrinsic to each can guide parents and educators about what virtues and social skills are best to encourage at each particular phase of life.

15

The Child's Sphere
of Love

THE WORLD A SON OR DAUGHTER INHABITS WITH HIS OR
her parents is the matrix of moral growth, the context out of which
homo sapiens fashion much of what makes them human. The dynamics of this world constitute the child's sphere of love. From the earliest
moments of life a child needs, yearns for and expects her parents' loving care. As she musters all her resources to bond with her parents—to
imitate as well as captivate her sources of life and love—she is building
an internal foundation for relating empathetically and responsibly to
others for the rest of her life.[1] The moral influence of the father and
mother never ceases, but becomes more internalized and indirect as the
son or daughter grows.[2]

Other significant adults also exert influence within the child's mind
and heart. Grandparents, aunts, uncles, neighbors and especially teachers are luminaries in the child's universe. Words of praise or rebuke fall
from such persons' lips with thunderous impact. To a child, a teacher is
someone to be adored and emulated. This yearning upward toward
mentoring adults, although sometimes disconcerting to them, is a natural endowment of the child's sphere of love and facilitates moral
growth. Better understanding of the heart of a son or daughter can
deepen educators' appreciation of their role in loco parentis in the moral
upbringing of youth.

Development in the child's sphere of love is not limited to early parent-child interactions. The old saying, "A son is a son till he takes a wife, a daughter's a daughter the rest of her life" is only half true. A son is a son for the rest of his life, too. The child's sphere of love extends throughout adulthood, offering new horizons as a child's wisdom and understanding of his parents' hearts deepens. What is more, the son or daughter's relationship to the parents colors his or her adult relationships with all authority figures and elders.

Moral Growth in the Child's Sphere

Eye contact, physical handling and caressing, tone of voice, laughter and gentleness on the part of the parents, especially the mother, give the infant reams of information about what other human beings are like. When his or her needs are met, the infant is reassured that the universe is a benevolent place. Psychologist Erik Erikson eloquently describes the importance of trustworthiness in the child's relational world and its impact throughout life.[3] From the foundational experience of trust, a worldview begins to emerge: "Others are good and loving. I am safe." This sets the stage for the individual to express goodness, hope and love in response.[4] The child's sphere of love begins the process, step by step, of the growth of other-centered love. It is the dawn of relationships and morality.

It is widely accepted among researchers that a warm, caring parent-child relationship aids in young people's moral development.[5] Secure attachment relationships are associated with healthy development,[6] empathy,[7] intelligence[8] and social-perspective taking.[9] James Q. Wilson describes the growth of conscience thus: "Conscience, like sympathy, fairness, and self-control, arises...out of our innate desire for attachment.... People with the strongest conscience will be...those with the most powerfully developed affiliation."[10] As the child's first attachments are to his parents, the parent-child bond is key to moral development.

Attachment also enhances the growth of heart. Dierdre Lovechy found that "developing the capacity to follow the parent's lead allows the child to experience empathy."[11] The ability to empathize—to recognize and feel another person's pain, suffering or joy as one's own—is the basis of the capacity to give love, take responsibility and have fulfilling relationships with others. Empathy emerges even in very young children who have a warm bond of attachment with a parent. Often, these are the children seen comforting others in day care or kindergarten situations. They are able to identify with and sympathize with a playmate's loneliness, and take steps to alleviate it.

Modern Psychology Affirms Ancient Wisdom

In Confucian philosophy, responsiveness to one's parents is considered the "root" or "fountainhead" of human-heartedness or *jen*. *Jen* is often defined as the ability to relate to others in a kindly, benevolent, altruistic and compassionate way. Having *jen* is crucial to being a fully realized human being. Mencius taught that if a person loves his parents, he would be kind to people in general and caring toward everything in the world.[12]

From Responding to Responsibility

Over time, the young child's responsiveness to the parents ripens into taking responsibility. Out of love for the parents, the child obeys. He or she learns to control impulses, especially aggressive ones, because this pleases the parents.[13] Researcher Selma Fraiberg writes, "There are obligations in love even for little children. Love is a given, but it is also earned. At every step of the way in development, a child is obliged to give up territories of his self-love in order to earn parental love and approval."[14] To continue to earn the parents' highly desired approbation, the child must take increasingly age-appropriate responsibility, such as taking care of her things, cleaning up and preventing messes, dressing herself, doing her schoolwork, and behaving respectfully toward others and property. These are legitimate claims parents can make on their children's love. In turn, as parents become confident of their child's character and trustworthiness, they feel free to give them greater responsibility.

Inch by inch, step by step, year by year, the parents' voices and instructions transmute from something outside of the child to something within. In increasingly independent situations from the parents, the child is able to say, "Inside of me, I know it is right (or wrong)." The child is now on her way to becoming an autonomous moral person. This development has been described as a five-stage process. First, the emotional bond with the child's parents pairs his sense of security and empathic responsiveness with a sense of moral obligation; next, he incorporates parental rules; then he develops an understanding of how empathy modifies strict rule following; he chooses ideals and idols that reflect earlier learning in primary relationships; and finally, he comes to visualize himself as a moral standard-bearer or teacher.[15]

Lessons learned in the child's sphere of love are the foundation for relationships in the next sphere of love—the sibling's sphere. Social and moral competencies will be further developed in relating with siblings and peers as the child practices truthfulness, sharing, taking turns, playing fair, learning not to hit, and respecting others' property. Moreover, children in the sibling's sphere do not "leave" the children's sphere; they still need the guidance and assistance of parents, mentors and other elders.[16]

Delayed Moral Growth

The sad histories of neglected and abandoned children have testified to the impairment that can result from an impoverished relationship with parents. In the 1940s, psychologist William Goldfarb did a study of seventy children who had been raised for the first three years of their lives in institutions. He found that they were inordinately cruel to one another and to animals and were severely lacking in impulse control.[17] Fraiberg, who studied abandoned babies, children raised in institutions, children shifted from foster home to foster home, and children torn from their families by war, remarks, "These children who had never experienced love, who had never belonged to anyone, and were never bonded to anyone except on the most primitive basis...were unable in later years to bind themselves to other people, to love deeply, to feel deeply, to experience tenderness, grief or shame."[18]

Yet even when parents are unable to provide the nurturing love needed for the child's moral growth, other adults can and do figure prominently in constructing or reconstructing a child's inner universe. The care of a responsible adult—a concerned teacher or coach, for instance—can repair a child's injured heart, helping even an at-risk child to rise to the occasion and succeed.

The Child's Sphere in Later Life

When the pull of peers becomes strong, when a marriage prospect comes into focus, when a baby of their own stakes a claim on their heart—these are challenging moments when older sons and daughters have to negotiate new ways of relating to their parents, based on deeper understanding and appreciation. The young child's accommodation to parental authority gives way to stormy and difficult relations as youth seek to define their identity, emotional boundaries and ideological vistas.[19] Socially, young adults are forging their own relationship to the larger society and world. As family moorings loosen, individuals may become emotionally tossed at sea, experiencing great dips and heights. Early positive bonds with parents can remain influential throughout adulthood, offering a secure base from which to make other significant relationships,[20] but the process of differentiation from parents is fraught with perils.

"Where do I belong? How do I fit in? What part of me is my parents and what part is me? Who am I anyway?"—these are the crucial questions of adolescence. Having attained what Piaget termed "formal operational thinking," teenagers search for meaning and imagine different ways of being.[21] Hence, adolescents may question the values his or her parents and society have taught and be quick to point out inconsistencies and hypocrisies.[22]

It is only too easy for individuals to separate from the parents too reactively, distancing themselves too far in order to prove their independence, as Jacob, a Kansas insurance agent, did with his father. "I didn't even realize what I was doing until the old man had a heart attack," confides Jacob. "I pretty much cut him off after college. Never communicated much. But really I was always playing to him in my head, trying to get his respect. I was afraid of how connected to him I still was, so I kept pretending I didn't care. When he almost died, I realized I'd gone too far. To really be my own man, I realized, I had to acknowledge how much I cared what he thought but not be totally driven by it."

Appropriate differentiation from the parents—meanwhile retaining and expanding the deep and special bond of child's love—is a major life task. It especially affects a person's marriage, where loyalty to the new bond with someone outside of the family of origin compels artful negotiation of the relationship with parents, with the parents of the spouse, and in accordance with the needs of the new family being formed.

Mature Devotion

The moral content of a child's love for the parents becomes more evident as the son or daughter gets older. Adult sons and daughters are moved to demonstrate filial love by acts of gratitude and service: the daughter who names her firstborn after her father, the son who builds a house for his mother, the brother and sister who take turns caring for the aging parents.

"We never know the love of the parent till we become parents ourselves." This observation by Henry Ward Beecher highlights how filial love evolves through growing and facing the responsibilities of an adult. New comprehension and sympathy for the parents may come as the son or daughter becomes a spouse, a breadwinner, a parent, a middle-aged caretaker of others, and a responsible community member. When children express their gratitude in later life for the good values and investment of time and loving effort that helped them build their character, parents feel the greatest pride. This mature heart of filial devotion says, "Thank you for giving me the foundation to create myself as a good person."

The moment may come when the grown-up child may have to literally change the diapers of the infirm parent, clear up old debts, settle the estate, and take on the role of patriarch or matriarch of the family while urging the parent to rest and do less. At such times, the son or daughter assumes an almost parental heart to his or her own parent. The child's sphere of love has come full circle.

Mature filial devotion is displayed by sons and daughters who seek to preserve and augment their parents' legacy. Sculptor Korczak Ziolkowski, who created the portraits on Mt. Rushmore, accepted a commission in 1947 to carve a massive tribute to the great Native American chief, Crazy Horse, out of a mountain in South Dakota. He devoted decades to the project but was able to complete only a portion before he died in 1982. However, his family comforted him before his death by committing their lives to carry out his promise. Seven of his 10 sons and daughters, and some of his grandchildren, now labor to bring this formidable project to completion.[23]

A child brings his parents pleasure even when he or she surpasses their accomplishments. At the time when Martin Luther King, Jr. was the rising star of the civil rights movement, an old friend of the family wrote an exuberant letter to King's father, who was a civic leader in his own right in Atlanta's black community: "I've heard you've got a son who can preach circles around you every time he mounts the pulpit. If so, it's an honor to you."[24] King, Sr. did see his son's accomplishments that way and was overwhelmed with joy when his son won the Nobel Peace Prize.

This is child's love in its optimal form—becoming a person who makes his or her parents proud. The Eastern tradition as taught by Confucius calls such child's love "filial piety." Confucius said, "True filial piety consists in successfully carrying out the unfinished work of our forefathers and transmitting their achievements to posterity." This was echoed in the Western poetic tradition by Thomas Macaulay when he wrote:

> And how can man die better than facing fearful odds
> For the ashes of his fathers and the temples of his gods.

The Child's Sphere in Society

Experiences as a son or daughter have a bearing on performing well in societal roles where one is in the position of a subordinate. A person's ability to follow instructions, humble himself, receive guidance, and support legitimate authority was first learned through his relationship with his parents. Conversely, the employee with "a chip on his shoulder" is likely to have residual resentment and mistrust towards his parents, and he projects it upon any authority he encounters.

Those who have developed a trusting rapport with their parents do not fear that supporting and serving will diminish them. They are the ones who often bring out the best in their teachers, bosses and other superiors. They may even come to inherit their positions. When Charles, a university student, realized that his microbiology professor had authored the college textbook, he became a fixture at his lab, auditing classes, asking questions, even staying after class to clean up. At first the cantankerous professor rebuffed him, but he persisted. "He scares people away so he can stick to his research, but I felt at home with him," says Charles. "He reminded me of my cranky uncle whom I won over as a kid." The two men spent more and more time together. When his professor needed a research assistant for a major project, Charles was a natural choice. His skill in establishing rapport with his professor in a father-son type of relationship stemmed from his successful experiences in the child's sphere of love.

16

The Sibling's Sphere of Love

THROWN TOGETHER BY FATE, SIBLINGS CAN BE THE BEST OF FRIENDS and the worst of enemies during the rough and tumble years of growing up together. In this intimate yet involuntary relationship, siblings are both allies and rivals, bound by the joys and sorrows of a shared family experience. Yet as time goes by, many siblings honor their relationships by labeling them relationships of choice: "You're my sister but also my friend," they tell each other; or they compare relationships of choice with this obligatory relationship: "I love my friend like a brother." In later life the very existence of a sibling, even if geographically far away, is a comfort and a boon.[1]

Daniel, a man from Michigan who is now in his 50s, recounted typical features of a sibling relationship: "When we were kids, my older brother Lance decided that if I wanted to tag along with him and his friends to the lake, I would have to know how to swim. They said they'd teach me when we got there. Well, they took me up high on the rocks and then, laughing, threw me in the lake. It was deep and cold and I had to swim or drown! I started dog paddling like crazy, and from there I taught myself." Surprisingly, the none-too-gentle ministrations of his older brother left no sense of acrimony. Daniel said, "Oh, heck, I knew he'd rescue me if I really got in trouble down there. Lance was always there for me. In fact, if there's anyone in the world I'd want to be in a tough situation with, it would be Lance." Most siblings feel similarly.

Like Daniel, they know they can count on each other in an emergency.[2]

Yet sibling relationships are among the most neglected areas of people's lives, and adults often long for improved relationships with their siblings. Like all relationships, sibling relationships require effort. They do not happen automatically; nor are they immune to the principles that govern all good relationships. By consciously investing in this significant relationship, people can be deeply enriched. Competence in the sibling's sphere provides essential foundations to enhance all subsequent relationships, and the sibling bond itself can take on increasing significance as time goes by.

Growth in Other-Centered Love

From the moment a sibling arrives on the scene, the dynamic of a family changes dramatically and forever. The child who used to be the sole focus of his parents' attention must share his or her parents' time, resources and affection with another. He or she may have to share a room, toys, games and activities. Thus, when the sibling sphere of love opens, it naturally pulls the older child toward greater other-centeredness.[3]

The older child has shed degrees of self-centeredness all along to respond to and keep the approbation of the most significant others—the parents. Now he or she is called upon to not only look upward toward the approval of the parents but to look to the side at the person next to him or her—the new little brother or sister.[4] It is an advance in other-centered love. Studies show that a warm and supportive sibling relationship fosters empathy[5] and prosocial behavior.[6]

Conversely, a younger sibling is born sharing. The older sibling has had a head start on garnering the attention of the parents and has greater command of the physical resources of the home. A younger sibling necessarily sheds degrees of self-centeredness in order to form an affiliation with the more powerful older one. He or she naturally looks to the older sibling for guidance on ways to be.

Parents help an older child become more other-centered by showing him continued affection while including him in the care of the new sibling. Many children respond to this with alacrity, eager to be of service. Older children who successfully manage the transition from only child to sibling are those who see the little interloper as someone who needs their care. They can experience pride, praise from their parents and a sense of accomplishment by helping out with younger brothers and sisters, even in little ways.

The sibling's sphere of love thus constructs the foundation for the future sphere of parental love. Pediatrician Benjamin Spock said, "One of the ways in which a young child tries to get over the pain of having a younger rival is to act as if he himself were no longer a child, competing in the same league as the baby, but as if he were a third parent." By encouraging the older child in this, "the parents can help a child to actually transform resentful feelings into cooperativeness and genuine altruism."[7] Many older children go on to the "helping" professions because of their benevolent experiences in caring for younger siblings. Such family experiences help people relate well to juniors and subordinates in other professions as well.

Mediating Sibling Rivalry

Young siblings often perceive each other as rivals in the central love relationship of their lives—their relationship with their parents. Parents are thus key in mediating sibling relationships.[8] It is not enough for parents to shower affection on each child. They have to understand how to affirm each child's value in a manner consistent with their naturally unequal positions as elder and younger. They see to it that while the older siblings command more respect and have more privileges, they also have more responsibilities.

There is already a hint of pride in the term "my older brother," and older siblings can enjoy this added respect as well as the extra "perks" that come with their position. They have the confidence and ear of the parents, for they share more in the parents' concerns. They may have considerably more freedom, a larger allowance, and may be in charge of their own study and recreation time. They may be allowed to go more places alone or accompanied by friends.

At the same time, older siblings shoulder more responsibility. Their parents ask them to watch the younger ones when they would rather be doing something else. Then, if things go wrong with a younger sibling, it is they who bear the brunt of their parents' disapproval. Older siblings also teach the younger ones how to swim, ride a bike or swing a bat. Studies confirm that older siblings are effective role models for younger ones, because they are often viewed as a respected source of knowledge.[9] If the older sibling takes on duties commensurate with his status, the younger ones feel protected and secure.[10] They are likely to respond with the adoration only a younger sibling can bestow.

Traditional societies emphasize family cooperation in shared tasks and tend to have less sibling rivalry than affluent societies where the prevailing ethic is one of equality, individualism and competition.[11] This norm continues with adult siblings, as they participate in the thick net of village relationships. When the cultural norms stress interdependence and loyalty, children feel natural about admonishing, protecting and helping one another. When Jim Barrall was in Ponce, Ecuador, he bought ice cream for a needy child named Heidi. But Heidi ate only half of the small dish. "I thought she either was full or didn't like the flavor," Jim thought. "But she told me she was saving the other half to give to her brother. Here was a child who had so little and yet could carry half a cup of melting ice cream home to her brother because she had something to give and share with him."[12]

In Asia, this distinction between the roles of elder and younger siblings is codified in the norms of the culture. The eldest son receives a greater share of the inheritance, but he is also expected to bear greater responsibility for the family's welfare. Younger children are expected to show deference to their elder brothers and sisters, but they can expect guidance, care and leadership from them. Such family norms create a context for harmony.

Sharon Goodman, the principal of a small private school in New York State, once worked overseas at a middle school for the arts in Seoul, Korea, where she served as a houseparent in a dormitory that mixed Asian and Western youngsters. The performing arts being what they are, there was a great deal of jealousy and competition. The staff recognized the need to instill a "brother-sister" mentality in the children. They adopted a policy that all students had to address each other based on age, using the honorific titles for older brothers and sisters embedded in the Korean language and used in Korean households. The Korean language provides a more formal way of addressing an elder than addressing a peer, even if the age difference is only slight. Elder boys are called "Oppa," which means "respected older brother," and elder girls are called "Onni," which means "respected older sister." The policy worked almost as soon as it was instituted. Peace came to the dorms. Rather than needing to lord it over their younger classmates, the older students felt secure in the respect shown to them. They began to coach and protect their juniors, even acting as mediators for them. Feeling protected and cared for, the younger students felt less need to assert themselves aggressively.

By successfully mirroring family traditions, this school improved peer relationships and elevated the moral atmosphere. Schools that encourage mentoring of younger students by older students are mirroring this positive family tradition. For their part, families can recover the lost tradition of a subtle hierarchy between siblings that balances privilege with responsibility.

Life Lessons from the Sibling's Sphere

The sibling sphere of love is relationship training for life. Moral development takes place through settling the issues of right and wrong that frequently arise between siblings—disputes over the use of possessions, taking turns, physical and verbal aggression and other moral issues. Even a bad older role model can help a younger sibling decide to go about life differently, and a good older role model will usually have a positive effect.[13]

Sibling relationships are also training for living in a world of diversity. Though born of the same parents, siblings often differ from one another widely in temperament, personality, tastes, preferences, talents and even political leanings. Living amidst a large or extended family provides training in tolerance, charity and acceptance of differences. It helps engrain the lesson that although people differ, they are fundamentally related and may still treat one another with respect and appreciation.

Cora, a woman in her thirties, says, "I'm a conservative and my sister is a liberal. We vote entirely differently and are on the opposite sides of the fence on most issues.... One time when we had an argument over politics, my sister called me up later and said in a choking voice, 'No matter what, you're still my sister.' That pledge of loyalty meant a lot to me. I've even come to see the other side as a necessary part of our nation's conversation."

Perhaps the most important lessons learned in the sibling's sphere of love are those that will aid in the later spheres of marriage and parenting. The care of younger siblings obviously develops parenting skills, yet living with siblings is an all-around humanizing experience and an asset for future marriage as well. Opposite-sex siblings see one another in a different light than they see their peers, whom they may romanticize. Brothers see sisters in their dishabille, in their tempers, when they are sick and when they are struggling with homework. Sisters see brothers in defeat at sports, vulnerable to other girls, and after they have messed up the bathroom. It is good practice for living on a day-to-day basis with someone in marriage.

Carl, a 21-year-old man from Kingston, New York, said that he learned a lot about women from his sisters. "Especially, I learned the chocolate trick. When one of them is really being cranky and nasty, I know it's her time of the month. I also know that chocolate helps get rid of cramps. When one of them starts acting that way, I go out and buy a box of chocolates for her. That wins her over and makes her feel good. My sisters say the girl who marries me is going to be a lucky girl. 'We trained you real good,' they tell me."

Sharing is a crucial lesson of the sibling's sphere of love that is invaluable practice for marriage. Marriage experts comment upon the amount of anger that is generated in marriage due to the incessant need to share. Like living with a sibling, living with a spouse requires constant sharing of the family's resources—allocating time, negotiating the family budget, using the same bedroom, bathroom, and taking turns with the family car. Some degree of privacy and autonomy is always sacrificed; some degree of self-centeredness has to be given over through sheer necessity. Learning to share with and accommodate the needs of siblings can help one have a tolerance for the day in and day out sharing of marriage.

Siblings teach deeper lessons, too. Jack, a man from Kentucky who had been a pest of a younger brother to his two older sisters said, "My sisters taught me what unconditional love was. Sometimes they were so kind, even after I'd done something awful to them, like put a frog in their room or read their diaries. Oh, they complained to my parents a lot, but when you've done that many bad things to someone and then the next Christmas they give you a super present signed 'Love, your sister,' you sort of melt. They taught me what forgiveness is."

A Bridge to the World of Friends

From the age of about eight years old, the race is on between parents and peers for influence. Parents are still prime movers in the preadolescent's universe, and their influence will be lasting and strongly felt. But by age twelve, peers rival and begin to overtake parental influences. By the time the child has reached puberty, friends are the greatest interest and greatest challenge.

The adolescent tasks of differentiation and integration require that the old affiliation with parents and the family of origin change in order to define the new person. New bonds with peers must be forged. Yet the old connections still call for allegiance and the new ones are sometimes problematic. Both yearnings—to be independent and yet included—are hitting teenagers at the same time, with magnum force. Add sexual awakening and the complexities of dealing with the opposite sex, and they have their hands full. No wonder they sometimes slam doors, sass back to their parents, storm out of the house and spend hours talking to one another on the phone.

Siblings serve as a bridge between the protective vertical relationship with parents and the need to explore horizontal relationships with peers. Sibling relationships, as an interim step, retain some slight vertical structure yet resemble peer relationships in many ways and serve many of the same functions. As sibling relationships are directly mediated by the parents, they are less risky than peer relationships and good practice for them. Without this practice, young people may be hard put to graduate from the strongly vertical, protective relationship of parent and child to the strongly horizontal and independent relationships of friendships and eventual marriage. The sibling's sphere of love, segueing into friendships and good peer relationships, is an important intermediate step that prepares a young person for relationships outside the family.

Siblings can provide needed familial support for venturing out into the world. Having a sibling in the same school can take some of the painful edge off peer relationships and their risks of rejection. "Even though I always acted like my brother was a total pain, it was good to see him at his locker and feel like our family was part of the school," says Jean, from Arizona. "When my friends started asking about him and saying how cool he was, I even started feeling proud and more confident myself. In addition, when I made the honor roll, he said, 'Well, now they know everyone in our family isn't stupid,' because his grades really weren't that great. It helped us both feel like we belonged."

Friendships

Friendships are an extension of sibling relationships, only they involve more choice, independence and equality. Friends take over where siblings leave off. Like sibling relationships, they offer ample opportunities for conflict and the building of conflict-resolving skills. Willard Hartup writes: "Peer relations contribute substantially to both social and cognitive development and to the effectiveness with which we function as adults. Indeed, the single best childhood predictor of adult adaptation is not school grades, and not classroom behavior, but rather the adequacy with which the child gets along with other children. Children who... cannot establish a place for themselves in the peer culture are seriously at risk."[14]

Friendships in childhood have at least four functions that strongly resemble sibling relationships. They provide: 1) emotional resources for having fun and adapting to stress; 2) cognitive resources for problem-solving and knowledge acquisition; 3) contexts in which the basic social skills of communication, cooperation and group entry are acquired or elaborated; and 4) they are forerunners of adult relationships, including relationships in the workplace and marriage—the "passionate friendship."[15]

Living with a roommate, creating camaraderie on the job, joining teams and group activities are all extensions of the sibling's sphere of love. Joining a club or service group can lead to friendships and foster cooperative skills. The club or group serves rather like a "parent"—it is the overarching context for the peer relationships and directs their growth. People working for a common purpose form special bonds that resemble those of siblings. Such experiences may even connect them to the interrelatedness of all people—a sense of the brotherhood of humankind.

Good friendships also provide surrogate sibling experiences for those who had negative ones in their families of origin, or few sibling experiences at all. Joey, a 15-year-old from Arkansas who had no sisters, recounted an experience during a service project in Guatemala: "We were all so tired, we would fall asleep in the bus that took us back to where we were staying each night. I saw this one girl's—Tracy's—face in the moonlight. She had a boy's haircut and she was very short and not pretty at all. But she looked so innocent sleeping, like a little kid. All she needed was a teddy bear. I felt my heart move and I felt so close to her. Watching the girls sweat and work so hard and get dysentery and go through all we went through on that project, I really discovered something. Girls are human, too." Because of this surrogate sibling experience, Joey gained a new perspective and respect for members of the opposite sex that ordinarily would have come through living with opposite-sex siblings.

Wrongful peer relationships, however, hamper development in this important sphere of love. The unfortunate trend of modern times is to jump from the child's sphere of love right into a physical relationship that more properly characterizes the spouse's sphere of love—a sexual relationship—without reaping the benefits of the sibling's sphere of love and its extension, peer friendships. The onset of sexual relations is occurring at ever younger ages, among children as young as ten, eleven and twelve. However, such sexual love is by definition love between two undeveloped people who are constitutionally unable to answer one another's needs. By skipping spheres of development, people do themselves no service. Unprepared for the emotional depths unleashed by a sexual relationship, underdeveloped children and teenagers flounder, hurting themselves and others. (See Chapter 24) Pre-teens and teens who understand the value of the sibling's sphere and its non-sexual friendships improve their chances of enjoying an intimate and rewarding marriage in later life.

The Sibling's Sphere in Later Life

Pursuing education, marriage and a career often pulls brothers and sisters out of contact with each other. Sometimes parents provide the main link, giving news about the siblings to each other and facilitating reunions. More fortunate are siblings who stay close geographically and maintain warm friendships. They provide invaluable support, extra financial reserves, and the kinds of allegiances and alliances that make responsible adulthood easier. Being part of a network of giving and receiving among siblings gives people pride, a sense of connection, and challenges them to meet the needs of others in unique adult ways. Research affirms that a link with siblings preserves a sense of well-being in middle and late life, even if actual contact is infrequent. Strong feelings and shared memories remain emotionally significant.[16]

For instance, adult siblings are the aunts and uncles of one another's children—important if underrated roles. Anyone with teenage children can attest to the need for good avuncular figures in their sons and daughters' lives to do what they cannot do. They are grateful to their siblings who play this valuable role in their children's upbringing. Avuncular roles thus naturally enhance relationships among adult siblings. They are another way for adult siblings to invest in their relationship, and to cultivate their heart and character in the process.

Taking an avuncular position to one's nephew or niece is itself a growth-enhancing and rewarding role in its own right. Uncles and aunts can help adolescents fulfill their particular need to differentiate from their parents and assess them objectively, weighing their opinions against those of other trusted adults. Frank Pittman observes, "Aunts and uncles are called to offer alternate realities to children."[17] Because they do not have the full burden of the parents' responsibility, uncles and aunts have less anxiety about outcomes. They can be freer about their honest feelings and thoughts. "With my nieces and nephews I could be myself rather than try to be whatever I thought a parent should be," notes Pittman. "At times I have liked them better than I have my own children; I've often felt I was a better friend to them."

The task of caring for aging parents usually falls to siblings later in life as well, calling for planning, assessment and sharing. Caring for and burying parents, and settling the parental estate often bring siblings into close contact to accomplish common goals,[18] and revitalizes the unique bonds they share. They are the longest survivors of the childhood family, the corroborators and keepers of family memories.[19] Loretta, a woman from Florida in her sixties, recounted: "In the end, it was just my brother Glen and I who placed the headstone on my father's property. Glen's wife had broken her hip; the kids had a gas leak in their car; someone else had a crisis at work they couldn't leave. It was just us, brother and sister, all alone on the property of our parents, where we'd grown up. It seemed very fitting somehow." After years of geographical separation and hardly seeing each other during the busy years of raising their own families, these siblings determined over their father's gravestone to start seeing each other several times a year. They felt, with their parents gone, they were each other's last link to their origins.

Brothers and sisters offer challenges and support that foster the growth of heart and character. Sibling relationships are foundational for peer relationships in the larger world; at the same time they form a particular bond that can increase in meaning and significance over a lifetime and serves as an important repository of a family's emotional legacy. The sibling's sphere of love is an important stage in life's journey, providing important lessons in relationships and heart that stand one in good stead in marriage, parenting and relating to the world at large.

17

The Spouse's Sphere of Love

THE SPOUSE'S SPHERE OF LOVE IS A UNIQUE REALM OF HEART AND and intimacy, distinctly different from any other kind of relationship. The relationship between spouses has dynamics, expectations and responsibilities that foster a specific kind of growth in other-centered love that is unattainable through other means. No other relationship has the same potential for human oneness, and thus no other relationship entails the same demands for surrender and entrusting of the self to another.

Marriage involves risk—the uncovering of deep relational fears, hopes and expectations. This is why it is often so difficult. To skirt these difficulties and risks, many couples opt to avoid marriage by merely living together. Yet the depth, breadth and tremendous potential for fulfillment in deep, satisfying interaction with one's complementary partner—in mind, heart and body—make the marital relationship unique and irreplaceable. It is worthy of honor and ceremony, as well as community support.

Marriage is a "form," says Elizabeth McAlister in her defense of traditional marriage. It is comparable to the poetic forms of the sonnet or haiku.[1] No one can doubt the power of haiku poetry, which is due in large part to the brevity of its form. The restrictions the form imposes unleash great forces and bestow great meaning on the few words that are said. The poet's artistic power is magnified because of the limits of the form. Likewise, the mutuality and strength of love is enhanced and deepened by the form of marriage. Its seeming constraints create the conditions for creativity, freedom and emotion that are without equal.

Success in the conjugal sphere of love is predicated in part upon experiences in the child and sibling's spheres of love. Marriage ideally takes place between two mature people, schooled through the challenges of the previous spheres in increasingly other-centered love. Character, moral values[2] and the habit of altruism are basic pillars of a successful and happy marriage. Character education in the younger years can thus help young people prepare for their marital journey.

Growing towards Unconditional Love

The traditional wedding vows reflect the unconditional aspirations of marital love and recognize that it is a lifelong commitment and process: "To have and to hold from this day forward, for better, for worse, for richer, for poorer, in sickness and in health, to love and to cherish, till death do us part." If a person can love another person day in and day out, under good conditions and bad, in all aspects of the other's being, the love they live out becomes unconditional. Lori Gordon, founder of PAIRS (Practical Application of Intimate Relationship Skills), describes conjugal love as "to feel that you can trust another person with your whole being, your laughter, your tears, your rage, your joy.... Its essence lies in total certainty that your partner is... open to you in body, heart and mind—and knowing that you are accepted and loved for what you really are, and knowing that you don't have to pretend."[3]

Loving a spouse in good times and in bad stretches one's character and capacity to love. As one husband in a long-term marriage said, "You've seen each other in every possible light, the very ugliest and worst and the most evil as well as the most divine and compassionate."[4] This does not mean that the spouse is acceptable no matter how he or she acts. It means that, barring any severe violation, the couple is willing to keep working on becoming closer and more understanding and caring toward one another as time goes by. Indeed, this is the definition of a good marriage endorsed by Marriage Encounter, a successful marriage enrichment program. A marriage is good if the partners are willing to keep working on it. Unconditional love is love that continues to try.

Sociologist Robert Bellah has noted that Americans are "torn between love as an expression of spontaneous inner freedom...and the image of love as a firmly planted, permanent commitment, embodying obligations that transcend the immediate feelings or wishes of the partners."[5] In successful marriages, couples' expectations incline towards the latter ideal. As marriage researcher Blaine J. Fowers points out, all the best techniques for improving marriages "have an ineluctable moral core."[6] It is this moral core that prepares couples for the challenges of parenting, where one is not only voluntarily bound up in another's life and well-being, one is eminently responsible for both.

Thus, the marital partnership is a shared journey that implicitly or explicitly holds before it an ideal of family love. Investment in the relationship and the other person's character growth as mate and parent pays off in increased love and understanding. This is important practice for the parent's sphere of love, when parental investment in a child may not reap visible fruits for many years.

The Challenge of Marital Love

With its thrust towards the unconditional, love in the conjugal sphere is far more genuine and true than its first appearance in the initial phases of dating and courtship. On dates, people put their best foot forward. They are usually freshly showered, dressed in attractive clothes and well-groomed. They have planned to spend money on a fun and interesting event; they are together for a limited amount of time and are on their best behavior. Often, they are still supported by their parents and thus are free of many worries and responsibilities.

In day-to-day married life, however, things are very different. The partners are financially independent and may have to struggle to make ends meet. They are not always at their best: tired and grumpy in the morning or exhausted after a long day at work. They may rarely find time to go out together on fun events; sometimes they cannot afford to. Marriage strips away the dating mask inexorably, and couples are sometimes quite disappointed when they begin to see the other person as a human being full of needs, vulnerabilities, faults, frailties and limitations. They may yearn for the romance of dating again, when everything seemed so perfect.

Nevertheless, a phase of disappointment and disillusionment is natural in the evolution of a marriage. Marital relationships are known to go through several predictable phrases.[7] Far from signaling that a marriage is in trouble, the disillusionment phase presents the opportunity to create a more authentic relationship and expand the couple's capacities in caring and giving. When couples understand this in advance, they can anticipate these phases and appreciate how these phases can contribute to a distinctive kind of personal growth toward a more highly evolved marital love.

First Phase—Romance or Infatuation

The initial phase of spouse's love has the sweet illusion of blissful oneness and mutual perfection. It is believed that these feelings will last, but they are only a temporary foretaste of the depth of love that becomes possible after the hard work of continual investment in one another and the marriage.

Second Phase—Conflict

With the passage of time, the realities of mutual immaturity and differences invariably break through the initial illusion of perfection. Both sides then have to adjust to each other and to the inevitable conflict, disappointment and anxiety. This phase presents an opportunity for spouses to know each other stripped of all illusions and to love each other as real, flawed human beings.

Immaturity and ignorance can cause couples in this phase to resign themselves to a marriage lacking in intimacy and escape into work, hobbies or their children. Some have an affair or decide to divorce, hoping to regain and sustain that initial phase of romantic love with someone else. The reality is that, should they marry again, such second unions have even higher percentages of divorce than first unions.[8] The way forward for couples in this phase is to make a new commitment to the marriage and labor to realize its initial promise on a higher level.

Third Phase—Recommitment and Cooperation

Wise spouses come to the realization that they must make real personal sacrifices for the sake of each other and the marriage. In this phase they begin to look within to take responsibility for their personal limitations—what they need to change, what they need to heal, and how they need to grow. Over time, a deep, secure intimacy emerges between them, even as they wrestle with old patterns of thought and behavior.

Fourth Phase—Creativity and Service

As their capacity to love grows and develops, couples are often moved from within to share with the world around them, which in turn enriches their relationship. Love in this phase has come to express the authenticity that Fromm described when he said, "Love is an attitude, an orientation of character which determines the relatedness of a person to the world as a whole, not toward one object of love... If I truly love one person, I love all persons, I love the world."[9]

It is due to the very exigencies of living with and for another person in the intensely close conjugal relationship that people can evolve into this higher level of concern and service. One husband of over thirty years described marriage as touching the "love that includes everything and everybody, the love that's universal... everything that is good about connectedness and caring for others."[10]

Gateway to Mature Relationships

A spouse is the gateway to mature relationships with the opposite sex. Since the husband or wife has all the qualities of masculinity or femininity, each spouse can understand the masculine or feminine world from an insider's point of view. Relationships with the opposite sex parent, opposite sex siblings, friends and associates may become easier and clearer as one gets to know and appreciate a spouse. Spouses begin to see each other in the light of many types of male-female relationships, not just that of husband and wife. They sometimes feel like brother and sister, parent and child, best friends, or colleagues. Multifaceted, the marital relationship becomes a source of endless fascination and learning.

Because of the mature character of conjugal love, spouses find themselves on a sympathetic new level with their own parents, who have tasted the joys and sorrows of marriage long before they did. Often, a new frankness and companionship grow up between parents and their sons and daughters once they are married. They sometimes even begin to enjoy each other socially, couple to couple, as if they were friends. A new sympathy also grows up between siblings, whose marriages borrow some of their flavor from, yet are distinct from, the family life they once shared.

Lack of Growth in the Previous Spheres

The foundations of mature love in the conjugal sphere are in the earlier spheres of love. A person whose heart and conscience has been nurtured through good parenting in the child's sphere has had ample opportunity to develop a trusting, responsive heart. The husband and wife relationship of his parents serves as a powerful model from which to draw lessons.[11] Living with siblings, especially when they are sick or struggling, is a humanizing experience and prepares a child for dealing with the vagaries of intimate life with another human being. Spouses who have had fulfilling experiences in the earlier spheres know the joys of living, breathing, eating together and bumping up against one another in the push-and-pull of family life. They know the happiness of everyday intimacy and are well acquainted with the sacrifices it entails. They are better prepared for married life.

Yet in reality, most people come to marriage with incomplete and unfulfilled experiences in the previous spheres and hence their abilities in love are limited. They may want to be mothered or fathered; succored or made excuses for, as if they were children. "He was so irresponsible—sometimes with not showing up for work, not paying his bills and not keeping his promises to me," says Susan, an aerobics instructor, of her former fiancé. "He seemed to be begging me to yell at him and lay down ultimatums, like a kid daring his dad to ground him and keep him out of trouble." Not having matured sufficiently through the previous spheres of love lies in the background of many relationship woes.

Several marriage counselors agree that the single most important factor in marital break-up is self-centeredness—expecting to receive love from the other rather than to give it. Gordon says, "Chronological adults who remain emotionally infants are basically self-centered. They expect to be taken care of and to get what they want when they want it, without having to give in return. They know only what they need, see others primarily as objects to meet their needs and are incapable of empathizing with the needs of others."[12] When the spouses have not matured through the child's and sibling's spheres to become capable of true love—living to be of service to others —they will unfortunately lack the depth of heart and relational skills required for building a successful and fulfilling marriage.

Unfinished business of the earlier spheres may also haunt spouses who see the commitment of marriage as an effort to take away their independence. Such people rebel against their spouses as a teenager rebels against his or her parents.

Deficiencies in the child's sphere of love can sometimes be remedied in the spouse's sphere through surrogate parental figures. Marriage mentoring is an excellent way to achieve this. Through a church or community group, younger couples are connected to older couples who have strong and lasting marriages. The couples meet and discuss typical issues that come up in marriage, and the older couple guides the younger couple over the rough spots they themselves have overcome. The mentoring couples act as parental figures to provide the kind of support the younger couples need.

Marriage itself is often restorative of previous spheres' deficiencies. Harville Hendrix believes that spouses choose each other based upon unconscious but potent needs to complete the unfinished business in their relationship with their parents. They tend to choose people who have the same qualities as their parents, in an inexorable cycle of history repeating itself. If the partners consciously apply themselves to understand one another and serve as healers for one another, they are able to break up negative cycles and fill in the gaps in their personalities, thus placing their marriage on a better footing where love can blossom.[13]

Strong attractions to persons other than one's spouse are often signals of deficiencies in the heart's development from an earlier sphere. People in such situations may assume that a new and different partner can heal the unsettled issues they sense but cannot articulate. Some are looking for a father or mother figure. Others are hurting in the sibling's sphere, with unfulfilled longings left over from adolescence.

Desmond, a man in his thirties, says, "I first saw Dana leading a demonstration at city hall. She looked so noble and fearless out there. I became extremely attracted to her and we began seeing each other, to the point where I was worried about my marriage. As it turned out, Dana steered me to join an environmental organization. Working with them has been great, the fulfillment of ambitions I've had since high school. I still bump into Dana once in a while but there's no big spark anymore. Now I realize my thing about Dana was more of a need within me."

Sex and the Spheres of Love

Each sphere of love has its unique expressions of physical affection. Breastfeeding, diapering, continual holding, lifting, dressing and bathing augment the emotional bond between mother and child. Parents continue to show physical affection for their growing children: a pat on the back, a quick squeeze, a gentle elbowing into laughter, etc. Siblings and peers express physical affection through sports, sleepovers, grooming one another or playful wrestling and tussling; this is peer-appropriate physical bonding.

Sex is the unique province of the conjugal sphere of love, its unique form of physical intimacy. On the basis of relationship skills and the growth of the heart attained in the earlier spheres, marriage can bear the intensity of sex without the partners' growth of heart in other-centered love being curtailed or damaged. This is something the other spheres are not equipped to do.

The painful results of sexualizing the child's sphere of love are demonstrated in cases of child sexual abuse. The plethora of books about sexual abuse by parents, family members, neighbors and caretakers depict the lifelong agony of the victims when the basic trust and innocence of the child's sphere is violated. John Sullivan, an expert on child safety, says, "The child who has been sexually molested is robbed of some of the basic psychological components of childhood."[14] Sex in the child's sphere of love damages the heart and can destroy a life.

Sexual relationships between siblings are known to be traumatizing—as well as genetically harmful for any ensuing children—but sexual relations between friends and other peers in adolescence are not so clearly prohibited. Yet the emotional and psychological consequences of uncommitted sexual relationships are legion. (See Chapter 24) Regardless of the partners' intentions, the heart's growth toward true and satisfying love is adversely affected when sex takes place outside of the conjugal sphere of love.

In marriage, a man and woman entrust themselves completely to one another. The sexual union between them is thus the physical manifestation of this openness and trust. It is the embodied pact of their commitment to utterly share with and be close to one another on all levels and for a lifetime. Sex outside of this commitment nevertheless implies this same message, leaving unmarried sexual partners with expectations, guilt feelings and attachments to one another they did not anticipate but which are psychologically very real. Because of its special bonding quality, sex is meant to be reserved exclusively for the spouse's sphere of love.

Throughout the Lifetime

Fulfillment in the spouse's sphere of love is a lifelong endeavor that grows and deepens over time into an irreplaceable richness of shared experiences. Over its lifetime, a marriage goes through many changes. Raging hormones give way to endorphins. Romantic delusions fall by the wayside. There are ups and downs, illness and wellness, temptations, financial plenty and financial woes. There are scintillating moments of soulful fusion; there are times when the two feel like strangers. There are the joys of having and raising children as well as the sense of overwhelming responsibility that it brings. Fine features and figures sooner or later go the way of all flesh. Beloved parents are dead and buried. Perhaps a child is, too. If a couple withstands all that and still stays together, it is clear that they have built a very special kind of love along the way.

In the musical *Fiddler on the Roof*, Tevya watches bemusedly as his daughters follow their passions and marry the men they choose. He has been married to his wife for a quarter of a century. It was an arranged marriage; they met for the first time on their wedding day. He asks his wife in song, "Do You Love Me?"[15] His wife hedges, thinking it a foolish question, but she answers. For twenty-five years, she says, she has cooked for him, cleaned for him, washed his clothes, shared his bed and borne his children. "If that's not love, what is?" she wants to know. The rich and soulful life they share is proof enough. The love between a married couple, increasing incrementally over time through mutual sacrifice, concern and caring, is a creative endeavor that successful couples can rightly be proud of.

In a marriage where the couple is committed to mutual understanding and intimacy, personal maturity and healing, and service to others, a lifetime is hardly enough to explore all the possibilities of love. The human psyche is vast, complex and profound. To know and truly love another human being in his or her entirety is an endeavor worthy of—indeed requiring—a lifetime of investment. As love advances toward the unconditional through the special growth available in the spouse's sphere of love, it provides the basis for launching into the most advanced sphere: the love of parents for their children.

18

The Parent's Sphere of Love

"I SAW THIS LITTLE BOY WALKING ALONG THE TRAIL. Suddenly I was overcome and just started to cry. I want one of those, I said to myself.... It was like I suddenly realized that I was no longer a child. I was an adult and I needed to have children."[1] After five years of an exemplary marriage, Nelson was overwhelmed by the sense that a new vista of love was calling to him. The parent's sphere of love beckoned to him as a compelling life need.

The need and desire to have children is more than a fact of biology. It arises from the heart's deep yearning to extend and multiply love. Instinctively, people know they need this life experience for the greatest fulfillment. They have a built-in need to give love on this level, and they will experience some frustration and emptiness if they do not. Those who cannot or do not have children will often adopt them. Connie, a woman in her fifties, explained why she and her husband had adopted four children: "We came to a point in our marriage where we knew we needed children to keep on growing." Others may mentor a young person through a community service program or "parent" surrogates, such as the youngsters who live in their neighborhood or a pet. They need an outlet for their maternal or paternal yearnings—their drive to give parental love.

The parent's sphere of love is the fullest, most profound and encompassing expression of the true love that has been developing throughout the previous spheres. It includes the special joys of grand-parental love. As the greatest of all loves, parental love serves as a good model for all moral love in society. This would include educators, social workers, those in the helping professions, and all those who contribute to the welfare of others.

An Other-Centered Life

Becoming a parent is probably the most life-altering event most people ever experience. Many feel themselves to be in a whole new world. "The birth of our first child was one of the high points of my life. There was something about Jack's birth and the things that happened around it that was really a passage," said one young father.[2] A young mother said that she felt she had been given the keys to an exclusive club, one she had not known existed until parenthood made her a member.

Whether in stores, on the streets or in neighborhoods, parents find common ground based upon their love for their children. Elizabeth, a 30-year-old mother from Michigan, says, "It is so much easier to strike up conversations with people now that I'm a parent. Other parents are more than willing to talk in the park and compare notes or even exchange phone numbers so our kids can get together. There's a lot of mistrust in society today because of all the things you read about in the papers, but parents seem to trust each other because we care about the same things."

Parents even constitute a kind of sub-culture all their own. One survey found that the most marked differences of attitudes on cultural issues are between those who have children and those who do not. These differences transcend economic, political, racial and other demographic factors.[3] Parents' attitudes on social issues take into account how those matters will affect the lives of the next generation, specifically their children, for whom they want the very best. This illustrates that parenthood marks a passage into a new way of looking at things that is powerfully focused on the welfare of another—significantly centered on true love.

Parental love calls forth the noblest and most unselfish emotions and actions from otherwise ordinary people. After Brian Volck, a successful pediatrician, adopted a Central American girl besides his own two healthy children, he began to reflect on his motivation for so doing. Children, he finds, "present me with opportunities to love when I would rather be alone, to be gentle when I would rather be efficient and to surrender when I would rather be in control."[4]

The highest level of human morality is to be willing to give one's life for the sake of others, and rare is the parent who would not sacrifice his or her life for the sake of the child. Travis, a father from Georgia, said that when he got a clean bill of health on a cancer test, he didn't care so much for himself. "If I had it, I had it, I figured. The only thing that concerned me was I didn't want my kids growing up without a dad."

Besides being insouciant about their own lives in comparison to those of their children, becoming a parent can help people find the moral strength to change a destructive lifestyle. A well-known actor gave up alcohol when he came in to his home drunk one morning and found his infant staring at him in pure amazement. He realized that he was out of sync with himself, with his child, and with any natural state of being. He roused himself up to start taking more responsibility.

In this way, parenthood can serve as a remedial influence on mistakes made in other phases of life. Many a spouse has been spurred to make more effort to make her marriage work for the sake of the children. Barbara, a woman in her sixties, found out in the first years of their marriage that her husband was extremely immature, but she stayed with him for her children's sake. "By today's standards," she remarked, "I probably would have divorced him long ago. But look what I got out of it. Harry and I have two good sets of relatives, financial stability, education and travel. The kids turned out well. When we talked about it together, we both wound up saying, 'Not such a bad deal!'" A good life was forged out of a problematic marriage held together by parental instincts to stay together "for the sake of the kids."

Because of this other-centered nature, the parent's sphere of love is most conducive to moral growth. No other role in life expands the heart and strengthens character like the experience of being a parent. Every step in raising children brings new challenges, demands more investment, and thus opens up new dimensions of heart and love. This is why the experience of parenting is crucial for a person's overall growth as a human being.

Challenges as Children Grow

Many parents find that caring for an infant is easier than caring for an older child.[5] An infant cannot walk, talk, assert his or her will, get into the china cabinet or chew on batteries left lying around. A toddler can, thus demanding more vigilance and teaching on the part of the parent. Many parents adore their babies but find themselves frustrated in dealing with older children. Yet if parents can stretch their love beyond the initial ease of bonding in the child's infancy, they will be infinitely rewarded as they witness and nurture the unfolding of a fully-fledged human being.

Parents are able to share more deeply with older children as their powers of understanding, reason and empathy grow. Their children listen as they explain what they believe and why, and impart a sense of who they are.[6] It is truly satisfying to parents when their child fully ingests a lesson. Sharing what they have realized, enjoyed and treasured, and seeing their child respond in kind creates a deep sense of unity on the path of life. It helps validate the parents' life experiences, enriching their sense of their own journey and legacy. On the other hand, a child's growing ability to notice and comment upon his parents' lapses and inconsistencies challenges parents to examine their own values and whether they are living up to their own preachments. Robert Coles points out that moral guidance is often a mutual experience between parent and child, one helping the other in different situations.[7] When parents raise their moral antennae and notice moral education moments in everyday living, children are likely to follow suit.

Parenting pre-teens and teenagers is often an emotional highwire act. Parents strive to accommodate the child's needs for peer approval and independence while protecting their child from harm. Particularly in today's culture—which many conscientious people see as adversarial to good parenting—parents no longer feel at ease letting their children have the freedom they clamor for. A fast-paced, competitive, individualistic, highly sexualized consumer society sends many negative messages to youth. Parents feel they cannot let their children watch television unsupervised; they must monitor popular music and now the Internet. With drug use and other negative behaviors penetrating to the middle school and even elementary school, parents need to know their children's friends well. They must be aware of where their children are and what they are doing at all times.

On the other hand, parents also have to deal with their teenage children's growing sense of identity as independent persons. They want to feel trusted as well as protected. One father confides, "When I asked my teenage son what we should improve in our efforts to lead him to adulthood, he replied without hesitation: 'You should trust me more that I am able to make the right decisions for my life and that I am ready to take on more responsibilities.'" The rueful father concedes, "Looking back, I have to admit that knowing the right measure for granting independence remains one of the more difficult tasks."[8]

This balancing act requires a lot of parents. It takes strength and discernment to set and enforce limits in a fair and growth-promoting way. It demands moral courage sometimes to say, "Why don't you stay home this evening?" It takes wisdom to guide a child to relate with peers who are upright or different rather than peers who are "cool." It requires a sacrifice of time to spend hours in joint activities with teenage children and to create a socially-rich family environment—two factors that have been shown to facilitate their moral growth.[9] Yet, with both parents working all day and facing home responsibilities all evening, it is all too easy to surrender the child to the culture in the form of video games, television, or over-reliance on peers to keep the child busy and happy while the parents catch up on sleep and precious time together.[10] These are challenges that try a parent's wherewithal.

While today's concerns may seem unique, parenting has probably always been an upstream swim. In less affluent days, parents had to worry how to feed, clothe and shelter their children, and in many parts of the world, they still do. No matter where and when fathers and mothers do their parenting, they face anxiety over their children's welfare and make courageous sacrifices to provide them with the opportunity for a better life.

Parenting is, as one mother said in Hillary Clinton's *It Takes a Village*, the decision to "have your heart go walking around outside your body."[11] To love as a parent loves carries risk, for there is always the possibility of loss. With each new step in the child's maturation, parents must brace for new risks. The parental heart aches the first time their child is out and about alone; the first time their teenage daughter goes on a date; the first time their son uses the car; the first year she is away from home at college. Most parents are hard put to control their emotions when their child marries, as they release the hand they have held for so long while another takes it. In all these ways, the heart of a parent beats for another.

Parents continue to guide, aid and advise their adult children as well as they can, yet they must exercise greater wisdom and caution as to when to hang on, when to let go, when to advise and intervene, and when they must honor their adult child's decisions whether they agree with them or not. Wise parents are accessible, yet they let their children lead their own lives. Less skillful parents either intervene too much or are consistently unavailable. The most effective and loving parents find that however far the umbilical cord stretches, it never really breaks, and the child comes back and back into the parents' orbits—a source of increasing affirmation, comfort and support.

Foundations in the Earlier Spheres

Parental love has its basis in social and emotional competencies developed in the earlier spheres of love. A good parent often was once a good child. Remembering when he was a child, he can identify with his own children's experiences and empathize with their feelings. Remembering the love he received in the child's sphere from his own parents, he imitates what they did for him. Christopher, a father in his thirties, says, "My mother always remembered from day to day whether I'd had a headache or stomach ache. She knew if I had a test that day in school and always asked how it had gone. I wanted to be as attentive a parent as she was, so I practiced remembering those little things about my kids' lives and asking about them. They were amazed that I remembered, and I think they felt cared for because of it."

Parenting teenagers commonly brings up difficult emotions, memories and feelings for mid-life adults. Their child's talents, intellectual prowess, physical energy and sexuality may confront them with their own inadequacies.[12] Observing how their own son or daughter fashions his or her life's goals and dreams, they may find themselves in a crisis of meaning as they recall unmet goals from their own childhood.

The sibling's sphere of love also provides invaluable lessons for parenthood. Andrea, a mother of two from Vermont, had been a "big sister" to a developmentally disabled child when she was a teenager. Michael was a crippled and sickly child who was always off by himself, unresponsive to everyone around him. Every day Andrea would hold Michael in her lap, press her cheek on his and rock him, but he showed no interest. One day as she was rocking him in her lap and absent-mindedly lifted her cheek from his, Michael's hand reached up and pressed her cheek back where it was. He smiled for the first time. Andrea realized that her care was reaching him. From then on Michael began to change. His face grew full of expression. As he laughed and played with other children, Andrea felt she had witnessed a miracle. "Sometimes now, when my own little boys are driving me crazy, I think about Michael and how persistent love changed him. Then I'm able to be more patient and loving with them," Andrea said. Those experiences in the sibling's sphere of love helped make her a better mother.

Strife in the spouse's sphere usually reduces parents' abilities to give to their children, as the parents' hearts and minds are embroiled in their own pain.[13] The son or daughter's neediness can be felt as an onerous burden rather than a call for compassion. Marital harmony, on the other hand, is one of the most effective parenting tools there is. Raising children brings many crises—a new baby, a serious illness, a teenager in trouble—when spouses need to draw on their deep well of character and good will toward each other. Success in the conjugal sphere of love brings strength and stability for dealing with the challenges of raising children, while successful parenthood affirms and augments the joys of marital love.

The lack of emotional and social development in the previous phases of life is key to understanding disabilities in the parental sphere. Parents well-schooled in other-centered love, who are sensitive, patient and psychologically mature, are more apt to meet their children's needs.[14] Many a parent has tiptoed into their child's bedroom and felt sorrowful when they looked down at the small, sleeping face after a conflict-ridden day. They may regret yelling at or punishing the child, realizing that they acted more out of their own fears, frustrations, ignorance and lack of experience than any serious fault in the child, and they begin to reflect on their own emotional stability and inner life. A reflective moment such as this often spurs a renewed sense of determination to invest and give more, thus expanding the reservoir of the parental sphere of love.

Grandparent's Love

An extension of parental love is the love of grandparents for their grandchildren. Although in the Western industrialized world the family has been reduced steadily down to the nuclear family, character is formed more completely and securely when three generations interact.

Grandparents are an invaluable source of rootedness for a child. Children who have relationships with their grandparents are more trusting, calmer and quieter than those who do not.[15] Grandparents are the link to all that has gone before and they give a sense of continuity and reassurance. They represent the past, while the parents represent the present, and the children represent the future. Grandparents help children to know what life was like long before they were born—where they have come from and the kind of people they have sprung from. They are the family's link to the chain of human history.

Having experienced the challenges of creating a family themselves, grandparents are a source of wisdom and a reassuring presence. "My grandparents gave me a deep sense that things would turn out right in the end," says one husband.[16] Grandparents can provide a "safe haven" when their children and grandchildren are experiencing turbulence in their relationships. Certain of who they are, grandparents stand for verities of the human experience that go beyond current fashions. The perspective of another generation, given with wit and candor, enriches and enlivens all.

The grandparental heart has an innate need to give from their lifetime storehouse of knowledge and experience to nurture and enrich the younger generations. Erikson and his colleagues have characterized the primary challenge in old age as one of "integrity versus despair," with the possibility of culminating in a profound awareness or higher sense of self.[17] In this last stage of physical life, individuals have the capacity to experience their personhood as that which "transcends time-bound identities."[18]

"The real point of having kids is to get the grandchildren," jokes Martin, 78, a retired restaurant proprietor in the Southwest. "Half the time I find myself thinking about how I can either help them or see them." Grandparents' hearts go out without reservation to their grandchildren, whom they commonly describe as "wonderful" and "perfect."[19] As they watch their grown children shoulder the responsibilities of adulthood, most are moved to help as much as they can. It is not unusual for grandparents to provide hours of free childcare, help with meals and laundry, monetary loans or gifts. It is their joy to give to their children and their grandchildren and to aid them in life's journey.

To fulfill their growth potential in this sphere of love, grandparents need and want opportunities to give. Teresa, a mother of two in Nebraska, met an elderly widow, Belinda, in her small town. Belinda was lonely and delighted to get to know Teresa and her two young children. She brought over jars of homemade jellies and jams and fresh vegetables from her garden. She gave the mother her phone number and told her to call any time she needed to. Belinda babysat for free and even offered to help Teresa clean house. One day Teresa couldn't help asking the elderly widow, "Why do you give us so much?" Belinda replied, "You give to me by letting me give to you."

For what they give, grandfathers and grandmothers in turn receive affirmation and comfort that their legacy will live on. The curious grandchild who absorbs their stories, their insights and their values becomes a keeper of the family's—and the community's—flame. In that way, they know they have made a difference and left some influence on the world. This is their link to immortality, and it is deeply gratifying.

Parental Heart in Society

Parental love is the prototype of mature love for others, and love in its fullest, deepest and broadest form resembles the love of a parent. It is evident in the best teachers and managers. Indeed, many historical figures whose lives have deeply affected others in a moral way came to be called "Father" or "Mother," signifying the parental quality of their leadership. Gandhi's followers called him "Bapu" (Papa) because of his great concern for them and for his nation. Abraham Lincoln became "Father Abraham" as he guided America through the darkness of the Civil War. "Mother" Teresa helped the poor and disenfranchised of India with a boundless compassion. "Mother" Cabrini became well-known for her charitable work in Chicago.

Regardless of his title or position, a person with a parental heart toward others is the true leader of any group or organization, the real embodiment of what the organization stands for. An exceptional teacher becomes more than an instructor in academics; he or she becomes like a second parent. Lydia, a 42-year-old woman who teaches in the inner-city schools of Newark, New Jersey, tells the story: "Mark had a real problem when he came to my class. He right away thought because I was blond I had to be a racist. I used to talk to him a lot after class, and after a while he started liking me. When he graduated from high school and went into the army, he would call me for encouragement and support. When he was on leave, he stayed at my house. If you look on my mantle at our family portrait, you see seven white faces and one black face—that's Mark! He calls me 'Mom.'" This teacher's maternal heart toward him changed Mark's life.

Nurturing a child from infancy to adulthood entails tremendous sacrifice and skill; it is an exercise of the heart second to none. Therefore, it is conducive to the most expansive moral growth. The parental sphere of love is the summit of the moral growth dynamic embodied in the family—the four spheres of love. Since this family-based dynamic is so central to education of the entire human being, character educators do well to be aware of it—to support, facilitate, learn about and cooperate with this powerful natural vehicle of human moral development.

Section 5

Building Healthy Families

JUNE SAUNDERS AND JOHN R. WILLIAMS

LOVING ANOTHER PERSON AND BUILDING A HEALTHY FAMILY together require prerequisite character skills, insights and understanding. If marriage and family are the settings for optimal moral growth, young people have a need to believe in them as institutions and as something at which they may succeed. This can come through marriage and family education that puts emphasis on character development in terms of achieving basic life goals. Character education and marriage/family resiliency are two sides of the same coin. Their confluent support of one another is highly desirable in preparing students for success in these core and morally important aspects of life.

19

Why Marriage?

In virtually every society into which historians or anthropologists have inquired, one finds peoples living together on the basis of kinship ties and having responsibility for raising children. The kinship ties invariably imply restrictions on who has sexual access to whom; the child-care responsibilities invariably imply both economic and non-economic obligations. And in virtually every society, the family is defined by marriage; that is, by a publicly announced contract that makes legitimate the sexual union of a man and a woman.

—James Q. Wilson[1]

THE UNIVERSALITY OF MARRIAGE THROUGHOUT HISTORY SHOWS its enduring power. As Wilson points out, marriage fulfills very real economic and social needs. It regulates sexual unions and provides for their results: children. There is much evidence that this regulation and provision is the backbone of a civil and prosperous society.[2] Furthermore, individuals are deeply drawn to marriage. Marriage holds the promise of answering profound psychological, emotional and physical needs. It appeals to the human need for community and belonging.

Yet marriage in modern times is under siege. It is no longer the accepted road to happiness and fulfillment; nor is it considered the only route to sexual satisfaction or the only context within which to raise children. It is rarely celebrated in the mass media or the entertainment industry. The survival of monogamous, lifelong marriage as an institution is, for the first time in human history, in doubt.

Is Marriage Obsolete?

Marriage rates have been gradually declining in most advanced countries. In the United States, for example, from 1960 to 1998, there was a 41 percent decline in the annual number of marriages per one thousand unmarried women.[3] In Japan and many European countries as well, people are putting off marriage for a variety of reasons. Some are postponing it indefinitely. Many factors contribute to the decline of marriage. Notable among them are several significant social and cultural trends: a rise in divorce, increasing acceptance of cohabitation and single parenthood, a widespread disillusionment with marriage, and the changing role of women in society.

Between 1960 and 1998 divorce rates climbed in the United States, more than doubling.[4] Divorce became a socially acceptable option, almost an inevitability. Marriage researcher John Gottman places the chances a first marriage will end in divorce over the course of forty years at 67 percent.[5] For the first time in history, more children became separated from one of their parents by parental choice than by death.[6] There are now so many divorces in America that public schools hesitate to teach that the two-parent family is the desirable norm. They fear to injure the self-esteem of over 50 percent of their students who are not in two-parent families.

In part as a reaction against the high divorce rate, many people choose to cohabit. One quarter of unmarried women between the ages of 25 and 39 are living with a partner at the present time, and a full 50 percent have lived with an unmarried partner at some time.[7] Cohabitation is so prevalent that a recent issue of *Newsweek* depicted the possible "death of marriage" on its cover.[8]

Since such living arrangements are easier to break up than a marriage, some couples believe that living together before marriage is a good way to "test drive" a relationship before fully committing to it and risking the trauma of later divorce. Yet in fact, living together neither helps people prepare for marriage nor does it prevent divorce. As researchers David Popenoe and Barbara Dafoe Whitehead report from their review of recent studies, those who live together before marriage are more likely to divorce after they do marry than those who married without living together first.[9]

There is a strong tendency in modern society toward social acceptance of unwed parenthood as well. One in three babies in the

United States are born to single mothers, and the rate in the African-American population is as high as four out of five. In Europe, the rate in France and the United Kingdom is also one in three, while in Scandinavian countries about half of all children are born to unwed mothers.[10]

Disillusionment with Marriage

Disillusionment about the prospects of marital happiness is widespread. Less than half of U.S. high school seniors believe that legal marriage will lead to greater happiness than cohabitation or staying single.[11] One young man from Copenhagen put the general European misgivings about marriage succinctly: "Marriage is like Christmas, a fairy tale. I just don't believe in it."[12]

The changing status of women has also brought disillusionment with marriage in its wake—and, where disillusionment already existed, the means to act upon it. Noreen Byrne of the National Women's Council of Ireland pressed for liberalized divorce laws, saying that many women feel that marriage is nothing more than the opportunity to "wash men's socks."[13] Young Japanese women are postponing marriage because they are disillusioned by the traditional model of the workaholic husband who is gone evenings and weekends and takes no part in childcare or housework. This reluctance to enter into marriage has caused Japan's fertility rate to plunge.[14] While the changing status of women has thrown traditional marriage conventions into question, it has provided few new models for marriage other than negotiation of every issue—a long, tedious and sometimes conflict-ridden process.

Yet in spite of their doubts as to its efficacy and chances for success, marriage remains a highly desired life goal for many people. The vast majority of people marry in their lifetimes and those who divorce remarry—usually within two years.[15] Strong majorities of American young people—83 percent and 73 percent of female and male high school seniors respectively—consider successful marriage and family life to be "extremely important" in their lives.[16] These statistics are particularly poignant since many of these young people have witnessed the dissolution of their own parents' marriages. In spite of widespread doubts about the permanence of marriage and its possibilities for happiness, the attraction of marriage remains strong.

Many unmarried people in their teens and twenties are open to and even eager to learn the competencies that can help them escape the divorce syndrome.[17] This is a hopeful sign, but the reality is that the lifestyles and attitudes of these young people almost preclude them reaching their goal of a happy lifelong marriage after a string of temporary sexual "hookups" and uncommitted relationships.

The Case for Marriage: Evidence from a Divorce Culture

Can a case be made for marriage? Is it a viable—even necessary—human institution? Statistically, a marriage culture is a far healthier, happier and safer place than a divorce culture. Marriage is a stabilizing social influence. Marriage even keeps crime rates down. But most importantly, a good marriage is the best setting within which to raise children. Since children are the key to the future, broken marriages have effects that resound far past the personal pain of the couples involved. Thus Hillary Clinton remarked, "Every society requires a critical mass of families that fit the traditional ideal, both to meet the needs of most children and to serve as a model for other adults who are raising children in difficult settings."[18]

Acknowledging the value of good marriages does not have to be intended to make divorced parents feel guilty; nor does it have to become a diatribe against single parents or stepparents. People in these situations are coping with life's complexities as best they can, and many are doing so with heroic self-sacrifice. Some have little choice about their situations; their difficulties were beyond the reach of easy or available answers.

It is also important to note that not all marriages are beneficial. Highly conflicted and stress-filled marriages are risk factors for many of the difficulties cited below as well.[19] "Intact" marriages do not guarantee good outcomes. However, it cannot be denied that "good enough" marriages—to borrow a phrase from David Blankenhorn in *Fatherless America*—are statistically some of the best social programs around. They are worth any and all efforts to build and sustain.

Damage to Children

The National Survey of Children, which followed the lives of a group of seven to eleven-year-olds for more than a decade, found that children living with one parent or in stepfamilies were two to three times as likely to have emotional and behavioral problems as children living in two-parent families. They dropped out of high school in higher proportions and are much more likely to abuse alcohol, marijuana, and other drugs. Girls are more likely to engage in teen sex and have an unwanted pregnancy. They are more likely to become violent or get in trouble with the law. These findings have been confirmed in study after study. Age, race, socioeconomic status, locale and educational level of the mother have little impact upon these statistics. The predicting factor is a broken family.[20]

Economically, children in single-parent homes are the poorest of all major demographic groups. Few children who were raised by their married biological parents experience poverty during childhood, but most children in single parent homes do. Experts have coined the phrase "the plunge into poverty" that women and their dependent children undergo after divorce. Forty-six percent of families with children headed by single mothers live below the poverty line, compared with only 8 percent of two-parent families.[21]

Family breakdown also has a negative impact on academic achievement. Rates for students who are forced to repeat a grade or who have been expelled or suspended from school are two times higher in single-parent homes and stepfamilies and three times higher in families headed by women who never married the father of their child. The 1988 National Heath Interview Survey on Child Health reported lower grades, poorer health, unsatisfying personal relationships, and even increased accident-proneness and speech defects among children of divorce.[22]

Karl Zinsmeister at the American Enterprise Institute is one of many experts who hold that the key to preventing social ills is rebuilding strong families. "There is a mountain of scientific evidence showing that when families disintegrate, children often end up with intellectual, physical and emotional scars that persist for life," he said. "We talk about the drug crisis, the education crisis, and the problem of teen pregnancy and juvenile crime. But all these ills trace back predominantly to one source: broken families."[23]

Non-Intact Marriages and Crime

Broken marriages have a bearing on crime rates as well. U.S. Department of Justice statistics show that 70 percent of young people in long-term prisons come from broken homes.[24] According to U.S. Census statistics, for each 10 percent increase in fatherless families, there was a 17 percent average increase in violent juvenile crimes.[25] Sociologist David Courtwright, who did a study of violence in America, concluded, "When stable family life has been the norm for men and boys, violence and disorder have diminished. That was one important reason why, during the mid-twentieth-century marriage boom, violent death rates showed a sustained decline."[26] Other studies have shown that crime rates in general are directly related to the numbers of divorced people, single parents and single people in communities. High marriage rates reduce crime and serve as a protective factor for women and children.[27]

Where fathers are absent from the home, more boys grow up to be violent—this link between non-intact families and social pathology can be found worldwide.[28] Studies in England and Germany have come up with similar conclusions. Researcher Norman Dennis at the University of Newcastle found that family breakdown was the significant factor contributing to the rise in crime in Europe. Because of divorce, he said, "Young men in England and Germany became much more prone to criminality, drug abuse and subcriminal disorder."[29]

Domestic violence and abuse is far more prevalent among cohabiting couples than among married ones. Some estimates place the chances of a woman being beaten by her cohabiting boyfriend as opposed to a husband as high as nine times greater. Sexual abuse of children by boyfriends of their mothers is also very high.[30]

Marriage helps channel male aggressiveness into the constructive pursuits of creating, raising, protecting and supporting a family. Males born and raised within the confines of marriage are less violent and crime-prone in society; they also go on to form families of their own, becoming stable society members. Anthropologist Margaret Mead quipped that every society faces the problem of what to do with the men. Socially speaking, the best answer to that dilemma seems to be: Marry them.

Personal Benefits of Marriage

Marriage brings great personal as well as social benefits. Marriage is good for people. In spite of the Hollywood myth that the single, swinging life brings more friends, more fun and more stimulation, married people generally enjoy better health and more happiness than do single or divorced people. An Oxford physician who has studied such health issues concluded that on all counts of physical health, married people do better than the unmarried, separated or divorced.[31] Married people have fewer diseases, and they often recover more quickly than a person without a supportive partner. When Robert H. Coombs, a behavioral scientist at UCLA, reviewed more than 130 published empirical studies conducted over the past sixty years measuring the effects of marriage and non-marriage on personal well-being, he found that married people live longer on average and tend to be healthier than those who are not married.[32] For instance, 90 percent of married women and men live to at least 65 years of age, while those unmarried for any reason—divorce, bereavement or never having been married—had only a 65 to 70 percent chance of living to age 65.[33]

Married people develop healthier behavior patterns. They monitor one another's health. It is often the spouse who finds the lump or mole that warrants attention, or who notices a spouse's shortness of breath. The couple may launch a diet or exercise program together as well. Researcher Linda J. Waite reports that married couples drink less alcohol and use fewer drugs.[34]

Married couples experience greater psychological health, too. They have the lowest rates of severe depression in the population.[35] Both married men and women report higher levels of personal happiness than the unmarried.[36] They also enjoy their sexual lives together, reporting higher levels of sexual satisfaction than either single people or cohabiting couples. The most rigorous sex survey ever undertaken in the United States, the University of Chicago study, reported that 88 percent of married people experience great physical and emotional pleasure in their sexual lives with their spouses.[37]

Married couples are also financially healthier than the single or the divorced. They have more than twice as much money, on average, as unmarried people. They save more, work harder and tend to be home and property owners. Among America's millionaires, most have been married to the same woman for all of their adult lives. Many cite the good character and support of their wives as important factors in their financial success.[38]

Springboard to Growth

The benefits of lifelong marriage for the individuals involved and its value as a healthy context for raising children are well known. Less often recognized is that marriage is a powerful instrument for personal growth. It is ironic that people sometimes view divorce rather than marriage as a source of personal liberation. In fact, the very opposite is true: marriage is a vehicle of psychological and spiritual liberation second to none. Deeply buried issues of the heart and psyche come to the surface in married life. In the context of a lifelong, total commitment, such issues can be resolved and healed. Marital therapist Harville Hendrix says, "I want couples to know that, in order to obtain maximum psychological and spiritual growth, they need to stay together not for three months or three years or even three decades, but for all of their remaining years."[39]

Marriage is an accepted, healthy and time-honored way for human beings to attain a sense of wholeness. The security of an unconditionally loving relationship provides an individual with the space to grow and to test new waters, without fear of rejection or disapproval. Psychologist Judith Wallerstein reports that the men she interviewed in her study of happy marriages claimed that they could access their feelings in new and deep ways thanks to the influence of their intimate relationship with their wives: "They felt as if they had recaptured a lost part of themselves. One man said, 'Because of her, I'm sure of how I feel. With her, I feel whole.'"[40]

Despite the stereotype about a wife being kept in her husband's shadow, many modern women find marriage to be a practical and realistic vehicle to greater independence and fulfillment. Social critic Diane Medved asserts that a supportive, loving husband can help a woman to challenge new arenas and take on more responsibilities as the security and stability of their bond gives her the strength and courage to take risks and experiment.[41]

Likewise, when a married woman is in contact with her "animus" or more masculine aspect through her deep relationship with her husband, she has more access to and moves about with more ease in the world of men. Linda, a newly married businesswoman in Los Angeles, says of her husband, Manuel, "It's been like the difference between night and day in my relationships with my male co-workers. I can face them and interact with them confidently because Manny's there, inside my heart, backing me up. No matter what happens or what others say, I know he will support me. I know I can go home to him and be safe and loved."

Marriage and Community

In recognition of the intensely personal side of male-female relationships, the contemporary view of marriage is an essentially private matter between the two people, unrelated to and not answerable to the larger communities and networks to which the couple belongs. This over-correction of past emphases on duty and obligation has lost sight of one of the chief purposes of marriage—as a building block of community.

Traditionally, a person marries into a network of neighbors and relatives linked by duties and obligations. Marriage marks the stage when adults shoulder community responsibilities to provide for children, help kinfolk and care for the elderly. In this cultural milieu, marriage is other-focused from the first. This marriage ethic implies strength and perpetuity. However, when people migrate from their hometown of origin in search of work and new opportunities, they loosen the family's connection to their kin and community. A recent demographic study shows that frequent migrations are associated with increased divorce rates.[42]

Conversely, community support for marriage presupposes that it will be a lasting and praiseworthy union. When a serious commitment is made before relatives and friends, they feel obliged to support it. However, when the vows are considered negotiable, the larger communities and networks in which the couple participates tend to feel less committed to the marriage as well. As columnist William Raspberry quipped, a son-in-law commands more of a father-in-law's assistance than does a live-in boyfriend. When wedding guests can't help wondering, even as the couple is walking down the aisle, how long the marriage is going to last, their support can only be lukewarm. Diane Sollee, executive director of the Coalition for Marriage, Family and Couples Education, said that she stopped giving the usual wedding gifts. She was tired of wondering who was going to get the lovely piece of china or the crystal vase once the marriage broke up. Instead, she gives couples tickets to marriage education seminars, hoping that they will help the marriage work out.

Ties that Bind

Marriage merges more than two individuals. It also merges two lineages, perpetuating a bloodline and providing a tangible link to all who have gone before and all who will come after. Marriage introduces entirely new networks of support, friendship and relatedness among people who would not even know each other but for a marriage among them. When author and history professor Richard Rubenstein expressed his delight with his Chinese daughter-in-law and grandchildren to an audience of visiting Chinese educators, one of them rose and said, "In the future, our countries will not only be friends—we will be in-laws!" It is hard to hate people to whom one is related by marriage and, via descendants, blood.

The role of marriage in forging bonds of peace and friendship between groups has been recognized for centuries. *Romeo and Juliet* is the story of marital love conquering the hatred of two clans. Alexander the Great consolidated his empire by encouraging marriage between his Greek officers and the vanquished Persians. He knew that marriage was the most effective way to make diverse peoples into one. As men and women of different national, racial and ethnic lineages blend together in marriage, they have powerful potential to reduce interracial and international strife.

"My mother was from Israel and my father was Egyptian," says Barbara, an interior decorator on the west coast. "We all know the problems in the Middle East. But growing up, I never felt those problems. When our families got together for holidays, no one knew terrorism, massacres, or prejudice. We all thought everyone was like us. I was surprised in my later years when I found out they were not!" Sydney, an African-American woman married to a white man, says, "Interracial marriage? Please! I can write the book. Being a black woman married to a white man in America has not been easy. But when I tell you it feels like we have solved the problems of slavery and resentment within the last 100 years in our marriage, I am not joking!" In cases such as these, the old saying "Love conquers all" has come true as people from diverse backgrounds come together in marriage.

Encompassing this kind of power and scope, marriage deserves to reclaim its central role in human affairs. Marriage has transcended all times and cultures. From a village temple outside New Delhi to St. Patrick's Cathedral in New York, people gather in groups to witness the vows of men and women planning to go on life's journey together. Marriage affirms the timeless, elemental relationship between man and woman and their role as progenitors of the future. It offers enduring and irreplaceable benefits to men, women and children as well as to society. To cheapen marriage and deny its efficacy is to disparage the totality of human experience. To honor marriage and affirm its implications is to elevate human life from atomistic chaos into creative, coherent community.

20

Preparing Youth for Marriage

For one human being to love another: That is perhaps the most difficult of all our tasks...the work for which all other work is but preparation.

—Rainer Maria Rilke

IN THE PAST, PREPARATION FOR MARRIAGE WAS DONE INFORMALLY by family and community life. In the present era, this traditional training is proving inadequate. Too many couples divorce and too many youth lack the confidence to enter into lifelong marriage. "I want to get married but I don't know what it looks like," said one teenage boy.[1] Indeed, some adolescents do not even know still-married adults to consult about how to make marriage last.

Nevertheless, teenagers and young adults are intensely interested in marital success. Psychologist Howard Markman reports they score higher than previous generations in interviews designed to gauge how committed they are to their relationships. "They know marriage is risky, but there's a stronger sense of commitment," he says. "The bad news is, they don't have a clue how to make their relationships work."[2]

It is ironic to contrast the sizeable investment of time and money young people make in preparing for career and financial success versus the meager investment put into conscious preparation for what is likely to be more critical to their future satisfaction—marriage. After their engagement, the average couple spends far more time and energy on organizing the one-day wedding ceremony than they do on readying themselves for the marriage itself, which they hope will last for many decades.

As a result, more and more schools are instituting formal classes in marriage preparation. Phyllis Hess, a counselor in Claremore, Oklahoma, decided to take action when she heard a teenager describing the plan for her life: "Go to college, get married, get divorced and then get married again." Hess says, "That spoke volumes to me."[3] A 17-year-old girl explains the rationale behind her class. "It's preventative.... They're doing this so we don't get divorced. Finally, society realized it has to do something."[4]

While marriage guidance still holds a stigma for older adults, the younger generation has fewer reservations about learning what research and experience can provide. "I want to find out everything I can," says Dipti, a high school senior. "Love is obviously not enough." Marriage education is romantic, asserts Diane Sollee. What could be more romantic than to say, "Beloved... I want to marry you and I love you so much that I want to learn everything the experts know about what makes marriage succeed or fail so that our love, and our marriage, has a chance to last"?[5]

Marriage Education Programs

Starting in 1999, the state of Florida mandated marriage education for all ninth or tenth grade students. In 1998, judges and lawyers in Oklahoma succeeded in getting a marriage preparation program developed by a divorce lawyer and the American Bar Association into all their high schools. South Dakota adopted statewide a relationships course developed by a high school psychology teacher. Minneapolis high schools now require a one-year program before graduation. Hundreds of other school districts nationwide likewise have adopted marriage preparation courses. Parents have generally applauded these programs. "I've had single moms and dads come back and say, 'This is great. I wish I had known this sooner,'" reports Char Kamper, teacher and curriculum designer.[6]

Elements of Marriage Preparation

Personal Resources for Marriage

· Becoming a good marriage prospect

· Sexual abstinence

Learning about Love

· Love as a decision

· Discerning kinds of love

· Insights about Marriage

Relational Resources

· Learning from parents

· Diversity of friendships

· Communication and conflict resolution skills

Courses in American universities are also popular. A new major, Marriage and Family Studies, is being offered at Philadelphia's Allentown College of St. Francis de Sales, aimed not at counselors but towards students aspiring to be good spouses and parents.[7] In addition, there is a surge of interest in marriage mentoring for engaged couples.[8] This represents an effort to reestablish the kind of informal modeling of elder couples to younger couples that the traditional extended family—of parents, grandparents and aunts and uncles—once provided.

Does marriage education work? Scott Gardner at South Dakota State University found that after a one-semester course, students were more likely to reason out arguments than resort to aggressive behavior.[9] Where cities have instituted the "Community Marriage Policy"—in which judges and clergy agree to conduct marriages only for couples who have received premarital education and counseling—divorce rates have dropped dramatically.[10]

There is also a natural synergy between the new marriage education programs and character education. Parents, teachers and others involved with character education find their task is most challenging in the upper grades. This is a time when adolescents no longer uncritically receive guidance from their elders and their attention is more focused on outward success, especially in romance, than on inner virtues. Education in matters of love, however, captures their interest; marriage preparation courses are consistently popular. Character can be promoted in this context as furthering their hopes for lasting marriage.

Personal Resources for Marriage

Young people dramatically increase their chances for future marital success when they develop requisite personal resources such as character, respect and integrity, when they have access to accurate information about love and marriage, and when they develop social competencies for maintaining healthy relationships.

Becoming a Good Marriage Prospect

Young singles looking for a romantic partner are typically attracted to external traits. Physical attractiveness, economic potential and social status are usually high on the list. These are not, however, the qualities that they are likely to value in their spouses after they marry. Happily married couples, when they evaluate each other, tend to emphasize inner qualities: caring, honesty, trust, fidelity, commitment, and self-sacrifice for the sake of the marriage. They value communication skills, companionship and humor.[11]

In a survey of 300,000 wives, most admitted they chose their husbands based on sex appeal. If they could choose again, 80 percent said they would put communication skills as the first criterion.[12] Good looks, moneymaking potential and social status can change, but the inner qualities of character are foundational for enduring relationships. Of course, they are the same qualities that are valued in any relationship, be it with family members, co-workers or friends. "Love as an act of giving," writes Erich Fromm, "depends on the character development of a person."[13]

The rosy glow of romantic love notwithstanding, young men and women do well to assess the character of a potential marriage partner. What is in his heart? What is her deepest motivation in life? What values does he hold dear? These are what endure over a lifetime. A potential mate who is selfish, unappreciative, lazy, ill-tempered or dishonest is unlikely to change after the wedding.

Students can get a foretaste of this in marriage preparation courses where they participate in a more serious variation of the childhood game, playing house. Students are paired up in pretend marriages lasting over the course of several class periods.[14] As the make-believe "spouses" have to work as partners to cope with a series of realistic problems involving issues such as money and children, they discover that even a make-believe marriage demands real-world virtues and relational skills—traits that have little to do with attractiveness or charm. Students complain, "My partner doesn't listen," "My partner makes all the decisions and doesn't ask me," "My partner doesn't do much around the house."[15] The exercise helps teenagers better realize the truth in the old saying that "Love is blind; marriage opens your eyes." Sometimes when dating couples that think they are in love enter into this pretend marriage, they discover things about each other that they didn't know and decide to break up.

On the other hand, even such imaginary adversities can reveal a student's deeper beauty. One boy saddled with the assigned difficulties of "widowhood," "low salary" and "six children" had to solve a family vacation challenge. He had his "family" camp out in his backyard, using borrowed equipment and a lot of ingenuity. These are unforgettable lessons for later life. The marriage class "made me think about my relationships with other people more in-depth than I did before," said Loni Estes, a high school senior. "Now, before I would let myself get close to someone, I would want to find out who they are, and their values and beliefs."

Ovid said, "To be loved, be lovable." Teenagers can appreciate that it is unfair to expect a potential spouse to have qualities that they do not have themselves. The paradox is that the best way for a person to attract a fine marriage prospect is to become that kind of person him or herself. Daily efforts to prepare their own characters to be a good and worthy mate are a worthwhile investment. Character traits cultivated through experiences in the child's and sibling's spheres of love can serve adolescents well as they anticipate making the transition into the world of married love. (See Chapters 15 and 16) Among these are integrity, personal development, respect for parents and sexual abstinence. Marriage education guides youth in self-assessments of their character and provides incentives to work on improving themselves with the goal of successful marriage in mind.

Integrity

The ability to follow through on the commitment of marriage is rooted in basic integrity. This is a fruit of general character education. When students at Virginia Institute of Technology were asked what they most treasured in a relationship, trust was by far the first choice.[16] Integrity breeds trust.

Having the habit of consulting the conscience when making decisions is a valuable asset to bring to married life.[17] It helps adults meet the constant challenge to set priorities among duties to spouse, child, work and community. Further, integrity figures in loyally living up to the marriage vows, even when the going gets rough.

Integrity also demands the practice of self-discipline. A key attribute of self-discipline is the ability to delay gratification for the sake of long-term goals. What could be more necessary for the mother who must work two jobs to support her family or the husband who will care for his ailing wife into their old age? When teachers ask students to consider the consequences of one spouse's reckless spending, alcohol abuse or infidelity on a family, this also helps them consider the role of self-discipline in married life.[18]

Personal Development

Good friends seek each other's company to share their abundance as well as to fill their needs, and so it is in a healthy marriage. The personal stability that spouses bring to their marriage makes it stronger. This is the paradox of each person needing to be a whole individual to be part of a whole union. Psychologist Les Parrott has his relationship education students recite: "If you try to find intimacy with another person before achieving a sense of identity on your own, all your relationships become an attempt to complete yourself."[19] It is better to approach marriage with a certain amount of maturity and independence. This calls for young people prior to marriage to make efforts to develop their personhood. Personal development involves issues of self-respect, interests and talents, solitude, self-knowledge and contentment.

Self-respect and self-worth are, in the words of the PAIRS for PEERS program, the "indispensable foundation" for relationship.[20] A deficiency leaves a person vulnerable. To fill the void he may end up trying to gain approval from his partner. This opens the door to self-deception and manipulation. No one can insist on being treated with respect and honor if he does not respect and honor himself. It is valuable for teenagers to understand when problems with friends and family are due to a sagging sense of self worth. Letting them identify their own admirable qualities and competencies, and giving them opportunities to make a positive difference in the lives of others, fosters their growth in this area.

Personal development naturally involves cultivating interests and talents. To avoid the tendency of married couples to fall into a deep boredom with each other, each spouse needs to be interesting and interested, to keep growing as a person and cultivating his or her hobbies and talents. A good time to start is in earlier years.

Perhaps a less-considered area of personal development is learning to use solitude well. Rather than being anti-social, this includes learning how to enjoy one's own company, being able to listen to one's own thoughts, feelings and conscience, and making peace with them. It means taking time to "identify individual goals, interests, friendships and dreams," as the Survival Skills for Healthy Families program advises.[21] In addition, it means knowing how to refill one's own cup of inner resources, to spiritually rejuvenate.[22] By occasionally foregoing the easy pleasures of socializing and entertainment and seeking out a quiet place, perhaps in nature, teenagers learn to face themselves and find renewal within.

Self-knowledge is another aspect of personal development. Natomas High School in Sacramento, California, uses a personality test to help students understand their own temperaments, strengths and weaknesses.[23] The Building Relationships program uses quizzes for self-discovery.[24] "My students are recognizing some of their own shortcomings," says a Chicago teacher employing the Partners program.[25] Adolescents love to learn about themselves, and this provides objective feedback that helps them to know what to work on, what challenges to expect for themselves in various circumstances, and what to look for in friends and a mate.

Counselors Judd and Mary Landis assert, "The most important characteristic of a marriageable person is the habit of happiness."[26]

This refers to another invaluable virtue for teenagers to learn: taking responsibility for their attitude in a given situation. Too often young people expect a spouse to fulfill them or that the marriage itself will solve all their problems. Psychiatrist Frank Pittman has quipped, "Marriage isn't supposed to make you happy. It is supposed to make you married.... You have a structure... from which you are free to make yourself happy."[27] To a great extent, individuals decide their own happiness, regardless of their mates.

Many marriage education programs help youth at all grade levels cultivate their basic emotional intelligence, the ability to identify and manage their own feelings.[28] A key skill is being able to admit their feelings to themselves, especially negative ones, and to know what to constructively do with them. PAIRS for PEERS introduces students to the layers of unpleasant feelings that can be bottled up in their "Emotional Jug" and how to release them without "popping their cork."[29]

Sexual Abstinence

The attitude and practice of sexual abstinence creates an excellent context for the other primary components of marriage preparation. It allows for the strengthening of character free from the moral compromises of sexual involvements; it allows for personal development free from sexual distractions; and it allows for friendship building free from sexual complications. These in turn tend to reinforce postponing sexual activity. Individuals with integrity, a close relationship with their parents, many good friendships and cultivated talents and interests find abstinence less of a challenge.

At the same time, those who practice abstinence tend to have a more positive view of marriage. Research found that virgins have more favorable attitudes toward marriage than do nonvirgins who had multiple sex partners.[30] No doubt both abstinence and pro-marriage attitudes reinforce each other. This reaffirms the affinity that marriage education and abstinence education have for each other. Boston University's *The Art of Loving Well* is a literature-based course that is used for both purposes.[31] Marriage education sustains the hope of a happy committed relationship, making the choice of saving sexual activity until marriage more viable and attractive. Even where marriage preparation courses do not have an explicit abstinence message, educators report that the very discussion of the demands and rewards of committed relationships reinforces the concept of abstinence before such relationships.[32]

Teenage Marriage: Making It an Option

Over 90 percent of American adults consider teenage marriage to be a disaster in the making.[33] In fact, contemporary high school health textbooks seem to favor unwed teenage parenthood over teenage marriage. The courage, commitment and social support recommended to help young single mothers cope are not considered sufficient to sustain young married couples.

Yet is adolescent marriage so hopeless? Sociologist Maggie Gallagher points out that though these unions are shakier than others, half of marriages among older teenagers currently do survive, as opposed to about 70 percent of those where the bride is at least 23 years old. With character, relationship and marriage education as well as greater community support, adolescents may do well to get an early start on realizing the rewards of marriage and family life.

For single girls who get pregnant, contrary to conventional wisdom, marriage is a desirable route. Research shows marriages to legitimate a pregnancy are on average no less grounded than other marriages. Marriage is also what these girls want, and if they do not marry the father the chances of a wedding are half those of their childless peers.[34]

Learning about Love

"I was a victim of poetry about marriage," admits Lynn Dixon, who teaches a high school marriage course in Philadelphia. Now divorced, she says she could have used such a program herself. "Love does not [just] flow like a river."[35]

Natural romantics, adolescents are eager for any insights into love that they can find. Yet love is so commonly misrepresented and misunderstood as to be probably the most significant source of confusion in marriage. Adolescents benefit immeasurably from knowledge about love's true nature, and what is required to sustain and enhance a love that lasts. The important understandings to convey about love have to do with its volitional component and how to distinguish true love (see opposite) from its look-alikes.

Love as a Decision

"While it sounds romantic to 'fall' in love, the truth is that we *decide* who we want to love," asserts the Connections program.[36] Marriage education typically seeks to counter the popular myth of "falling in love": that an overwhelming, irresistible feeling that springs up spontaneously between two people leads to true and lasting love between the partners. The challenge is merely to find the right person who arouses this feeling. If problems arise later, the assumption is that it was the wrong person after all and the relationship should end.

This neglects the volitional aspect of loving, as marriage expert Gary Smalley suggests in his book, *Love Is a Decision*. A mature and genuinely loving person is committed to being loving whether or not he or she feels loving at the time.[37] It is true that the feeling aspect of love—as a strong state of liking—is beyond control.[38] However, the other aspect— as a chosen attitude and behavior—is not, and can influence the other. In other words, the decision to love can encourage the feeling of love.[39]

Understanding love as involving an act of will brings in the element of choice. This can be a source of freedom and security for adolescents. Teenagers often struggle with fears that certain flaws mean no one can love them or that married love will someday vanish. "If we fall out of love," they wonder, "how can we bring it back?" They can learn it is possible to generate love even when it is not readily flowing. In addition, if it is indeed true that it is not whom they love that counts as much as how they love, then they don't have to be waiting helplessly to bump into the "right one." They can be getting practice and building confidence in becoming loving persons. Finally, the notion of love as an active verb helps teenagers grasp the key difference between maturity and immaturity—the immature focus on being loved; the mature focus on giving love.

Discerning Different Qualities of Love

Infatuation or Self-Centered Love	True Love
Prefers to be receiving	Enjoys giving
Judges the other according to how well they make them feel loved	Judges themselves and how they can give more to the other
Focuses on the other's—and their own—external traits, such as looks, income and status	Cherishes the other most for their good heart and character
Makes the other feel anxious	Makes the other feel secure
Starts up quickly and ends just as quickly	Grows steadily and ends slowly if at all
Separation and time weakens the bond	Separation and time intensifies the bond
Fosters self-absorption within the couple and exclusion of others	Encourages reaching out to others
Relationship has priority over virtue	Virtue is a basis of the relationship
Hinders productivity	Enhances productivity
Quarrels crop up with increasing frequency and severity	Quarrels arise less and less over time, with less intensity
Conflicts poison and can destroy the relationship	Conflicts deepen the partners' mutual understanding and intimacy

Discerning Kinds of Love

One of the most fundamental insights adolescents want to learn is how to distinguish between true love and its precursor or counterfeit: crushes, infatuation, or unhealthy attachments. They can come to recognize that only when the heart's impulse filters through a strong and virtuous character will love prove true and lasting.

Loving Well and other curricula help adolescents reflect on different kinds of love.[40] Leon and Amy Kass, both University of Chicago professors and husband and wife of 40 years, conduct a college seminar on love and courtship that offers readings from Shakespeare, Plato, Aristotle, the Old Testament, Jane Austen and other sources to inspire discussion about "noble examples of romance."[41] "Love must be learned, and learned again and again; there is no end to it," remarks author Katherine Anne Porter.[42] Adults can help adolescents by giving them a good map for their explorations.

Insights about Marriage

There are certain objective realities about marriage itself that too few people know. Passing these on can help teenagers better comprehend the marriage commitment in its fullness. They will also more realistically anticipate its many challenges and rewards and not interpret its inevitable ups and downs as evidence that there is something fundamentally wrong with either them, their spouse or the relationship.

One valuable if unromantic piece of information concerns marriage and divorce laws. Martin Luther High School in Philadelphia teaches about this with the aid of a nearby legal office. The public implications of such a private matter as marriage are a revelation to many teenagers. For instance, it is sobering for young men to learn that the law requires them to finance any child they might have for 18 years, even if they choose not to marry or if they would have a divorce.[43] Thus youth can better understand how society holds them accountable for the commitment they will make.

It is not commonly recognized that marital relationships pass through several predictable phases—romance, conflict, recommitment and service—before reaching the goal of deep oneness of heart that is so attractive in couples of enduring love. (See Chapter 17) Marriage courses encourage students to reflect on the inevitable seasons of all relationships, including marriage, with such questions as, "How has your relationship with your parents changed as you have matured?" Teenagers can be dismayed by the degree to which even minor issues can generate conflicts in their own relationships and in the marriages they see around them.[44] When they understand in advance that the initial romantic phase will inevitably give way to a phase of disillusionment and tension, which in turn presents the opportunity to find union on a deeper level, they can avoid the mistake of giving up when difficulties arise. They can better appreciate the necessity of traits such as patience, resilience and tolerance, and that some pain is a necessary part of the real work of creating the basis for lasting love. They also gain the perspective to better interpret the committed relationships around them. "My parents would have benefited from a program like this," says a 17-year-old son of divorced parents.[45]

Relational Resources

Research has shown that strong relationships with parents, teachers, mentors, elders, siblings, cousins and friends build up a sense of self-worth and meet a young person's needs for love and acceptance. Improving relations with friends and relatives can lessen the appeal of premature romantic or sexual involvements and strengthen chances for marital success. Strong foundations in the sibling's and child's spheres of love—solid friendships, good relationships with parents and teachers, and the insights and social skills that go along with them—are invaluable resources to bring to a marriage.

Learning from Parents

Parents' love and guidance remains an important anchor, even as their son or daughter explores romantic love and prepares for family life. A young person's relationship with his parents helps fortify his identity and value system, to better ground his character. Moreover, it is a lifeline by which the parents can guide him and help him avoid serious mistakes in love.

Positive experiences with their opposite-sex parent teach adolescents how they should treat and expect to be treated by the other gender. "I don't know why some of my friends put up with what they put up with from boys," says Yukimi, a high school junior. "My Dad treated my mother and I like we were special, and I expect the same kind of respect from any boy who expects to have a serious relationship with me." Adolescents also learn from observing how their parents relate to one another.

Naturally, parents do not always provide good models. When their parents fall short, young people can compensate by looking elsewhere for parental role models as well as learning from their parents' mistakes. Jamie, a student at Iowa State University, reflected about the impact of her parents on her concerns about marriage. She has always felt close to her mother, but her father was an unhappy, brooding man, inclined to take out his anger on the children with emotional and sometimes physical abuse. Realizing that her father could not be her best role model in his present state, Jamie decided to accommodate this need in her life through her church pastor, a happily married man whom she respected and trusted. Throughout her late teens she came to rely on him for guidance and wisdom. Describing him as "my mentor," Jamie still calls him now and then even though she has been away at college for almost two years.

Adolescents who are distant from their parents, especially the opposite-sex parent, are more susceptible to unhealthy obsessions with the opposite sex. Researcher Carole Pistole suggests that teenagers often turn to one another for love when their parental attachment needs are not being met.[46] The girl starved for her father's attention is particularly vulnerable to the selfish sexual advances of boys. The boy who is longing for the tender comfort of his mother is more tempted into infatuations with girls and to seek comfort sexually. Adolescents who are aware of this may be more alert to their vulnerability, and they can try to improve their connection to their parents or other elders.

Parents are a valuable source of wisdom on matters of love and selecting a potential mate. Adolescent sons and daughters are torn between wanting guidance and asserting their independence, especially in matters as personal as romance. Still, there are ways for teachers and other adults to encourage them to seek their parents' help and approval in selecting someone to date and marry. One simple, nonthreatening exercise is to have students ask their parents to list the qualities they see as most desirable in a spouse, and discuss why. "I have to confess; my Mom made more sense than I expected," says Jameel, a middle-school student. "I can see some of the 'hot' girls aren't really so hot." Through such discussions, they may recognize that their parents have objectivity and wisdom in matters of love that they lack.

Diversity of Friendships

If the best marriages are great friendships, it stands to reason that developing qualities of a good friend will help anyone succeed in marriage. Competency in making and keeping friendships includes learning how to relate harmoniously with many different types of people—older and younger, male and female, from different backgrounds and walks of life. After all, a great variety of people will become permanently a part of their world when they get married. The spouse, in-laws and even their own children will present personality traits and points of view that can be quite challenging.

This is why a popular marriage preparation course at Seattle Pacific University coaches students in negotiating the full spectrum of relationships, "making bad relationships better and good relationships great." It challenges students to reflect on such issues as:

> Of the four qualities that keep friendship going—loyalty, forgiveness, honesty and dedication—which one is most important to you and why?

> Relationships fail because of change, neglect or betrayal. As you consider your own failed friendships, what can the cause tell you about finding the "cure"?

> When it comes to the practical side of mending a broken relationship...which [possible step] would be most difficult for you to take and why?[47]

Friendships help develop the necessary marriage-building skills that sustain relationships over time. A marriage commands loyalty and sacrifices even if the people within it sometimes do not seem deserving.[48] Educators can encourage students to stick with teammates or a particular friendship despite how the team member or friend may have disappointed them.

Any relationship demands regular maintenance, some sort of regular shared activities, whether play, work or conversation. These have to be adjusted and renewed as circumstances shift. The skills spouses need to keep their connection to each other[49] —and what parents need to stay current with their older children[50]—are best honed in earlier friendships. Teenagers can also notice the greater depth and resilience of friendships forged within the context of unselfish service to others. If the desirable final phase of marriage involves service to others, it is only wise to orient the young in this direction. Thus, service learning augments marriage preparation, though it is seldom a part of a formal marriage program.

Relating with the Opposite Sex

Just as students benefit from learning how to deal well with a diversity of people, "crossing the gender line"[51] helps them to respect, understand and appreciate members of the opposite sex. Many marital difficulties arise because men and women are so different from one another—in the way they process information, communicate, respond to crises and in other areas. These differences can either grate on each other or complement each other, depending on how men and women respond. Just being aware of these differences helps students to accept as normal certain challenges in the partnership of masculinity and femininity that is marriage.

The insights needed to understand the other gender are best gained in relationships free of the disruptive influence of sexual gamesmanship. Of course, making friends with the opposite sex without sexualizing the relationship is not always easy.[52] To do this requires knowing how to recognize sexual attraction, cool down the relationship and rechannel the energy away from romance and towards friendship.

Dating is, of course, one component of relating to the other gender. Most marriage programs lead adolescents to reflect upon and develop healthier dating attitudes and practices. However, especially for young or pre-adolescents, engaging in one-on-one dating does not necessarily serve youth's best interests. Getting involved in intense relationships when there is no prospect of commitment serves no healthy purpose. Some have described early dating as training for divorce, since there must be necessarily a series of broken involvements.[53] Certainly, dating increases pressure to engage in unnecessary levels of physical intimacy. Research correlates earlier dating with earlier sexual encounters.[54]

Furthermore, the artificiality of dating is a detriment. It discourages natural connections based on shared values and activities. Since on a date people tend to be on their best behavior, it tends to conceal an individual's real character and makes it harder to evaluate a prospective spouse. Dating encourages a starry-eyed view of the other person that invites undue emotional involvement, infatuation and physical intimacy.[55] This is one reason why the Single Volunteers program in Washington, D.C. has young people meeting while doing community service, "with no make-up on and up to their knees in mud," according to co-founder Dana Kresierrer. "It's about who you are, not what you look like or how much money you make." Participants say they make solid friendships there that sometimes lead to marriage.[56]

Group dating is a noteworthy new trend at universities, where students socialize in unpartnered groups.[57] Group dating not only avoids the complications of one-on-one dating but offers many practical advantages: less pressure to have to relate to only one person, the sharing of expenses, transportation and responsibility for planning activities, and so on. Many parents appreciate school support in helping them guide their teenagers as to what to wear, planning fun activities for the date, how to recognize when a situation is unsafe and when to leave, and other relevant points.

Also promising is the rising courtship movement, which sets out guidelines such as this one by Karla Griffin, director of a prominent courtship-training and singles service in Denver: "Instead of going out on dates, do things with your friends and family."[58]

In addition, adults can encourage adolescents to spend time with the opposite sex in situations that foster friendships. "I think dates are weird," says Selena, a teenager in New Jersey. "I work on the stage crew at the community theatre and you can meet boys there and it's a lot more natural way to get to know them.... You have something to talk about." In some towns, parents, school personnel and community leaders provide chaperoned, drug- and alcohol-free settings where teenagers and young adults may constructively socialize. The Mountain Pointe High School in Phoenix, Arizona, for example, creates a plethora of supervised activities for teenagers to enjoy on Prom Night as an alternative to the typical circumstances that invite unhealthy behavior.[59]

Communication and Conflict Resolution Skills

"Lack of communication" is the classic relationship killer. The prominent marriage courses all feature training in listening and communication skills.[60] (See Chapter 21) These techniques reflect and reinforce the character traits that facilitate strong relationships and are often used to rebuild empathy and understanding when the connection has broken down. Through the PAIRS for PEERS program, Chicago teenagers are learning a simple technique for sustaining relationships. This consists of addressing five categories of connection that married couples share regularly, even if only for a few minutes: expressing appreciation, conveying news, constructive complaining and requesting changes, asking questions and sharing hopes. Awareness of these intimacy-builders helps remove the mystique from what it takes to make and sustain an emotional connection. After the course, a student reported, "I appreciate people more and I don't take them for granted."[61] Closeness is seldom sustained by magic; it has to be intentionally engineered into a relationship.

Learning how to handle tensions skillfully is a great advantage, tested no more vigorously than in marriage. Effective marriage education programs give coaching in the essential points of reducing conflict,[62] such as defining the issue clearly and sticking to it, and not bringing in old points of dispute that confuse and escalate the conflict. They also provide practice in avoiding such poisonous practices as personal criticism, contempt, defensiveness and stonewalling. Helping teenagers recognize these behaviors and develop habits that are more constructive is preventive of harmful marital mistakes later. "You have to try and compromise. This told me how to go about it," says an Illinois high school girl about her class.[63]

Marriage preparation education is an investment that not only bolsters family stability and community well-being; it also fulfills the dreams of all young people for enduring love. "The degree to which adolescents believe in being in love is absolutely extraordinary," says sociologist John Gagnon. The vast majority of American youth want to marry and raise children. And though not every one of them is capable of excelling in business or academics or other areas of life, each has a chance to excel at creating a loving marriage and a beautiful family.[64] Thomas Langridge, 16, said of his marriage education course, "All students should take a class like this. If they do, they won't just jump into marriage. They'll think about it, know each other better and know what to expect from each other."[65]

21

Character and Skills for Resilient Marriages

STRONG MARRIAGES ARE ESSENTIAL IN CREATING THE WARM, stable home environment that is central to children's moral development. They model healthy, harmonious interactions that are necessary for children to attain loving relationships in their own lives. Marriage programs such as Marriage Encounter, Family Wellness, Imago, PAIRS for PEERS, Prepare/Enrich, etc. have done wonders for couples by providing new research-based information with proven principles of relationship-building that make for fulfilling marriages.

Most of these principles and techniques have moral implications. The skills most effective in facilitating relationships are those that also foster character growth and the unselfish habits that enable people to sustain long-lasting and satisfying marital relationships. Thus, just as character education is interconnected with marriage education for youth (see Chapter 20), so it is with marriage enrichment programs for couples. Developing character and the associated relational skills is a lifelong endeavor. This is self-evident from the perspective of the Basic Life Goals and the Four Spheres of Love model of moral development through the family. Marriage enhancement efforts thus support the task of character maturation in adult life even as it helps couples deepen their intimacy and develop resiliency in the face of the inevitable challenges that they will encounter.

The Anchors of Commitment and Fidelity

Establishing lifelong intimacy and joy in marriage does not come about serendipitously. It is achieved through the practice of virtues and gaining competency in managing a long-term relationship. "It took me a while to catch on," recalls Josh, 32, a realtor in the Midwest, about his first year of marriage. "After the first few months, I started getting upset when Tamar didn't automatically make me feel as important and do things for me as I wanted and I got pretty demanding. My Dad tipped me off: Nothing is automatic. I've got to give respect and earn respect just like when I started my business."

The foundation of character is primary. Virtues such as forgiveness, respect and self-control help fortify a marriage. Their cultivation strengthens the relationship to stand the test of time and provides the life satisfaction couples earnestly desire. Yet above all else, the fundamental anchors of a marriage are the moral values of commitment and fidelity.

Commitment and fidelity function as both an axis and a compass for marriage. Commitment is like a cornerstone, and fidelity offers ethical boundaries. Girded with these foundational virtues, couples are deeply united and fulfilled. They can enjoy trust, intimacy and freedom because they feel confident of each other's total loyalty and support.

Commitment

A marriage based solely upon changeable, romantic feelings of love is hard put to weather the inevitable storms that are characteristic of all marriages and of life itself. There are times in every marriage when the partners need to persevere through the challenges that arise. Only commitment can see people through the moments when they no longer feel like going on, when disillusionment sets in, when conflicts are hard to resolve.

At the same time, commitment means more than a clenched-teeth determination to endure the marriage no matter what, as people have done in the past. John from Iowa, who is in his sixties, recalls a time when his grandparents did not speak to one another for an entire year. Divorce was then a socially unacceptable option, so couples endured whatever they had to in order to avoid breaking up the marriage—even if it meant complete emotional separation within the same house. No contemporary couple would dream of enduring such a situation.

Commitment to marriage today means dedication to making it work by seeking the help, skills training, support and mentoring needed for mutual fulfillment. Commitment involves the willingness to do what it takes to maintain a partnership through challenging circumstances and continually work to enrich it in times of normalcy.

Sometimes weathering the storm is the best solution. Such was the case for Ellen, a 34-year-old mother, and her husband Jack. Ellen had suffered a series of illnesses after the birth of her daughter. Jack was supposed to inherit his father's chemical company, but had been pushed out by the partners. He felt overwhelmed; he was unable to pay the doctor's-bills, he had trouble finding another job, and he complained bitterly of his wife's sour personality. They faced bankruptcy and lost their home, hitting "rock bottom." Ellen felt she had to endure the pressures these setbacks caused to their marriage for the sake of her daughter, even though she was tempted to divorce. By the end of the following year, however, their fortunes had changed considerably. Not only was their economic situation better, their marriage was, too. Commenting to a friend at her daughter's fifth birthday party, Ellen said, "I am so glad I didn't give up on Jack or our family. It was a very dark time and we are just beginning to believe in each other again, but at least we're still a team."[1]

Commitment also means refusing to indulge in escapism. Those who have escape hatches ready and available are less likely to do the work and apply the will necessary to get through difficult periods. There are many subtle ways to escape in marriage, from preoccupation with work or children to indulgence in endless television watching or other hobbies to avoid facing difficult emotions or subjects. Escaping is a survival tactic that temporarily may keep the peace but is unlikely to lead to fulfillment as a couple. Commitment requires that couples have the courage to face their difficulties consistently and creatively.

Consistency, dependability and trustworthiness build emotional safety and allow the relationship to thrive. It also provides the context to begin fully appreciating another person, a process that takes place over time. In fact, many couples feel that one lifetime is hardly enough to explore all the possibilities of loving another person. At the same time, it is long-term commitment that discloses what character and talents there are to admire. James, the 68-year-old husband of 70-year-old Lorna, said after fifty years of marriage: "She has so many fine qualities, I have even come to love her faults."

Fidelity

Marriage experts find that the two major relational fears people experience in intimate relationships are fear of abandonment and the fear of loss of autonomy. Once a partner has the safety net of the other's fidelity, he or she will slowly shed the fear of abandonment. A partner who is assured of his or her partner's faithfulness will be less dependent and clinging; hence, the other partner will feel more freedom and have a greater sense of autonomy. Fidelity assuages fear and gives the partners in the marriage a sense of security that comes from each spouse's unconditional support. It is essential to a happy and trusting marriage.

Most people agree that infidelity is destructive to a marriage.[2] Although some marriages can survive infidelity, it threatens conjugal resiliency to its very depths. One therapist who specializes in cases of infidelity describes in his patients a "volcano of pain" when they discover their spouse's cheating.

Infidelity usually involves deception of the spouse. A husband named Lewis described his affair, "I invented so many stories to explain my whereabouts; it was amazing that I was able to keep them straight. My secretary covered for me dozens of times. When my wife called, she'd tell her I was out of the office for an appointment, in a meeting that couldn't be interrupted, or unexpectedly tied up." Lewis wove a web of lies that compounded the pain his adultery had caused. The marriage counselors who treated Lewis and his wife said that spouses suffer as much from the feeling of being lied to and duped as they do from the sexual betrayal itself. "How can I ever trust him (her) again?" is the most frequently asked question they hear in such cases.[3]

Loving relationships depend on trust. Fulfillment and personal growth in marriage require the safety that mutual trust engenders. Partners reveal their innermost thoughts, fears and dreams to one another, and thus the risks of rejection and ridicule are felt most profoundly. Childhood fears, adolescent rejections, anxiety about attractiveness, aging, and one's own masculine or feminine adequacy all come to the fore in one way or another via the intimacy of marriage. Only if the marriage bed is inviolate can two vulnerable beings meet and become as one. Educator Catherine M. Wallace affirms that, "Intimacy arises only as fidelity is established and only to the extent that fidelity is realized. Intimacy is not possible except between two people who have a profound faith in one another. Sexual fidelity is a practice intrinsic to the happiness of a happy marriage.... [It] is a growing, living thing that interacts with and reorganizes all the other ingredients of the marriage."[4]

Healthy Attitudes for Lasting Relationships

Internally, there are certain attitudes that make for peace and growth between couples. Chief among them are acceptance, continual giving, and focus on a higher purpose. These particular dispositions strengthen a marriage by reducing self-centeredness and promoting altruistic, other-centered living.

Acceptance

Steven Wolin, author of *Resilient Marriages*, studied why some marriages failed and others bounced back from every conflict and adversity. Among his factors of resiliency, he listed the virtue of acceptance.[5]

The play *I Love You, You're Perfect, Now Change* describes the attitude of many people going into marriage. Yet, there are many things about a spouse that cannot be altered. Their essential personality is not going to change, and neither is their sense of humor. Their lifelong tastes and predilections will probably continue as is, along with many personal habits. This is not to say that in areas of serious fault such as alcoholism, drug addiction, the use of violence, infidelity and other serious breaches of the marital contract a partner should not speak up and strongly request change. It means that, barring such serious difficulties, marital partners learn to accept, encourage and support each other's growth.

Spouses who have a particular strength can help their partners develop this strength themselves. A spouse proficient in social skills for example, can patiently encourage a timid partner to relate to people more confidently. Partners learn to appreciate the other's good qualities and overlook imperfections or their different way of doing things. Transformed through acceptance, Margarita, a wife from Europe, shared her views on an Internet website for couples:

> The biggest change in our marriage came when... I put into practice the principle of acceptance. I began to see my husband in a new light. I saw and accepted him for who he

was—not someone I thought he should be.... To my amazement, I found a new spark ignited between my husband and
me.... In return, I am receiving the love I so desperately
longed for from him. We're just falling in love all over again,
only this time it's better because we know it's for real.[6]

The fact that the husband likes to watch football and the wife
wants nothing more than to sit in silence and sew is not a serious difficulty, but it can certainly lead to friction. The couple can pursue their
hobbies in different rooms and come together again later, refreshed.
Or the husband can learn to watch with the volume down while the
wife learns to sew in less than perfect silence. Or they can decide to skip
their habitual hobbies and go out and do something new they both find
pleasurable. Wolin said resilient couples come to accept and enjoy each
other in spite of their differences. They say to one another, "We're different. We've always been different. We'll always be different. Let's
dance."[7]

Paradoxically, once husbands and wives do not feel pressured to
change and feel accepted as they are, they are often less resistant to
making the effort to change in ways which will please their spouses.
Genuine acceptance, of course, cannot harbor this ulterior motive.
Change is an unexpected bonus of giving unconditional love.

Continual Giving

A marriage may be thought of as a garden that needs constant
tending. Gary Smalley offers another analogy. He advises couples to
think of giving to the relationship as an investment in a "marital bank
account."[8] A kind word or deed, a favor or service, a sympathetic ear or
sincere sharing of personal thoughts and feelings—these are deposits.
A harsh word or inconsiderate deed, a criticism or attack, neglect, and
putting up barriers to intimacy are withdrawals. Like a real bank
account, if the emotional reserves of the marriage are continually drawn
upon without being replenished, the couple's love will go bankrupt.
John Gottman recommends five deposits for every one withdrawal, or
a ratio of five positive interactions to one negative one.[9]

Giving tends to beget more giving, and the returning of the favors.
"When my wife Cathy is feeling neglected, when she wants us to get
closer, and even when she is mad at me, she takes the initiative to give
to me," says Robert, a writer and husband of 18 years. "Cathy will make

a special meal, offer me a massage, or rent a video I'd like. Now I notice: what she is giving is maybe what she'd appreciate getting from me. And it sure is easier to give back." Cathy confides, "When I'm feeling distant from Robert about something and don't feel like giving, I do it anyway and that helps me somehow warm up to him. I feel closer to him and it's easier to give some more." This habit of generosity is helpful in sustaining and reviving love.

In her study of good marriages, Judith Wallerstein found that the happy couples "were not envious of what they gave to the other. They did not dole out kindness with the expectation of immediate reimbursement. They did not weigh their gifts or keep records. Supporting and encouraging the other was a given. They accepted this major task not only as fair but as necessary to make the marriage succeed."[10]

One husband in a successful marriage commented, "I know many people who are divorcing, and I've noticed...that people expect more from their partner than they're willing to give themselves."[11] True love, it was noted, is to act with a warm heart for the benefit of the other. (See Chapter 4) Love is easy when the exchange is mutual, but it requires maturity and character strength to deal with the periods in a relationship when one partner has to "carry" the other when there is no emotional return. Honing the art of loving when the benefit is not immediately felt is a valuable individual goal for the sake of the partnership. It can spark the process where both become happily engaged in a circle of giving and receiving—the never-ending circle of a successful and fulfilling marriage.

A Higher Focus

"Love does not consist in gazing at each other but in looking together in the same direction," penned author Antoine de Saint-Exupery.[12] If the couple honors some ideal higher than their own pleasure in one another, they will be more resilient in the face of obstacles and difficulties. This ideal can be many things—the welfare of the children, religious faith, inner growth, or public service. A veteran of a thirty-year marriage, Bo Lozoff says, "I can be just as corrupt and wretched as anybody else. But the context—our shared belief in the search for truth—has always pulled us through."[13]

A focus on something beyond themselves helps smooth partners' exchanges and avoid friction. Pat and Eric, a couple from Philadelphia, were having guests over for dinner. They were quarreling over everything before the dinner guests arrived—the placement of the chairs, the color of the candles, whether the guests' coats should be hung up in the closet or put on the master bed. Of course, when the guests came to the door, the bickering ceased, and the couple made their best efforts to be polite to everyone and to each other. The evening turned out splendidly. Everyone had a good time. When the guests had gone home, Pat and Eric turned to one another and asked, "What were we fighting about?" Neither of them could remember, and with a shrug, they let it go. Because they had taken their focus off themselves and extended it to others—their guests—the couple found that their differences had evaporated.

Whether it is taking a neighborhood youngster under their wing or giving their time to a charitable organization, public service is the secret of many strong couples. Such an overarching cause can help them transcend temporary tensions and help them see each other in an admirable light. Tricia from Georgia recounts her parents' happy marriage of over fifty years:

> I always had this sense that their marriage was greater than the sum of its parts, more than just two individuals together. One time when they really believed in a presidential candidate, I hardly saw them in the weeks before the election. They were out canvassing and going to meetings, working hard for what they believed in. They often talked over the dinner table about society and politics. Whenever a crisis came up, they talked over their standards, their beliefs, how they thought it should be handled. They had ideals and they tried to live up to them. Their love was, as the old saying goes, "bigger than both of them."

Relational Skills

Good communication is basic in any cooperative endeavor, and working on communication skills is a cornerstone of most marriage enrichment programs. However, studies demonstrate that only 7 percent of communication is words. The rest comes through more subtly, through tone of voice, body language and the invisible but perceptible qualities of one's character. As Smalley observes, "When... courage, persistence, gratefulness, calmness, gentleness and unselfish love are... in a person's character, it is easier to receive his or her words."[14]

Nevertheless, communicating well is an art, and communication skills that build upon the foundation of good character are supportive of lasting marriage. There are proven techniques to improve one's ability to listen to one's partner. There are poisonous tactics to be avoided, as well as the common "communication traps"—those phrases and ways of speaking that multiply rather than solve problems. Couples also benefit from learning to choose the best time to discuss a sensitive topic and how to separate an issue from its emotional freight.

Identifying Relationship Poisons

John Gottman has identified the most virulent relationship poisons that come through during times of conflict. These threaten the very survival of the marriage if allowed to spread. He calls them "the Four Horsemen of the Apocalypse": criticism, contempt, defensiveness and stonewalling.[15] Any relationship displays these negative characteristics occasionally, but the danger comes when they take up permanent residency in a marriage.

These destructive tactics do not necessarily follow one another in exact order, although one certainly leads to another. They do feed on and encourage one another: for instance, criticism leads to contempt, which leads the other partner to display defensiveness and/or stonewalling. Complaint is reasonable when it targets a specific behavior or lack of one. But criticism is character assassination—laying on blame and making global judgments about the person, often using sarcasm, sneering, mockery and disgust. Understandably, the partner reacts with defensiveness. Defensiveness, in essence, denies that the problem lies with the accused party and tries to shift the blame back onto the other. Eventually, one partner may shut down and begin to stonewall. He or she will avoid the conflict altogether by physically getting out of the situation or by acting impervious to what the other spouse is saying. Unfortunately, stonewalling only drives the other partner into more virulent attacks, thinking the message of criticism and contempt is simply not getting through.

The antidote to these poisons is learning how to speak clearly and listen attentively, and communicate both with manner and words in a respectful, fair and constructive way.

Attention to the Message

Quite often what is left unsaid, or the attitude with which words are spoken, either prolongs peace or provokes strife.[16] For instance, Amanda and Harold, married over 10 years, had the following exchange:

Amanda: I just say one little thing and you fly off the handle. All I said was could you please move the stuff out of the way of the staircase.

Harold: You said could you *please* move the *stuff* out of the way of the staircase!? You were impatient and mad. The phone was ringing, I'm expecting an important call, the kids were all over the place and I just got home. I meant to move it; I just haven't had time.

Amanda: Okay, okay. I'm sorry. Please move it when you get a chance.

In this case, Harold accurately noted the emotional subtext beneath Amanda's words that amounted to an accusatory attitude on her part. Amanda admitted to this and, when apprised of Harold's stressed situation, became amicable instead of criticizing him.

A non-accusatory attitude is an important part of good communication. Cultivating a habit of appreciation—and expressing it often—prevents the harboring of accusatory and critical thoughts that may slip out in casual dialogue or explode during an argument. If necessary, a spouse can keep a running list of the other's good points to keep positive and appreciative feelings flowing. Expressing kind words to and about the spouse helps reinforce good feelings.

Lara, a 32-year-old dental technician, was complaining about her husband over the phone to a friend. The more Lara discussed his faults, the angrier and more hurt she became. As her feelings spiraled downward and she piled criticism upon criticism, the friend said mildly, "Is he really all that bad?" Lara stopped and thought; then she said slowly, "No, he isn't. In fact, there are a lot of things I appreciate about him." The friend suggested she name several, and Lara quietly counted off a handful of qualities she loved about him. Her mood changed. "I'm actually a pretty lucky girl," she commented as she signed off to make dinner for him.

Avoiding Communication Traps

The classic marital advice given by experts is to use "I" rather than "you" messages when communicating with a mate, especially about sensitive areas. Targeting the specific behavior without drawing conclusions about the overall character of the person is the idea. The speaker casts the message in terms of how it affects the person speaking. Saying, "I get nervous when the monthly bills start to pile up. I wish you would pay them promptly," is far less provocative and far more effective than saying, "You never pay the bills on time. I have to worry about everything!" "You" messages all too frequently turn into accusations, whereas "I" messages share useful information about how the behavior affects the partner. Such expressions invite the listener to access his or her concern for the spouse and to evaluate his or her behavior in light of this.

"Always" and "never" are provocative words and of little use in communication. Regardless of the issue, the person who consistently hears that he or she "always" or "never" does something is bound to be defensive about such global statements. Much energy and time is wasted disproving this exaggeration—"I don't always do that!" Meanwhile, the issue at hand is lost. By the same token, it is constructive to attempt to solve one issue at a time and avoid dredging up past grievances or unrelated topics.

Sometimes one partner will bring up past complaints in order to gain more points, to "win." Yet the cost of winning a battle could be high when it perpetuates a conflict that hinders harmony and intimacy. By thrashing out the issue with the goal of resolving it, partners can achieve a "win-win" outcome.

Reflective Listening

A structured dialogue is perhaps the most widespread and relied-upon marital communication tool available in both therapy and couples courses. It helps to heighten emotional safety by controlling explosive reactions and minimizing the chance for bad listening habits to interfere with communication. Thus it codifies into practice the self-restraint, patience, honesty, fairness, generosity and prudence that characterize loving and constructive exchanges.[17]

This method allows only one partner to speak at a time. Some couples use an actual piece of floor tile to literally "give the other the floor." The spouse who does not have the floor listens carefully, focusing his or her attention on what is said and paraphrasing it back accurately. This is known as "reflective listening." After the listener has "reflected" what the other has said accurately, the speaker affirms, clarifies, and then goes on to elaborate more. This technique requires the listening spouse to concentrate to make sure he or she understands. It helps the speaking spouse feel truly heard, and often helps him or her get in touch with deeper thoughts and feelings. Here Alex and Toni try the technique, with Toni as the speaker:

> *Toni:* I feel hurt and humiliated when you question my disciplining the children right in front of them. I think it undercuts my authority and makes me look foolish.

> *Alex:* You feel hurt and humiliated when I argue with you in front of the girls and it undercuts your authority. And it makes you look foolish. Is that right? Is there more?

> *Toni:* Yes. It makes me want to defend myself and attack you. I don't want to do that. Especially in front of the children. I want to feel we are together on this, on the same team.

> *Alex:* You don't like that it makes you want to defend yourself and attack me. You want to feel I am your ally, on the same team, raising our children. Right?

> *Toni:* Yes, that's right. I'm glad you understand how I feel.

Once Toni is finished, Alex takes his turn to respond, with his wife reflecting it back. Of course, spouses with good relationships do not often need to converse in this artificial style. Still, this kind of communication is a highly effective technique to use when discussing emotionally sensitive issues, even for couples who consider themselves close.

Reflective listening trains couples in listening to one another from the other person's perspective. Often, people assume they understand what others are saying when they do not. Because spouses are very familiar with each other, they easily "tune out" important details. They tend to listen to the other person's points selectively—solely what they want to hear—often reacting only to the statements that reinforce their own viewpoint. They also tend to be preoccupied with preparing their reply. This kind of listening prevents the other person from feeling fully understood, validated and cared about. As a result, he or she may expend a lot of energy in counterproductive efforts—nagging, shouting, and arguing—in an effort to be heard. Reflective listening begins with considering the other's perspective first. Characterized by empathy, a natural monitoring of nonverbal cues, and by the strong desire for understanding and cooperation, reflective listening helps resolve issues on a deep emotional level.

Practicing Good Timing

Good timing when discussing potentially volatile issues exercises the virtues of wisdom and patience. It requires considerable emotional poise to postpone a potentially conflictual discussion to a more fortuitous time. Kevin and Lisa found themselves discussing Lisa's parents in the middle of peak hour traffic, with their children in the back seat of the car. In-laws are often a touchy issue, and as Kevin's remarks grew more irritable, Lisa said, "This is a sensitive topic with a lot of potential for a big argument. There's an awful lot of traffic too. I suggest we talk about it tonight, when circumstances are better." Kevin agreed, and a fight was avoided. If tempers are beginning to flare, asking for a cooling off period is helpful, to give one or both spouses the opportunity to regain emotional control. It also communicates that the spouse does want to resolve the issue, but under circumstances more conducive to a good outcome.

Depersonalizing the Issues

Depersonalizing difficult issues also prevents quarrels from escalating. It requires self-control to suspend an initial defensive reaction, and insight to see into the deeper underlying issues. Gender differences often play a large role in marital difficulties, for example. Men and women are very different in their emotional and physical makeup. Harmonizing masculinity and femininity is one of the joys of marriage, yet also a source of considerable friction.

Spouses can learn to recognize that not all angry words or sneering looks are actually directed at them. Sometimes they are merely projections of the partner's negative self-talk and inner struggles. Before marriage, the spouse may have had bitter experiences—betrayal, ridicule and loneliness—that continue to affect him or her. The intimacy and expectations of the marriage relationship can awaken those old but vivid feelings and thoughts. The spouse may appear as a mirror in which the other's own unlovable feelings or disturbing memories are reflected back.

This has nothing to do with the spouse; it has more to do with the internal world of the other person. "When I remembered how the men in her family had put her down all the time," recalls Kenton, about his wife, Grace, "I realized that when she raged she wasn't really yelling at me. She was yelling at her Dad and brothers. I just needed to reassure her of my love and respect, not defend myself." If a spouse has the maturity of character to see the other's spiteful words as stemming from inner hurts rather than as a personal attack, the spouse avoids an emotional reaction and even respond with compassion.

Many couples are unprepared for the extent of the conflict they find in their marriage and think it is a reflection on the quality of their relationship. However, both happily and unhappily married couples experience conflict. The difference between happy couples and unhappy ones is that in happy couples, negative feelings and conflicts do not overpower the basic affection they have for one another. Such couples have built enough meaning, friendship and enjoyment into their marriage that negative exchanges do not overly detract from it. More importantly, they have cultivated the character to anchor their partnership and weather its inevitable storms. They have learned the art of maintaining intimacy and affection that deepens over a lifetime.

22

Parenting with Love and Authority

BECOMING A PARENT MEANS ENTERING A WHOLE NEW REALM of caring and responsibility. Earlier phases of life, having taught their lessons of love, are foundational for success in this important endeavor. Yet parenting presents its unique challenges, and parenting in modern times is especially daunting. Children have access to media information—both good and bad—in ways their parents couldn't even dream of. Both parents often work, leaving them little time to devote to their children. What is more, society is just beginning to recover from more than thirty years of questioning its most basic values, leaving parents to wonder which direction is best for their children.

Clearly, parents stand in the position of the primary moral educators, yet schools and the community can support parents in giving proper guidance to their children. The most effective parents, teachers and community leaders recognize this and do their best to support and supplement one another. Parents are helped by the efforts of good teachers and community mentors, and in turn the school and community gain from well-reared children.

Teachers and parents benefit from a strong mutual support system. In the past, parental support for teacher authority was so solid that it was common for a child who had been disciplined at school to be disciplined again at home. The parents did not even need to know what the child had done. "If the teacher says you did something wrong, you must have done something wrong," was the parents' philosophy. Nowadays, the parent is more likely to call the school and demand an explanation, sometimes putting teachers and administrators on the defensive and fearful of possible litigation. This lack of support takes its toll. Older teachers comment on the marked difficulties in discipline they face due to students' changed attitudes toward authority, most of which derive from the home.

Parental Authority

Society has swung like a pendulum on issues of authority. People rightly reacted to the authoritarianism that produced well-behaved yet insecure youngsters whose preoccupation with protecting themselves from punishment stymied their growth in love for others. Yet permissive, child-centered parents who rejected authoritarianism contributed unwittingly to wanton behavior in their offspring.

A balanced approach to authority pairs high levels of compassion and care with an equally high degree of firmness. Psychologist Diane Baumrind calls this "authoritative parenting." She found that children of authoritative parents are the most well-adjusted and well-behaved. Children raised in an authoritarian manner—which is characterized by high levels of strictness and low levels of warmth and supportiveness— are also well-behaved, but they tend to be so out of self-protectiveness rather than moral conviction. Children of permissive parents—high in warmth and supportiveness but low in control—fare the worst of all, engaging in the most negative behaviors and showing the least social adjustment.[1]

When children catch the message, "*Because* we love you, you must do as we say," they are already deeply assured of the parent's love and regard for their ultimate well-being. Out of this understanding, there is a greater sense of willingness to respect and comply with their parents' directives.

Parenting as Partnership

The two sides of authoritative parenting—high levels of both warm supportiveness and fairly strict control—are seemingly embodied in the parenting partnership of a mother and father. The often-heroic efforts of single parents notwithstanding, the father and mother team is best suited to provide this balance of warmth and strictness. A partnership allows the parents to integrate the complementary dimensions of parental love—the "soft" maternal side and the "hard" paternal side.

Mothers tend to provide comforting, nurturing love. Maternal affection seems to be given without condition, for who the children are rather than for what they do. "He'll always be my baby," a mother may say, even on her son's wedding day, and that's more than enough reason for her to adore him. A mother's arms are comforting and healing; she will tend to be less strict and more forgiving. A mother's instincts are to protect her child, urging the child to be careful rather than to explore too much and experiment with independence.

A father's love, on the other hand, tends to be more challenging. Paternal affection looks more conditional, since it may be withheld until the son or daughter meets certain expectations. Fathers are inclined to be stricter, but they also encourage a child to take more risks and to try more things. A child about to climb a tall tree may hear his or her mother's caution, "Oh, don't! Be careful!" while the father says, "Go ahead and see if you can do it. Just stay on the thicker branches."

Of course, mothers and fathers slip in and out of these two kinds of love, and circumstances sometimes force one parent to try to give both kinds. Generally, however, paternal and maternal love balance each other well and provide enriching contrast. The cooperative and loving interplay between a mother and a father enhances their parenting. With both kinds of love, a child has a safe haven from which to venture out and achieve. This is why fostering and sustaining a good marriage—strengthening the parenting partnership—is part and parcel of the parenting task.

Love—The Basis of Legitimate Authority

As leaders of their family, parents necessarily have to have a healthy sense of their own authority. On the one hand, power and authority over anything is usually granted to its originator. The author of a book, for instance, is the one who knows best what the book's purpose is, how it can be utilized, interpreted, etc. As the "authors" of a child, parents have a natural authority.

On the other hand, as the anti-authoritarian voices of the 1960s and 1970s pointed out, authority is sometimes abused. They served as a reminder that genuine and trustworthy authority belongs to those who care about their charges and willingly sacrifice for their sake. In any project, business or school, authentic leaders earn their authority through care, investment and sacrifice. The same is true of the child-rearing enterprise. Parents best wield authority on a foundation of deep, demonstrated love for the child. Otherwise, the child will have trouble receiving the parents' directives.

"Without a strong, healthy love-bond with his parents," observes psychologist Ross Campbell, "a child reacts to parental guidance with anger, resentment, and hostility."[2] Power used without an appropriate amount of love can produce a person who eventually resents all authority. To such a child, authority is linked with exploitation. A child who knows she is deeply loved, on the other hand, will readily accept her parents' directions, identify with them and make their values her own. Furthermore, a positive relationship with parents predisposes a child to respect legitimate social institutions and civil laws and the just authority they represent. Thus, good parenting extrapolates into society.

Building Up a Child's Foundations

Caring deeply about their children is not a problem for most parents. As Theodore Reik expressed poetically, "Romance fails us—and so do friendships—but the relationship of mother and child remains indelible and indestructible—the strongest bond upon this earth."[3] Even so, this profound connection requires continual investment to keep it strong. As new parents can testify, parental love deepens as they care for the child. The first feedings, first bath, the first time the crying child is successfully comforted all augment a bond that is fast on its way to becoming unbreakable. As the son or daughter grows in independence and will, the parents' investment and commitment must grow likewise.

Psychologist Steven Stosny asserts that the fact that children emerge from the womb expecting to be well taken care of shows empirical evidence for the existence of the heart—the part of each person that is inherently good, true, just and worthy. However, unless this sense of worth is nurtured by the love of parents, it may remain dormant. "We learn how valuable and worthy of love we are almost exclusively through interactions with attachment figures, especially parents and children," he observes.[4] M. Scott Peck agrees, "When children have learned through the love of their parents to feel valuable, then it is almost impossible to destroy their spirit."[5]

Awakened by the selfless devotion of the parents, the son or daughter's heart learns its worth and naturally sees others as being similarly worthy. He or she will then behave in a manner that is just and kind toward others when out in society.

Parental investment thus builds up a child's foundations in two ways: first, it cultivates the parent-child bond, which opens up the child's sphere of love. (See Chapter 15) This bond serves to enhance moral and cognitive development. Second, it fosters a sense of inherent value and worthiness—and, by extension—the value and worthiness of others. Attachment to parents and sense of self-worth are both healthy expressions of the child's budding heart and essential foundations for moral growth.

Consistent and Continuous Giving

Although parents invest in their children to build up these foundations of a moral self, they may not necessarily see immediate results from their efforts. They give and give, and then forget what they have given and give still more. This is why parental love is the very definition of the unconditional. Yet even though fathers and mothers cannot anticipate how their children will turn out, their continual caring is the surest lifeline for even the most incorrigible child.

Jan Smith of Stamford, Connecticut, learned to deal with the emotional turbulence of her rebellious teenage daughter by applying unswerving love. Her daughter's rebelliousness culminated late one night when the police called Jan to tell her that she had to come to the police station to pick up her daughter, who was arrested for drunk driving. Mother and daughter did not speak until the next afternoon. Jan broke the tension by giving the girl a small gift-wrapped box. The teenager nonchalantly opened it and found a small piece of a rock. "Cute, Mom. What's this for?" she said, and then she noticed a card inside. It read, "This rock is more than 200 million years old. That's how long it will take before I give up on you." She responded by giving her mother a big hug.[6]

Parental Modeling

The most powerful teaching is by example.[7] Children are more likely to do as a parent does than what a parent says. According to psychologist Joseph Pearce, the greater part of the child's mind-brain structure is imprinted with the character and example of significant people in their lives. Only about 5 percent is available to respond to words and instruction.[8] Thus the expression, "Who you are speaks so loudly I can't hear what you are saying."

Of course, parents are children's first and most significant role models. Children closely observe their parents' interactions with each other, other family members, friends and neighbors. From this they learn how to treat other people. Likewise, families with parental conflict and unresolved anger tend to have children who are more aggressive.[9] Parents teach respect through modeling respect, caring through modeling caring, responsibility through modeling responsibility.

Consider the moral lessons modeled by Claire and Warren as they help their daughter Jenna grasp the intricacies of a weaving kit project. Warren is calm and a natural teacher but knows nothing of weaving; Claire knows the craft but her character tends to be high-strung and impatient. When the mother's tension begins to mount, the father distracts them both with humor and asks Jenna to show what she has learned. After the short break, Claire resumes the lesson. In this way they model to the daughter how a husband and wife cooperate to build on their strengths and compensate for each other's weaknesses. In addition, she has experienced her parents' loving devotion to her. The next day in school, Jenna spontaneously volunteers to help a boy in a lower grade with his reading, using many of the same patterns of speech and behavior that her parents used with her.

Imitation can be the sincerest form of flattery when parents hear children dealing with people politely and well in imitation of their own good manners. They are considerably less flattered when they hear their child use a harsh tone of voice on a pet or younger sibling in imitation of the parents' own impatient utterings. Parents are "on display"—including all the contradictions in their own attitudes and behavior. For example, when the phone rings, instructing the child to tell whoever is calling that the parent is not home sets an example of untruthfulness. Going through the express check-out line posted "10 Items or Less" with fifteen items in the grocery cart sends a powerful unspoken message about cheating. In the end, a virtuous example is the most effective character education.

Rules and Expectations

The power of example, of course, does not mean parents have no need to impart firm ideas of right and wrong as well as appropriate limits. Moral instruction is one of the greatest investments a parent makes in a child. It is like planting a seed that bears fruit later in life. While a young person may not seem to appreciate or absorb moral instruction, in fact, parents may be assured that a significant amount is sinking in, even if the child does not let on. By explicitly passing on rules and morality, the parent informs the child's conscience—the cognitive aspect of morality—which will eventually serve as a portable parent. The conscience will set off some alarm bells when basic values are being transgressed.

"It was funny," admits Xavier, a 19-year-old student at a midwestern college. "I'd roll my eyes when my Dad talked about drinking when I was younger. I didn't mess around with it much anyway when I was in high school. But in my first year at college, alcohol was like *everywhere*. Suddenly I had to take a look at what I was going to do and not do and what I would say to my Dad. I ended up deciding to pretty much draw the line he used to say I should." Strict limits provide parameters in youth's moral universe.

Some limits take the form of rules. Once a rule is made, it has an authority of its own. "The rule in this house is…" carries a great deal of weight. Children and teenagers actually appreciate rules. Rules help them know what is expected and keep them from spinning off into chaos. If children are accustomed to obeying rules when young, they are more apt to observe guidelines as teenagers in more sensitive areas such as drug use and sexual experience.

Children want and need moral guidance from their parents; adolescents are often crying out for it.[10] If rules and expectations are laid down in the home, children feel more protected. They also have a good excuse when facing down peer pressure: "My Mom and Dad freak if I'm out after nine o'clock. That's their rule. I know it's a drag, but that's the way they are. They'll kill me if I don't come home." The parents can be the "bad guys" and let the child keep his or her cool image.

When setting up rules and expectations, it is necessary for parents to agree on both standards and enforcement. This may require extensive private discussion. It also may mean that one parent may support the other in front of the children even if he or she disagrees with how the other parent is handling a situation. Children, even the nicest ones, can be manipulative, and even very young children learn that if they can divide their parents, they can conquer them.

Taking Time to Parent

Caring for children takes large amounts of time and energy—precious commodities for modern working parents. This led to the notion of "quality time," which was widely embraced by family theorists and parents alike. Only a small amount of parental investment is necessary per day, they thought, as long as it is high quality. Yet others believe that "quality time" is a myth. One mother, a successful lawyer, had a rude awakening one day when doing the family grocery shopping with her children, a task the babysitter usually did. They was sliding on their knees down aisles, screaming, asking for everything and creating an embarrassing disturbance. The cashier said, "Oh, so *you're* the mother," as if the children's terrible behavior were well known at the store. She realized, "Babysitters don't raise children; parents do," and she immediately decided to cut back on her career to have more time at home with her children.[11]

Parents serve their children best by being with them in a relaxed state and giving them the gift of their full presence and attention. Doris, a mother in Pittsburgh, stated that she raised three children in the public school system, and they were all drug and alcohol-free by the time they graduated. A younger friend asked her for advice about whether or not she should home-school. She wanted to protect her children from negative peer influences, but bewailed the amount of time it would take. Doris replied, "You have to take a lot of time with them anyway. I had to detox my kids every day from all the negative peer influences, explaining over and over again why they can't do what their friends are doing and to give them the strength to keep resisting." The older mother had worked for years at a low-paying, part-time job just so that she could be home when her children returned from school.

Most youth problems in the United States occur between the hours of three in the afternoon and six o'clock at night—unsupervised hours when the children are out of school but the parents are not yet home from work. These are the times when children tend to experiment with undesirable behaviors.

Talking to Children about Sensitive Matters

Talking to young people about drugs, sex and violence is never easy. But physician Victor Strasburger reassures parents, "What you say isn't nearly as important as the fact that you are willing to discuss the subject in the first place. That... makes it far more likely that your child will come to you with questions in the future."[12] The following are guidelines about discussing sensitive matters:

· *Initiate discussion early.*

Early discussions have the effect of immunizing youth against hazards.[13] Even kindergarteners see their parents take pills and this can begin an education about use and abuse of drugs. When parents initiate the discussion, as they might about brushing teeth or bicycle safety, they establish their position as the primary source of guidance and understanding about these matters. They also indicate their approachability, so that children come to them in the future with their concerns.

Topics should be discussed in an age-appropriate manner. When Nick's 4-year-old son asked him, "Where did I come from?" Nick explained that he came from his mother's belly. When his 8-year-old daughter asked the same question, Nick wanted to be truthful yet protect his daughter's natural modesty. He said, "Your mother and I truly wanted a child. Our desire and love grew so strong that eventually a tiny seed was planted in Mommy's belly. It grew, and after nine months a beautiful little girl was born." She was very satisfied with this answer, which fit with her stage of cognitive and emotional development.

· *Give honest answers.*

Parents need to answer all inquiries to the best of their knowledge, and when stumped, offer to find out the answer. "My Dad used his connections with the police department to get me in to see the jail," recalls Kyle, now in college. "It definitely left me thinking long and hard about the pressures to join a gang."

When speaking to adolescents about sexual matters, using correct terms helps to remove the unhealthy mystique from the topic.

Part of honesty is dealing with questions of the parents' own experiences with the forbidden behavior. Personal confessions are unwarranted and only burden and distract children, but parental sharing about how they thought and felt in their youth can comfort a child and enhance parents' credibility.

· *Help children think.*

To help the young resist unhealthy influences, it is helpful to invite them to practice explaining their views and reasoning out a responsible response. Saying, "I'd like to know what you think about that situation," and "What do you think should happen now?"—and respectfully listening to their replies—not only helps parents know how to guide their children; it also encourages the child to craft his or her moral code and articulate it to others.[14]

· *Show unconditional support.*

Educator Patty Stark recommends giving the message, "Let's put together a game plan to help you manage the pressure and come through this a winner. We believe in you, and we will be with you every step of the way."[15] At the same time, they need to know that whenever they feel uncomfortable or scared—regardless of where the are, who they're with or what time it is—they can call their parents to get them, without facing an interrogation.

Parents must sometimes make hard choices, like Doris did, in order to devote time and effort into their children's well-being. Schools and communities can help matters by offering quality after-school programs that both attract and protect youth. Yet even organized after-school activities sometimes cut unduly into the family's time together. William Doherty, director of the marriage and family therapy program at the University of Minnesota, works to organize parents to "take back family life from overscheduled family hyperactivity and the consumer culture."[16] Even though enrolling the child in several different sports, lessons and extracurricular activities seems to enrich the child's life experience, some families find themselves on the run constantly to keep up with their schedules, with no time for relaxed or thoughtful interaction—something which is ultimately more valuable for the child.

Turning Off the TV

One way to allow for more healthy family interaction is to turn off that thief of family time, the television. A Nielsen study in 1996 indicated that the average child in the United States spent thirty-five hours per week viewing television as opposed to thirty-five *minutes* of meaningful conversation with his or her parents.[17] Turning off the TV frees up hours to read to or with children, converse with them, play games, put on plays, bake with them—a whole host of things that build relationship, teach skills and at the same time encourage more brain activity and creative thinking. This will also shield them from being overly influenced by programs and commercials that rarely reflect parental values, glorify consumerism and materialism, and desensitize children to violence.[18]

While families may want to watch some TV, it is appropriate to carefully regulate viewing. Program viewing is best scheduled ahead of time, with family members agreeing not to turn the TV on at random throughout the day. Watching the television is regarded as a privilege, not a right, and permission is required. Like other appliances in the household, it is natural for the television to be left off most of the time.

Parents and children benefit when they watch worthwhile programs together. If objectionable content comes on, it is a chance to explain why it is unacceptable and even discuss the commercial reasons why TV producers show such content. This is imparting "media literacy."

Regulating the television is an area where schools can specifically support parents. Not only can they sponsor times for families to do without TV and award students who do, schools also help indirectly by promoting reading programs like "Book It!" where the local Pizza Hut offers free pizzas to children who read a certain amount within a month.

Family Meals and Rituals

Family meals are a valuable opportunity for parents to share with their children. A study by the Cincinnati Children's Hospital Medical Center showed that teenagers who ate at least five meals a week with their families were at lower risk for bad behavior, did better in school, were better socialized and enjoyed better relationships with peers than teenagers who did not eat together with their families on a regular basis.[19]

Alysson, a medical transcriptionist in the Northwest, takes a few moments to light candles at dinner and plan conversation. She thinks beforehand of positive topics to introduce, stories she wants to tell, and questions she wants to ask. She asks her two children, 10 and 13, and her husband, "What was the best thing that happened today?" and "What was the worst thing?" to draw out deeper responses than "It was okay," when she asks them how their day went.

Bedtime, suppertime, movie nights, religious observances, and holidays are some of the occasions for family rituals that provide stability amid the hectic pace of modern life. Small children especially will get upset if rituals are interrupted. A bedtime ritual of bath, story, lullaby and kiss will comfort a child immeasurably, and is well worth the time. Studies confirm that bedtime is a chance for strong parent-child bonding, even for teenagers.[20] Many remember their parents' nightly routine for the rest of their lives. Annabelle, a middle-aged woman from West Virginia, says, "My mother would always pull the blanket up under my chin, smooth it down, and kiss me on the lips. She'd say, "Goodnight, angel!" and then kiss me again on the forehead. I would not let her vary or abandon this routine until I was 18 and off to college."

The soothing power of routine and ritual tends to have a cumulative effect, taking on more power and significance as time goes by. When a ritual is missed, all the family members feel a loss. Family rituals around holidays create and sustain family bonds and a sense of belonging and continuity in a changeable world. "That first Hanukkah after Mama died was awful," recalls Rachel, an accountant on the West coast. "But my brothers and sister and I gathered anyway at my house and we tried to do everything the same way as if Mama and Papa were there. We did it mainly for the kids. In the end, though, it was the only way we adults were able to get through the holiday."

The Family with a Purpose

Stephen Covey suggests that creating a statement of the family ideal or mission together is a valuable family-building activity.[21] A mission statement is a declaration of the family's vision and its values. It can be as elaborate as a page-long essay or as simple as "The Jacksons keep their word, care about people and get the job done." Since it is arrived at by consensus, creating such a statement of the family ideal may require a lot of time and reflection by all members of the family. Once written, the statement of the family ideal can be prominently displayed—on the wall, on the refrigerator, or even on tee shirts—as a reference to keep the family on course. Some families make a weekly ritual of reading their family ideal and renewing their pledge to fulfill it.

Many family mission statements include a clause about how the family will serve neighbors or contribute to their community or the nation. The Singh family of Reno, Nevada mentions their "Pennies with a Purpose" collection, which is earmarked for a needy Indian child they sponsor. Such altruism boosts family pride. Although it seems paradoxical, the family that belongs to benevolent organizations, hosts guests, helps out neighbors and volunteers for community causes finds that the bonds with one another are strengthened by the time and energy they give to others outside of the home.

Family Meetings

Family meetings are also a good way to build family togetherness through focusing family members' attention on planning trips, chores, service projects or addressing issues that have come up. With a snack or treat added, some stimulating questions and some laughs, family meetings can be wonderful and memorable times of sharing as well as learning how to treat each other fairly and respectfully.

Family meetings are most successful when they occur at regular times, are only about an hour long, and acknowledge the rights of everyone to contribute, even the youngest member of the family. The rule can be established that each person is allowed to have his or her say with the respectful attention of the others and without criticism or teasing. While the parents' decisions on important issues are final, recognition of the children's contributions and suggestions affirm that they are a valued and vital part of the family team.

Parenting with Compassion

Regardless of what they do and the time they take to do it, if parents demonstrate care and compassion for their children, almost anything they do will turn out all right, according to Stosny.[22] Compassion is an expression of love that means literally to feel strongly with someone, and includes a willingness to share his or her difficulties. A father or mother's compassion for his or her children means patience and understanding of their developmental limitations, a benevolent outlook on the child, and relying on support and encouragement rather than shame or harsh punishment to awaken the heart and conscience and reestablish good behavior.

A compassionate parent looks beneath the bad behavior of a child to the motivating factors. An otherwise angelic child can become a veritable monster when deprived of a nap. A hungry child can be cranky and rude. Going deeper, a child who has just lost a ball game or been ridiculed by peers may be too ashamed to tell his or her parents, but his or her behavior that evening may be hard to put up with. Harsh punishment and unrealistic demands only layer hurt on top of hurt without addressing the underlying emotional need.

Educator and author Jane Nelsen was out hiking with her family and some friends. Their 10-year-old son became tired and started complaining that his backpack was rubbing his back raw. His father, a former Marine, urged his son to "Be a man" and stand up to the pain. The boy tried to obey his father, but after a while he couldn't to go on. Jane knew it had probably hurt and angered her son that his father had not taken his situation seriously. She asked his father to stop, and together the parents jerry-rigged some padding for the boy's back that protected the sore spot. He made the rest of the journey without incident or complaint, supported by the empathy of his parents. Through compassion and understanding, they had reached into their son's world, helped him through the difficult feelings, and administered the care and support he needed to accomplish the climb.[23]

Parental Sacrifice

As any father or mother well knows, attending to children's needs often comes at a personal cost—the sacrifice of the parent's interests, plans and desires. Most parents recognize that on the deepest level it is a joy to make sacrifices on behalf of their children. Nevertheless, being a good parent means putting up with the mess of an art project on the kitchen table. It means answering the fiftieth question in a row while trying to prepare dinner. It means resisting the impulse to resort to "Because I said so, that's why!" when confronted with a defiant 15-year-old demanding to know why she is not allowed to stay out late when *everyone* else in school does it. It means forgoing that new car to pay for a son or daughter's college expenses. More than any other activity in life, parenting means self-sacrifice. David Elkind, a child psychologist at Tufts University, said, "If it is to be done well, child-rearing requires, more than most activities of life, a good deal of de-centering from one's own needs and perspectives."[24]

It's the Heart that Counts

There are times and circumstances when fathers and mothers are simply too busy to give much time to family activities or companionship with their children. Struggling to make ends meet, coping with a chronic illness, being called out of town for long periods in the military service or on business—these may keep a family apart. Once again, the important thing is that the sons and daughters know that their parents' hearts are with them even when their physical presence is not. Then the children will be better able to honor and appreciate the sacrifices their parents are making.

Kwi Soh Young, a teenager from Seattle, affirmed that although she and her siblings endured prolonged separations from her father due to the demands of his work as a public defender, their suffering was ameliorated by his actions and attitude. She said, "I always knew he was thinking of us, no matter where he was. He would make sure to call us from the office or when away on trips. He even sent cassette tapes sometimes telling us about what he was doing and seeing, and he'd sing us a bedtime or birthday song. We knew he was thinking of us and missed us, that he was concerned about us all the time, so we didn't feel deprived." The basic relationship of heart was intact even if the father's responsibilities took him away from home.

The Parent as Hero

Only a dad with a tired face,
Coming home from the daily race,
Bringing home little of gold or fame
To show how well he has played the game;
But glad in his heart that his own rejoice
To see him come and to hear his voice...

Only a dad, but he gives his all
To smooth the way for his children small,
Doing with courage stern and grim
The deeds that his father did for him.
This is the line that for him I pen:
Only a dad, but the best of men.

—From "Only a Dad" by Edward Guest[25]

Character-Building Responsibilities

Another aspect of parenting is educating children to shoulder responsibility, with the objective of raising them to be productive and sacrificial adults themselves. This requires the judicious use of chores and a little adversity.

Household Chores

Chores and household duties help produce resilient children who will grow up to be responsible, self-respecting adults. A loving and wise parent requires that the child reciprocate for all the parents do for him or her. When parents ask children to contribute their fair share to the family, it inculcates the values of reciprocity and responsibility.

One Harvard study that followed the lives of almost 500 boys well into middle age showed that the children who did chores turned out to be healthier, happier, more productive and more satisfied in personal relationships than those who had no home or yard responsibilities in their younger years.[26] Even very small children can do simple chores such as placing the napkins on the table or corralling stray shoes into a neat line. Older children can take on more ambitious responsibilities.

Assigning children chores is perfect for the family in which both parents work, since the parents do not have time to do all the household tasks. When children pitch in, the parents have more time to spend with the children as they work together, engage in meaningful conversation, and share experiences and views. Boys and girls working side by side with their fathers and mothers absorb practical skills, feel a sense of companionship and worth, and inherit the traditions of generations before them. Thus the value of chores is not only measured in work done, but in the way they build bonds and character.

Codifying and writing down the chores for display multiples the chances of children fulfilling them. Parents can note when they are done with a check mark or sticker, and reward the children periodically. Jarmo and Anita, parents of three in the Appalachian Mountains region, got their children interested in chores by assigning them "pet points" for each chore done with a cheerful attitude. The children had been begging to have a dog, and the parents held a family meeting to discuss the possibility with them. They outlined all the responsibilities involved in caring for a pet and declared firmly that neither parent would have time to fulfill them. If the children wanted a dog, they would have to take care of it, and prove beforehand that they would take this responsibility seriously. Therefore, they would have to earn 500 "pet points" each by performing regular chores, at a point each, for some time. The promise of a dog provided the youngsters with the incentive to learn self-discipline and perseverance, and the couple hoped the habit of responsibility would be engrained enough, as the points accumulated on the chart, that they would be ready to care for a pet.

The Uses of Adversity

Psychologist John Rosemond recommends that parents give children all of what they need, but a small—very small—amount of what they merely want.[27] Giving a frugal allowance, limiting TV and video game hours, limiting treats and entertainments, and enforcing rules and responsibilities in the end benefit a child enormously. "Sweet are the uses of adversity," said Shakespeare. Indeed, the child who faces no challenges, who has every path cleared, who always wins and never loses and always gets his or her way, is unprepared for life as an adult.

What Price for a Man's Character?

Captains Courageous is the story of a spoiled boy's character being built by adversity. Harvey Cheyne, the son of a very rich man, was spoiled, pettish, weak, unhealthy and disrespectful to his elders. He believed that he could buy his way in or out of any situation. When Harvey was swept off the deck of an ocean liner by a wave, a fishing trawler and her salty crew picked him up. His bribes and entreaties availed him nothing with the sailors. He was expected to obey, conform and help in the rigorous work. In his first encounter with captain Disko Troop, Harvey was punched in the face for his incessant whining and complaining.

Disko and his crew were fair, honest, tough, hard working and well schooled in the difficult codes of the sea. At their none-too-gentle hands, Harvey received the education of his life: "I worked like a horse and I ate like a hog and I slept like a dead man," he said. He learned sacrifice, gratitude and obedience; he learned of the fellowship of shared dangers and hard work. At the end of the novel, he spoke of how much he owed the captain, who in essence made him into a man of character.

For all of his millions, Harvey's father could not repay Disko for what he had done. What price can be paid for a man's character? It can only be bought with love that dares to demand that a young person earn respect by showing respect and by stretching himself to the limits to be useful to the people around him.[28]

This type of education is particularly necessary in developed societies where many hardships of the past no longer exist. In prior times, life was so difficult for adults and children alike that children had to form good character traits or suffer massive defeat in life. They had to work hard, they had to help out; often they were key to the family's income. They had to "make do and do without"—an exercise in creativity that produced the special joy that comes from self-reliance. A wise grandfather wrote a letter to his grandchildren:

We tried so hard to make things better for our kids that we made them worse. For my grandchildren, I'd like better: I hope you learn to make your own bed and mow the lawn and wash the car. And I really hope nobody gives you a brand new car when you are sixteen. I hope you get a black eye fighting for something you believe in. I hope you have to share a bedroom with your younger brother. And… when he wants to crawl under the covers with you because he's scared, I hope you let him. These things I wish for you— tough times and disappointment, hard work and happiness.[29]

Parenting is among the most demanding tasks on earth. To accept the children as they are and yet challenge them to be better, to set rules and give responsibility yet show compassion when they are in difficulty, to give continuously and yet create opportunities for the children to give in return—these are not easy to balance. Ultimately it the parents' heart of sacrificial investment and love that both guides them to maintain the right balance—and which wins their children's natural respect for their parents' legitimate authority.

Part III

Challenges
Facing Youth

Section 6

Ethical Sexuality

JOHN R. WILLIAMS

SEXUALITY, WHEN DIRECTED BY LOVE AND RESPONSIBILITY, has the capacity to enhance inner growth and the pursuit of meaningful life goals. Misdirected, its harm to the heart, conscience, relationships and career can be uniquely painful and hard to reverse. Given these inevitable moral implications, education about sexuality is rightly addressed from the perspective of character and values. Indeed, character education can hardly avoid the topic, particularly when addressing teenagers for whom sex is frequently an all-absorbing focus.

There is a promise of synergy between character education and sex education that can promote good character and support responsible sexual behavior at the same time. Yet for this to happen, it is necessary to go beyond traditional norms to find agreement on an ethic of responsible and healthy sexual love. Such an ethic recognizes the moral implications of sexuality and the deeper need for enduring love. Educating for such an ethic furthers character development: not pressuring others for sex demonstrates respect; waiting until the appropriate relationship requires self-discipline; resisting negative peer pressure demands courage. Though adults hold reservations about advocating abstinence to the young, an updated expression of this ethic addresses these concerns.

23

An Ethic of Responsible Sexual Love

SEXUALITY REPRESENTS A UNIQUE CHALLENGE TO CHARACTER and culture. Arguably the most formidable power that human beings have at their disposal, sexuality is inextricably intermingled with the impulse to love, the creation of life, and the passing down of genes and lineage.[1] Indeed, because it taps into the deepest aspects of being human, sex is something that borders on the sacred. As such, sexuality inescapably involves issues of right and wrong, responsibility and irresponsibility. For these reasons, organizations such as the Character Education Partnership have proposed the integration of sexual ethics into character education.

The Four Spheres of Love paradigm implies a sexual ethic. (See Section 4) It proposes that sexual intimacy is a feature of the spouse's sphere alone. It suggests that respecting this guideline facilitates an individual's character development and social maturation, while violating this standard hinders it. This implied ethic is worthy of further elaboration.

Love: The Deeper Need

Decades after the sexual revolution, people are reconsidering the prevailing sexual norm. The sexual revolution promised men and women more love, happiness and freedom. It did not deliver on these promises. Since the breakdown of the monogamous norm, society has been plagued with staggering epidemics of sexually transmitted diseases and unwanted pregnancies. More insidious have been the emotional agonies of broken relationships, disillusionment and divorce.

Under intense pressure to perform sexually and to be sexually attractive at all costs, people these days are arguably less comfortable and contented in their relationships with the opposite sex and with their own sexuality than ever before. Ironically, sexual dysfunction in the form of lack of desire was the most widely reported sexual malady in the highly eroticized culture of the United States in the last decade. Author Peter Marin concludes, "We have been liberated from the taboos of the past only to find ourselves imprisoned in a 'freedom' that brings us no closer to our real nature or needs." Why did the bright ideals of the sexual revolution fail so abysmally?

A central reason is that the revolution emphasized sex and the body rather than love and the heart. Psychologist Rollo May differentiated between the impulse for love and the drive for sex, saying, "For human beings, the more powerful need is not sex per se but for relationships, intimacy, acceptance and affirmation."[2] Frank Pittman explains that most extramarital affairs take place more over the telephone than in the bedroom.[3] Adultery's main allure is the hope of satisfying the loneliness of the heart, not the sexual impulses of the body.

Ironically, when sex is overvalued, eroticism itself is the casualty. "Somehow I missed the boat on the pleasure cruise to carefree, guilt-free sex," a young college student writes in a popular woman's magazine, after sampling the campus sex scene. Liaisons that are "void of emotion" and hence dull, she noticed, are "the all too common basis of an active sex life." Now, "with all the fuss about sexual freedom, it's a little hard to stand up and admit it's not what everyone imagines." Indeed, sex without the love and loyalty that give it meaning is empty and ungratifying. Some people respond to this emptiness by trying a variety of positions, of partners and practices, but this leads to even more jadedness and lack of feeling.

If the deeper human need is a heart-to-heart connection, sexual union can only be a supplement, not a substitute. However, since love and sex are so interconnected, people often mistake a sexual attraction for "the real thing." Their yearning for intimacy propels them into sexual relationships in hopes of finding true love. Yet sex can obscure the meaning of love. Often these relationships wind up hurting them and hurting others, damaging their ability to love and be loved in a deep and authentic way.

Philosopher Elisabeth Haich captures the confusion of sex and love in insecure relationships well: "Sexuality mimics love. It compels tenderness and embraces; it forces the lovers to hug one another, to allay one another's pain through the revelations of sexuality, as when true love is exchanged. What follows such experiences? Disappointments, a bitter after-taste, mutual accusations or bleak loneliness, feelings of exploitation and defilement. Neither of the two gave true love but only expected to receive it, therefore neither received it!"[4]

A sexual norm that respects the needs of the heart and conscience as well as the body—that harmonizes unselfish love and passionate sexuality—represents a more complete, enlightened and responsible ethic of sexual love. Such an ethic is sorely needed in contemporary times, when the old taboos are gone but few new standards for behavior have been set up as guideposts.

Ethic of Intimacy

Sexual ethics, of course, have been evolving since the celebration of blatant promiscuity in the 1970s. Now there is the more restrained practice of serial monogamy—having a series of exclusive sexual relationships that last for some time. The *Playboy* ethic has given way to an "ethic of intimacy."[5] "I want to feel very emotionally attached to someone before I have sex with her," says Oliver, a sophomore at New York University. Love is now the main reason why both young men and women enter into a physical relationship.[6]

Sexual activity is still regarded as morally neutral; motivation decides its morality. A certain definition of affection now legitimates sex, according to popular ethicists. As long as there is intimacy, care, emotional vulnerability and at least some degree of commitment, the sexual relationship is considered justified. The only immoral sex is that which is deemed "loveless" or "meaningless."[7] This is typified by the advice that Kelly, a young dental hygienist from Connecticut, gives her three younger sisters. "I say, "Don't avoid sex. Just make sure that each sexual encounter matters.""[8]

Certainly this represents a retreat from the trenches of the sexual revolution and an awakening of an incipient new sexual ethic. It remains, however, too vague to be of any real help. If mutual consent, tolerance and a loose definition of love and intimacy prevail, this legitimates temporary liaisons based on fickle feelings. Perhaps this precludes the most overt exploitation, but the more subtle kinds of hurting—including where the victim is a willing if foolish participant—are given free rein. Ultimately the innate desire for true and lasting love is left unsatisfied as well. A clearer standard is necessary.

Philosophical Roots of the Sexual Revolution

If any written reference can be identified as the foundation of the prevailing sexual ethic, perhaps it is the "*Playboy* philosophy." Championed by Hugh Hefner beginning in 1954 and trumpeted through his *Playboy* magazine and related enterprises, the *Playboy* philosophy has shaped the sexual attitudes of several generations. Hefner ridiculed marriage and parenthood as restrictive of personal freedom and asserted that any kind of sex is a private matter between consenting partners. He popularized the notions that recreational sex and masturbation with pornography are healthy activities for adult men. Prior to Hefner, most college-educated men felt that such activities were juvenile or immoral.[9] In this way, the *Playboy* philosophy rationalized the worldview of adolescent boys. It legitimated the impulse to seduce and discard women and to prefer bachelor pleasures to the pursuit of responsible and unselfish partnerships with women.[10]

Hefner sought to disseminate the notions of Alfred Kinsey, the most influential sex authority in the world.[11] His 1948 *Kinsey Report* purported to be the first objective research into human sexuality. Its morally "neutral" tone influenced people to begin to think of sex divorced from ethical implications. Kinsey asserted that human beings need frequent sexual "outlets" or they will suffer from psychological problems.

The context of sexual release was irrelevant—marital relations, premarital sex, infidelity and even incest and exploitation of children were all equivalent. Further, he declared that illicit sex was far more common than people had suspected. Many decent people began to question their moral reservations about sex outside of marriage, since they believed they were missing out on pleasures others were enjoying. In addition, Kinsey claimed evidence of the sexual nature of young children and thus opened the doors to legitimating child sexual abuse.

Recent discoveries now confirm that Kinsey misrepresented American sexual behavior, relying on biased methods and unrepresentative samples.[12] For example, one in four of the people he interviewed for this report were prisoners or ex-convicts, hardly examples of normal human behavior. Five percent of these were male prostitutes. More sinister, he presented data on the sexual activity of children based solely upon the reports of one pedophile's abuse of over 300 victims. Despite a "neutral researcher" persona, there is substantial evidence that Kinsey had a clear agenda to legitimate homosexuality, pedophilia and promiscuous sexual behavior, activities in which he and his colleagues participated.[13]

Through Hefner, Kinsey's sexual ideology penetrated deep into the male psyche. By 1972, *Playboy* reached half of all male professionals. As recently as 1985, *Playboy* was found to be America's "most widely read sex education resource."[14] Its views helped turn sexual mores—and legal codes—upside down. Given its roots in pseudo-science and its fruits of dubious freedom, the ethic of "sexual liberation" is due for replacement by one based on valid research, universal values and a higher vision of love.

The Moral Component of Sexual Love

Loving sexual expression is other-centered, an act of sharing. Someone motivated by true love does not put his or her beloved in jeopardy in any way. Healthy sexuality therefore inevitably involves morality—the way people treat and affect others.

Sexual encounters are not a casual matter, a purely physical activity that simply ends when it is over, like enjoying good food. Sex encompasses the partners in their totality, touching their minds and hearts as well as their bodies. It is the very "language and embodiment of commitment" between two people who have pledged to spend their lives together.[15]

Sexual relations also have implications for many other lives—friends, parents, other potential life partners, and, of course, any resultant children. Consider this all-too-typical scenario: Max and Leanna, both 20, met and soon after began a sexual relationship. When Leanna became pregnant they thought to abort, but assurances of support from their parents and relatives as well as their own affection for each other led them to decide to have the baby. Six months into her pregnancy, though, when they realized that they were unprepared to commit themselves to each other and to the child, they put the baby up for adoption. An infertile middle-aged couple began adoption procedures and brought the infant home when he was born. Soon, however, Leanna's parents asserted that they wanted to raise the child themselves. Relations among Max, Leanna and their families became stressed to the breaking point. The adopting couple surrendered the baby and went through an agonizing series of rising hopes and shattered dreams as the parties argued the issue out. The child spent the first few weeks of his life shunted between an angry mother, irate grandparents, and the adoptive couple who were afraid to give their hearts to him.

This illustrates how the impact of sexual relations often has little to do with the partners' intentions. They may have cared for each other and meant each other no harm. They may have had no wish to conceive a child. They may have wanted to spare their family and community any disruption. It also does not matter whether or not the partners had the capacity to cope with the consequences. They may have been only young and foolish.

Like fire, sexuality is a powerful force. It can either enhance or impair people's lives, based solely on whether or not it is released in the circumstances that can fully contain and direct it constructively.

Healthy and Ethical Sexuality

"It was a tough situation," said Rick, a professor in his 30s, of his moral dilemma. "I was working late every night for weeks on a special proposal for my department. My wife Yolanda was fighting a bad case of flu and so when I got home she was wiped out. We hadn't made love in over a month. I was feeling pretty lonely, I guess. Then one of my grad students started coming to my office in the evening with her dissertation questions. She admired me a lot and she was pretty, in her late-20s and single, it turned out. On one occasion too many she leaned very close to me and I could smell her perfume. Her eyes said she was willing...."

Rick is grappling with the central question in a discussion of a sexual ethic: What is healthy, ethical sexuality? Researcher and psychologist Archibald Hart describes ethical and healthy sexuality as sexual response "at the appropriate time and towards the right person when the right conditions are fulfilled."[16] It is helpful to elaborate on the components of this definition.

"At the appropriate time and towards the right person" represents self-control in the workplace, at social functions and within the family. A healthy, mature person is able to focus his or her sexual arousal on the chosen partner and limit arousal towards others. He or she can also wait until a proper time not only in terms of other responsibilities but also relative to the partner's needs and preferences.

A further elaboration is "when the right conditions are fulfilled." Right conditions involve many elements. There is the matter of the partner's preferences for the context of lovemaking. But clearly more important are the moral and relational components—primarily unselfish love and lasting commitment. Significant too are such social factors as adequate economic resources and the support of parents and relatives. Only meeting these conditions will contain all the potential consequences of sexual union for the partners, their families and society. At the same time they create the safety and security necessary for the greatest sexual satisfaction for both partners.

What then is unhealthy, unethical sexuality? Turning the previous definition on its head yields some insight. It can mean a response at an inappropriate time—when too young and unmarried, when other responsibilities beckon or when the spouse does not want it. It can mean a focus on an inappropriate person—someone else's spouse, an unmarried peer, a child. This implies that encouraging arousal—or at least not discouraging it—by fantasizing or flirting is also not ethical.

To sum up, unhealthy, unethical sexuality is physical union under the wrong conditions: wrong time, wrong person, wrong motives. These represent insufficient concern for and commitment to the welfare of all who would be involved and hence is immoral. Rick finishes his story: "I caught a glimpse of the picture of Yolanda and my son on my desk and got my bearings. I made up some excuse to go home and from then on I met that grad student in the library."

Sex and Marriage

For spouses, sex fulfills several important roles:[17]

Sex strengthens the bond between husband and wife. Sex fosters the growth of a special kind of friendship and intimacy in marriage. It reinforces the uniqueness of the conjugal relationship. Physical union symbolizes and reinforces the union of the partners' lives in all the other aspects—emotionally, financially, as parents and in destiny.

Sex is a special way to express love. Sex conveys love in a unique way, though it cannot replace other signs of affection. It remains a shared and exclusive experience between the spouses even if there is little else in common. At times of emotional distance during the shifting seasons of marriage, sex can be a reassuring point of connection until emotional intimacy can be reestablished.

Sex reinforces the exclusivity of the relationship. When daily life pulls the attention and energy towards children and other people in the home and community, sexual relations can reaffirm the central place the spouse occupies in a couple's lives.

Sex provides a sense of emotional security that promotes happiness. Physical affection calms and reassures in a way that complements verbal expressions of caring and acts of thoughtfulness.

Sex helps to overcome conflicts and to mend rifts. The non-verbal physical communion of sex is a relief from heated arguments and petty divisive issues and helps to remind the couple of their essential commitment and companionship. Especially in the beginning of marriage when many conflicts arise, the excitement of exploring sex together serves as a grounding experience that carries the couple through difficulties.

Sex reduces stress and anxiety by releasing tension. The feeling of togetherness and physical release provide a welcome relief from the stresses of daily life.

Simply, sex is a powerful bonding force that affirms and celebrates the special intimacy between husband and wife. Through sex, spouses express their affection for each other and comfort each other amidst the strains of daily life.

Role of Sex in Uncommitted Relationships

Uncommitted partners, after their first sexual encounter, sense a line has been crossed. Their relationship has irrevocably changed. Traditionally the partners were said to have "lost their innocence"; they can be said to have exited the sibling's sphere. However, without the mental and emotional backbone of lifelong commitment to one another, they are unprepared to handle the myriad relational obligations—spoken and unspoken, accepted and denied—thrust upon them. Participating in the conjugal sphere on an inappropriate foundation, they are caught up in issues that damage the heart and hinder growth.

Sex outside of marriage holds great allure, of course. It can seem to function as in marriage: expressing affection, bonding the partners, adding sparkle to their relationship and helping it to feel special. Unfortunately, it can also bring about practically the exact opposite of what sex does in marriage. It can highlight the underlying sense of emotional insecurity, introduce and aggravate conflicts, and increase stress and anxiety—effects so subtle as to be initially overlooked.

Sexual involvement without the lifetime commitment that marriage represents is only a symbolic experience of the partner in his or her totality. It frustrates the desire for authentic oneness. It can bond people who do not belong together, creating a false intimacy that deceives them into investing time and energy that would be better spent elsewhere. It can eclipse other means of relationship building and communication, eroding the basis for sustaining the relationship long-term. It can aggravate the tendency of immature couples to turn inward and neglect other people and responsibilities as well as other growth-promoting relationships and activities. Thus, uncommitted sex carries a host of hazards for the relationship as well as the individuals involved. (See Chapter 24)

A New Sexual Counterrevolution

"The time is ripe for a sexual counter-revolution and a renewal in love that leads to marriage," says Amy Kass, author and professor of a course on romantic love at the University of Chicago.[18] Indeed there are many signs of a shift in the currents of young love. Eric Nielson, a student at Rutgers, is unashamed to announce he is a virgin and he figures half his friends are too.[19] He is among the ever greater numbers of adolescents and young adults who are resisting the pressure to engage in unmarried sexual activity.

High school virgins are in the majority for the first time in twenty-five years in the U.S.[20] Significantly, the increase was more than twelve times greater among boys than girls.[21] This represents a swing in male youth culture towards self-restraint. Attitudes have changed as well. A 1997 UCLA survey finds the majority of college freshmen disapprove of casual sex, an increase of 10 percent in the last decade.[22] Almost half of teenagers believe sex before marriage is "always wrong"[23] and 60 percent advocate teaching abstinence to unmarried adolescents.[24]

Virginity is becoming a source of pride. The media calls "teenage celibates" the "fastest growing youth movement."[25] More than 2.3 million youth—13 percent—have pledged to save their virginity until marriage.[26] Music celebrities join them in that pledge[27] and the professional organization called Athletes for Abstinence includes basketball and football stars within its ranks.[28] Television shows showcase committed virgins. Over 20 contestants for various state beauty contests in 1999 used abstinence education as their platform and several won.[29] Books and periodicals signal this shift[30] and note an emerging trend toward earlier marriage, without cohabiting or many prior sex partners.[31]

There are hints of a global trend. Marriage is burgeoning in France, where the average age of first intercourse has risen to 18 in general and age 20 for the middle class.[32] From Japan to South Africa, a pro-abstinence movement is gaining ground.[33]

The trend is not unambiguous, of course. U.S. sexual activity and cohabitation rates for the young remain higher than before the sexual revolution. But youth now have a vantage point unavailable to prior generations—they can see the hazards as well as the pleasures of sexual expression. "They're far less willing to take the risks," says Kirsty Doig, of a New York market research group. "They've seen... the huge consequences: death, divorce."[34] Researcher Rosalind Miles writes that these offspring of the sexually permissive generation "currently display in their conversation, in their behavior, in their music and culture, a fierce faith in monogamous, exclusive, lifelong love and mutually faithful partnership."[35] Market researchers call it "neo-traditionalism" and note youth mores may well resemble their grandparents' more than their parents'—"Picture Eisenhower but with a pierced eyebrow."[36]

Celebrating Abstinence Outside of Marriage

Premarital abstinence liberates young people from unnecessary burdens and ensures the freedoms that all young people want to enjoy. Tara Roberts, a 24-year-old virginal woman explains, "I [want] to be in control of and empowered by my sexuality."[37] She points out that "virginity" is "derived from a Latin root meaning strength, force, skill." Says Dawn, 19, of Tucson, Arizona, virginity is "a matter of self-respect, and also the respect of my real friends."[38]

An abstinent lifestyle encourages teenagers to make friendships with many kinds of people, including the opposite sex. It gives them the space to learn creativity in expressing affection without physical intimacy. This fosters good social skills, a boon to later marriage and parenthood. At the same time it facilitates finding a marriage partner by protecting promising relationships from the misunderstanding, selfishness and distraction that sex can introduce.

Concerning future marriage, abstinence contributes to a person's financial stability before and after marriage since it frees energy to work on their careers and prepare in other ways for what will be expected of them as spouses, as parents, and as productive citizens. "As a father of four," says author Daniel Gray, "I am reaping the dividends [of investments made] years earlier when I heard and put into practice the message of abstinence before marriage."[39] These dividends include moral authority in guiding his children. More directly, premarital abstinence builds a foundation of trustworthiness and the habit of fidelity.

Those who no longer have their virginity can reap some of the advantages of abstinence by simply deciding to change. "I wanted to [become celibate] because sex had become such a... controlling factor in my life," confides a male university student. "I felt I could rise to higher levels... mentally, if I wasn't so focused on it."[40]

After two years of sexual intimacy with her fiancé, Ray, Susan sensed that sex dominated their relationship. She called off the sex as well as the engagement. Ray came to realize they needed to change. The couple later began their relationship again, this time grounded in a commitment to friendship and premarital abstinence. "Now I am happily married to Ray," Susan says. "Waiting until marriage to have sex [has] been worth it."[41]

Sexual Love Entails Responsibilities

When asked why he was still a virgin, 26-year-old Neal Bernards replied, "To me, intercourse implies a commitment that translates into a willingness to spend a lifetime with my partner and/or the children we create."[42] These words suggest the inherent responsibilities of sexual love that an enlightened ethic would affirm. They are basically three: to the conscience, to the present or future spouse and to the present or possible future child.

1. Responsibility to the Conscience

Honoring the conscience means living out moral convictions and respecting universal values regarding the larger meaning of sexuality. It encompasses responsibility to the individual's parents and grandparents—some might call this family honor—and to the larger community. "I've come this close at times to going too far," admits Ramon, a 23-year-old electrician, putting his thumb and index finger almost together. "But my fiancée and I have held the line at kissing and things like that. Partly it would be against what I believe in, and partly I'd be too ashamed to face my parents. My Dad's first and only woman was my mother. It was the same with his dad and mom. Dad once told me he almost cheated on Mom once, but one reason he didn't was because he did not want to set that kind of example for me. Times are very different for me than they were for Dad, but I still feel I want to uphold my family's values."

Furthermore, being responsible to the conscience involves the determination to achieve maturity of heart and character, to become a person of sufficient integrity to be able to fulfill the other two responsibilities of sexual love.

2. Responsibility to a Spouse

This recognizes the obligations of an enduring partnership. For single people, this means to be mindful of their future husband or wife and practice fidelity to them in advance. "I've had an empty frame near my bed since I was 13," says Tashika, a junior in an East coast high school. "I imagine it's my future husband and I sometimes write letters to him when I get lonely. It helps when my friends tell stories of having sex and stuff with their boyfriends and I start to get jealous and left out. Then I think about how I want to be when I face my future husband and I realize I want to save the excitement for him." For married couples, it is a commitment to cherish and care for their spouse and to preserve trust—the foundation for love—by being faithful to each other.

3. Responsibility to Children

Entering into sexual union implies the commitment to the potential result—a new person. The parents have a responsibility to the child they have chosen to create, to lovingly nurture him or her to his or her maturity. A loving marriage is the most secure foundation for the care of children. Children naturally want and need their parents to love each other and to be together, not only for their physical and emotional nurturing but also as an affirmation of their identity and value. Moreover, marriage is a worthy anchor for the lineage being created. It passes on a sound legacy and a healthy tradition for the descendants to inherit, imitate and build upon. "My parents have their shortcomings," says Jane, a mother in her mid-40s, "but you've got to hand it to them: 50 years of marriage, that's something to brag about." All children deserve to be proud of the love that conceived and raised them.

Only an ethic of committed, lifelong, mutually faithful monogamy—fidelity in marriage and abstinence before marriage—fulfills these three inherent responsibilities of sexual love. Such an ethic allows the nurturing and cohesive power of love to bind individuals, families, and ultimately a society together in strength.

Awakened to the downside of the permissive sexual ethic, society grapples with fashioning an ethic of healthy and responsible sexual love. A viable ethic recognizes the moral implications of sex and the deeper need for enduring love. It understands that sex in marriage not only heightens the sense of bonding, exclusivity and security between the partners, but it also addresses all the responsibilities inherent in physical intimacy. It celebrates the freedoms that premarital abstinence affords young people: to reach personal maturity and prepare for family life and their roles as citizens. It affirms these realities, not out of tradition, but out of a critical evaluation of the emotional, moral and social dimensions of this powerful and far-reaching act.

A high school senior, when sharing about her sexual experiences, concluded she'd like to be married the next time. "I'd want something permanent before having sex again, some stability, a reason he won't leave or I won't leave."[43] A progressive and yet responsible expression of the ethic of monogamy helps young people avoid the many pitfalls of sex outside of marriage (the subject of the next chapter) and find the surest route to romantic satisfaction, happy family life and personal maturity.

24

Consequences of Sex Outside of Marriage

I cannot here enumerate... the young men and women whom I once saw as a therapist and teacher, who, barely out of adolescence, had slept with so many people that they found themselves frigid or unresponsive beside those whom they genuinely loved.

—*Peter Marin*[1]

LETHAL SEXUALLY TRANSMITTED DISEASES AND UNWED parenthood garner attention from parents, teachers, legislatures and public health officials. Lost in this focus is the reality that even if disease and pregnancy are avoided, every sexual encounter outside of a mature and lifelong commitment—marriage—carries the risk of negative psychological, relational and social consequences. This risk is inherent to the nature of sexuality and therefore unavoidable.

Because the prevailing permissive ethic is grounded in a certain non-judgmental tolerance, the deeper, non-physical levels of harm and therefore the more subtle forms of abuse within sexual relations receive little acknowledgement. Patricia Dalton, a clinical psychologist in Washington, D.C., speaks of her clients displaying "an almost breathtaking lack of awareness of the price they stand to pay for casual sex."[2]

To admit that people are hurting and being hurt in these relationships would mean that some activities have to be deemed wrong. Instead, those suffering have often been left to doubt themselves, to blame their anguish on their residual inhibitions left over from the "dark ages" of traditional values.

These more subtle consequences of nonmarital sexual expression fall into categories roughly reflecting the three basic life goals. There are effects upon the individual, upon the pursuit of loving relationships and family, and upon the wider culture. Therefore, the issue is relevant not only to sexuality education but also to character and marriage education as well.

Impact on the Individual

As first explored by educators Thomas Lickona and Josh McDowell,[3] the emotional and psychological harm of sex in insecure relationships may be perceived only semi-consciously at the time, eclipsed by the pleasures and supposed benefits of expanded experience. Too often the real price paid is discovered after much of the damage is done. One woman psychiatrist recounts the impact of her promiscuous teenage years: "That sick, used feeling of having given a precious part of myself... to so many and for nothing, still aches. I never imagined I'd pay so dearly and for so long."[4] The effects of sex outside of marriage on psychological health, especially among adolescents are many:

Hindered Personal Development

Getting involved in sexual activities prematurely and in insecure relationships drains youth of the energy needed for emotional, moral, creative and intellectual growth. Sex under these circumstances becomes a powerful distraction away from important tasks that adolescents need to complete on the way to personal maturity, creating a family and pursuing their careers.

Julia, a college sophomore at a Midwestern university, reflects upon her first two years away from home: "When I get involved with a guy that way, it seems like everything else stops. I don't see my friends or make new ones or join in any extra activities—everything gets absorbed in him. The funny thing is that the times between boyfriends are the times when I really start to grow as a person. That's when I take the time and go to the trouble to get together with girl friends, do volunteer work, go to plays, take long walks." Since she noticed this, Julia has opted for a celibate lifestyle that frees up time and energy to pursue creative growth.

Derailed Character Growth

In marriage, sexual intimacy supports the partners' mutual love, while in uncommitted relationships among youth, it is mainly to boost the partners' egos.[5] Premarital sex thus often compounds self-centeredness, rather than supporting the developmental task of learning unselfish love.

Worse than hindering character growth, nonmarital sex is a corrupting influence. It's no secret that people will lie and cheat to get sex. In one group of 75 middle-class 19-year-old male students, most admitted that they had used force or other means to get sex, according to a University of Connecticut study. Sixty-five percent of the young men had gotten young women drunk for that purpose. More than half had arranged to enter their date's apartment and 40 percent had used verbal intimidation. One in five had used force or threats of violence.[6]

About half of University of California students surveyed admitted to lying in order to get sex. A quarter of those men who were sexually involved with more than one person at a time said their sexual partners did not know.[7] In a separate California study of male students tested for AIDS, many confessed they would conceal even a lethal disease—25 percent would not tell sex partners if they were found to be HIV positive.[8]

Middle school students are inheriting callous moral attitudes when it comes to sexual matters. In a national survey of students in grades six through nine, over 65 percent of boys and girls said it was acceptable for a man to force sex on a woman if they have been dating for six months or more." One third said it was all right to rape a woman if she was not a virgin.[9] When people treat others as objects to be exploited, they actually end up debasing themselves.

Regret, Guilt and Shame

College counselor Carson Daly comments, "I don't think I ever met a student who was sorry he or she had postponed sexual activity, but I certainly met many who deeply regretted their sexual involvement."[10] Several surveys suggest that half of sexually experienced students report "tremendous guilt" as part of the aftermath.[11] People intuitively feel that to give away their virginity in an unworthy relationship, and to possibly continue to abuse their sexuality, is a profound violation of self. This becomes a source of shame. The shame is deeper still if they have violated their parents' trust and feel compelled to keep their sexual activity a secret.

Physical Impact: Teenage Unwed Pregnancy

Adolescent girls becoming pregnant and bearing children has always been commonplace; until the recent past they were typically married. Though the younger the girl the greater the health risks to both her and the baby, the greatest hazards of pregnancy to an unwed teenager are less physical than psychological, relational and economic—mainly due to her being unmarried.

Pregnancy can generate a great deal of emotional distress, not the least of which is tension between the teenagers and their parents and between the partners themselves. Nine out of ten American adolescent boys abandon their pregnant girlfriend, even if reluctantly. Suicide is seven times more likely for the pregnant girl.[12] Economically, girls who choose to bear their child are far less likely to complete higher education, to marry and to escape poverty. Indeed, mothers who are unmarried, under 20 years old, and without a high school diploma are ten times more likely to raise their child in poverty in America than those who are not.[13]

If the girl aborts the pregnancy there are risks as well. Physical complications—scarring, infection, or damage to organs—are not uncommon. Emotionally there is a hazard of chronic grief and guilt. Over 80 percent of teenagers in one study reported preoccupation with the aborted fetus, and half had nightmares.[14] Boys who are involved can be troubled by the event as well.[15] There have even been cases of babies surviving the abortion and being born, to haunt the young parents with their abortion-related disabilities.

A ruined reputation only aggravates the shame. One girl explains: "I get asked out all the time and I'm sick of the creeps who just want to make out all the time. I am also sick of myself. I'm only 17, and my reputation is not worth a dime.... Whenever I meet a new guy I wonder how much he has heard."[16]

Worst of all, if someone has knowingly—or even unknowingly—used another only for the pleasure of sex and then witnessed the partner's heartbreak after being discarded, this can generate guilt that can linger over a lifetime. A young man recalls his first sexual involvement as an adolescent: "I finally got the girl into bed... but then she started saying she loved me.... [When] I finally dumped her... I felt pretty low."[17] Jacques, a Canadian in his 20s, recounted how he had had his first sexual encounter with a woman after an evening of drinking together. "What I can't forget is how she said she'd never been so happy in her life." This evidence that the sexual relationship had meant so much more to her than it did to him haunted him, and his guilt followed him for years.

Lowered Self-Respect and Self-Esteem

A reliable casualty of nonmarital sex and multiple partners is the sense of self-respect and self-esteem. Jennifer Grossman, 30, candidly shares one reason: "The acceptance, even encouragement of premarital sex makes it very difficult to sustain the fantasy that we are loved alone."[18] When sex is a matter of making conquests or negotiating favors, or using and being used, youth cannot help but lose respect for themselves, even if they are not conscious of the loss for a long time. William, a good-looking college student who had had numerous sexual encounters, was disturbed after watching a 1950s movie and the modest way people dressed back then. "They had so much dignity. I've lost that, and I don't know how to get it back."

Further, making sexiness and sexual prowess an important basis for romantic connections amplifies the tendency to judge people on what they do and how they look rather than on who they are.[19] Thus anxiety is built into insecure relationships. "Do I still please you? Do I still look good?" There is always the legitimate fear that someone else will perform better or look more attractive when sexual utility is the criteria for attention.

Sexual Addiction

Mae Williams, a senior at Howard University, commented, "I don't have time for casual sex, it's too addictive. I've seen people fall into a pattern of nonrelationships. Those are worries I don't want."[20] Adolescents are always facing the temptation to seek an easy escape from the challenges of growing up and taking responsibility for their lives. Like controlled substances, sex is addictive—there are estimated to be over 13 million sex addicts in the U.S.[21] As with any addiction, sex can take over relationships and overwhelm other interests.

Depression and Destructive Behavior

All infatuations or romantic involvements of some duration are painful when they break up. When sex is introduced, the emotional ties as well as expectations are intensified. Sex is like powerful glue that, once bonded, has no way to release its grip. Hearts that have bonded through sex, even in a casual encounter, are unlikely to disengage without being torn in some way. Psychologists have pointed out that breaking off such relationships can precipitate an emotional crisis that resembles that of a divorce. This is exemplified in the words of one girl, who said, "I didn't know how to live without him. I wanted to curl up and die when we broke up."

This heartbreak, compounded with the sense of having given themselves so totally for such a paucity of return, not to mention the fallout of a pregnancy, abortion or an STD, can help drive young men and women to the brink of despair. One tragic result is teenage suicide, which has tripled over the past 25 years in the U.S.—the same period during which the rate of teenage sexual activity rose so sharply. Statistically, non-virginal girls are six times more prone to suicide than are virgins.[22]

Adolescent premarital sex is also associated with other destructive behaviors. Sexually experienced girls aged 12 to 16 are 18 times more likely to run away from home than virgins. They are 9 times more likely to be arrested by the police. The probability of being suspended from school is 5 times greater. Non-virginal girls are 10 times more likely to use marijuana, one of the gateway drugs. Similar correlations are found among non-virginal boys.[23]

Physical Impact: Sexually-Transmitted Diseases

While public attention is often drawn to the danger of AIDS, it is small in numbers compared to the massive epidemic of other sexually transmitted diseases (STDs). There are 300 new STD cases for every new AIDS case in the United States.[24] Of the total population infected with any STD, two-thirds of these cases are youth under the age of 25.[25] It is estimated that half of nonvirginal Americans can expect to be infected during their lifetime. More than one in five teenagers and adults currently has an incurable viral STD, apart from AIDS.[26]

People remain largely unaware of the risks and consequences of STDs. Condoms are largely ineffective with common infections like genital herpes, gonorrhea, human papilloma virus and chlamydia.[27] Viral diseases have no cure. Many people are even unaware that they have an STD. Like AIDS, these diseases can show no symptoms for quite a while.

The potential consequences of STDs include chronic pain AND psychological distress. In one study over half of herpes victims reported fear of rejection and depression during their most recent outbreak.[28] More serious consequences include infertility, a greater susceptibility to cancer and HIV, and difficulty in getting married.[29]

Young people have the highest risk of infection. Girls' bodies are more vulnerable to infection than those of adult women. The cervical mucous of a girl is more conducive to microorganisms.[30] Girls are ten times more vulnerable to pelvic inflammatory disease, an affliction accompanying chlamydia and gonorrhea that threatens fertility.[31] Most of those with the chlamydial form of the disease will face pelvic surgery of some kind, whether to remove organs or to help conceive a child.[32] Sexually active girls under 17 years of age have double the rate of cervical cancer of grown women. Cervical cancer is also linked to having many sexual partners.[33] It does not occur in girls who remain virgins.

Youth are at greatest risk also because those who begin sex early will likely have more sexual partners over a lifetime. It is this—not whether each of those relationships was mutually exclusive at the time—that increases the probability of contracting such lethal diseases as AIDS. Medical realities affirm that people, especially the young, are not suited for sex outside of a lifelong monogamous relationship.

Rage and Fear

Finally, the emotional explosion over a sexual betrayal can turn into rage, leading to violence against the former partner or the new lovers. News accounts of teenage murders often describe a broken sexual relationship as the chief motive. Anna, a junior at a northwestern college, tells of a broken sexual relationship veering into fear and violence. When she broke up with one young man, Bill, and started dating a friend of his, she says, "They got into a fight over me right on the street, yelling at each other and circling each other." Police intervened but it was little comfort. "Bill knew where I lived, and I wondered if he was going to start stalking me or something. I wondered if I'd be safe in my own neighborhood."

Daly summarizes the mental and emotional impact of uncommitted sexual intimacy by citing her long experience:

No one prepares young people for these effects: the lowered self-esteem; the despairing sense of having been used; the self-contempt for being a user; the embarrassment of having a reputation that puts you outside the circle of people with true integrity; the unease about having to lie or at least having to conceal one's activities from family members and others; the extreme difficulty of breaking the vicious cycle of compulsive sexual behavior; and the self-hatred of seeking, after each break-up, someone else to seduce in order to revive one's fading self-image. No one tells students that it sometimes takes years to recover from the effects of these sexual involvements—if one ever recovers.[34]

Impact on Relationships

"Sex always changes the dynamics of a relationship," observes McDowell.[35] When uncommitted adolescents appropriate a distinctive part of the spouse's sphere—sexual bonding—for a relationship that is essentially an extension of the sibling's sphere, they have the worse parts of both worlds. They can no longer enjoy the full growth and pleasures of their friendship nor can they reap the rewards of married love. Beyond the partner, their relations with friends, other peers and potential marriage partners are compromised, as well as the bond with parents and other elders. Premarital sex jeopardizes even the most promising relationships, and its impact can extend into a future marriage as well.

Stress with Parents and Friends

When their children enter into sexual relations outside the formal process of marriage, parents can feel disrespected and hurt, their intrinsic interests ignored, their values compromised. The breach can be difficult to mend. "When my father found out I was having sex, he was really hurt. It's not like he disowned me, but our relationship hasn't been the same," says Sarah, 17, from Indianapolis. Though she feels she loves her boyfriend, "I love my father, too, and I never thought about how he'd feel."[36]

Friendships are certainly affected too. Krista, a high school senior from Kentucky, tells of how a sexual relationship changed a circle of friends: "We just used to hang out at each other's houses, all very casual. My best friend was eyeing Buddy but he wasn't really interested. But then Buddy and I got more involved and pretty soon we got into a physical relationship. I'll never forget my best friend's face, all tear-streaked and angry, when she said, 'Did you sleep with him?' She eventually went and made another best friend. Nobody hung out together anymore. It was just Buddy and me. Then his family moved to another town and we broke up."

Sexual involvement can turn close friends into bitter enemies overnight. Nothing—not power, money or beliefs—is as divisive as sexual jealousy. Indeed, sometimes a crowd of adolescents can feel like a sticky web of sexual attraction, possessiveness, jealousy, rivalry and betrayal. All intentions become suspect. Is this just a hug or an invitation to something more? Does she want a friend or a sexual partner? Or is she just trying to make someone else jealous?

Problems with Partners

The expression, "Once burned, twice shy" applies to many people who emotionally withdraw and refuse to trust anyone as a potential partner after the heartache of the breakup of a sexual relationship. The remembered pain of betrayal stands in the way of giving themselves trustingly to anyone else. As a Rod Stewart song of the sexual revolution era termed it, everyone becomes "Scarred and Scared." A college senior described how a night of sex ruined what had been a promising friendship in high school, and the pain of that break-up damaged his ability to trust and to find love for many years: "I didn't go out again until I got to college. I've had mostly one-night stands in the last couple of years. I'm afraid of falling in love."[37]

Frequently, the introduction of sex derails a warm and caring friendship that might well have been a good basis for marriage. Ryan, a teacher in Vermont, recalls his long-time close friendship with the "girl next door" that everyone thought would lead to marriage. "We didn't need sex and didn't want it. But everyone expected us to be sexually involved, so finally we decided maybe we were missing something.... [We had sex and] afterwards our relationship changed. We felt different about each other and what we had just faded away. I still regret that."

At the same time, the bonding power of sex can also lead people to prolong an unhealthy relationship that is based on physical attractiveness or a need for security. Consequently, some teenagers feel trapped in a relationship they don't really want but don't know how to get out of. One girl confessed, "I truly regret that my first time was with a guy I didn't care that much about. I am still going out with him, which is getting to be a problem. I'd like to end this relationship and date others, but after being so intimate, it's awfully tough."[38]

What enhances unselfishness in a committed relationship can multiply selfishness in an insecure one, leading to more tensions and conflict. The pleasures of sex too readily invite rationalization of expectation and demand. "Since that first night, he expects sex on every date, like we are married or something. When I don't feel like it, we end up in an argument. It's like I owe it to him," Denise, a high-school junior complains. In fact, sexual involvement outside of marriage, especially among live-in lovers, is associated with more violence and other forms of abuse than among the married.[39] (See Chapter 19)

Physical intimacy leaves the heart yearning for comparable emotional intimacy. Yet ironically, sex makes that longing harder to fulfill.[40] Sex can easily come to overpower any meaningful communication or other healthy activities together. A 22-year-old male student, a virgin, said, "I've seen too many of my friends break up after their relationships turned physical. The emotional wreckage is horrendous because they have already shared something so powerful. When you use sex too early, it will block other means of communicating love and can stunt the balanced growth of the relationship."[41]

Consequences for Future Marriage

The effects of premature sexual experiences do not end when young people enter into the world of marriage and parenthood. A person rarely forgets a sexual partner, even if he or she wants to. Those who have engaged in premarital sex may find that they are haunted by the images of past partners, even in the marriage bed. This involuntary comparison of previous lovers to their spouse can be not only disturbing to them, but also disconcerting to the spouse, if known. Who likes to have their husband or wife comparing their body or performance to a lover in the past? One young husband observed, "Whenever I kiss my wife or engage in love play, my memory reminds me that this girl could kiss better than my wife, that that girl was better at something else, and so forth. I can't concentrate on loving my wife with all that I have—there have been too many women in my life to be wholly committed to one."[42] Likewise, these days there are many young wives who develop a feeling of scorn for their husbands who cannot measure up to idealized memories of past partners.[43]

Worse, studies show the habit of surrendering to sexual feelings before marriage can prove to be a serious problem at some stressful time with a spouse.[44] If young men and women are unable to practice sexual integrity before marriage, what will guarantee their ability to do so after the wedding? At that point, succumbing to the old habit would be devastating to the mate, marriage and child.

After many uncommitted relationships, sex may lose its power to build intimacy with the one chosen to be a lifetime companion. Like glue, sex does not bond as well when reused again and again. The bonding power may grow feebler after having already imprinted the heart and mind with previous partners. An opposite problem emerges when early disappointing experiences can lead either to an aversion to sex or a feeling of boredom with it. This can take years to overcome, even after becoming married.

"Sexual activity only celebrates what is there. Sex cannot deliver what does not already exist," states William McCready of the University of Chicago.[45] In the context of a committed marriage and the mutual trust and unconditional love it provides, sexual relations amplify the already present atmosphere of understanding, acceptance and intimacy. Without that commitment, sex only aggravates insecurity, lack of trust and misunderstanding, making real intimacy harder to attain.

The Culture of Uncommitted Sexual Relationships

Most adults who are uncomfortable with teenage sex clearly see its negative consequences. They agree that immature teenagers should be encouraged in abstinence, in their own self-interest and in the interest of society.[46] Yet, when adolescents decide on sex outside of marriage and unwed parenthood, are they not simply following the example of their elders?

Most of the social problems associated with nonmarital sex involve adults. Over 80 percent of pregnancies outside of marriage in the U.S. are to women over 20. Teenagers under 18 account for only 13 percent.[47] The numbers are similar for abortions,[48] and most STDs are also among adults.

It is certainly not easy to explain why the same behavior that is so risky and irresponsible for a girl on one side of age 20 is merely a "personal decision" for a young woman on the other side. Are the prospects for a typical 23-year-old single mother and her baby considerably better than those facing an 18-year-old single mother? Are all the other negative psychological, relational and social consequences significantly different for adolescent boys and girls as opposed to men and women?

The first generation shaped by the sexual revolution thinks they are. While three out of four Americans frown upon teenagers having sex before marriage, less than half believe that it is always wrong for adults to do it. The majority under age 45 thinks that sex outside of marriage is generally beneficial for finding a good spouse and for other reasons apart from pleasure.[49]

Here lies the heart of the problem: adult attitudes and behavior favoring non-monogamy. If adults do not expect marriage to be the context to find romantic and sexual fulfillment and to raise children, then why should teenagers behave differently? This is especially true when society accepts that a good marriage is a dim prospect.

Teenage Sex and the Loss of the Marriage Culture

What is striking about teenage birth rates today as contrasted with those in the 1950s and 60s—besides being actually lower—is that in the past teenage parents used to be married.[50] The issue today is not how many get pregnant but how few get married. The decline of adult respect for marriage as the context for sex has left little incentive for youth to postpone sex. Setting age as the guideline does not work. Certainly being told that before a magic age, having sex or a child—or even getting married—is a bad idea but afterwards anything goes is "hardly likely to capture their moral imagination," as Maggie Gallagher put it. "Does it capture yours?"[51] If marriage is not the decisive event worth waiting for, then why is an arbitrary age?

What's worse, once marriage is no longer expected, engaging in particularly hazardous sexual behavior may even seem to be a substitute way to show special love and loyalty. Gallagher observes, "If it is not marriage that confers special meaning to the sexual act, then perhaps it is [a girl] giving the gift of unprotected sex, or making a baby." Indeed, in one avant-garde movie about a man who died of AIDS, the camera reveals him making love with his girlfriend and then pans dramatically to the unused condom on the bedside table. An unused piece of latex now represents the nobility of a lover's sacrifice.

Given a culture allergic to committed monogamy, adolescent sexual relations are not hard to understand. To be sure, it is harder to fathom why they would want to wait.

Adult Complicity in Teenage Sex

Some experts are blunt about adult complicity in youthful exper-imentation. "The 'raging hormones' argument is nonsense," says John Gagnon. "Society elicits sexual behavior in kids."[52] However, the criti-cal role the adult sexual ethic plays in the sexual behavior of the young is a reality hard for parents, teachers and other adults to accept. Even prominent advocates of character education and traditional family val-ues are reluctant to take a stand on the issue of adult sex outside of marriage.[53] If making hard and fast guidelines for adolescent sexual behavior is a divisive issue, doing the same with adult sexual behavior is for many out of the question.

A society that is ambivalent in its sexual standards for adults can-not expect its youth to live moral and healthy sexual lives. Example is the strongest teacher. The single mother whose date slept over last night, the teacher physically involved with a student, the coach having an affair with a married woman—not to mention the movies and music endlessly depicting the glories of unmarried sex—none of this goes unnoticed.

Sexual permissiveness also makes it harder to establish other moral boundaries. "Sex before marriage has proven to be the runaway horse of traditional values. Once it took off, all the other old-time mores became more difficult to keep in their place," concludes author David Whitman.[54] In fact, virtue becomes turned on its head. A consistent theme in articles on celebrity parenthood out of wedlock is that it is, in the words of Barbara Dafoe Whitehead, "not only...a way to find hap-piness but also as a way to exhibit such virtues as honesty and courage."[55] Uncommitted sex is conveyed as downright ennobling.

Related to this is the way tolerance of nonmarital sex undermines parents' and other adults' sense of moral authority. Afraid of appearing hypocritical, elders may feel helpless to advise youth to act in ways they themselves have not and are unable to do. The net effect is that adolescents are denied the clear sexual guidance they want and need. "People say 'Use a condom,'" says Stephanie Brown, a Planned Parenthood teen clinic director in Northern California, "but not 'Why are you having sex with this person?'" As author Nellie Bernstein observed, "We talk to young people as if their genitals are a matter of public concern, but their souls are none of our business."[56]

Adult tolerance of teenage sexual activity can also be more self-serving than it is comfortable to face. It can be easier for elders to remain silent or merely help a boy or girl acquire contraceptives rather than to risk being judged by their own standards and face changing old habits. William Galston, board member of the National Campaign to Prevent Teen Pregnancy, concedes: "We believe what we believe about premarital sex because it is convenient for us to do so."[57]

Certainly it facilitates the exploitation of girls by older men. A fact expediently underplayed in the discussion of "teenage" pregnancy and disease is that many are encounters between minors and adults or near-adults. The majority of pregnant girls began their sexual activity as a result of being raped or abused by men 27 years old on average.[58] California research suggests that over half of births to girls 11 to 15 involve males over 19.[59] National studies indicate that one in five births to teenage mothers 15 to 17 years of age involve men over 21.[60] There is evidence that most cases of girls infected with STDs are due to liaisons with adult men, who are four times as likely to be infected as boys.[61] To help "prevent junior high sex," researcher Mike Males points out, it is necessary "to lecture grown-ups."[62]

Of course adults retain their prerogative to make personal sexual decisions; this is a given. However, it serves no purpose to pretend that apart from the grossest of abuses, these decisions are morally equivalent and of less consequence to the young than they really are. What adults do—what they are—always affects others around them, especially the next generation. Committed monogamy in marriage honors this moral reality. If the sexual culture of even a small but influential group of adults—perhaps parents and teachers—shifts towards a healthy and responsible sexual ethic, the sexual attitudes and behavior of the young can also change.

Today's pervasive culture of sex outside of marriage has made virginity into an act of deviance. Adult virgin Neal Bernards asserts that sex has become the "drug of choice," and those who abstain are seen as "aberrant, abnormal and even dangerous."[63] Yet young people drawn into the maelstrom of nonmarital sex are at risk. Beyond the commonly recognized risks of pregnancy and disease, there are psychological hazards and damage to future relationships. These risks are often overlooked, yet they take a very real toll.

To spare the young these hazards, a progressive and responsible norm is necessary. Setting up two separate standards for youth and adults based on arbitrary ages is unworkable. So is grounding it in self-assessments of maturity or states of feeling or other subjective and unreliable criteria. The only viable standard is one based on an act of will, a promise that establishes a definite reference point for the partners and for the many others who are affected. In truth, a responsible ethic of sexual love would have to assert the currently unpopular notion that all sex in insecure relationships is self-defeating and irresponsible. If sexuality is to be fully enjoyed and its fruits love-enhancing and life-enriching, then its context can only be committed, lifelong, mutually faithful monogamy—in other words, marriage.

25

Addressing Objections to Monogamy

THE STANDARD OF COMMITTED, LIFELONG, MUTUALLY FAITHFUL monogamy[1]—that is, abstinence before marriage and fidelity within marriage—has traditionally been exalted as the virtue of chastity. Excesses and injustices in enforcing this traditional code have contributed to its rejection in recent times. Many commonly held notions pose obstacles to parents, educators and others interested in reinvigorating this norm. These are notions about sexual needs, knowledge, pleasure and regard for the body, personal growth, the double standard, and guilt. In addition, some adults have qualms about being hypocritical if they advocate marriage and abstinence to the young. Educating for healthy and responsible sexual love necessarily means addressing these concerns and objections.

Issues of Human Nature

Can people meet their sexual needs while practicing premarital abstinence and marital fidelity?

A 1991 sex survey of students at a northeastern college found that about 20 percent affirmed the statement, "the more fun a person has, the sounder he or she will be psychologically."[2] This reflects the belief that sex is not only an urge but also a need that must be met, like food or sleep, or else there is a risk to mental and physical health. It follows that it is unreasonable to expect people to forego sex, especially if they are in difficult situations—a bad marriage, widowhood, unable to marry, and so on. The argument goes that because of this need, a large proportion of people have always engaged in premarital and extramarital sex, even if it was kept a secret.

The notion that sexual inactivity in itself is a threat to psychological health is dubious. Hundreds of thousands—3 percent—of Americans have remained celibate throughout their lives[3] and millions have waited to begin sexual involvement until age thirty and beyond with no proven ill effects. Over 80 percent of Americans under age 60 have had either one or no sex partner in a given year.[4] A corollary is that among married couples, cheating is the great exception.[5] When opportunity for sex is not available for long periods of time—in military service for example—interest in it has been known to drop off to nil.[6] Furthermore, sex experts say that one reason married couples may find themselves having little or no sex is that they simply get out of the habit.

Sexual abstinence is, in the words of Gabrielle Brown, author of an exhaustive study of celibacy, "the rest state of sexuality, where the sexual response becomes more diffuse, expanding in many directions beyond a simple genital response." Rather than a state of repression or frustration, it can simply represent a redirection of sexual impulses.[7] As Masters and Johnson have stated, "In one respect, sex is like no other physical process... [it] can be denied indefinitely, even for a lifetime." In fact, some experts question if it is even a drive at all since it is so amenable to learning and will. "Sex is a natural urge, but the role it plays in your life and the importance you attribute to it... is a matter of free choice," concludes psychologist Peter Koestenbaum.[8] The notion of compelling sexual needs comes chiefly from discredited studies conducted in the 1950s, notably the specious work of Alfred Kinsey, who is coming under increasing fire for bias and using unsound sampling techniques.[9] (See Chapter 23)

Controlling the sexual urge is obviously what most people must do most of the time. Even when a partner is available as in marriage, circumstances such as illness, work, pregnancy, menstrual cycle and the demands of parenthood dictate a large measure of self-control. Thus, any reasonably functional person needs to learn sexual self-restraint.

The prevailing view assumes people need physical gratification more than they do, and this produces its own negative fallout. In the past those with strong sexual desire struggled with feelings of abnormality and those with few scruples had to justify why their partner should give in. Now the situation appears reversed. Single and married people wonder if they are abnormal if they do not desire sex as much as they hear they should. Those with lower desire or reservations about sex outside of marriage face pressure to satisfy the demands of more aggressive partners, because it is after all "healthy" and "normal."

Unreasonably high expectations of sexual interest and readiness produce as much pressure as the past taboos,[10] with perhaps more destructive results. The chief worry of girls 12 years and older is sexual pressure, not only from boys but also from other girls, friends and the media.[11] Thus young people push themselves into sexual involvement earlier and in more insecure situations than they would otherwise be inclined to. One 23-year-old woman had her first sexual experience because "virginity was like a tiny but oppressive burden that I always carried around with me; it was great to get rid of it."

Isn't monogamy unnatural?

"Homo sapiens is a promiscuous species," asserts clinical psychologist Jules Older.[12] Arguments abound that biology dictates that men and women pursue a variety of sexual partners, like polygamous primates. Therefore, self-restraint is not only difficult, it is almost hopeless.

However, this argument does not hold when considering the basic difference between humans and promiscuous primates like chimpanzees. Male chimpanzees are not concerned about the welfare of their offspring, or even which baby is theirs. Human fathers on the other hand love their sons and daughters. And well they should, from a biological perspective; human children require a great deal of parental nurturing. If human fathers want their children to thrive, they need to make a sizeable investment in both the children and their mother. The mother needs to make a similar investment.

In unstable communities where crime, early death and other conditions create extreme stress, it might make genetic sense for males to impregnate as many females as possible and for females to have babies unmindful of the fathers—in other words, to act like chimpanzees—to ensure that some of their offspring might survive. But a healthy human norm it is not. Monogamy and marriage support the prospering of the human species and favor the individual's posterity. It is no accident that enduring societies worldwide have affirmed the marriage norm. The myth of more "natural" sexually permissive societies propagated by an earlier generation of anthropologists like Margaret Mead has been exposed as wishful thinking.[13]

The Social Value of Monogamy

Since the dawn of time, enduring societies, including those most economically successful, have been monogamous.[14] Cambridge professor J. D. Unwin studied eighty-eight societies and discovered, contrary to his expectations, that all favored premarital abstinence and marital fidelity. When they abandoned this sexual ethic they perished within a few generations.[15]

A key reason why monogamy works best is that it is "democratic." Every man has an equal opportunity to have a woman and have children. "Polygamy creates a clear social order, with distinct winners and losers," especially among men, observes sociologist William Tucker. Outwardly attractive men—those with looks, money and status—get as many women as they can afford. Other men lose out, even those with the inner traits that would enable them to be better husbands and fathers. The scarcity of women encourages such practices as the bride price which further narrows the chances for less affluent men, or arranged marriages between older men and younger girls, which creates an unlikely context for a happy marriage.[16]

Thus, there arises the "bachelor herd" of single men with no legitimate way to meet their heart's need to enter the conjugal and parental spheres of love, or even of their physical desire for sex. These discouraged men end up fighting for alliances with the high-status men and for dominance among themselves, not to mention taking out their frustrations by terrorizing the populace. In the U.S., single male teenagers and young adults commit 90 percent of violent crime.[17]

Monogamy, on the other hand, reduces sexual competitiveness among men. This makes male cooperation possible, and allows men and women to work together in a non-sexual setting. In this way, monogamy permits and sustains democratic government and the generation and distribution of wealth. Since it is also better for the nurturance of children, it naturally cultivates stronger and more productive citizens. Middle-class families, aspiring to better themselves, tend to prize premarital abstinence and marital fidelity. With much to gain and much to lose, they are neither secure enough to be cavalier about sexual norms, nor hopeless enough not to care. It is when the middle class abandons this innate caution and begins to imitate the racy lifestyles among the class above or below them that society is most at risk.

Monogamy—and the constellation of attitudes and practices that uphold and protect it—is not only good for individuals, spouses and children. It is good for society, too. "The long-standing, almost universal dislike and disapproval of child-bearing out of wedlock, of sexual infidelity, of public prostitution and pornography... these are not just irrational intolerances," asserts Tucker. "They are the ancient, forgotten logic that holds together a monogamous society."[18]

Doesn't this ethic reinforce ignorance and superstition?

There is truth to the criticism that traditional norms inhibited open discussion of sexuality and thus encouraged ignorance. Yet while contemporary attitudes have eliminated old superstitions—that women do not enjoy sex, for example, it has created new ones—that consensual sex is always beneficial or at least harmless. The assumption that the more permissive ethic is more rational and informed by social science is a shaky one. Recent decades have brought an avalanche of hard data on human sexuality that explodes many contemporary myths—that sex is best for young singles, that cohabitation is beneficial, that men lose out in marriage or that most spouses cheat.[19]

An enlightened sexual ethic today recognizes the importance of knowledge and understanding about love and sexuality. These need to be conveyed in an age-appropriate way and within an ethical framework. The ample evidence for the benefits of marriage, even for sexual satisfaction, also deserves a complete airing.

Isn't this ethic ultimately anti-sex, anti-body and anti-pleasure?

For some, the fear of dampening sexual pleasure is greater than any other. "Parents worry less about preventing their children's sexual activity than they do about inhibiting their sexual feeling," observes Helen Kaplan, director of the Human Sexuality Program at the Cornell Medical Center.[20] Ironically, sex in insecure relationships generates its own problems in this area. One experienced teenager says she gets "a massive body headache" just thinking about sex. Others say they "freak out" either beforehand or afterwards, contemplating the possible fallout.[21] Is this conducive to sexual pleasure?

A progressive yet responsible expression of the ethic of premarital abstinence and marital fidelity is "sex positive." It can point to the enhanced eroticism and pleasure available through a monogamous relationship. Over 85 percent of married people report enjoying great sexual pleasure, and as many speak of being quite emotionally gratified as well.[22] The safety, trust and familiarity of a lifelong partner set up the context for fully exploring the possibilities of sexual love. Sexuality deserves to be appreciated and celebrated in all of its depth and power, neither trivialized nor demonized. Within its rightful context and in the spirit of ethical love, there are no limits to exploring and enjoying its profound meaning, beauty and joys.

Doesn't monogamy restrict personal growth?

Implicit in this objection is a positive regard for diverse experiences of any kind. Therefore, enjoying various sexual partners is considered more enriching and broadening. Indeed there is even the connotation that it is more courageous to do so, demonstrating a greater desire for self-actualization. In the survey of college sexual attitudes noted above, more than half of the students agreed with the notion that "Premarital sex is all right if it increases the capacity to trust, brings greater integrity to personal relationships, dissolves barriers separating people, enhances self-respect, and fosters a zest for living."[23] However, as discussed in the previous chapter, premarital sex actually has the opposite effect a great deal of the time.

A related idea is that sexual satisfaction is a growth-producing phenomenon in and of itself. In this view, exploring all the dimensions of sexual experience is a positive good. One partner is considered unlikely to provide the full range of potential sexual experiences. To be sure, uncommitted sexual encounters can be revealing about love and the self. However, the truth is that monogamy is far more demanding and growthful. To wait for and invest in one person in such a way as to sustain and renew love may seem impossibly demanding, but it is precisely this context that stretches every faculty and promotes the greatest personal growth. (See Chapter 17)

It is only too easy to run to another partner instead of facing the deeper issues that real and enduring intimacy demands. In the words of human potential philosopher George Leonard, "It is easy to associate multiple sexual partners with personal change and monogamy with personal stasis.... But extramarital affairs and pursuit of recreational sex are far more likely to be associated with the avoidance of change."[24] In a lifelong commitment, a person must face him or herself deeply— there is no escape. This leads to authentic expansion of the heart and building of the character, not the superficial changes that come about in more temporary and uncommitted relationships. This is why psychiatrist Viktor Frankl maintained that monogamy fosters the inner growth needed to share true love.[25]

Personal growth logically relates to maturity. Psychologist Abraham Maslow noticed that one trait of self-actualized people was a deep appreciation of sexual love, yet the ability to tolerate its absence well.[26] A full definition of maturity naturally includes self-control in the sexual arena just as it includes self-control regarding time, anger, sleep and other matters. Most adults would be embarrassed to oversleep for an appointment, to shout in a business meeting, or worse, to be unable to control their toilet habits. Yet they can be unashamed of sexual indiscretions.

Indeed, sexual self-discipline is a defining task of instinctual control during adolescence. It is similar to toilet training for the young child. Just as the child feels proud and "grown up" when he or she has mastered continence, so the teenager can learn to find pride in and equate maturity with sexual abstinence. "My dad says a real man controls himself. I'm strong enough to wait," says Makeem, a high school senior.

In addition, monogamy supports the fundamental integrity that comprises maturity by keeping the body aligned with the conscience and deepest heart. The body has its own language: a fist means hostility; a smile signifies good will. If a smile conceals malice, it is a deception, a misuse of the language of the body. In this vein, sexual coupling represents the total union of hearts, minds and lives. When physical union is merely for pleasure or as an expression of warm feelings, this too can be considered a deception. Dishonesty like this is incompatible with reaching moral wholeness and maturity.

Doesn't the sexual modesty and restraint that this kind of ethic implies encourage sexual inhibitions?

The current sexual climate assumes it is better to be rid of artificial boundaries between the sexes and to be frank about people's sexual desires and the naked body. Progressive men and women are supposed to be comfortable with nudity and sexual talk, and to prefer a straightforward negotiation of sexual favors.

However, sexual restraint in dress and manners is innate in people cross-culturally, even among peoples who wear few clothes. Western women who are scantily dressed often exspend a lot of energy trying to keep themselves as covered as their clothes allow. Sexual modesty has the effect of preventing distractions and leaves men and women free to relate to each other as personalities instead of bodies.[27]

In a world that denies modesty, like many college dormitories where men and women daily share bathrooms and bedrooms, young people end up tuning out the eroticized environment in order to survive. With this goes some capacity for emotional closeness as well. Even attempts at serious romantic relationships end up, in ethicist Daniel Mahoney's words, "oddly disengaged"—emotionally cool while physically hot.[28]

Sexual modesty is protective. It is the corollary to the sharing of confidences only with intimate friends. It reflects the privacy of hopes and dreams, the withholding of the deepest recesses of the self only for a worthy person.

Doesn't this ethic encourage guilt?

Opponents of the monogamy ethic point to the harsh way people are stigmatized for trying to cope with their sexual urges, especially those not happily married. This is said to produce such guilt that even between husbands and wives neurotic attitudes persist and damage sexual satisfaction.

It is true that past taboos in support of monogamy could be cruelly applied even against victims of rape. It is also true that setting any kind of standards means a certain stigma is inevitable for those who breach them. In the present climate, there are still people being stigmatized, only now it is those who resist uncommitted sex. "Virgin" has become an epithet. Girls who favor marriage over racking up a complex sexual history have had to hide their "dark" secret.[29] Boys who want to respect themselves and girls by being abstinent feel the need to lie about it or have their sexual orientation or normality questioned.

An ethic of healthy and ethical sexuality stigmatizes what is unhealthy, hurtful and irresponsible. At the same time victims of sex crimes deserve compassion. This is possible when the goal is not punitive but to help people find their way to optimal satisfaction, health and growth.

Neurotic guilt can be a real hazard for romantic and sexual happiness. Encouraging self-control without promoting neurotic guilt is the goal of all who would guide young people. But, of course, not all guilt is unhealthy. Healthy guilt has its roots in empathy and connectedness to others.[30] It protects sexuality by keeping it humane and meaningful.

The solution to unhealthy guilt is not to lower moral standards. Instead, it is to convey a sense of normal desires and struggles, so youth can better put their situation in perspective. Second, adolescents can learn how to handle their mistakes with compassion towards themselves. Parents and educators do this by modeling that sensitivity.

Issues of Relationships

Isn't sex a natural way to express love?

It is true love to want only the best for the beloved and the relationship. Sexual expression in an uncommitted relationship will expose both partners—not to mention a host of others close to the partners—to emotional, physical and relational risks neither can control. These consequences may last much longer than the warm feelings do. Premarital abstinence as a lifestyle, on the other hand, enhances the capacity to give unselfish love. Therefore, partners who genuinely love each other wait until they can create the setting where the physical intimacy can only enrich each other's hearts and lives in the long term.

Isn't a committed relationship equivalent to marriage?

It is understandable that when singles lack the confidence to formalize their commitment, when the divorce-weary would rather not go through it again, when some people are unable to legally wed, this question arises. Isn't living together sufficient commitment to legitimate physical intimacy?

The issue is whether an informal arrangement is able to contain all the potentially life-changing results of sexual union—a pregnancy, the birth of a child, emotional bonds and expectations. Unstable relationships do not allow the trust needed even for maximum sexual satisfaction, let alone handling a pregnancy and other possible outcomes. Given that even half of engagements break up, a committed relationship that will not pledge loyalty before the mate, family and community is simply not very committed. (See Chapter 19)

Doesn't prior sexual experience make for better marital sex?

"You should be good in bed with someone before you marry him," says dancer Nicole, "and you probably should sleep with a few people so you know what it's all about."[31] It is a prevalent belief that sexual experience at least with the prospective spouse will make a person a better lover when married.

This application of "practice makes perfect" may sound logical but research does not bear it out. One survey suggests women who are virgins when they marry report a greater degree of sexual pleasure and satisfaction, while women who began their sexual activity as unwed teenagers have more dissatisfaction with their sexual experiences as adults.[32] Given sexual "flashbacks" and the many other disadvantages of premarital sex and cohabitation discussed in the previous chapter, sexual experience before marriage is far from helpful.

Exclusive Claims of Sexual Love

A study found that men had an involuntary negative reaction to the thought of their mate having sex with another man; the women reacted negatively to the idea of their mate having a strong emotional involvement with another woman.[33] This is not surprising. Studies indicate one of the most universal of taboos in all societies worldwide is infidelity. Men and women react viscerally to the idea of their partners sharing themselves intimately with someone else.

Mature human love differs from animal love in that it is keenly aware of the unique individuality of the beloved. No matter how promiscuous people may be, few want to feel that they are replaceable in the eyes of their lover. Even the unfaithful would prefer that their spouse be faithful to them.

It is a curiosity of romantic love that lovers have a sense of belonging to the beloved. "You own my heart," they say to each other. Thus they make promises of undying commitment and share their fortunes and futures, all they have and ever will have with one another. The most treasured gift is their exclusive affection and trust, and implicit is exclusive sexual involvement.

In this sense, the genital organs symbolize the desire of the heart for conjugal union. Neither the heart nor the sexual parts can find complete fulfillment without the beloved. Indeed, they are connected, one moving the other. There is a mysterious link of reinforcement between the communion of lovers' hearts and union of their genitals.

This is why a husband and wife feel a natural claim on both their beloved's love and sexual expression. Legal codes have historically recognized these expectations as "conjugal rights." This sense of entitlement or proprietorship, of course, is necessarily in the spirit of respect and care.

From this perspective, a sound ethic of sexual love can be reduced to a simple universal code: an individual's sexual expression is reserved solely for his or her spouse.

What about the double standard?

Monogamy is often tied to an entire system of male domination of women. "Marriage was a business deal," say authors Susan Jonas and Marilyn Nissenson. "Since women were regarded as property, a defiled bride meant...'damaged goods.'"[34] Males have been free to indulge themselves at the expense of females, who were perceived to have limited sexual desire. Women would seldom find sexual satisfaction yet they would pay the price for any illicit liaisons through stigma as well as pregnancies and other burdens. One extension of this view is that to counteract this injustice, women have to claim their right to sexual pleasure and beat men at their own game of sexual domination. Female promiscuity is thus the exercise of women's power and independence.

The problem with this argument is that the double standard is abandoned in favor of a lower standard for both genders. Feminist Sally Cline asserts women are trying to inherit men's innate weakness—the penchant for separating the body from the heart and sex from responsibility and love—instead of passing on feminine strengths.[35]

Girls are now expected to want many sexual partners. Boys are expected to treat girls as if they do. The result is many females have to deny their more relational and monogamous romantic inclinations. They also have to deny their natural instincts of self-protection: birth-control or not, females carry the greater burden of sex outside of a secure relationship. And the double standard still prevails in the "safer sex" world, where they face the greater responsibility to supply condoms or otherwise use contraception.[36]

A fair ethic of premarital abstinence and marital fidelity applies to both men and women. Obviously, men cannot be rewarded for promiscuity while women are penalized and held solely accountable for controlling them. Nor can the pretense be maintained that males and females are the same in sexual response and needs or in bearing the consequences of sexual acts.[37] Even in the present sexually permissive climate, women think in terms of fewer sexual partners than men do. One study revealed that the number of partners single men desired in the following two years was six, while for single women it was only one.[38] Not all sexual differences are the result of oppression.[39] These intrinsic gender strengths and weaknesses require some consideration.

This is the origin of the traditional codes of male and female honor. Men agree not to use their superior physical strength to take advantage of women, nor to exploit the female susceptibility to promises of love and security. Women agree not to use men's vulnerability to visual arousal and emotional manipulation against them. These codes made distinctions between the genders, and so they were laden with sex discrimination. Nevertheless, they also protected men and women and thus created the context for greater freedom and trust between them.[40] One look at contemporary culture suggests that some form of these codes needs to be revived. Young people, in Mahoney's words, "worry about date rape, because nobody knows what is permitted and what is not. Sex has become like a football field without any lines; sure, you can't step out of bounds, but it is not clear how to play the game anymore."[41]

The ethic of monogamy sets up rules binding upon both genders equally. It helps avoid mutual exploitation, using the opposite sex as an emotional crutch, pawn or object of revenge.[42] As such it represents real power, freedom and independence for women as well as men.

Issues of Advocacy

How can adults advocate abstinence outside marriage when they did not or do not practice it themselves?

Many well-intentioned parents, teachers and others responsible for youth hesitate to promote abstinence because they themselves did not practice it when younger or are even now violating that standard. They fear to be judged a hypocrite. This is reminiscent of the issue often faced by those involved in character education: How can teachers advocate such high standards when so many adults fail to live up to them? Sexual abstinence and marital fidelity, like honest business practices, truthful journalism and a host of other norms, represent high standards that are worth striving for. When conscientious people fail to keep a certain standard, they feel remorse, make amends and try again. They continue to advocate it for themselves and others; they do not deny its validity simply because it is hard.

No parents want their child to repeat their mistakes. Just because adults did or do not exemplify the healthiest and most responsible standard in their lives does not mean they can do nothing to teach youth how to live better than they did. The sorry smoker will try to steer her students clear of tobacco. The repentant career criminal will encourage his nephew towards an honorable occupation. The now wiser unwed single mother wants her daughter to find a boy to marry before having a child. This is only natural.

The once-promiscuous parent may say, "I regret the bad choices I made in the past. You can understand these matters better than I did at your age and avoid my mistakes. This is your advantage." Adults who admit their mistakes win the admiration of young people and reestablish their moral authority as well.

At the same time, this assumes the adults are making a sincere attempt to practice what they are now preaching. Concern about hypocrisy is valid. Those who are in a position to influence youth have reason to examine their behavior from the standpoint of a parental heart. Is it what they would really want the young to emulate?

Just as adolescents are wary of hypocrisy, they are also alert to self-serving evasiveness. They respond to sincerity and honesty. A high school student appealed to an audience of parents and educators to "tell us your experiences, your hard times with love and sex and what you've learned."[43] Elders have no need to give detailed confessions, but they can share from the heart about their successes and failures and why they advocate the highest standard.[44] It is the nature of the younger generation to want to do better than their elders. By encouraging their best instincts, adults are at the same time fostering a healthier ethos over the long run that will make the optimal standard easier and easier to live by.

How can adults encourage youth to marry when many of them can't model it themselves?

As with the abstinence standard, many adults who have divorced or otherwise have not been successful in establishing a satisfying marriage feel uncomfortable advocating a marriage norm. For some it is more than concern about hypocrisy. They are genuinely ambivalent about the chances of young people to do better in marriage than they.

No one wants to foster false hopes, yet again the parental heart naturally focuses solely on one question: "What is in this young person's best interests?" When adults convey that finding a suitable mate, marrying and sustaining the marriage are too difficult, they are giving up on the young and relegating them to lives of unsatisfying liaisons that at best mimic what they really want. However well meant, this is ultimately a betrayal.

The alternatives to monogamous marriage are not ones that most would wish on youth. There used to be the myth of the swinging 20-something single life full of self-discovery and sexual experimentation followed by marriage or a committed relationship and possibly children when 30-something. This, however, has not been played out in reality. Without even considering the emotional scars, STDs, infertility due to waiting too long and other issues, the painful reality is that many single adults in their 30s and 40s, especially women, find themselves unable to find a marriageable mate or are unwilling to accommodate a partner in their current lifestyle.[45] They are facing the prospects of a lonely old age that no amount of social acceptance of singlehood can ameliorate.

Adults are presenting, Nellie Bernstein observes, "fewer and fewer coherent models for conducting and sustaining intimate relationships." Though some may question whether lifelong marriage is viable, at least such a norm has "the advantage of being imitable" and clear.[46]

Divorced adults may not know all about how to make a good marriage work, but they do know something about how it does not work. They have learned much from their experience and teenagers and young adults want to hear it. Adults serve young people when they encourage their dreams of lasting love, steer them away from dead ends and give them the benefit of their experience, not their cynicism.

In addition, there are good reasons to be optimistic about the younger generation's prospects for satisfying marriage, even apart from the declining rate of divorce. The exploding field of marriage education arms youth with more insight and skills than previous generations have ever known. (See Chapter 21) This, coupled with character and abstinence education, can help them achieve the success in love that has so far eluded many of their elders.

An ethic of responsible sexual love can reclaim monogamy and its associated virtues. In the words of educator Mary Patricia Barth Fourqurean, such a perspective and practice is "an empowering strength" that liberates young men and women "from the mixed signals of sexual games" to enjoy relationships of intimacy, trust and lasting love.[47]

Still, unless youth have the depth of heart and strength of character to resist sexual pressure, they do not have the capacity to actually choose abstinence and fidelity. This is why abstinence education is inescapably linked to effective character education. And unless young people have the understanding and skills to create healthy relationships leading to marriage, they cannot have sufficient hope to choose the responsible ethic either. For this reason, marriage preparation education is a boon. Character education, abstinence education and marriage education form a protective triangle for the support of youths' moral development and their success in achieving loving relationships and sound families.

Section Seven

Supporting a Healthy Lifestyle

JOHN R. WILLIAMS, ANDREW WILSON
AND JUNE SAUNDERS

TEENAGE PREGNANCY, SEXUALLY TRANSMITTED DISEASES, DRUG abuse and violence: these problems afflicting young people have elicited focused educational programs and interventions in the form of sex education, substance abuse prevention and conflict resolution. Approaching these issues from the perspective of heart and character yields distinctive insights. It happens that all these problems are part of a constellation of risky behaviors that is impacted by character and the familial relations that are meant to foster it. Hence, prevention begins with general character education from the early grades. Character-based approaches go beyond giving information about risky behavior; they empower students to take responsibility. Just as importantly, they situate the behavior within a larger context of life's meaning and purpose, thus giving a perspective that examines consequences far beyond the concerns of the moment. Character-based programs that focus on core motivational factors, including the search for meaning and value, give added protection to youth.

26

Character-Based Sexuality Education

MARGARET MURPHY, A NURSE AT A MIDDLE SCHOOL IN A suburb outside Chicago, has two weeks to present her proposal to the school board. The time has come for the school to select a formal sexuality education program. The pregnancy of an eighth grader has galvanized the community, and the several health presentations in physical education class are no longer enough. The superintendent favors an abstinence-oriented program. A vocal member of the school board wants birth control information to be center stage. What should Nurse Murphy do?

Stopping further pregnancies is an immediate concern. Even making condoms available to the students is an option to consider. Yet crisis management has to be weighed against long-term goals, she realizes. The school has just begun a character education initiative. What approach best supports the kind of ethos they are aiming for, one of respect and self-restraint, that precludes irresponsible sexual experimentation?

Murphy takes her role as a health advocate and educator very seriously. What is the optimal health message regarding teenage sexual behavior? In short, what is the program her conscience could live with? Margaret Murphy has entered the controversial world of sexuality education. It is a world of competing philosophies, sometimes-conflicting claims of research, and passionate feelings on both sides.

The fundamental postulate guiding this volume is that character issues deserve priority in education. This suggests as a corollary that a character-based approach is most appropriate in the area of sexuality education as well. After reviewing this approach and the competing model of sexuality education, the advantages of character-based sexuality education will be examined in terms of its effectiveness and its compatibility with general character education.

Contrasting the Approaches

Two competing models of sexuality education influence how both teachers and parents socialize youth about sex. One emphasizes technology and techniques to reduce the harmful consequences of sexual relations. This contraceptive-based sexuality education is also often called the comprehensive or "safer sex" approach. The other model focuses on self-control to prevent adolescent sexual activity. This model is commonly called the abstinence-based approach to sex education. The most up-to-date methods of abstinence education, however, frame the message of abstinence with a view to developing character and inculcating a positive vision of love, marriage and family. Therefore, this model is more accurately called a character-based approach.

There are essential differences between the two approaches. Contraceptive-based sexuality education, on the one hand, sees responsible and healthy sexual relations as based on mutual consent and including birth control and prophylactics.[1] Risk-reduction of physical consequences through increasing use of protective devices is considered the only viable objective, since the approach assumes teenagers will inevitably experiment with sex. This attitude is typified in the words of Susan Newcomer, director of education for the Planned Parenthood Federation of America, "Teens are having intercourse, they have always done so, and no amount of exhortation will cause them to stop."[2] Educators promote birth control and prophylactics and make them available to all students. The immediate appeal of "safer sex" education is its pragmatic simplicity.

On the other hand, character-based sexuality education sets the desirable standard as no sexual relations until marriage.[3] "We teach that abstinence from sexual intercourse outside of lawful marriage is the expected social standard for unmarried, school-aged persons," said

Stephen Pryor, spokesman for the Mobile County, Alabama, public schools.[4] Its objective is risk-elimination, consistent with policies regarding other hazards, such as smoking, substance abuse and weapons at school. Contraceptives are not promoted; they are seen as conveying adult expectations of sexual activity. When educators discuss contraceptives, they clarify their limitations. In addition, this approach stresses prevention of the psychological, moral and relational risks of premarital sex.[5]

The character-based approach holds an intuitive appeal in its resonance with parents' and educators' task to encourage strong character in the young. Fostering self-control, personal integrity, compassion and altruism, as well as a deep sense of meaning and purpose, is the deeper and longer-term solution to not only pregnancy and disease but also all problematic behaviors of youth: truancy, substance abuse, and violence.

View of Marriage and Family

Character-based sexuality education holds that marriage and the two-parent family is the norm and the only acceptable goal to be advocated by family life educators dealing with the general population. The value of marriage has an objective basis in research and cross-cultural studies.[6] The marriage norm in turn provides the basis for advocating premarital abstinence as the sole responsible sexual ethic.[7]

Contraceptive-based education sees this differently. It asserts that in a pluralistic society, views on marriage and family are so diverse that students must interpret them individually in counsel with various sources of guidance.[8] Thus this approach presents information within the context of various views of sexual morality. Students are encouraged to develop their independence and own moral guidelines. These are based on being well-informed and assessing alternatives and consequences as well as consulting trusted authorities.[9] In the words of Susan Wilson, executive coordinator of the New Jersey Network for Family Life Education, it is better to "support the decision to say 'yes' as well as 'no' to sexual involvement." Sex educator Mary Lee Tatum advises, "encourage abstinence but not to the exclusion of other decisions people might make."[10]

The character-based approach recognizes that sexuality is inherently morally laden. Teenagers need not only information but also

The Two Approaches at a Glance

The following chart offers a thumbnail sketch of the contrasts between the two models:

Character-Based	Contraceptive-Based
Norm is no sexual relations until marriage	Norm is sexual relations by mutual consent & use of protection[11]
Contraceptives not promoted, as would undermine abstinence[12]	Contraceptives promoted as effective protection[13]
Appeal as character-building	Pragmatic appeal
Supports most parents' values	Tolerates diverse values
Morally directive	Non-directive[14]
Assumes teenagers respond to abstinence message	Assumes teenage sexual activity is inevitable
Abstinence defined as no genital activity[15]	Abstinence includes "low risk" sex[16]
Age-appropriate discussion respects natural modesty	Explicit discussion to instruct in contraceptive use
Supports parents without reservation[17]	May support students' privacy against parents[18]

unambiguous guidance. "With drugs or tobacco we are crystal clear. How can we be vague about sex which can potentially mess up their lives even worse?" asks a California father. "Children hunger for this moral clarity and direction from adults," says Thomas Lickona.[19] They are able to positively respond to the challenge and protection of the abstinence message.

Modesty and Parental Involvement

To facilitate contraceptive education, "safer sex" educators advocate explicit discussion about sexual anatomy and practices in mixed-gender settings from a young age.[20] This desensitizing technique lowers barriers to dealing with issues surrounding contraceptive use. A widely used Rutgers University program, *Learning about Family Life,* advocates telling children in kindergarten, "The man puts his penis in the woman's vagina and that it feels really good for both of them."[21]

Further, it advocates allowing students health services—such as receiving contraceptives and abortions—without the parents' knowledge when the parents' right to know clashes with the child's right to private decisions.[22]

Conversely, to protect the natural modesty of young people, character-based education favors accurate yet discreet, developmentally appropriate instruction. Pre-teenagers often receive discussion in separate-gender settings.[23] In addition, educators encourage parents' protective interests by supporting their right to know about their children's circumstances without reservation.[24] It recommends involving parents in designing the program and reviewing every element before it is presented.

Comparing Program Effectiveness

The rate of births to unmarried girls aged 15 to 19 recently declined for the first time in 25 years.[25] During the five-year period from 1991 to 1996 abortions declined as well, as did overall sexual activity. At the same time, condom use rose 33 percent.

Was this improvement due more to the increase in condom use or to greater abstinence? More specifically, should the "safer sex" approach or abstinence education receive the credit? Though research is sometimes ambiguous and the abstinence-oriented programs are too new for extensive testing, an association representing 2,000 health professionals, the Consortium of State Physicians Resource Councils, attributed the decline in the birth rate to the increase in abstinence-focused education and "increased cultural acceptance of abstinence."[26]

Why? Before surveying the evidence it is helpful to note the record for the contraceptive-based approach. Although it has enjoyed the lion's share of funding and time to prove itself, it has not been shown to be effective. "The 20 to 30 years of contraceptive education... did not show a decrease in sexual activity... pregnancy rates and... STD rates," concludes Reynolds W. Archer, former director of family planning and sex education programs for the U.S. Department of Health and Human Services.[27]

One comprehensive 1997 overview by the World Health Organization of over 50 studies of contraceptive-based programs gave a dismal outlook.[28] Over half—27—found the programs under review to have no impact at all on behavior or attitudes. The remaining studies deemed such programs to be somewhat successful in delaying sexual activity, reducing the number of partners or reducing unwanted pregnancies or STDs. However, these were minimal improvements based on small samples. In one case, only 12 students out of a comparison involving a total of over 430 were found to have resisted sexual activity, and even this gain was lost in the following months.[29]

The Achilles heel of "safer sex" education is its objective to increase consistent contraceptive use. This is extremely difficult to achieve. Even among couples where one spouse is HIV-infected and they are continuing to have sexual relations, only about half of these highly motivated adult couples could be bothered with using condoms.[30] Given this resistance, what level of diligence can be expected of teenagers who have no evidence that their partner is infected? Researcher Douglas Kirby concedes, "It may actually be easier to delay the onset of intercourse than to increase contraceptive practice."[31]

Yet even when the consistent use of condoms increases, rates of pregnancy and disease do not necessarily decline. One reason is that condoms and other devices are unreliable or even useless against certain important hazards. Condoms are in fact poor birth control, exhibiting between 13 to 27 percent failure rates in students under the age of twenty.[32] Indeed, the recent statistics about adolescent sex during 1990 to 1995 show teenagers' increase in rates of condom use was matched by their increase in rates of out-of-wedlock births.[33]

Condoms are even worse as disease control. In the case of the most prevalent viral STDs such as genital herpes and human papilloma virus, condoms are virtually useless.[34] Rates of chlamydia transmission have been found to be identical whether condoms are used or not.[35] Against deadly HIV, overall failure rates range from 10 to 30 percent for consistent adult condom users, in a comparison of five different studies published since 1993. "It is a disservice to encourage the belief that condoms will prevent the sexual transmission of HIV," concludes researcher Susan Weller in her analysis of multiple studies.[36]

In contrast, character-based programs offer 100 percent reliability against pregnancy and disease when they can succeed in reaching young people with the abstinence message. They have yielded dramatic results in reducing teenage pregnancies and delaying the onset of sexual activities.

"Low Risk" Sex?

Perhaps the fatal flaw in the logic of contraceptive-based education is best revealed by the advocacy of so-called "low risk" sex activities—those short of intercourse. Debra Haffner, executive director of the Sex Information and Education Council of the United States (SIECUS), recommends teaching adolescents about "oral sex, mutual masturbation" and other techniques "to help them delay the onset of genital intercourse."[37] Since these behaviors carry less risk of conception or transmission of disease, enjoying them as an alternative to intercourse is considered a benefit. Of course, common sense would suggest the opposite. These activities are otherwise called foreplay and lead to strong arousal, putting the couple at great risk for actual intercourse. No evidence has ever been shown to the contrary.

The recent proliferation of the practice of oral sex among middle and high school American students would seem to be the realization of these advocates' hopes. Yet it is not bringing positive results.

On one hand, such non-penetrative activity still holds a significant measure of risk of disease. More than 5 percent of AIDS infections are transmitted by oral sex.[38] A young teenage girl was admitted to a New Jersey hospital with such severe genital herpes she could not stand because of the pain. She received the disease from oral sex.[39] On the other hand, most of the non-physical risks of sex—the psychological harm, the link to substance abuse and suicide, and the impaired preparation for committed relationships—are unmitigated. Adolescents still report regret, shame, a sense of degradation and deepened loneliness as a consequence of "low-risk sex."[40]

Actual promotion—not just tolerance—of sexual activity apart from the context that makes it safe and responsible reveals the deep-seated bias that adolescents should be free to experience sex prior to maturity and marriage. Peggy Brick of

Planned Parenthood has said that "pleasure, sexual satisfaction... and orgasm" are important to be emphasized to
adolescents, even without reference to marriage.[41] Sex is
seen as a natural right and potentially enriching experience,
and therefore no blanket prohibition is warranted.

As long as these attitudes persist among educators, the contradictory effort to encourage youthful sexual experimentation while trying to contain the negative consequences will
continue.

Pregnancy Reduction through the Character-Based Approach

Best Friends, a character-based program in Washington, D.C.,
reduces the rate of unwed pregnancies within a high-risk, lower class
urban population. Of the 600 Washington girls in grades nine through
twelve who participated for two years or more, only 1 percent became
pregnant, as opposed to a 25 percent citywide rate for girls of comparable age.[42]

A 74 percent reduction in their teen pregnancy rate was reported
in East St. Louis, Illinois after the first year of their character-based educational experiment.[43] Character-based programs at Jefferson High
School, located within the Washington, D.C. area, resulted in a significant decline in high school pregnancy rates over five years, as well as
an overall improvement in school performance.[44]

Some of these programs only indirectly could be called sex education efforts. As with the best character education initiatives, a character-building context is created and the constructive results—whether
reduced substance abuse, violence or pregnancies—flow from that. The
National Longitudinal Adolescent Health Study noted that youth attending schools implementing intentional character education enjoyed addi-
tional protection against early sexual activity.[45]

The Teen Outreach Program of general character building through
service learning began in 1978 and is now used in 120 middle school
classrooms in over two dozen cities with over 6,000 students enrolled.
A careful four-year evaluation reports a 40 percent reduction in pregnancies among teenagers in the program, as contrasted with their counterparts who applied for the programs but were not selected by lot-

tery.[46] Kirby concluded in his landmark 1996 survey, "This is the best evidence we have that any single program can actually reduce teen pregnancy."[47]

Decline in Adolescent Sex

Besides reducing pregnancies, other measurable areas for evaluation are the delay in the onset of sexual activity, reduction of sexual activity itself, and the promotion of attitudes favoring abstinence. Character-based education excels in all three of these areas.

Over 90 percent of the virgins participating in the *Art of Loving Well* course were still abstinent two years later, as compared with about 70 percent of non-participating counterparts.[48] "If it weren't for Loving Well, I would be a father!" wrote one eighth-grade boy in Dudley, Massachusetts.[49]

Among teenagers in the Best Friends program, only one in five lost their virginity before twelfth grade, contrasted with three out of four comparable girls who did not participate.[50] Similarly, there was five times the protection of the students' virginity among 4,500 eighth-grade girls who participated in Postponing Sexual Involvement, an abstinence-oriented health program used in Atlanta, Georgia.[51] 70 percent of the girls said they learned that they "can postpone sexual activity without losing their friends' respect." The protective influence persisted into the following year.[52]

An evaluation of two programs, Facing Reality and Choosing the Best, involving over 6,800 Illinois middle and high school students from 76 schools, showed an increase in the number of students who believed that sexual urges could be controlled and that saving sex until marriage is valuable.[53] Surprisingly, this change in attitude was greater among the sexually experienced and those virgins whose circumstances would suggest a higher risk for premarital sex.[54]

Thus, evidence affirms the intuitive expectation: cultivating the heart and strengthening the conscience of youth helps them to better resist all influences not conducive to their best interests. Character-based sexuality education helps to reduce unwed teenage sexual activity and pregnancies and other harmful consequences that follow.

Focus on the Cause

Why are the character-based programs effective? There may be many factors, but certainly the chief virtue of character-based sex education is its focus on the actual cause of the problem. It looks squarely at the fact that except in cases of rape, teenage pregnancy is essentially the result of lifestyle and is in the realm of choice. Teenage pregnancy is but a symptom of the deeper problem of teenagers having sex outside of the maturity and commitment that characterize marriage. The same holds true for sexually transmitted diseases, which persist despite the widespread availability of contraceptives and advances in medical technology. As physician Farzin Davachi states, STDs are "a moral problem [requiring]... a moral remedy."[55] Those practicing abstinence before entering into a lifelong, monogamous marital relationship face a negligible risk of contracting AIDS or any other STD.

The temptation to focus on preventing pregnancy and STDs, rather than addressing the sexual behavior that causes them, is understandable. Addressing teenage pregnancy and sexual diseases in themselves are not as contentious as the emotionally charged issue of premarital sex. Besides, there is a known route—promotion by physicians and the media, for example—for getting a population to use technology to protect themselves. However, targeting the consequences rather than the causal behavior—stressing a secondary level of prevention over the primary one—is ultimately inefficient and ineffective.

The Teen Outreach Program serves as an example of the elegance and efficiency of the character-based approach. Yet this relatively simple and inexpensive program devotes less than 12 percent of its time to discussion of sexual issues. Its effectiveness is due to its addressing the pillars of character in a way that supports the three basic life goals.

The program addresses young people's need to make a meaningful contribution. Joseph Allen, a University of Virginia psychologist, observed in the teenagers a significant change in self-perception: greater self-respect and an enhanced sense of self-worth by finding a more valuable role to play in the community. "When they learn to take care of others, they learn to take care of themselves," he remarks.[56] In addition, they learn the benefits of altruism: what is given is received.

The program also meets the need for warm peer relationships and a sense of belonging. TOP integrates discussion and group spirit building with the volunteer activity. When teens get involved in meaningful friendships with a wide circle of peers, the narrow and inward focus offered by one-on-one dating and sexualized relationships holds less attraction.

Characteristics of the Character-Based Approach

"Sex education is... about character and formation of character, says former U.S. Secretary of Education William Bennett. "A sex education in which issues of right and wrong do not occupy center stage is evasive and irresponsible."[57] Research shows that values determine sexual choices more than information does.[58] Teenagers who agree with such statements as "It goes against my values to have sex" and "There are many benefits to saving sex for marriage" are much more likely to practice self-control than those who do not.[59]

For example, one feature of several character-based programs is a pledge of commitment to abstinence—what the National Longitudinal Study on Adolescent Health found to be the single factor most associated with the delay in early sexual activity.[60] Then to help teenagers realistically meet the challenges of abstinence, the programs boost moral reasoning, a sense of empathy and commitment, wisdom about love and social skills. Thus, character-based education sets a clear moral norm and then actively prepares young people to meet it.

The Character Education Partnership advocates character-based sexuality education with these characteristics:[61]

- Guides youth to discern right and wrong regarding sexual choices

- Cultivates the virtues, skills and strategies needed to practice abstinence

- Fosters the value system and moral reasoning that favors abstinence

- Clarifies the difference between sex and love

- Addresses the physical, social and emotional needs of students in a holistic way

- Promotes marriage and the value of saving sex until marriage

- Encourages non-virgins to recommit to self-restraint

- Fosters the cooperation of home, school and community in strengthening marriage and family life.

Moral Directiveness

Moral ambiguity regarding sexual choices undermines the resolve needed to achieve the optimal health choice, premarital abstinence. If feelings of love, a sense of need, use of birth control or being married are all morally equivalent bases for sexual relations, why choose the most demanding standard? If abstinence is simply pragmatic for certain age groups, then why is it morally superior?

Character-based education assumes that parents and teachers are inescapably involved in giving guidance by virtue of their elder position. Whatever they do or do not emphasize is itself a statement of moral advocacy. Therefore, clear guidelines are in order as a starting point for setting standards for the young. Successful programs such as Facing Reality prod students' moral reasoning with questions like these: "Is it possible that two individuals could agree to use each other? What effect do you think an arrangement like this would have on personality?" "Why does maintaining a family require self-mastery and unselfishness?" "How might a self-centered sexual choice hurt a family?" "What motives would parents have for setting age limits on dating?" "How can girls make guys feel esteemed and admired for choosing the wise course [of avoiding sexual activities on dates]?"[62]

Advocating abstinence echoes the great religious and moral traditions of the world—which unanimously recommend premarital abstinence and marital fidelity. This gives adolescents the benefit of thousands of years of human wisdom and protects them from having to learn from painful trial and error.

Modesty and Conscience

The sense of privacy and sexual modesty are youth's allies in avoiding premature sexual involvement. These are innate,[63] universal traits necessary to abstinence.[64] Like a prompting of the conscience, sexual embarrassment is a valuable signal that indicates a moral and relational boundary is being threatened. Without it, adolescents are weaker and have, as author Wendy Shalit observes, "nothing to protect what is human in them."[65]

Girls and boys are shy about sex because they sense its mystery, its gravity and their own intense interest and potential responsiveness. When modesty is not socially supported—when they feel they must succumb to the sexual pressures to fit in—they have little choice but to try to close down their sexual awe and emotional vulnerability. They may adopt a matter-of-fact attitude towards even the most intimate of behaviors, as the peculiarly dispassionate nature of much of contemporary teenage sex shows.[66]

Responsible sexuality education thus protects adolescents from situations of embarrassment or overstimulation. Effective teachers exercise care not to let a precocious or reckless few set the tone for an entire classroom. In middle school settings, they often arrange separate discussions for boys and girls to allow gender-specific issues to be brought up and to discourage sexual acting out of insecurities between the genders.[67]

Supporting Hopes for Lasting Love

The dominant reason sexually experienced teenage girls gave for their physical involvements was not pleasure but a search for "true, monogamous, permanent... love."[68] Tying this innate hope of teenagers for lasting love to the challenge of abstinence—indeed any challenge of character—is a smart way to motivate them. Most adolscents hope someday to be married. (See Chapter 19) Abstinence educator Richard Panzer tells of routinely asking classrooms of teenagers, "How many of you see the possibility of marriage in your future?" and having almost all hands go up.[69]

Young people can respond to the realism of the abstinence message especially if it is combined with an inspiring vision for a more passionate and lasting love.[70] They naturally want the highest they can believe in for themselves and are capable of sacrificing for what captures their idealism and sense of romance.

"You don't have to have sex until you get married. There's always going to be the peer pressure and there's always going to be the urge, but it's a matter of... how strong you are," says Jeremy Smith, 16.[71] Young newlyweds Michael and Tina of Concord, New Hampshire, concur. "If you never give [sex] to anyone else, except for the person you marry, on your wedding night, then that is the ultimate act of love."[72]

Delayed gratification is possible when youth see themselves as part of a heroic journey to realize true love.

Of course, this appeal is predicated on students seeing happy marriage as a reachable goal for themselves. Otherwise, why should they—how can they—wait? This is why character-based abstinence education is naturally more effective when coupled with marriage preparation guidance. (See Chapter 20) Effective abstinence programs often have such a component.[73]

Valuing an Abstinent Lifestyle

Character-based programs help students understand the psychological, moral, relational and physical risks involved in premarital sex and the greater sexual and emotional satisfaction to be experienced within marriage. They arm students with strategies for controlling sexual urges and how to distinguish between love and infatuation. Abstinence educator Mike Long finds that teenagers appreciate his Love Test: "Ask the partner to wait until marriage for sex and by their response you'll know if he or she loves you."[74] Given the romantic idealism and naïveté of adolescents, such discussion is fascinating.

Character-based programs such as No Apologies present abstinence as a "whole person commitment,"[75] a natural part of a lifestyle reflecting respect and responsibility and a manifestation of unselfish love. (See Chapter 23) They celebrate abstinence as liberating adolescents from unnecessary burdens and ensuring the freedoms that all teenagers should be able to enjoy.

Those who are no longer virgins are encouraged to recommit to abstinence to enjoy many of these benefits. Among those teenagers labeled "sexually active," many have had sex only once or twice,[76] and over half of them express regret.[77] Gynecology professor Marion Howard found that 84 percent of the non-virginal girls at Grady Memorial Hospital, in Atlanta, wanted to know how to say No without hurting the boy's feelings.[78] Thus they can be readily persuaded to shift towards the healthy ethic and gain the character strength to practice it.

"Saving Sex" Plus "Safer Sex"?

Some educators recommend an abstinence-oriented approach supplemented by contraceptive instruction, sometimes called "abstinence plus" or "dual message." Advocates claim that teaching about contraceptives will not put the abstinent students at risk, while it helps those who are already involved in hazardous activities.

Certainly it is not unreasonable to inform adolescents about contraceptives. The issue is not in discussing them but in promoting them to make their use attractive to young people. This means maximizing their advantages and minimizing their disadvantages. Herein lies its potential for compromising the character and abstinence focus. Can educators paint a compelling vision of the value of self-control, the beauty of saving sex until marriage and the connection between true love and abstinence while portraying condom use as responsible and loving as well?

When signals collide, which one wins? Teaching both "saving sex" and "safer sex" at the same time is equivalent to telling students not to smoke cigarettes, but if they do, to use a filter, or don't inhale deeply. It is like telling them not to drive while drunk, but if they do, to use seat belts.[79] For adolescents eager for new experiences and who think they are ready to enter the adult world, the abstinence message can be less exciting, concrete and memorable than a discussion of contraceptive devices. Even one session of giggling students fumbling with putting condoms on bananas can neutralize many classes emphasizing self-restraint and the benefits of abstinence. As Baltimore teacher Deborah Roffman remarks, "Any teacher knows that when students get mixed messages from adults, they test."[80]

"Melanie," a middle-aged health educator, tells of her experience of sexual promiscuity as a teenager. Her abusive home life drove her to engage in petty crime just to enjoy the relative safety of jail. It was there where a counselor visited her and she told him of her risky sexual habits. His response was to guide her towards greater self-respect and self-discipline. Melanie took his advice and changed her life. She eventually became a happily married wife and mother and a speaker of international fame. "What would have happened," she asks, "if that man had given me a condom instead of believing in me?"[81]

Comprehensive Character-Based Sex Education

The broader the character-based, abstinence-oriented initiative, the greater the results. Programs such as Best Friends are school-wide. The effort is even more effective if it involves coordination among parents, school and community. An integrated kindergarten through twelfth grade abstinence education curriculum in Denmark, South Carolina engaged parents, clergy and other community leaders and media coverage involved the entire community. As a result, the pregnancy rate was cut by more than half after the first year and remained low in subsequent years.[82] The "Not Me, Not Now" initiative of Monroe County, New York, is aimed at helping youngsters aged nine to fourteen to postpone sexual involvement. It encompasses a television and radio campaign, a student-friendly website, a peer-led classroom program, parent coaching and a research and evaluation component. Such comprehensive school-wide and community-wide efforts create a culture supportive of the marriage norm and provide numerous protective influences around adolescents.

Too often, early sexual experimentation comes as a result of loneliness and a desire for attention. Sex not only looks like a way to attract and hold a partner but it can score points in impressing friends as well. Therefore, successful programs cultivate a peer culture supportive of non-sexual relationships. Free Teens generates positive peer pressure by setting up student clubs and having older students in high school or university serve as teachers and mentors to younger ones. Not only do the younger students respond, but also the older students deepen their conviction regarding abstinence. "None of my friends are having sex," says Sarah, 17, of Portsmouth, Washington. "Usually kids at school push you to ignore your parents' beliefs and it's really hard to resist, because everybody wants friends. But having friends who are also waiting until marriage helps me know it is really right for me, not just my parents."

Parental Involvement

Pro-abstinence parental influence is probably the strongest safe-guard for youth. "Intimacy, responsibility, trust, integrity, the difference between love and lust, behavioral expectations—these are not 'taught' by specialists," observes educator Patty Starks. "They are 'caught' in the course of kids' daily lives from those who influence them the most—their parents."[83] Parental disapproval of sex and contraceptive use is powerfully associated with postponement of teenage sex.[84] This is why it only makes sense for sexuality educators to reinforce the link between parent and child as much as possible as well as help compensate for its deficiencies.

Character-based educational programs create a partnership with parents, inviting them to preview materials in advance of presentation to their children. They dispense homework that invites parental partic-ipation, and coach the parents in passing on their sexual morality. The Teen-Aid program, Sexuality, Commitment and Family, invites teenagers to discuss with their parents such issues as "How should a marriage partner be selected?" and "What does commitment mean?"[85] Practices like this encourage a more open and honest relationship between parent and child.

Parents often need and appreciate encouragement and help to successfully share their insights and sexual ethics with their children. After all, teenagers require more than a "Just Say No" button from their parents[86]—they need time with them, an emotional connection, and the guidance necessary to address their deepest concerns. Some schools coach parents in talking to their children about sex, monitoring their children's friends, delaying and supervising their dating, and regulating exposure to various kinds of media and entertainment. The support, reassurance and research base of a dedicated school program can strengthen parental backbone.

In the end, Nurse Murphy is likely to join the trend of schools towards character-based abstinence education. "School policy at the local level really does promote abstinence overwhelmingly," said Cory Richards, co-author of a recent Alan Guttmacher report. Currently, one in three schools employs an exclusively abstinence-oriented program. Many districts have shifted from a neutral stance concerning abstinence to one of promoting it.[87]

Respect for both the power of sex and the character potential of youth spells a character-based approach. This approach is more effective against unwed pregnancies; it recognizes the mental and moral consequences of even protected teenage sex; and it reduces the causal problem of sexual activity itself. It works even with youngsters considered to be at highest risk.

Such an approach reinforces the strengths in a young person's character and supports the positive elements in his or her home and school environment to provide the best protective influence. When schools take a moral stand for abstinence and involve parents and the community in comprehensive efforts, they are taking steps to change the popular culture away from one that celebrates casual sex towards one that uplifts the value of character and true love.

27

Substance-Abuse Prevention

Drug use is a misguided attempt to find the meaning of life. It is a great deception because it gives users a false and temporary sense of transcendence, of power and control. The drug problem is fundamentally a moral problem in the end. It is seeking meaning in a place where no meaning can come.

—William J. Bennett[1]

THIRTY YEARS AGO, DRUG PREVENTION PROGRAMS PRIMARILY warned youth about the dangers of substance abuse. They relied on the theory that students would act rationally to avoid drugs once they knew the facts. Warnings alone are indeed sufficient for some. Yet despite widespread drug education in middle schools and high schools, and countless anti-drug messages on television, the trend towards substance abuse did not abate.[2] Few were addressing the underlying reasons why people take drugs.[3]

Today, the theory that merely dispensing information about the dangers of substance abuse—or any dangerous or antisocial behaviors—would be motivationally strong enough to deter youth has been discredited.[4] The so-called "targeted" approaches at prevention that deal narrowly with the behaviors to be prevented are ineffective as compared with more "general" approaches that broadly aim to address risk and/or protective factors. The latter are aimed at adolescents and pre-teens at the time when they are at greatest risk for engaging in the problem behavior but before they have actually started doing so.[5]

Newer, more effective substance prevention programs employ comprehensive strategies that target a variety of risk factors for drug abuse. They continue to provide information, but they also address the deeper personal and interpersonal factors that predispose adolescents to abuse drugs.[6] The Drug-Free School Recognition Program sponsored by the U.S. Department of Education has determined that successful drug prevention programs do more than provide accurate and age-appropriate information. They also train in social resistance skills and a broad repertoire of personal and social skills such as decision-making, anxiety reduction, communication and assertiveness. Most importantly, they promote positive values, a sense of self-worth, and a vision of life's meaning in which drug use is not the norm.[7]

This is the hallmark of a character-based approach. Indeed, it turns out that the same character and interpersonal factors that predispose adolescents to substance abuse also correlate with increases in other risky behaviors, including dropping out of school, early sexual intercourse, and attempted suicide.[8] Thus, character-based prevention programs help prevent a broad spectrum of undesirable behaviors, substance abuse among them.

What are the deeper reasons why people take drugs? The physical mechanism of drug action is to mimic or interfere with the natural chemicals of the brain and central nervous system. In this way intoxicants artificially create the feelings, emotions and moods that people normally experience in the course of a gratifying life. Drugs, therefore, become a substitute for the natural satisfaction that derives from fulfilling the basic aspirations of human life.

As clarified previously, these aspirations are: first, to achieve personal maturity; second, to give and receive love; and third, to make a contribution to society. As people achieve these basic life goals, they gain a sense of joy, competence and well-being. This requires years of effort. On the other hand, instantly and without any effort at all, a person can experience analogous emotions by taking drugs, though the effect is short-lived. Therefore, when a young person loses his way or finds his path to authentic fulfillment blocked, he does not cease to desire the joys that fulfilling the basic life goals would afford. He may turn to intoxicants in the desperate hope of filling the emptiness inside.

The Human Face of Drugs

Drug abuse has a human face; it wreaks havoc in the lives of famous personalities. John Belushi, a well-known American comedian and actor, died from cocaine and heroin use. The American rock artist Kurt Cobain committed suicide by a heroin overdose.

South American soccer star Diego Maradonnna led Argentina to victory in the 1986 World Cup. When on his game, he was a sports legend on the level of a Pelé or a Michael Jordan, but drugs laid him low. Living in the fast lane, by age 24 he had developed a cocaine habit. In 1991, while playing for Italy, he tested positive for cocaine and was banned from playing for 15 months. Despite a brief comeback, he couldn't stay off drugs and in 1994 was suspended once again. According to doctors, his addiction has caused irreversible brain damage.

Gia Caranji was one of the world's top models, appearing on the covers of *Vogue* and *Cosmopolitan*. However, she acquired a serious heroin habit. At 26 years old, she was reduced to an unemployed street junkie injecting herself with dirty needles. She died of AIDS within a year.[9]

Jennifer Capriati at 14 years old was on top of the world of tennis. An Olympic gold medalist, she was making millions of dollars in prize money and endorsements. Then she began using drugs, and in 1993 she dropped out of professional tennis. Although she kicked the habit, she spent years floundering in the basement of the tennis world.[10] But having beaten her drug habit, her story may have a different ending. With family support and considerable determination, seven years later she is on her way to becoming a contender once again.

Detour on the Road to Personal Maturity

Mature character is not achieved automatically as the body grows. It is rather the outcome of individuals making the effort to cultivate the conscience, practice self-control, and learn to take responsibility for their actions. (See Chapter 7) These efforts are difficult and must be pursued continually, yet the result is a satisfying sense of self-respect that accompanies each step on the path to maturity.

Drugs can impart the illusion of maturity and of being in control, and inspire the false sense of confidence to go with it. Thus, substance abuse can be viewed as a misguided attempt to fulfill a legitimate inner need by taking a dangerous detour. When the illusion subsides, the user finds his or her life falling apart. In reality, substance abusers have done nothing to build up their inner resources; they have only avoided working on themselves and on their problems. Hence, their character development is arrested. Kathy, a 26-year-old recovering substance abuser, gave up drinking and smoking marijuana only to discover to her dismay that all her old problems were still with her:

> I started drinking when I was twelve, and two years later I was a regular user of marijuana. When I couldn't cope with things I would get high to make it through. The next thing I knew was that as a twenty-year-old I was getting nowhere. I thought if I gave up the stuff then everything would some-how be all right. But the reality was that I had all the same problems... I did... when I started. Nothing had changed except that now as an adult I still had the same insecurities and emotional disposition as when I was twelve.

Another way to look at personal maturity is in terms of attaining a balanced personality. Human beings have physical, intellectual, emotional and moral aptitudes in diverse measure. All these faculties function together in a balanced way in a healthy, mature person. They support the moral reasoning, feeling and action that make for strong character. Neglecting to develop one of them affects all the others and detracts from optimum wellness.[11]

A star athlete or a science prodigy who has focused on developing one aspect of his or her self may leave other aspects underdeveloped. Such an imbalance can lead to difficulties for themselves and others. One of the tasks of character development is to help students identify and challenge their limitations, resisting the tendency to rely too much on their strengths rather than remedy their weaknesses.

When people find it too painful to face their shortcomings, they may turn to intoxicants for relief. This can blind them to the many negative effects that such substances have on their personality and character—impairing the intellect, disturbing the emotions and weakening the will.

Weak Character: A Risk Factor

Therefore, the factors that make for a weak character are also major risk factors for drug abuse. As Peter Benson has noted, "failure to pay attention to the development of our young goes a long way toward explaining the proliferation of health-compromising and future-jeopardizing behaviors among young people that unnerve all of us."[12] It stands to reason that people who have poor impulse control will have less ability to resist drugs' lure of immediate gratification, that those with a limited sense of responsibility will be less concerned about the consequences of their actions, and that those without positive life goals will be less averse to drugs as harmful to their future.

Indeed, some of the factors associated with weak character that have been found to put young people at risk include aggression, academic failure, low commitment to school and low religiosity,[13] as well as a low stage of moral decision-making[14] and an impoverished sense of personal meaning that does not regard drugs and alcohol as harmful to their life's goals.[15] Other verified risk factors include poor social skills[16] and drinking alcoholic beverages at an early age.[17] Conversely, even youth born into challenging situations have a stronger tendency to resist drugs when they have well-developed intellectual abilities, social and interpersonal skills, and close friends for support.[18]

It follows that the components of a strong character—a high moral standard, obedience and respect for parents and elders, self-discipline, the ability to manage time well, responsibility, and a sense of life's meaning—are protective factors against substance abuse. People exhibiting these character traits have the power to resist the allure of drugs, whether from peer pressure, messages from the media, or the blandishments of drug dealers. They understand that substance abuse interferes with their long-term goals. Says Tina, a West coast teenager, "I want to be a veterinarian, and I can see how the kids using drugs are real losers. If I am going to get where I want to go I can't afford to spend my days wasted."

For these reasons, drug prevention begins with education for character. The Child Development Project (CDP) has helped reduce the use of tobacco, alcohol and marijuana in 5th and 6th grade students, while in matched schools that did not use the program students' use of the same substances remained constant or increased.[19] "We try to help schools provide children with a stronger sense of autonomy, belonging and competence—a new sense of the ABCs," says Eric Schaps, program founder. This program focuses on school discipline practices, parental involvement and school climate. Hall monitors report on peers' behavior, and a buddies program places older students with students from younger grades to support them during the school year. Family involvement is encouraged through events such as the Family Read Aloud Night and homework assignments that draw on family experience.[20] CDP is typical of comprehensive character education programs, implemented from the early grades, that effectively address the underlying risk factors of substance abuse even when drugs are not explicitly the issue. In fact, once the issue of drugs has taken center stage, providing stopgap measures and giving warnings may be too little too late.

Detour on the Road to Loving Relationships

All people desire the joy that comes from giving and receiving love. The key to fulfillment in love lies in developing the ability to share oneself with others. Traversing the emotional terrain of relating to others with integrity, courage and unselfishness allows young people to experience authentic human interaction and belonging.

Normally, people's craving for love pushes them toward making greater efforts at relating well. However, drugs—including alcohol—give the illusion of facilitating social relationships and putting people at ease with one another. They provide a false sense of sociability and a sham sense of belonging, simulating the emotional satisfaction that comes from strong relationships without the hard work of caring and investing. Yet the end result is often isolation and loneliness, as the user discovers he or she has alienated family and real friends in favor of the false friends whose concern is only to enjoy the stupor of intoxication. Drugs thus become a well-camouflaged detour from the path towards fulfilling the life goal of loving relationships and family.

Gateway Drugs

Despite widespread usage and acceptance, alcohol and tobacco are classified as drugs. They are responsible for more health and social problems than all other drugs combined. For this reason, there is a worldwide trend to restrict the consumption of cigarettes, especially to minors.

Moreover, there is a strong link between alcohol and tobacco use and the use of hard drugs such as cocaine and heroin. A person under the age of twenty-one is far more likely to try hard drugs if he or she has already known the intoxication of alcohol or marijuana. They are more prone to try marijuana if they have already put tobacco smoke in their lungs.[21]

Not every smoker will go on to use cocaine. Nevertheless, the probability that a 12–17-year-old teenage smoker will one day use cocaine is 19 times greater than a non-smoker. A teenage drinker is 50 times more likely to someday use cocaine than a teetotaler. A teenager who smokes marijuana is 85 times more likely to use cocaine at some point than one who never smokes marijuana.[22] Thus, tobacco, alcohol and marijuana are called "gateway drugs."

Research has found that if students perceive the use of marijuana as "risky," then drug use declines; if not, then the converse is true.[23] A tolerant attitude toward "softer" drugs only encourages abuse of the hard, addictive drugs.

Unhealthy Family Environment: A Risk Factor

Given the pivotal role of family experiences in moral growth, families that fail to instill self-discipline and self-worth and provide training in respect and reciprocity leave youth more at risk for substance abuse. Domestic violence, lack of affection and care between the husband and wife and between parents and children, absence of parental discipline—

these all take their toll. Research in criminology and child development indicates that family deviance, including substance-abusing parents, affects the developing child, because such families are likely to tolerate and model deviance for children.[24] Drug abuse can arise as a reaction to neglect or lack of intimacy between parents and children, as the adolescents try to fill an unmet emotional need.[25] Likewise, teenagers who consistently spurn the guidance of elders and do not establish a bond with at least one adult, such as a grandparent or teacher as a positive role model, are also at greater risk to take drugs. FBI statistics indicate that three-fourths of young people in drug treatment centers come from single-parent homes.[26]

After college basketball star Len Bias died of cocaine, his mother Lonise began speaking to young people about drug abuse and learned that many of them could not deal with troubles at home: "They told me many of them used drugs because they cannot cope. I asked them what they meant by that, and they say, 'My mom and I don't get along,' or 'My mom and dad are divorced.' Parents who couldn't cope with each other are expecting children to be able to cope. We need families where the children can see the mom and dad trying to do their best and young people will emulate the parents."[27]

Educators can take a proactive approach by identifying such at-risk children early on and offering assistance. This remediation works best if it begins in the primary grades, long before the temptation to substance abuse enters the children's lives. Elementary school programs with a component of individual mentoring, such as the CDP program described above, can give students the emotional support they lack at home and teach them the ways of good relationships.

Healthy Family Environment: A Protective Factor

Conversely, a healthy family is a protective factor against substance abuse. A warm, emotionally close relationship with a parent that includes open communication,[28] bonding,[29] quality time spent together and parental assistance with problem solving help protect youth from drug use.[30] Where there is affection, harmony and respect among family members, children become secure and confident that they are loved and learn the ways of getting along well with others. These family experiences are invaluable assets in resisting the allure of intoxicants.[31]

In this regard, it is a protective factor if family members set the example of being drug-free themselves. Children raised by parents who smoke cigarettes are far more likely to become smokers themselves, while children raised by non-smokers are less likely to take up smoking. The same applies to alcohol[32] and drugs.[33]

Current drug prevention strategies target family environments and their impact on potential drug abuse in children.[34] Government-sponsored advertising campaigns advise parents about talking to their children about drugs. A project in Louisville, Kentucky that focuses on parental training and support was found to delay the onset of alcohol and drug use in high-risk teenagers ages 12-14.[35] Encouraging parents to be more involved with their children and to maintain open channels of communication where they can express their values about substance abuse is key.

Peer-Helping Strategies for Drug Prevention

School-based substance-abuse prevention programs likewise benefit from attending to relationship needs. Peer influence is strong on adolescents, whose life focus is on the sibling's sphere of love. Thus, peer leadership can be an effective strategy for drug and alcohol prevention programs in schools.[36] The National Commission on Drug-Free Schools identifies programs that combine "positive peer influence with specific skills training" as effective to "change the drug use behavior of nearly implacable high-risk populations."[37]

When peers dispel the myth that "everyone is using drugs," the message is received with greater impact. A 20-session program for over 1,000 seventh-grade students from 10 suburban New York junior high schools that involved such activities as role-playing, interpersonal exercises and active feedback from peers, led to a significant reduction in drunkenness.[38] At Dundee High School, where peer leaders were trained to lead the drug prevention classes, students voiced such remarks as, "I feel more comfortable talking to seniors than adults" and "We felt we could tell them more than we could tell a teacher and we were more likely to listen to them."[39] Project Northland, a seventh-grade program implemented in 20 northeastern Minnesota schools, included a peer participation program in which student groups planned supervised, alcohol-free activities for themselves and their classmates. Program goals included (1) providing peer leadership and social support for non-use of alcohol, (2) creating opportunities for alternative behaviors to alcohol use, and (3) creating a norm of non-use.[40]

Critical to the success of peer-helping programs is the selection of suitable peer mentors. Effort is made to identify prospective student leaders who are helpful, trustworthy, concerned for others, good listeners, and positive role models. Recommendations from teachers or interviews with a project staff member and a teacher can identify students with moral leadership potential. A school-wide focus on character education provides more fertile ground for the cultivation of such individuals, who can then lead their at-risk classmates away from the blind alley of substance abuse.

Detour on the Road to Making a Contribution

Young people want to excel—on the athletic field, in the classroom, and in their careers. They yearn to develop their talents. They hope their accomplishments will gain the approval of their elders and their peers. They look forward to the power, money and prestige that come with success. More importantly, they want the inner satisfaction that comes with making a difference in the world.

The basic life goal of making a contribution to society is closely linked to mastery—competence in the skills and knowledge to do a job well and create things that people value. Thus mastery too is a fundamental human aspiration. Hence, when it is frustrated, people are liable to turn to a substitute. Taking intoxicants can give a person the illusion of brilliance, competence and power. Yet in reality it sidetracks them from the path to true mastery and social contribution.

Creativity also figures into making a valuable contribution. Few experiences are more satisfying than to be recognized and appreciated for a work of genuine self-expression. This is especially true of people with an artistic bent. When circumstances constrain their self-expression, when their work goes unappreciated, or when their creative well is stagnant, they may in frustration turn to drugs. An accomplished classical musician recounted, "My first big break was with the orchestra of *Cats*, but after a week I began to lose confidence I could deliver night after night. A friend turned me on to meths. They made me feel confident, really great. The problem was that I wasn't playing up to par;

I was disrupting the whole violin section. And by the time anybody told me I couldn't take it; I was a bundle of nerves. They let me go after five weeks."

Social Impediments to Youth's Aspirations: Risk Factors

Risk factors for substance abuse include the limitations within the community that discourage young people's ambitions to mastery and their hopes of making a difference in the world. Schools plagued with discipline problems, dull programs and aloof teachers are an obvious example. Regardless of how strongly adults preach an anti-drug message, if a student feels that they don't genuinely care about him, his achievements and his future, he will be at risk.

Moreover, even gifted students are at risk in environments such as the inner city that lack jobs and opportunities for career advancement. Frustrations fed by perceptions of "dead end" jobs tempt students to seek an escape through intoxicants. One school principal who runs a successful drug program says, "Teaching kids the skills they need to get along in society isn't enough; you must provide opportunities for them to practice and develop those skills. To be successful we must help young people find options, avenues, and alternatives that enrich their lives and alter their lifestyles."[41]

Lack of constructive recreational and artistic opportunities is another risk factor. Whether on the athletic field, in the art studio or at a wilderness campground, students can blossom when they have incentives and opportunities to work on their skills, express their creativity, and find a meaningful way to relate to their world. The unavailability of such outlets makes the allure of drug abuse that much stronger.[42]

Communities can include arts and recreational organizations in their drug prevention efforts. At Ailey Camp in Baltimore, children attend a dance camp where they learn discipline and self-confidence.[43] Students from the "Just Say No" to Drugs Club in Cherryvale Elementary School in Sumter, South Carolina organized themselves into a dance group.[44] The "Rope Not Dope" program trains inner-city girls in the skill of Double-Dutch jump rope and prepares them to participate in national competitions.[45]

When teenagers are busy honing their skills and striving for success, they are naturally less likely to be attracted to substance abuse. Life Skills Training (LST) is a program that builds adolescents' ability to deal with life's challenges rather than escaping them through drug use. Lessons teach such life skills as dealing with stress, resisting advertising pressure, and decision-making that considers the long-range consequences of behavior. Lessons in conversation skills and manners are supported by out-of-class behavioral "homework," such as encouraging students to introduce themselves to five new people. The fifteen LST classes in the seventh grade are supplemented through "booster" classes in the eighth and ninth grade. Program developer Gilbert Botvin tracked 3,600 LST students in 56 rural and suburban public schools in New York State. Six years after being coached in the program, they were less likely to use alcohol, drugs and cigarettes than those who had not been so trained.[46]

Community and cultural norms condoning the "gateway drugs" of alcohol and cigarettes and glamorizing the harder drugs can also put young people at risk. Project Star, a five-year program adopted by the Indianapolis schools, reaches out to parents and the community with prevention education. In the first year, students are taught drug awareness and resistance skills. In the second year, parents are involved with the aim of creating stronger family rules. In the third year, schools sponsor community-wide prevention activities such as "smoke-outs" and alcohol-free sporting events. In the fourth year, program participants work for policy changes such as creating a tax on beer and drug-free school zones. In the fifth year, they target the mass media to deliver anti-drug messages in advertisements and talk shows. Programs like Project Star that address community norms are more successful in curbing substance abuse than school-based programs lacking this component, according to school psychologist Mary Anne Pentz, who developed the program. It has been shown to lower occasional use of gateway drugs throughout high school and to quell heavier use, such as daily drunkenness and chain-smoking.[47]

Drug Highs and Natural Highs

Everyone wants to experience the peak experiences or "highs" of life. Natural highs are intense, exhilarating experiences that affirm the best in oneself. People often take drugs to experience an artificial version of such exhilaration. Indeed, research at the University of Kentucky and Indiana University shows that drugs excite the neural reward system in the brain that is normally activated by novel and stimulating experiences.[48]

Substance-induced ecstasy is a very poor substitute for natural highs, extracting a terrible toll. When drugs affect the central nervous system, they cause physical and psychological dependence that can harden into addiction. Natural highs, on the other hand, extract no toll: they are physically, emotionally and mentally constructive. They are the body's way of rewarding an individual for accomplishments on the path to maturity, love and success in life.

One example of a natural high is graduating from college. When the student receives a diploma, the moment is euphoric. Society is celebrating the achievement of a personal goal. All of the hard work and discipline she had invested to pass exams and get good grades is appreciated and validated. The student's family, too, is proud of her accomplishment and showers her with praise. In terms of the basic life goals, this natural high reaffirms her family relationships and validates that she is qualified to contribute to society.

Sports provide natural highs that come with scoring a goal, winning a tournament, or earning a trophy. The ability that allows one to seize that moment and perform so admirably is the culmination of years of physical discipline and training. Yet, that one moment of success makes it all worthwhile. It is even more satisfying when the individual is contributing to a team effort or bringing victory to his school—when his personal mastery contributes to a social purpose. Greg, a high school senior, remarked, "I experienced the greatest natural high after we won the basketball championship. When the final buzzer rang and the whole crowd was on their feet cheering and clapping, the emotional atmosphere was incredible. It was such a powerful experience. I was so high that I wasn't sure if it was all real. At one point everything seemed to suddenly go silent, and I felt like I was floating on air. It was only for a moment, but it was the best feeling I have ever had."

Experiences that reach the peaks of human value—love, truth, beauty and goodness—reinforce positive behavior leading to fulfillment of basic life goals. Musicians experience a natural exhilaration when their music is in perfect harmony; it gives them incentive to strive for even greater performances. A couple experiences a natural euphoria when their first child is born; it opens their hearts to the experience of parenthood, which will demand much of them. Walking in the woods in the springtime can be a natural high, instilling a life-long environmental awareness and bond with nature.

Drug-induced intoxication does none of this. Natural highs enhance and encourage growth towards sound character and social skills, whereas drug-induced highs distort and impede growth by short-circuiting the path to psychological and social maturation. Natural highs lead to improved health and well-being, whereas drug-induced euphoria leads to a deterioration of physical and mental health and well-being. The only thing drug-induced exhilaration reinforces is further drug abuse, leading to ever-greater dependence and ultimately addiction.

In the last analysis, the drug problem is primarily a moral problem. More than any outward allure, contributing factors lending attractiveness to drugs lie in deficiencies in the moral formation of young people. That is why substance abuse prevention programs have a better chance of succeeding when centered on a moral dimension. There is thus a natural synergy between drug prevention and character education.

Youth who are taught and encouraged in self-discipline, kindness, delayed gratification and hard work toward desired goals are insulated against the dangers of drug use. They experience the natural highs and sense of self-building their accomplishments bring them. Such youth can recognize drugs as illusory and growth-inhibiting substitutes for the real happiness and bona fide success in life they are busily garnering.

28

Causes and Resolution of Conflict

IN THE WAKE OF THE SHOOTINGS AT COLUMBINE HIGH SCHOOL in April of 1999, popular opinion about protecting students from conflict includes support for such measures as installing metal detectors in schools. Yet most of the conflicts that affect youth—and which affect youth all over the world—take place under far more ordinary circumstances. Children and teenagers suffer from quarrels between their parents, discord within their neighborhoods, and clashes with schoolmates. Indirectly, children suffer from the workplace disagreements their parents cannot leave behind as well as marital quarrels; these drain parents of the energy and aplomb needed to optimally care for their children. These conflicts take their psychological and emotional toll on young people, affecting them deeply, cumulatively, and often permanently.

Understanding the causes of conflict and the means of resolving it are ways to lessen this psychological toll and help children grow into maturity with secure inner working models for forging good relationships even in the midst of the inevitable tensions they will face.

The Value of Resolving Conflict

Conflict is a fact of life. Under ordinary circumstances, conflict is neither good nor bad in and of itself. It is the way people respond to conflict and handle it that determines its outcome. If conflict is feared and regarded as negative, it has little growth-promoting potential. Conflict, like all adversity, is best looked upon as an opportunity for character growth—a chance for individuals to call upon and refine their inner resources—to challenge themselves to new frontiers of empathy and relationship skills.

Conflict is a symptom and sign that the emotional subtext of a relationship needs correction and improvement. Tensions may even be welcomed as a herald of potential to deepen a relationship. Many a couple feels closer and more intimately connected to each other after a dispute has been resolved. Friendships are often strengthened by successful resolution of a disagreement. New bonds have been forged in the fires of conflict in all types of relationships.

Unfortunately, many people respond to the presence of conflict by seeking to terminate the situation where they find it. They quit jobs, leave schools, divorce, sever friendships, never go into a certain store again or stop speaking to a relative. These avoidance methods bring temporary relief, but in fact, unresolved conflicts inevitably return to haunt the person. They often reappear in a new form or with new people, continuing to resurface until resolved. Conflict cannot be compartmentalized. Until the problem is healed on the deepest levels of the human heart, it inevitably permeates a person's interactions with others.

Dawn, a mother of three, had an altercation with a neighbor over her children playing in the back of his parked truck. He strongly urged her to ground her children for the offense. Dawn remembered, however, that he often let the children play in the truck when he was in a good mood. How could he be so inconsistent? Dawn was angry with the neighbor and decided not to punish her children. Yet when her husband and children came home, she found herself yelling at them over every minor offense. Dawn realized her unresolved anger over the incident with the neighbor was causing her to lash out at her family.

Resolving conflict is desirable for many reasons. The cessation of tensions removes the paralyzing impasse that leaves both sides feeling isolated and stagnant. It opens the doors to forgiveness and reconciliation, which in turn free up time and energy for creativity and progress. The amount of emotional energy lost in maintaining friction—the defensive moves and retaliations—could be more efficiently directed toward living a full and productive life and promoting more gratifying relationships.

Peter from New Haven recalls the sense of renewal and resurgent relationship upon resolving a difficulty as a child. "When I was a small boy I used to play every afternoon with my best friend. Our favorite game was setting up our army of tin soldiers. I was especially proud of a little army truck my father had given me. I even marked it in a special way. Then one day, the truck disappeared. What was worse, I discovered that my friend had taken it. Because of the little mark I had made, there was no doubt in my mind that this was my truck. I said nothing and my friend said nothing, but our happy little world lay in ruins. I knew that he took it, and he knew that I knew that he took it. We could not face each other. We could not play together. Then, in a day or two he came up to me and said, 'I'm sorry. I took your truck. Please forgive me.' There was a moment of silence. 'Oh, forget about it,' I answered. 'What do I care?' Suddenly all the world around us was bright and happy again."

A person is able to make his or her world of relationships better by seeking the means to resolve conflict. Part of this resolution involves understanding that there are often deep underlying emotional and psychological needs beneath the surface of disputes.

Causes of Conflict

Among school children, disputes arise over personal possessions and school resources, cliques, differing ideas and opinions, cheating, bullying, and such abusive moves as shoving for a better place in line, using put-downs and name calling. Many schools have conflict resolution programs in place to deal with such everyday issues,[1] but schools with character education programs are already teaching their students the basics of respect, courtesy, manners and the treatment of all people as equal and worthy, proactively addressing the issues that underlie much conflict. (See Chapter 12) Such preventative efforts keep clashes from arising in the first place.

In the home, disagreements occur over such common issues as discipline and obedience, parenting styles, money, sibling rivalry, homework and grades, children's possessions and teenagers' desire for independence. Conflicts tend to escalate when self-control, patience, forbearance, long-sightedness and other virtues are deficient. Thus, building healthy marriages and giving children the foundation of good parenting reduce conflicts. (See Chapters 21 and 22)

Conflicts in families are exacerbated and amplified by substance or alcohol abuse. In addition, certain destructive patterns such as schizophrenia and alcoholism tend to run in families, producing strife. Negative patterns of family interaction—violence, insults and sarcasm, among others—tend to be imitated from generation to generation until one member of the family has enough perspective and courage to change it in his or her generation. People who have interrupted the negative cycles of neglect and abuse in their personal histories to become loving, respected parents to their own children sometimes feel they are literally altering fate, breaking up the bad "karma" of their family line.[2]

Tensions with a History

Individuals and families in neighborhoods and communities are often affected by hostilities stemming from actions, past and present, by or against their ethnic, racial, religious or national group. Sometimes crimes were committed against a certain group as part of a national mindset or policy. The result is that succeeding generations inherit a legacy of racial and ethnic resentments and prejudice. Such tensions fuel fires that can escalate simple interpersonal conflicts into community conflagrations.

One such incident happened on a sunny summer day in New York, when eleven-year-old Steven pushed ten-year-old Joey to the ground and kicked him hard in the ribs during a dispute over a game. When Joey's mother went outside, she found him on the ground, in pain and gasping for air. Fortunately, Joey's asthma medicine restored his breathing, and a doctor's visit showed that he had a bruised rib, not a broken one. That, however, was not the end of the incident.

Steven's family had come to the United States from Puerto Rico, and the only housing that had been available to them when they first came was in a ghetto area where Steven had quickly learned to defend himself and his brothers. He and his family already felt that white people were against them, and that feeling was exacerbated when neighbors grew cold after the incident with Joey. For their part, the white neighbors feared Steven's ferocity and viewed him and his growing brothers with suspicion, wondering about a future Puerto Rican gang, as they'd read about in the newspapers. The ethnic mistrust that permeates American society hardened the families' attitudes toward one another, reinforcing old prejudices and leading to catcalls, rudeness and minor scuffles whenever paths crossed. Thus, due to racial prejudice, a simple playground fight polarized a whole neighborhood.

Recurring Effect of Unresolved Conflict

Tensions over racial inequities is a prime example of how an issue of conflict will resurface repeatedly until it is finally resolved. Although the United States was founded upon the highest ideals of democracy and freedom, translating these ideals into practical reality has been a continuous challenge throughout its history.

The issue of slavery was never dealt with during the founding of America. Thomas Jefferson said slavery kept him awake like an alarm bell in the night, foreboding the death of the Union.[3] George Washington predicted that this unfinished business would someday divide the nation. His guilt and uneasiness over slavery led him to free his own slaves upon his wife's death and to work for the education of all slaves. "I clearly foresee that nothing but the rooting out of slavery can perpetuate the existence of our union," he said,[4] and vowed that if the nation ever divided on the issue, he would fight on the side against slavery. Yet Washington's efforts to better the lots of slaves in Virginia were fruitless. The unresolved issue raised its head again, as these presidents predicted it would, several generations later. The Civil War was fought over the issue of slavery, at the cost of half a million lives.

Abraham Lincoln vowed to fight slavery to the end, even "until every drop of blood drawn with the lash shall be paid by another drawn with the sword."[5] He believed that the war was payment for long unresolved injustices. But even though the Civil War was consciously fought to right an historical wrong, the issue of inequality between races was not settled and was left to another generation to resolve on a deeper level—the level of the heart.

One hundred years after the Civil War, Martin Luther King, Jr. and others worked to establish civil rights and equality for all races. King's soaring oratory and his courage through a campaign of non-violent demonstrations called America to her conscience on race relations. Many whites experienced a genuine change of heart. Legislation was passed, and as they had in the Civil War, federal troops were called in to defend blacks' rights to participate in democracy. African-Americans entered mainstream national life in unprecedented numbers and ways. Although race relations are far from what they should be, King and others catapulted race relations forward through the peaceable resolution of conflict, bringing the ideal of human equality closer to actuality.

If social problems and crises are not dealt with thoroughly and well, they will inevitably resurface in the future until they are properly resolved. There have been many cases where one side won a war only to be re-engaged in battle years later because the original animosities never were addressed. Physical force may stop an aggressor in the moment, but it does not stop the enmity and resentment that caused the aggression in the first place. Defeating an enemy does not answer his or her grievances or end hatred. Unless the defeated one's desire for vengeance is abated by kindness and fairness, sooner or later the urge for revenge will rise again, often in an even more destructive form. This is why history often appears to repeat itself. Until the deep, underlying factors are resolved, the conflicts will arise again and again.

Conflict needs to be dealt with on the deep, causal emotional level before peace can be well and fully established—whether it is peace between nations, races, societies, communities, students, families or within an individual. The heart of the problem is the human heart.

Conflict and the Human Heart

When people feel their human dignity has been violated, the reflex is to strike back. According to psychologist Steven Stosny, anger and the desire for vengeance stem from a sense of diminishment of self. The person feels disempowered and belittled. Therefore, he seeks to re-empower himself. Too often, such empowerment is attempted through counter-productive means.[6]

A nation may feel stung by actions that threaten its sovereignty, impugn its motives, or threaten to harm its well-being through interdiction of goods and services. That nation may go to war. On the community level, some individuals feel disenfranchised by the system. They feel left out, deprived, treated unequally. Such individuals may resort to crime and become even further marginalized.

After the Columbine massacre, fellow students reported that Columbine killers Eric Harris and Dylan Klebold had been the victims of brutal teasing. They were badgered, shoved up against lockers, bashed into walls, and people cut in front of them in line, acting as if they did not exist.[7] Erik Veik, a friend of the pair, reported that Klebold and Harris said they wanted to get revenge for the constant hazing. "They were tired of those who were insulting them, harassing them. They weren't going to take this anymore, and they wanted to stop it. Unfortunately, that's what they did."[8]

Police psychologists Marisa Pynchon and Robert Fein interviewed other students now in jail for school shootings and found that they, too, were often the victims of harsh teasing. Luke Woodham, convicted for shooting his girlfriend in school in 1997, stated, "They'd call me stupid or fat or whatever. Kids would sometimes throw rocks at me and push and kick me and hit me." These psychologists emphasize the need for adults to understand the intensity of teasing and similar conflicts between students at school.[9]

People who are marginalized or disrespected naturally seek to reassert their importance and value. While nothing can justify the actions of these students, it is possible that an atmosphere dedicated to the resolution of conflict and respectful treatment of others could have encouraged them to seek the help they so desperately needed instead of resorting to their horrendous actions.

Authentic empowerment comes from accessing the intrinsically good and most fundamental part of the self: the heart. Others' careless and thoughtless words do not—indeed cannot—diminish this core value of a human being. As Eleanor Roosevelt once said, "No one can make you feel small without your cooperation." Difficult circumstances may tarnish the "shine" from a person's heart but ultimately cannot destroy its potential to love and relate in a healthy way.

Stosny teaches children this concept with a coloring book that depicts "My Good Heart" and helps children get in touch with their best selves through drawings and questions. When asked, "What happens when people are not in touch with their good hearts?" children invariably draw pictures of people hitting each other, yelling at each other and committing acts of violence—scenes of escalated conflict.

Yet accessing the heart is not always easy. Without proper cultivation, the heart remains buried and often tangled in conflicting desires. Martin Luther King, Jr., commented on such intrapersonal tensions—tensions within the person himself: "Each of us is something of a schizophrenic personality, tragically divided against ourselves. A persistent civil war rages within all of our lives."[10] This inner divisiveness between the individual's best impulses and his worst ones is the root of conflict. This has been described and dramatized in countless ways throughout history.

Plato described the human personality as a charioteer with two willful horses pulling in opposite directions. Psychology depicts it as a battle between the socialized self and the infantile self. Some cultures have characterized it as a battle between the animal self and the human self. Poets, artists, philosophers and the religious have often seen it as a war between metaphysical forces of good and evil. However it is viewed, this inner struggle is inevitably reflected in quarrels with others, whether within the family, in the school, or in the community. When people are not at peace with themselves, it is easy to clash with others. The quarrels between spouses, strife between groups, and hostilities among nations are all reflections of the conflict within each individual.

One way to access the heart is to affirm such universal values as respect and the interrelatedness and common humanity of all people. Indeed, universal values lie at the core of peacemaking and rebuilding a sense of connection and community. Kay Pranis of the Minnesota Department of Corrections said, "Communities are value-laden structures. Resilient, sustainable communities are built on respect, caring, taking responsibility, fulfilling obligations, a sense of shared fate."[11] Any attempts to arrive at peace that are not value-driven are usually ineffective.

Universal values include the notion that every person is worthy of respect. This respect extends to the one who is considered the offender in the conflict too. The offender, even in the wrong, is a human being responding to pain—a person in need of correction, but in need of support and help as well. To bring the offender back into good standing with the others he or she has affected is the goal. This means healing the rift rather than just meting out punishment. Ideally, it means restoring the relationship on the level of the heart.

Steps to Resolving Conflict

Mohandas K. Gandhi, the great peacemaker of India, discovered in his early law practice that everyone benefited if his motivation was to bring the parties together rather than to "win" his cases. Indeed, if restoring the warring parties into a good relationship is the basic motivation of conflict resolution, the problem is already well on its way to being solved. There are three distinct phases or steps that characterize all good conflict resolution efforts:

Step One: Reflection and Reorientation. This step involves getting in touch with the heart and higher motives as well as considering the ways in which one might have been at fault.

Step Two: Reversal and Restitution is the step of acting upon these better impulses to ameliorate some of the injury and separation.

Step Three: Reconciliation and Renewal is the experience of coming together again and making a fresh start.

Whether consciously or not, conflict resolution goes through these steps naturally. People clash and separate. After they cool off and calm down, they often find themselves having regrets and even charitable feelings toward the other party. These sentiments gently prod them to renew the relationship. They approach the other person with an apology or other expression of sorrow over the incident. Then the two parties begin to restore some degree of harmony and good feeling.

Step 1 – Reflection and Reorientation

Upon reflection, those who have been involved in a conflict may realize how their own conduct contributed to the problem in some way big or small. Rueful second thoughts about their own words or behavior—or the motivation behind them—are often part of this process. So is clarifying why the other person or group affected them in such a way. Parents and educators can guide students to consider such questions as: "What could I have done differently? What is the real problem here? What do I really want and need? Where do I need to change myself? How did I contribute to the problem?"

Students usually need special help with this process. When emotions are running high, a teacher can encourage reflection by first helping the parties cool down and think. The Falk Laboratory School at the University of Pittsburgh in Pennsylvania has developed a creative program called Conflict and Resolution Education (CARE) that helps students to think things through by use of a traffic light image. The red light reminds students to stop and "Cool Down" and recall the "Ground Rules." "Tell Your Side" and "Listen" are labels for the yellow light. The green light exhorts them to "Brainstorm Ideas" for solving the problem.

At the end of the first year, teachers reported that conflict resolution had taken on a collaborative problem-solving dimension. One primary grade teacher found that students were applying techniques taught and practiced in classrooms at home. One insightful seven-year-old student urged his parents to use the conflict-resolution traffic light because "it works in school."[12]

Another technique to encourage reflection and reorientation is taught by Volunteers of America. It is called "Have a SODA." Students at odds are given a picture of a large ice cream soda and asked to sit down and reflect on the meaning of the acronym. S means "Stop." O means consider the "Options"—"If I do this, this will result, and if I do that, that will result." D stands for "Decide" which option to take, and A stands for "Act" according to a good decision.

Step 1: Reflection and Reorientation

- Identify one's contribution to the problem

- Recognize how it affected the other's feelings

- Evaluate one's attitude and behavior in light of universal values

- Consider how one might have better dealt with the problem

- Decide to take responsibility for one's contribution to the problem

- Plan how to make amends

Thinking about Values and Outcomes

The reflection phase also includes thinking about values: Do I believe in fighting? Are angry words, harsh gestures and unforgiving attitudes conducive to good human relationships? Are all people inherently worthy of respect and fair treatment—even my so-called enemy of the moment? Am I worthy inside, no matter what the other person has said or done? Such reflection can often calm a person down and motivate him or her to take responsibility to heal the conflict.

In the upper grades at New Hope School in Bridgeport, Connecticut, behavior journals function as a method to cool off, gain perspective and process negative feelings about a situation that made a student angry or agitated. When teens are overwhelmed by feelings of unfairness, frustration, impotence or anger, their ability to reflect on goals and values is greatly compromised. In their journals students describe their view of what happened, the variety of emotions surrounding the experience, and to consider the implications if "everybody responded that way." Then they identify a value or action that will help resolve the conflict.

This technique worked well for one student, Steve. During the stressful time of his parents' divorce, he yelled a racial slur at the school janitor, and later defended his action by claiming that the janitor had previously called him names and spread rumors about him. Steve's teacher did a lot of work to help him get to the heart of the matter—his own pain and frustration—and to see the value of practicing respect even though he might not feel adults always deserve it. After begrudgingly writing an apology to the janitor, Steve began to feel true remorse and decided to apologize face to face.

Reflection also means to clarify the desired outcome of the conflict and to consider means to bring this about. In a thoughtful moment, a person may realize that some types of vengeful actions or expressions of anger will not bring about the results they really desire and might even have an opposite effect.

For instance, Patricia, a mother of two elementary school children, was enraged when her nine-year-old son came home from school saying that his teacher had accused him of lying, in front of the class. The boy had expressed confusion and concern at home about test scoring, and when his father had called the school to inquire, the teacher had become defensive and thought the boy had gone home with tall tales about unfair test scoring practices.

Patricia and her husband were angered on behalf of their son, but they reflected upon what they wanted to come out of the ensuing parent-teacher conference. What they really wanted, they decided, was for their son to receive a sincere apology in front of the students who had heard the accusation and for the teacher to be more charitable toward him (and other students) in the future. They did not want to take him out of school in the middle of the academic year. They decided to work toward these ends.

Upon reflection and discussion with the principal, the teacher decided that she had been in the wrong. She adopted the policy that when an issue came up with a parent, she would first discuss the issue thoroughly with the parent and the principal before confronting a child. She reoriented herself toward giving children the benefit of the doubt.

The Role of a Mediator

A mediator may be needed in the case when the parties involved need help in getting the process started. A mediator is a neutral and mutually trusted figure who is not personally involved in the conflict. The mediator helps the disputing sides find a common basis—points of agreement—for constructive interaction. Thus the mediator encourages both sides to take the first two steps of restoring peace and find their way towards reconciliation and renewal.

An effective mediator affirms the value of both parties and thus helps each to affirm the other's value. The goal of the mediator—although it is not easy—is to achieve a collaborative, win-win outcome where both sides can feel satisfied. The mediator helps the parties find possibilities for cooperation and mutual benefit.

School mediation is typically led either by teachers or peers. Six basic steps of successful teacher-led mediation are as follows:

1. Initiate mediation: Approach the conflict and make a statement, stop aggressive behavior, neutralize any object of conflict by holding it (i.e., a disputed piece of sports equipment will be appropriated by the teacher).

2. Gather information about the victim's feelings and aggressor's wants and assure the disputants that each will be heard.

3. Define the problem in terms satisfactory to both sides by paraphrasing their feelings and concerns.

4. Generate alternative solutions by encouraging suggestions from disputants and observers and allowing ample time for them to come up with ideas on their own.

5. Agree on a solution: paraphrase it and spell out how the solution will be implemented.

6. Follow through by arranging someone to monitor the implementation and announce its success when this has occurred.[13]

Some schools have success with peer mediation programs for older students. The Mediation for Kids training program[14] trains young mediators how to see both sides, remain impartial and not react to the excesses of emotion involved in the disagreement, and assert values over vengeance. It provides an activity format to guide students through the mediation process.

Properly trained, peers can be understanding and helpful mediators, though they need the support of the administration, teachers and other adults to be effective. Peer mediators are uniquely placed to find and understand the underlying emotional and psychological needs operating in their peers and to help them "save face" and survive in the school environment.

Step 2 – Reversal and Restitution

Reversal and restitution is the substantial attempt to right the wrong that was done to the other party and to reverse whatever caused him or her to feel hurt or violated. It is a sincere effort to soothe the sorrow and pain that was caused. It is an admission of wrong and a gesture of good will which strives to make amends and reconnect with the other person by whatever means are necessary to make an opening to renew the relationship. In the case of Patricia's son, the teacher issued an apology to the boy in front of the class and from that time on treated him with more kindness.

Often, the motivation to restore a damaged relationship and forgive cannot be awakened without an actual gesture showing sorrow or compunction. Such a gesture serves as payment or indemnity for losses incurred. In common incidents, it is a peace offering: the enraged heart of a neighbor is assuaged when the boy who put a ball through his window offers to pay for it; the wife who is angry at her husband's neglect is mollified by a huge bouquet of roses.

This concept of making concrete reparations, called "restorative justice," is enjoying increasing popularity in the criminal justice system.[15] Some offenders are being held financially liable to their victims for the losses and damages they caused. In other cases, the offender not only pays compensation in the form of service to the community or in fines or incarceration, but also he or she meets with the victim and their representatives and listens to their story of how the offense affected their lives. In many cases, this leads to greater understanding between the two and reduces recidivism as the offender is schooled in empathy. The victims also feel relief at having been heard.

Restitution may take the form of lesser compensation, such as an apology or an act of kindness in a relationship that is basically sound. On the other hand, there are situations where "equal" restitution is necessary. If property is damaged, it may have to be repaired or replaced for the full value of what it was worth before it was damaged. In some cases, the restitution required may be greater than the original injury.

A $50 debt that is left unpaid may be increased to $60 to cover the delay and frustration of the creditor. Someone who has made a hurtful remark to someone they do not know well may have to make many gestures of sincerity before the person is able to trust them. Insincerity or failure to fulfill an earlier promise may increase the time and amount of restitution required. This is one reason why it is desirable to resolve conflict when it first crops up.

Step 2: Reversal and Restitution

- Reverse whatever caused the other to feel violated

- Make restitution to correct injustice and repair damage done

- Be open to receive restitution

A Change in Attitude

Sometimes a reversal in a person's attitude and behavior is the key to restoring harmony. Certain attitudes provoke friction. Arrogance is one of them, and practicing humility reverses it. Humility involves being able to admit to not always having the superior or correct view and being receptive to learning from others. Often, a stubborn insistence on being right hinders people from seeing events from another person's point of view. A person with humility defers to the common humanity of all people, recognizing that everyone, including herself, has shortcomings and can improve.

"I hadn't talked to my brother Piet for a year after we had a big blow-up in a restaurant over his claiming to be out of money again and asking me to pay," recalls, Joan, a middle-aged illustrator. "I went ballistic after all the money I've lent him that he still hasn't paid back. When he finally called me up and apologized for that, I found myself admitting to myself that I once owed Dad quite a bit of money, too. Somehow I could let it go and enjoy talking to Piet." Thus does humility often beget more humility. If a person can bring him or herself to humbly admit to wrongdoing or a bad attitude, the other person is much more inclined to forgive—or even to sheepishly admit to his or her own weakness or role in the problem.

Generosity reverses greed. An episode on a popular television series showed how a woman had undercut a talented friend in order to take center stage and become a star. When confronted with her greed, the star generously allowed her friend to go on stage in her place, giving her a moment in the spotlight. She also helped her friend's daughter succeed in a stage career. In this way, she reversed and made up for her self-centered and hurtful actions.

Feeling themselves superior to others, people sometimes treat one another in cruel or unjust ways, spawning resentment, anger and a desire for retaliation. An attitude of service reverses the pain caused by such actions and attitudes. A hospital orderly on the West coast tells of one episode of service removing resentment. "The doctors sometimes march around like little kings and never even notice you. But I'll never forget the first time a doctor remembered my name, thanked me, and even gave me a present later for my new baby. I was stunned. I felt different after that."

Anger is reversed by compassion. A program for New York City bus drivers designed to help them cope with stresses and frustrations on their jobs helped them develop compassion toward their passengers through changing their frame of reference. The bus drivers were shown a film clip of a woman getting onto a bus very slowly and holding up all the other passengers, as well as traffic. The bus drivers found this maddening. Couldn't the woman understand the pressures of traffic and route timing that the drivers were under? Why was she deliberately moving so slowly? Then it was explained to the drivers that the woman had a disability which was not visible but which caused her to walk slowly and with much pain. Back on the job after such training in compassion, the bus drivers all reported a decrease in tension, anger and conflict. Some of them even felt sorry about the way they had treated customers in the past and began to deal with their customers with more empathy and understanding.[16]

Two Sides to Every Story

Taking responsibility for restitution is not the sole burden of the offender. Often it is not even easy to determine who is the offender and who the offended. In most clashes, both parties wind up hurting each other, or the present offender might think that he or she is only evening up the score from a previous injury committed by the other party. Sometimes, too, the apparent offender lacks the maturity or clarity of mind to make any gestures of reparation, and if the relationship is valued enough—as between family members—the offended may need to make the first move if any restoration of the relationship is going to occur. "Realistically, I knew my mother was bullheaded and proud and she wouldn't budge even if it killed her," says Matt, 38, a stock analyst in Canada. "Not coming to my wedding just tops a long list of insults. But she is my mom and I want my kids to have a grandma, so I've made overtures and even apologies so she can be part of our lives without admitting she did wrong." It is wise for both sides of a conflict to think in terms of how each may take responsibility to rectify the problem; however, in the end it may well be that whoever has the heart to do so has to initiate efforts to repair the relationship.

Consciously applying the strategy of Reversal and Restitution shows people what to do when they are feeling stymied by conflict. Though they may not feel inclined to do so, once they have made a gesture of restitution, they are likely to experience a great release of good feeling and a strong sense of renewed relationship. This is the transition to Step Three of conflict resolution—Reconciliation and Renewal.

Step 3 – Reconciliation and Renewal

In the case of Patricia mentioned above, although the teacher had apologized for the miscommunications that had led to the altercation over test scoring, this mother still felt distant from the school and brooded over whether she should keep her child there. She realized upon reflection, however, that she had been feeling distant from the school for a long time before the incident and had not been cultivating a relationship with her child's teacher as much as she should have. At the next opportunity, she went up to the teacher after school and sincerely apologized for her part in the conflict, presenting a small gift. The teacher was a conscientious woman who had deeply regretted the incident, and when Patricia apologized to her, she had a hard time holding back her emotions. Mother and teacher promised to work more closely together in the future. Patricia felt a rebound of loyalty and affection for the school and began to think of ways she could contribute as a volunteer.

This third step in peacemaking is a result of the work done in the first two steps. It is a transitioning from broken relationships to restored ones: reconciliation. Often, the restored relationship is stronger than it was before the conflict happened. Based on reconciliation, there may be renewal. Once the parties understand each other better, new avenues of friendship and relationship open. Having had an emotional experience together, people who have successfully resolved a conflict may feel closer and more bonded than ever before. Reconciliation means people have had to take a closer look at one another and at themselves; it is often a spur to new levels of understanding and sympathy.

Step 3: Reconciliation and Renewal

- Give up claim to retaliation
- Forgive and be open to forgiveness
- Support the other's reform
- Foster good will

The Element of Forgiveness

Forgiveness is an essential aspect of reconciliation to bring tensions to an end. Forgiveness means to give up the claim to retaliation and to allow positive energy to flow in the relationship again. Forgiveness does not excuse the wrongful or hurtful actions; nor does it mean that repetition of such actions is acceptable. However, forgiveness means that the actions no longer stand in the way of relating. The blockage is at least partially removed.

It is also well to note that forgiving is as beneficial to the one who forgives as to the one who is forgiven. Forgiveness brings relief. Letting go of the resentment, ill will, residual desires for revenge and negative expectations of the other brings a new sense of freedom.

"I'll never forget the feelings I had when the airplane started to shake and dip," said Toby, a woman in her late twenties, who was flying from California to New York at the time. "I gripped the seat handles and thought, 'What if I die?' Then the next thought that came was, 'Who haven't I forgiven?' I realized I hadn't forgiven Jesse, who had jilted me after a year's engagement. He'd approached me several times afterward, trying to be friends, but I'd just spurned him. In those moments before I thought we were going to go down, I thought, 'Jesse, I forgive you. I let you go.' Well, the plane didn't crash, but after that I found that whenever thoughts of Jesse occurred—less and less as time went by—I felt peace in my heart. I've heard he's married now, and I wish him well."

Forgiving is not easy. It requires the individual to find a certain amount of trust that he or she will not lose by forgiving. Forgiveness is easier if the second step of Reversal and Restitution has been done sincerely and well. Yet, even without these steps, the forgiving person is the one who finds the greater peace within and more gratifying relationships with people in general.

It is easier to reconcile when one person is able to see the other as a vulnerable fellow human being. Reconciliation and renewal are humanizing processes. The other person may be operating from a base of fear or pain or deprivation, and once this is understood, it is easier to forgive. As Henry Wadsworth Longfellow wrote, "If we could read the secret history of our enemies, we should find in each man's life of sorrow and suffering enough to disarm all hostility."[17]

A woman in her sixties had been shaken upon discovering a homeless man who had broken into her basement and lived there for three days. The sight of the man and the mess he had made of her basement had terrified her. When she saw him again, this time in court, however, she felt sorry for him. The man had gone through a rehabilitation program and now humbly apologized, telling her he understood her feelings of fear and violation. The woman suddenly saw him as a person like herself, not a threatening figure at all. She realized that his crime against her property had been more a result of his own confusion and helplessness rather than an attack upon her. She said, "I saw him as another human soul trying to put sense into life. I see that person as myself in many ways, that frightened, sometimes beaten soul."[18]

The heart is where conflicts become embedded, and they will proliferate and rise again until truly resolved on this profound level. Conflict need not be feared or avoided, but rather seen as an opportunity for deeper relatedness. After proceeding through three discrete steps, conflict resolution can welcome people firmly back into the camp of human belonging, resulting in hope and resurgent relationships.

Notes

Chapter 1

1. Alcestis Oberg, "Values Education Wins Supporters," *USA Today,* April 19, 2000, p. 27A.
2. Norman Dennis, "Europe's Rise in Crime," *The World & I* 12 (October 1997), p. 28.
3. William J. Bennett, "Is Our Culture in Decline?" *Education Week* 12/28 (April 7, 1993), p. 32.
4. Arnold Toynbee, *Civilization on Trial* (Oxford: Oxford University Press, 1948).
5. Ron Stodghill, "Everything Your Kids Already Know About Sex—Bet You're Afraid to Ask," *Time,* June 15, 1998, p. 54.
6. Marc Silver, "Sex and Violence on TV," *U.S. News & World Report,* September 11, 1995, pp. 62, 66.
7. Sylvia Ann Hewlett and Cornell West, *The War Against Parents* (New York: Houghton Mifflin, 1998), p. 44.
8. Robert N. Bellah, et al., *Habits of the Heart: Individualism and Commitment in American Life* (Berkeley: University of California Press, 1985).
9. Christopher Lasch, *The Minimal Self: Psychic Survival in Troubled Times* (New York: Norton, 1984).
10. Roy F. Baumeister, *Meanings of Life* (New York: Guilford Press, 1991).
11. Peter L. Berger, *The Sacred Canopy: Elements of a Sociological Theory of Religion* (Garden City: Doubleday, 1967), p. 3.
12. Stephen Covey, et al., *First Things First* (New York: Simon & Schuster, 1994), p. 181.
13. Daniel Goleman, *Emotional Intelligence* (New York: Bantam, 1995), p. 162.
14. This terminology also varies by country. Thus in the United States the current favorite is "character education," while in Great Britain the preferred term is "values education" and in Japan the term "moralogy" is in wide use. Sometimes the choice of terms is influenced by political concerns; thus "character education" gained currency in the United States partly to overcome the older religious connotations of the term "morality" and also to distance it from the values clarification approach normally implied by the older term

"values education." See Marvin W. Berkowitz, *The Education of the Complete Moral Person* (Aberdeen, Scotland: Gordon Cook Foundation, 1995).

15. *Protagoras* 325c-e.
16. Mortan A. Kaplan, "Higher Education, Lower Standards," *The World & I* 10/3 (March 1995), p. 357.
17. Goleman, *Emotional Intelligence,* p. 36.
18. Haim Ginott, *Between Teacher and Child* (New York: Avon, 1976).

Chapter 2

1. Deb Brown, "Learning and Living the Character Message," *The Fourth and Fifth R's Newsletter* 4/1 (Summer 1998), p. 4.
2. See George Gallup, "The Twelfth Annual Gallup Poll of Public Attitudes toward Public Schools, *Phi Delta Kappan* 62 (September 1980), p. 39; H. Spears, "Kappans Ponder the Goals of Education," *Phi Delta Kappan* 55 (September 1973), pp. 29-32.
3. For analyses of the causes of this decline, see William Kilpatrick, *Why Johnny Can't Tell Right from Wrong* (New York: Simon & Schuster, 1992); also Kevin Ryan and Edward Wynne, *Reclaiming Our Schools: A Handbook on Teaching Character, Academics and Discipline* (Columbus: Merrill, 1993).
4. Frederick Rudolph, *The American College and University: A History*, 2nd ed. (Athens, GA: University of Georgia Press, 1990), p. 6.
5. Noah Webster, "On the Education of Youth in America" [1790], in Frederick Rudolph, ed., *Essays on Education in the Early Republic* (Cambridge: Harvard University Press, 1965), p. 63.
6. John Silber, "Exploring Models of Character Education," International Educational Foundation International Educators' Conference, Washington, D.C., June 12-18, 1995.
7. From Gong Dafei, *Chinese Maxims: Golden Sayings of Chinese Thinkers over Five Thousand Years* (Beijing: Sinolingua, 1994).
8. See Thomas Lickona, *Does Character Education Make a Difference?* (Salt Lake City: Utah State Office of Education, 1991); L. Nucci, "Challenging Conventional Wisdom about Morality: The Domain Approach to Values Education," in L. Nucci, ed., *Moral Development and Character Education: A Dialogue* (Berkeley: McCutchan, 1989).
9. Sidney Simon, Leland Howe and Howard Kirschenbaum, *Values Clarification: A Handbook of Practical Strategies for Teachers and Students* (New York: Hart, 1972). See also Louis E. Raths, Merrill Harmin and Sidney Simon, *Values and Teaching* (Columbus: Merrill, 1966).
10. Alan J. Lockwood, "The Effects of Values Clarification and Moral Development Curricula on School-Age Subjects: A Critical Review of Recent Research," *Review of Educational Research* 48/3 (Summer 1978), pp. 325-64. Cf. J. S. Leming, "Curricular Effectiveness in

Moral/Values Education: A Review of Research." *Journal of Moral Education* 10/3 (1981), pp. 147-64.

11. Thomas Sowell, *Inside American Education: The Decline, the Deception, the Dogmas* (New York: Free Press, 1993), p. 65.

12. Simon, Howe and Kirschenbaum, *Values Clarification: A Handbook*, p. 30.

13. Thomas Lickona, *Educating for Character* (New York: Bantam, 1991), p. 237.

14. Simon, Howe and Kirschenbaum, *Values Clarification: A Handbook*, pp. 38-57.

15. William J. Bennett, *The De-Valuing of America: The Fight for Our Children and Our Culture* (New York: Simon & Schuster, 1994), p. 56.

16. See Milton Rokeach, *Beliefs, Attitudes and Values* (San Francisco: Jossey-Bass, 1968). He defines a value as "an enduring belief that a specific mode of conduct or end-state of existence is personally or socially preferable to an opposite or converse mode of conduct or state of existence."

17. Raths, Harmin and Simon, *Values and Teaching*, p. 48.

18. Ruth Bell, et al., *Changing Bodies, Changing Lives* (New York: Random House, 1987), p. 90. Quoted in Kilpatrick, *Why Johnny Can't Tell Right from Wrong*, pp. 39, 53.

19. Bell, *Changing Bodies, Changing Lives*, p. 49.

20. Merrill Harmin, "Value Clarity, High Morality: Let's Go for Both," *Educational Leadership* (May 1988), pp. 24-30.

21. Howard Kirschenbaum, *100 Ways to Enhance Values and Morality in Schools and Youth Settings* (Needham Heights, MA: Allwyn & Bacon, 1995).

22. Howard Kirschenbaum, "A Comprehensive Model for Values Education and Moral Education," *Phi Delta Kappan* 73 (1992), p. 773.

23. Carl Rogers, *Freedom to Learn* (Columbus: Merrill, 1969).

24. Abraham H. Maslow, *Motivation and Personality*, 2nd. ed. (New York: Harper & Row, 1970), p. xx.

25. Kilpatrick, *Why Johnny Can't Tell Right from Wrong*, pp. 103-106. Cf. Jean-Jacques Rousseau, *Emile*, ed. Alan Bloom (New York: Basic Books, 1979), p. 39: "Natural man is entirely for himself. He is numerical unity, the absolute whole which is relative only to itself or its kind. Civil man is only a fractional unity dependent on the denominator; his value is determined by his relation to the whole, which is the social body."

26. The connection between Rogers' psychological theories and the cultural changes of the 1960s is well documented. Many of his ideas were refined at "encounter groups" at the Esalen Institute, a celebrated center of the counterculture where psychedelic drugs were in abundant supply. See Kilpatrick, *Why Johnny Can't Tell Right from Wrong*, pp. 31-32.

27. Analects VII.8. Arthur Waley, *The Analects of Confucius* (New York: Random House, 1938).

28. Kirk Johnson, "Self-Image Is Suffering from Lack of Esteem," *The New York Times*, May 5, 1998, p. F7.

29. Johnson, "Self-Image Is Suffering."

30. Lawrence Kohlberg, "Moral Stages and Moralization: The Cognitive-Developmental Approach," in Thomas Lickona, ed., *Moral Development and Behavior* (New York: Holt, Rinehart and Winston, 1976); See also Lawrence Kohlberg, *The Psychology of Moral Development* (San Francisco: Harper & Row, 1984).

31. Ann Higgins, "Research and Measurement Issues in Moral Education Interventions," in R. Mosher, ed., *Moral Education: A First Generation of Research and Development* (New York: Praeger, 1980), pp. 92-107; F. Oser, "Failures and Mistakes in the Just Community Process," American Educational Research Association annual meeting, New Orleans, April 1994.

32. Lickona, *Educating for Character*, pp. 241-42.

33. Ibid., p. 243.

34. Educational researchers favor the approach, as dilemmas are easy to administer in tests and scores are quantifiable. Therefore, the Kohlbergian paradigm pervades much research in moral education, even though it may be too narrow to encompass all aspects of moral selfhood.

35. Christiana Hoff Sommers, "Teaching the Virtues," *The Public Interest* 111 (Spring 1993), pp. 3-14.

36. Lickona, *Educating for Character*, p. 51.

37. Kilpatrick, *Why Johnny Can't Tell Right from Wrong*, p. 85.

38. A. Colby and W. Damon, *Some Do Care: Contemporary Lives of Moral Commitment* (New York: Free Press, 1992); D. Hart and S. Fegley, "Prosocial Behavior and Caring in Adolescence: Relations to Self-understanding and Social Judgment," *Child Development* 66 (1995), pp. 1346-59.

39. Lickona, *Educating for Character*, pp. 249-57.

40. Charles E. Finn, *We Must Take Charge: Our Schools and Our Future* (New York: Free Press, 1991), p. 285.

41. Kevin Ryan and Karen Bohlin, "Values, Views, or Virtues?" *Education Week*, March 3, 1999.

42. Philip Fitch Vincent, lecture to the Canandaigua City School District.

43. Sommers, "Teaching the Virtues."

44. Philip Fitch Vincent, quoted by Alcestis Oberg, "Values Education Wins Supporters," *USA Today*, April 19, 2000, p. 27A.

45. "Character Education—A Growing National Movement," *CEP Character Educator* 7/2 (Spring 1999), p. 6.

46. Roger Rosenblatt, "Who'll Teach Kids Right from Wrong," *The New York Times Magazine*, April 1995, p. 37.

47. Mary M. Williams and Eric Schaps, "Character Education: The Foundation for Teacher Education," Association of Teacher Educators Commission on Character Education Report, Character Education Partnership, 1999.

48. "The Child Development Project: A Brief Summary of the Project and Findings from Three Evaluation Studies," Developmental Studies Center, Oakland, California September 1998.

49. "Schools of Character: Reclaiming America's Values for Tomorrow's Workplace," McGraw-Hill Companies and Character Education Partnership, p. 15.

50. "National Schools of Character, Best Practices and New Perspectives," Character Education Partnership, 1999, pp. 16, 20, 40.

51. For more assessments, see James S. Leming, "Whither Goes Character Education? Objectives, Pedagogy, and Research in Education Programs," *Journal of Education* 179 (Spring 1997), pp. 11-35; James Leming, "Current Evidence Regarding Program Effectiveness in Character Education: A Brief Review," *Character Education: The Foundation for Teacher Education, Report of the National Commission on Character Education*, Mary M. Williams and Eric Schaps, eds. (Washington, DC: Character Education Partnership, 1999), pp. 50-55.

52. William J. Bennett, *The De-Valuing of America: The Fight for Our Children and Our Culture*, (New York: Simon & Schuster, 1994), p. 357.

53. James S. Leming, *Character Education: Lessons from the Past, Models for the Future* (Camden, Maine: The Institute for Global Ethics, 1993), p. 21.

54. Ivor Pritchard, "Character Education: Research Prospects and Problems," *American Journal of Education* (August 1988), pp. 469-95.

55. James S. Leming, "In Search of Effective Character Education," *Educational Leadership* (Nov. 1993), p. 70.

Chapter 3

1. C.S. Lewis, "Right and Wrong as a Clue to the Meaning of the Universe," *Broadcast Talks* (London: Centenary Press, 1942), p. 11.

2. Rushworth M. Kidder, *Shared Values for a Troubled World: Conversations with Men and Women of Conscience* (San Francisco: Jossey-Bass, 1991), p. 103.

3. Kieran Egan, *Educational Development* (New York: Oxford University Press, 1979), pp. 164-65.

4. E. Turiel, *The Development of Social Knowledge: Morality and Convention* (New York: Cambridge University Press, 1983), distinguishes moral values, which are intrinsically and universally prescriptive, from "social-conventional values," which are by social agreement. Yet these two domains overlap, as will be noted below.

5. Marvin W. Berkowitz, *The Education of the Complete Moral Person* (Aberdeen, Scotland: Gordon Cook Foundation, 1995). http://www.uic.edu/~lnucci/MoralEd/aotm/article3.html.

6.   Milton Rokeach, *Beliefs, Attitudes and Values* (San Francisco: Jossey-Bass, 1968).

7.   Compare, for example, Thomas Lickona's case for "values education" in his seminal 1991 book, *Educating for Character* (New York: Bantam, 1991), pp. 3-22; with Kevin Ryan and Karen Bohlin's call for a "virtues-centered approach" to moral education in their 1999 book, *Building Character in Schools* (San Francisco: Jossey-Bass, 1999), pp. 25-52.

8.   John Graham, *It's Up to Us* (Langley, WA: The Giraffe Project, 1999), p. 108.

9.   "Connecticut's Assets-Based Character Education Conference," Central Connecticut State University, New Britain, CT, March 5, 1999.

10.   Doctrine of the Mean 14.1-2, *English Translation of the Four Books, Revised from the Translation of James Legge* (Taipei: Council of Chinese Cultural Renaissance, 1979), p. 28.

11.   Confucius also had a theory of revolution to deal with the question of unjust norms.

12.   Cf. James A. Ryan, "Moral Philosophy and Moral Psychology in Mencius," *Asian Philosophy* 8/1 (March 1998), pp. 47-65.

13.   http://info.csd.org/staffdev/chared/prep.html.

14.   Rushworth M. Kidder and William E. Loges, "Global Values, Moral Boundaries: A Pilot Survey," Institute for Global Ethics, Camden, ME, 1997.

15.   Marvin W. Berkowitz, "Integrating Structure and Content in Moral Education," in L. Nucci, *Developmental Perspectives and Approaches to Character Education*, AERA symposium, Chicago, March 1997.

16.   See *World Scripture: A Comparative Anthology of Sacred Texts*, ed. Andrew Wilson (New York: Paragon House, 1991).

17.   Analects 15.23; Matthew 7:12; Anusasana Parva 113.8; Yoruba proverb. See *World Scripture*, p. 114.

18.   Matthew 5.44.

19.   Qur'an 41.34.

20.   Dhammapada 223.

21.   Tao Te Ching 49.

22.   See Martin Heidegger, *Being and Time*, trans. Joan Stambaugh (New York: SUNY Press, 1996).

23.   Mencius II.A.6, in *Mencius Vol. 1*, tr. D. C. Lau, *The Chinese Classics: Chinese-English Series* (Hong Kong: Chinese University Press, 1979), p. 67.

24.   On the universality of Kohlberg's stages of cognitive moral development, see Ann Colby and Lawrence Kohlberg, *The Measurement of Moral Judgment* (Cambridge: Cambridge University Press, 1987); J. R. Snarey, "Cross-cultural Universality of Social-moral Development: A Critical Review of Kohlbergian Research," *Psychological Bulletin* 97 (1985), pp. 202-32.

25.   Carol Gilligan, *In a Different Voice: Women's Conception of the Self and*

Morality (Cambridge: Harvard University Press, 1977).

26. L. J. Walker, "Sex Differences in Moral Reasoning," in W. Kurtines and J. Gewirtz, eds., *Handbook of Moral Behavior and Development, Vol. 2* (Hillsdale, NJ: Lawrence Erlbaum, 1991); L. J. Walker, R. DeVries and S. Trevethan, "Moral Stages and Moral Orientations," *Child Development* 58 (1987), pp. 842-58; M. Brabeck, "Moral Judgment: Theory and Research on Differences between Males and Females, *Developmental Review* 3 (1983), pp. 274-91; K. Deaux and B. Major, "Putting Gender into Context: An Interactive Model of Gender-Related Behavior," *Psychological Review* 94 (1987), pp. 369-84. One difficulty with this research is that the content of the dilemmas presented—e.g., abortion, confronting a bully—often brings out gender differences that skew the findings.

27. *The Great Learning 1.4, English Translations of the Four Books*, pp. 3-4.

28. *Doctrine of the Mean* 12, in Lin Yutan, *The Wisdom of Confucius* (New York: Random House, 1938), p. 108.

29. Christian de Duve, "The Meaning of the Universe," in *Vital Dust: Life as a Cosmic Imperative* (New York: Basic Books, 1995).

30. Edward O. Wilson, "The Biological Basis of Morality," *Atlantic Monthly* 281/4 (April 1998), pp. 53-66. See also Robert Wright, *The Moral Animal: Evolutionary Psychology and Everyday Life* (New York: Pantheon, 1994); Frans de Waal, *Good Natured: The Origins of Right and Wrong in Humans and Other Animals* (Cambridge: Harvard University Press, 1996).

Chapter 4

1. Daniel Goldman, "Exclusive Interview with John Dean," *Comment*, Boston University School of Law, February 1979, p. 7.

2. The Loving Well Project, *The Art of Loving Well: A Character Education Curriculum for Today's Teenagers, Teacher Guide* (Boston: Boston University, 1993), p. 48.

3. Samuel P. and Pearl M. Oliner, *The Altruistic Personality: Rescuers of Jews in Nazi Europe* (New York: Free Press, 1988), p. 171.

4. Thomas Taaffe, "Education of the Heart," *Cross Currents* 45 (September 1995).

5. Taaffe, "Education of the Heart."

6. James Q. Wilson, *The Moral Sense* (New York: Free Press, 1993), p. 127.

7. Mencius II.A.6.

8. Alexander Solzhenitsyn, *The Gulag Archipelago* (New York: Harper & Row, 1985), p. 312.

9. Mencius II.A.6.

10. See Daniel Goleman, *Emotional Intelligence* (New York: Bantam, 1995).

11. Quoted in Thomas Lickona, *Educating for Character*, p. 60.

12. Kieran Egan, *Educational Development,* quoted in Gabriel Moran, *No Ladder to the Sky: Education and Morality* (New York: Harper & Row, 1987), p. 10.

13. Pamela B. Joseph and Sara Efron, "Moral Choices/Moral Conflicts: Teachers' Self-Perceptions," *Journal of Moral Education* 22/3 (1993), pp. 201-20.

14. See A. Bandura, *Social Learning Theory,* (Englewood Cliffs, NJ: Prentice-Hall, 1977).

15. Anton A. Bucher, "The Influence of Models in Forming Moral Identity," *International Journal of Educational Research* (1997), pp. 619-27.

16. Joseph and Efron, "Moral Choices/Moral Conflicts."

17. G. Kochanska, K. Murray and K. C. Coy, "Inhibitory Control as a Contributor to Conscience in Childhood: from Toddler to School Age," *Child Development* 68 (1997), pp. 263-77.

18. Mark Twain, "The Facts Concerning the Recent Carnival of Crime in Connecticut."

19. Elena Mustakova-Poussardt, "The Ontogeny of Critical Consciousness," Ph.D. dissertation, University of Massachusetts at Amherst, 1996.

20. John C. Gibbs, Karen Basinger and Dick Fuller, *Moral Maturity: Measuring the Development of Socio-Moral Reflection* (Hillsdale, NJ: Lawrence Erlbaum, 1992), pp. 1-33.

21. Stephen G. Post, *Spheres of Love: Toward a New Ethics of the Family* (Southern Methodist University Press, 1994), p. 5.

22. Carol Gilligan and colleagues have explored the difficult transition for women who have conceived their responsibility as that of self-less caregiver to include the needs of self in the caring for others. See Jane Attanucci, "In Whose Terms: A New Perspective on Self, Role and Relationship," in Carol Gilligan et al., *Mapping the Moral Domain* (Cambridge: Harvard University Press, 1988), pp. 201-24.

23. Source: Inspirational Stories website.

Chapter 5

1. Alisdair MacIntyre, *After Virtue,* 2nd ed. (South Bend: University of Notre Dame Press, 1984), p. 144.

2. Elena Mustakova-Poussardt, "The Ontogeny of Critical Consciousness," Ph.D. dissertation, University of Massachusetts, Amherst , MA, 1996.

3. Steven Covey, *First Things First* (New York: Simon & Schuster, 1994), p. 45.

4. Thus the life goals listed by Milton Rokeach, *The Nature of Human Values* (New York: Free Press, 1973), can be classified under:
   Personal maturity: 2) freedom, 4) happiness, 5) an exciting life, 6) wisdom, 8) self-respect, 15) inner harmony, 16) pleasure

Loving relationships, and family: 3) equality—brotherhood, equal opportunity, 9) mature love, 13) true friendship, 17) family security

Contribution to society: 1) a world at peace, 7) a comfortable life, 10) social recognition, 11)sense of accomplishment, 12) national security, 14) a world of beauty.

5.   Richard Livingstone, *Education for a World Adrift* (Cambridge, 1943).

6.   The Character Education Partnership, *Character Education in U.S. Schools: A New Consensus* (Alexandria, VA: The Character Education Partnership, 1996).

7.   Kay O'Connor and Kerry Chamberlain, "Dimensions of Life Meaning: A Qualitative Investigation at Mid-Life," *British Journal of Psychology* 87/3 (August 1996), pp. 461-77.

8.   Kurt L. De Vogler and Patricia Ebersole, "Categorization of College Students' Meaning of Life," *Psychological Reports* 46 (1980), pp. 387-90; "Adults' Meaning in Life," *Psychological Reports* 49 (1981), pp. 87-90; "Young Adolescents' Meaning in Life," *Psychological Reports* 52 (1983), pp. 427-31.

9.   Sydney K. Baum and R. B. Stewart, "Sources of Meaning through the Life Span," *Psychological Reports* 67 (1990), pp. 3-14; Irvin D. Yalom, *Existential Psychotherapy* (New York: Basic Books, 1980); De Vogler and Ebersole, "Adults' Meaning in Life."

10. Victor E. Frankl, *Man's Search for Meaning* (New York: Washington Square Press, 1963); Yalom, *Existential Psychotherapy*.

11. Peter Bertocci, Boston University philosophy lecture, September 1980.

12. William Kilpatrick, *Why Johnny Can't Tell Right from Wrong* (New York: Simon & Schuster, 1992).

13. Chenyang Li, "Filial Morality Revisited," *Philosophy East & West*, 47/2 (1997), pp. 211-33.

14. William Damon and D. Hart, *Self-understanding in Childhood and Adolescence* (New York: Cambridge, 1988); Anne Colby and William Damon, *Some Do Care: Contemporary Lives of Moral Commitment* (New York: Macmillan, 1992); Antony Blasi, "The Development of Identity: Some Implications for Moral Functioning," in G. G. Noam and T. Wren, eds., *The Moral Self* (Cambridge: MIT Press, 1993), pp. 99-122.

15. Kevin Ryan and Karen E. Bohlin, *Building Character in Schools* (San Francisco: Jossey-Bass, 1999), p. 40.

16. Even teachers in religious schools tend to curtail discussions with moral and existential content; see K. G. Simon, "The Place of Meaning: A Study of the Moral, Existential and Intellectual in American High Schools," unpublished doctoral dissertation, Stanford University, 1997.

17. Character Education Partnership, *Character Education in U.S. Schools*.

18. Thomas Lickona, *Educating for Character* (New York: Bantam, 1991), p. 51.

Chapter 6

1. Stephen Covey, *Principle-Centered Leadership* (New York: Simon & Schuster, 1991), p. 18.
2. Stephen Covey, *Seven Habits of Highly Effective Families*, (New York: Golden Books, 1997), p. 15.
3. The Great Learning 5, *English Translation of the Four Books, Revised from the Translation of James Legge* (Taipei: Council of Chinese Cultural Renaissance, 1979), p. 8.
4. M. Scott Peck, *The Road Less Traveled* (New York: Simon & Schuster, 1978), p. 82.

Chapter 7

1. Kevin Ryan and Karen E. Bohlin, *Building Character in Schools* (San Francisco: Jossey-Bass, 1999), p. 11.
2. Steven S. Tigner, "Aristotle's *Nicomachean Ethics*, an Outline Guide for Educators," Montclair Kimberley Academy, 1997, p. 6.
3. Erik Erikson, *Identity, Youth, and Crisis* (New York: W.W. Norton, 1968); Lawrence Kohlberg, "Stage and Sequence: The Cognitive-Developmental Approach to Socialization," in D. Goslin, ed., *Handbook of Socialization Theory and Research* (Chicago: Rand McNally, 1969), pp. 347-480.
4. Anne Colby and William Damon, *Some Do Care: Contemporary Lives of Moral Commitment* (New York: Macmillan, 1992).
5. Elena Mustakova-Poussardt, "The Ontogeny of Critical Consciousness," Ph.D. dissertation, University of Massachusetts, Amherst, MA, 1996.
6. John Graham, *It's Up to Us* (Langley, WA: The Giraffe Project, 1999), p. 76.
7. Aristotle, *Nichomachean Ethics* 2.1, tr. W. D. Ross.
8. Thomas J. Stanley and William D. Danko, *The Millionaire Next Door* (Atlanta: Longstreet, 1996), p. 208.
9. D. Baumrind, *Child Maltreatment and Optimal Caregiving in Social Contexts* (New York: Garland, 1995).
10. Stephen Covey, *Seven Habits of Highly Effective Families* (New York: Golden, 1997), pp. 277-78.
11. Antony Blasi and K. Milton, "The Development of the Sense of Self in Adolescence," *Journal of Personality* 59 (1991), pp. 217-42.
12. Uichi Shoda, Walter Mischel and Philip K. Peake, "Predicting Adolescent Cognitive and Self-Regulatory Competencies from Preschool Delay of Gratification," *Developmental Psychology* 26/6 (1990), pp. 978-86.
13. S.E. Samenow, *Inside the Criminal Mind* (New York: Random House, 1984), p. 160.
14. James Q. Wilson, *The Moral Sense* (New York: Free Press, 1993), p. 11.

15. William Bennett, *The Book of Virtues* (New York: Simon & Schuster, 1993), pp. 21-23.
16. Laurence Steinberg, with B. Bradford Brown and Sanford M. Dornbusch, *Beyond the Classroom: Why Schools Reform has Failed and What Parents Need to Do* (New York: Simon & Schuster, 1996).
17. The philosopher Rene Descartes propounded a strict dualism—the body as extension and the mind as thought. But his philosophy floundered on the question of how mind and body could interact, as they would have nothing in common.
18. Jack Canfield and Mark Victor Hansen, eds., *A Second Helping of Chicken Soup for the Soul* (Deerfield Beach, FL: Health Communications, 1995).
19. Erik Erikson, *Childhood & Society* (New York: Norton, 1963).
20. John Battista and R. Almond, "The Development of Meaning in Life," *Psychiatry* 36 (1973), pp. 409-27.
21. W. M. Phillips, "Purpose in Life, Depression, and Locus of Control," *Journal of Clinical Psychology* 36 (1980), pp. 661-67; Gary T. Reker, "The Purpose-in-Life Test in an Inmate Population: An Empirical Investigation," *Journal of Clinical Psychology* 33 (1977), pp. 688-93.
22. P. R. Pearson, and B. F. Sheffield, "Purpose in Life and the Eysenck Personality Inventory," *Journal of Clinical Psychology* 30 (1974), pp. 562-64.
23. Sheryl Zika and Kerry Chamberlain, "On the Relation between Meaning in Life and Psychological Well-being," *British Journal of Psychology* 83/1 (February 1992), pp. 133-45.
24. Anne Colby and William Damon, "The Development of Extraordinary Moral Commitment," in *Morality in Everyday Life*, ed. Melanie Killen and Daniel Hart (New York: Cambridge University Press, 1995), pp. 361-62.
25. Deb A. Brown, *Lessons from the Rocking Chair* (Chapel Hill, NC: Character Development Group, 1997), p. 23.
26. R.N. Cassel, "Critical Contributions to Human Motivation Theory," *Psychology* 11 (January 1974), pp. 58-64.
27. A. Bandura, *Self-Efficacy: The Exercise of Control* (New York: W.H. Freeman, 1997); B. J. Zimmerman, A. Bandura and M. Martinez-Pons, "Self-Motivation for Academic Attainment: The Role of Self-Efficacy Beliefs and Personal Goal-Setting," *American Education Research Journal* 29 (March 1992), pp. 663-76.
28. Stephen R. Covey, et al., *First Things First* (New York: Simon & Schuster, 1994), p. 138.
29. See G. T. Reker and P. T. Wong, "Aging as an Individual Process: Toward a Theory of Personal Meaning," in J. E. Bitten and V. L. Bengston, ed., *Emergent Theories of Aging* (New York: Springer, 1988), pp. 214-46; P. E. Lacocque, "On the Search for Meaning," *Journal of Religion and Health* 21 (1982), pp. 219-27.
30. Viktor Frankl, *Man's Search for Meaning* (New York: Washington Square, 1984).

31. Graham, *It's Up to Us*, p. 1

32. Thomas Lickona, *Educating for Character* (New York: Bantam, 1991), p. 51.

33. William M. Hendryx, "Profiles in Courage: Rescue on the River," *Family Circle*, February 1, 1998.

34. Jerome Kagan, *The Nature of the Child* (New York: Basic Books, 1984).

35. Martin L. Hoffman, "Empathy, Social Cognition, and Moral Action," in W. M. Kurtines and J. L. Gewirtz, eds., *Handbook of Moral Behavior and Development. Volume 1: Theory* (Hillsdale, NJ: Erlbaum, 1991), pp. 275-302; Nancy Eisenberg and Patricia A. Miller, "The Relation of Empathy to Prosocial and Related Behaviors," *Psychological Bulletin* 94 (1987), pp. 100-31.

36. Source: Inspirational Stories website.

37. Aristotle, *Nichomachean Ethics* II.9, 1109a25.

38. Bennett, *The Book of Virtues*, pp. 441-42.

39. Stephen R. Covey, *Seven Habits of Highly Effective People* (New York: Simon & Schuster, 1989), p. 202.

Chapter 8

1. Michael D. Resnick, et al., "Protecting Adolescents from Harm: Findings from the National Longitudinal Study of Adolescent Health," *Journal of the American Medical Association* 278 (1997), p. 10.

2. Teilhard de Chardin, *The Phenomenon of Man* (New York: Harper & Row, 1959), p. 264.

3. Ibid., p. 41.

4. Denis Waitley, *Chicken Soup for the Soul at Work*, ed. Jack Canfield, Mark Victor Hansen, Maida Rogerson, Martin Rutte and Tim Clauss (Deerfield Beach, FL: Health Communications, 1996).

5. Mencius VII.A.4.

6. Galatians 6:7.

7. Qur'an 39.10.

8. Robert Kane, *Through the Moral Maze* (New York: Paragon House, 1994), pp. 20-24.

9. Courtesy of Nadine Andre.

10. Thomas J. Stanley and William D. Danko, *The Millionaire Next Door* (Atlanta: Longstreet, 1996), p. 228.

11. Provided by Anne Ipparaguirre.

12. Erin White, "Lessons in Shaking Hands, Twirling Spaghetti Await Some Workers," *The Wall Street Journal*, Tuesday, December 7, 1999.

13. In a sentence with a transitive verb, the subject is the actor and the object (direct or indirect) is the person or thing acted upon; thus "Jack threw Tom the ball." A similar meaning is captured in the suffixes "-er" and "-ee." An interviewer is in the subject role and the interviewee is in the object role. This is not to be confused with

other meanings of "subject" and "object" in philosophical discourse.

14. Note that the teacher does not thereby relinquish her authority over the content of the curriculum. This was an issue for values clarification. (See Chapter 2)

15. From Daniel Goleman, *Emotional Intelligence* (New York: Bantam, 1994), p. 148.

16. John Rosemond, *A Family of Value* (Grand Rapids: Zondervan, 1995), p. 66.

17. J. M. Cooper, "Aristotle on Friendship," in A. O. Rorty, ed., *Essays on Aristotle's Ethics* (Berkeley: University of California Press, 1980), p. 302.

18. Blaine J. Fowers, "Psychology and the Good Marriage," *American Behavioral Scientist* 41 (January 1998), pp. 516-43.

19. Erich Maria Remarque, *All Quiet on the Western Front* (New York: Fawcett, 1991), p. 212.

20. Ross Campbell, *How to Really Love Your Child* (Wheaton, IL: Victor Books, 1977), p. 57.

21. Amitai Etzioni, *The Spirit of Community* (New York: Simon & Schuster, 1993), p. 12.

22. James Q. Wilson, *The Moral Sense* (New York: Free Press, 1993), pp. 162-63.

Chapter 9

1. John Graham, *It's Up to Us* (Langley, WA: Giraffe Project, 1999), pp. 7-8.

2. Robert Kane, *Through the Moral Maze* (New York: Paragon House, 1994) pp. 73-79.

3. Thanks to Nadine Andre.

4. Cheryl Norwood, at "Heartwarmers4u," Inspirational stories website.

5. Amitai Etzioni, *The Spirit of Community* (New York: Simon & Schuster, 1993), p. 10.

6. Graham, *It's Up to Us*, p. 14.

7. Mary Beth Grover, "Daddy Stress," *Forbes*, September 6, 1999, pp. 202-208.

8. *Doctrine of the Mean* 14.1-2.

9. Jeanne-Marie Christman, "Mama Hawk Hawkins," *Family Circle* 109/13 (September 17, 1996), p. 13.

10. Carol Hymowitz, "Racing onto the Web, One Manager's Secret Lesson Is Simple: Listening," *Wall Street Journal*, February 8, 2000, p. B1.

11. William Bennett, *The Book of Virtues* (New York: Simon & Schuster, 1993), p. 348.

12. Thomas J. Stanley and William D. Danko, *The Millionaire Next Door* (Atlanta: Longstreet Press, 1996).

13. Alfie Kohn, "In Pursuit of Affluence, at a High Price," *The New York*

Times, April 1999.

14. "World Conservation Strategy: Living Resources for Sustainable Development," Nevada, IUCN/UNEP/WWF, 1980.

15. See Michael J. Caduto, "Ecological Education: A System Rooted in Diversity," *Journal of Environmental Education* 29/4 (1998), pp. 11-16; John Sandlos, "The Storied Curriculum: Oral Narrative, Ethics, and Environmental Education," *Journal of Environmental Education* 30/1 (1998), pp. 5-10.

16. "Catherine Sneed," Giraffe Project Website.

17. Wing-tsit Chan, *A Source Book in Chinese Philosophy* (Princeton: Princeton University Press, 1963), pp. 86-87.

Chapter 10

1. "CEP Urges States to Carefully Consider Character Education Mandates," *Character Educator* 8/3 (Spring 2000).

2. David Wangaard, "Character Education Program Components in a Public Elementary School: A Case Study," Ed.D. dissertation, University of Northern Colorado.

3. Gordon Vessels, *Character and Community Development: A School Planning and Teacher Training Handbook* (Westport, CT: Praeger, 1998).

4. Philip Fitch Vincent, ed., *Promising Practices in Character Education* (Chapel Hill, NC: Character Development Group, 1966), p. 7.

5. Vincent, *Promising Practices*, pp. 2-3.

6. Andrea Billups, "Academy in Harlem Enforces Strict Rules," *The Washington Times*, March 27, 2000.

7. Vincent, *Promising Practices*, pp. 12-14.

8. "1999 National Schools of Character: Best Practices and New Perspectives," McGraw-Hill Companies and Character Education Partnership, 1999, p. 23.

9. Ibid., p. 16.

10. Vincent, *Promising Practices*, pp. 57-58.

11. Remarks given at the *Business Week* Schools of Character Awards Dinner, New York, April 27, 1998.

12. Vincent, *Promising Practices*, p. 33.

13. "Character Education—A Growing National Movement," *Character Educator* 7 (Spring 1999), p. 1.

14. William J. Bennett, *The De-valuing of America: The Fight for Our Children and Our Culture* (New York: Simon & Schuster, 1994), p. 53.

15. Michael Rutter, B. Maughan, P. Mortimore, J. Ouston and A. Smith, *Fifteen Thousand Hours* (Cambridge: Harvard University Press, 1979).

16. Susan Pelis, "Book Bags: One Simple Way to Bridge School and Home," *Responsive Classroom: A Newsletter for Teachers* (Summer 1999), p. 5.

17. Vincent, *Promising Practices*, p. 13.

18. "Schools of Character: Reclaiming America's Values for Tomorrow's Workplace," McGraw-Hill Companies and Character Education Partnership, 1998, pp. 2-3.
19. "1999 National Schools of Character," pp. 2-3.
20. "Schools of Character: Reclaiming America's Values," p. 38.
21. Lawrence J. Walker and John H. Taylor, "Family Interaction and the Development of Moral Reasoning," *Child Development* 62 (1991), pp. 264-83.
22. Joseph W. Gauld, *Character First: The Hyde School Difference* (Rocklin, CA: Prima, 1995).
23. Josephine Hauer, "Class Teachers in Russia: Lifelong Mentors and Partners in Moral Education," paper presented at the Moral and Social Interdisciplinary Colloquium, University of Utrecht, Netherlands, July, 1999.
24. "Schools of Character: Reclaiming America's Values," p. 5.
25. Ibid., p. 10.
26. "1999 National Schools of Character," p. 40.
27. "The Child Development Project: A Brief Summary of the Project and Findings from Three Evaluation Studies," Oakland, California: Developmental Studies Center, September, 1998.
28. Elizabeth Shepard, "How You Can Help a Child," *Parade*, September 1998, p. 6.
29. Thomas Lickona, *Educating for Character* (New York: Bantam Books, 1991), pp. 35-36.
30. Ibid., p. 402.
31. Cindy J. Christopher, *Building Parent-Teacher Communication—An Educator's Guide* (Lancaster, PA: Technomic, 1996), p. 33.
32. "Schools of Character: Reclaiming America's Values," p. 9.
33. Henry A. Huffman, *Developing a Character Education Program—One School District's Experience* (Alexandria, VA: ASCD, 1994), pp. 64-70.
34. D. A. Johnson, et al., "Relative Effectiveness of Comprehensive Community Programming for Drug Abuse Prevention with High Risk and Low-Risk Adolescents," *Journal of Consulting and Clinical Psychology* 58 (April 1990), pp. 447-56; R. C. Lefebrere, T. M. Lassater, R. A. Carleton, and G. Peterson, "Theory and Delivery of Health Programming in the Community: The Pawtucket Heart Health Program," *Preventive Medicine* 16 (1990), pp. 80-95.
35. I. Goldenberg and H. Goldenberg, *Family Therapy: An Overview* (Pacific Grove, CA: Brooks/Cole, 1991).
36. Lickona, *Educating for Character*; Wangaard, "Character Education Program Components."
37. B. Moody and Linda McKay, "CHARACTER PLUS—A Process, Not a Recipe," *Educational Leadership* 51 (1993), pp. 28-30; C. E. Carlson, "HIIP: A Comprehensive School-Based Substance Abuse Program with Cooperative Community Involvement," *Journal of Primary Prevention* 10 (April 1990), pp. 289-301.
38. "1999 National Schools of Character," p. 34

39. Ibid., p. 37.
40. "Schools of Character: Reclaiming America's Values," p. 12.
41. Ibid., p. 5.
42. "Utah Project," http://www.usoe.k12.ut.us/curr/char_ed/.
43. "1999 National Schools of Character," p. 35.
44. Report by Gary M. Smith at the Cooperating School Districts conference, "For Home, School, Community and World," St. Louis, MO, July 8–10, 1999.
45. "1999 National Schools of Character," p. 52.

Chapter 11

1. Kevin Ryan and Karen E. Bohlin, *Building Character in Schools* (San Francisco: Jossey-Bass, 1999), pp. 94-97.
2. Thanks to Jack Lapolla of Wilton, CT.
3. Karla Cook, "Children's Maturity Plays Key Role in Talking about Sex Scandal on TV," *The Star-Ledger*, January 24, 1998, p. 9.
4. "Schools of Character: Reclaiming America's Values for Tomorrow's Workplace," McGraw-Hill Companies and Character Education Partnership, 1998, p. 7.
5. "Schools of Character: Reclaiming America's Values," p. 10.
6. "1999 National Schools of Character: Best Practices and New Perspectives," McGraw-Hill Companies and Character Education Partnership, 1999, p. 16.
7. "1999 National Schools of Character," p. 23.
8. Thomas Lickona, *Educating for Character* (New York: Bantam Books, 1991), p. 173.
9. Ibid., pp. 167-168.
10. Bruno Bettleheim, *The Uses of Enchantment* (New York: Vintage Books, 1977), p. 8.
11. *The Giraffe Heroes Program*, Giraffe Project, Langley, WA, 1999.
12. Lickona, *Educating for Character*, p. 117.
13. "1999 National Schools of Character," p. 17.
14. Chip Wood, Northeast Foundation for Children, Greenfield, MA.
15. Thomas Lickona, "Educating for Character: A Comprehensive Approach," in A. Molnar, ed., *The Construction of Children's Character* (Chicago: University of Chicago Press, 1997), p. 52.
16. Ibid., p. 55.
17. "1999 National Schools of Character," p. 16.
18. David H. Elkind and Freddy Sweet, "Lessons from Producers of Successful PBS Talk Shows," *Live Wire Media*, San Francisco, CA.
19. John C. Gibbs, et al., *The EQUIP Program: Teaching Youth to Think and Act Responsibly through a Peer-Helping Approach* (Champaign, Illinois: Research Press, 1995).
20. M. Shure, *I Can Problem Solve: An Interpersonal Problem-Solving Program* (Champaign, IL: Research Press, 1992).

21. *Second Step: A Violence Prevention Curriculum: Preschoool-Kindergarten Teacher's Guide* (Seattle, WA: Committee for Children, 1992).

22. Gordon Vessels, *Character and Community Development: A School Planning and Teacher Training Handbook* (Westport, CT: Praeger, 1998), pp. 136-37.

23. From www.inspirationalstories.com.

24. From a discussion with teachers at Kimberley Academy, Montclair, New Jersey, September 1997.

25. "1999 National Schools of Character," p. 49.

26. Jerome Bruner, *Acts of Mind* (Cambridge: Harvard University Press, 1999); Alisdair MacIntyre, *After Virtue* (South Bend, IN: Notre Dame University Press, 1981); Robert Coles, *The Call of Stories* (Boston: Houghton Mifflin, 1989).

27. Pablo Paolicchi, *La morale della favola* (The Moral of the Story) (Pisa: ETS, 1994); Pablo Paolicchi, "Narrative and Education: A Different Story," paper presented at the Moral and Social Interdisciplinary Colloquium, University of Utrecht, Netherlands, July 1999.

28. E.L Deci and R. M. Ryan, "A Motivational Approach to Self: Integration in Personality," in R. Dienstbier, ed., *Nebraska Symposium on Motivation, Perspectives on Motivation* (Lincoln: University of Nebraska Press, 1991), pp. 237-88.

29. E.L. Deci, H. Eghrari, B.C. Patrick and D.R. Leone, "Facilitating Internalization: The Self-Determination Theory Perspective," *Journal of Personality* 62 (January 1994), pp. 119-42.

30. Deci and Ryan, "A Motivational Approach to Self," pp. 237-88.

31. Georg Simmel, *Essays on Sociology, Philosophy, and Aesthetics*, Kurt Wolff, ed. (New York: Harper and Row, 1959); Stanford Lyman and Marvin Scott, *A Sociology of the Absurd*, 2nd ed. (New York: General Hall, 1989); Jennifer Hunt, "Divers' Accounts of Normal Risk," *Symbolic Interaction* 18 (1995), pp. 439-62.

32. Lori Holyfield and George Fine, "Adventure as Character Work: The Collective Taming of Fear," *Symbolic Interaction* 20 (1997), pp. 343–64.

Chapter 12

1. H. Stephen Glenn and Jane Nelson, *Raising Self-Reliant Children in a Self-Indulgent World* (Rocklin, CA: Prima, 1989), p. 155.

2. Maurice J. Elias, et al., *Promoting Social and Emotional Learning* (Alexandria, VA: Association for Supervision and Curriculum Development, 1997).

3. Trygve Bergem, "The Teacher as a Moral Agent," *Journal of Moral Education* 19 (May 1990), pp. 88-101.

4. Erwin Staub, *Positive Social Behavior and Morality: Social and Personal Influences* (New York: Academic Press, 1978); D. Solomon,

M. Watson and V. Battistich, "Teaching and Schooling Effects on Moral/Prosocial Development in Virginia," in *Handbook of Research on Teaching, 4th Edition* (Washington, D.C.: American Educational Research Association, in press).

5. Fritz Oser, "Editor's Introduction: Moral Context and Moral Self," *International Journal of Educational Research* (1998), p. 536; Thomas L. Jetton and P.A. Alexander, "Instructional Importance: What Teacher's Value and What Students Learn," *Reading Research Quarterly* 32 (March 1997), pp. 290-308.

6. Thomas Lickona, "Becoming a School of Character," *The High School Magazine* 5 (November-December 1997), p. 8.

7. Thomas Lickona, "Character Education: Seven Crucial Issues," *Character Education: The Foundation for Teacher Education* (Washington, D.C.: Character Education Partnership, 1999), pp. 40-45; Rita Devries, "Implications of Piaget's Constructivist Theory for Character Education," *Character Education: The Foundation for Teacher Education* (Washington, D.C.: Character Education Partnership, 1999), pp. 33-39.

8. Ann Higgins, "Teaching as a Moral Activity: Listening to Teachers in Russia and the United States," *Journal of Moral Education* 24 (February 1995), pp. 143-59; Ken Schroeder, "Authoritarian Teaching," *Education Digest* 58 (January 1992), pp. 74-76; Judith A. MacCallum, "Teacher Reasoning and Moral Judgment in the Context of Student Discipline Situations," Eric Document No. ED332973, 1991.

9. Gordon Vessels, *Character and Community Development: A School Planning and Teacher Training Handbook* (Westport, CT: Praeger, 1998), pp. 84-100.

10. Joseph Seeman, *Preventing Classroom Discipline Problems* (Lancaster, PA: Row-Peterson, 1998), p. 84.

11. "The Child Development Project: A Brief Summary of the Project and Findings from Three Evaluation Studies," (Oakland, CA: Developmental Studies Center, 1998).

12. Thomas Lickona, "A Comprehensive Approach to Character Education in Catholic Schools," *Catholic Education: A Journal of Inquiry and Practice* 1 (December 1997), p. 173.

13. Lori S. Wiley, *Comprehensive Character-Building Classroom* (DeBray, FL: Longwood, 1998), p. 83.

14. Lickona, "Becoming a School of Character," p. 8.

15. Thomas Lickona, *Educating for Character* (New York: Bantam Books, 1991), p. 99.

16. Ibid., p. 100.

17. Glenna Hess, "Relationships: That's My Buddy," *Caring Matters—The Child Development Project—Creating a Caring Community of Learners* (Spring, 1998), p. 6.

18. J.W. Keating, "Sportsmanship as a Moral Category," in W. J. Morgan and K. V. Meier, eds., *Philosophic Inquiry in Sport* (Champaign, IL:

Human Kinetics, 1988), p. 40. Cited in Duane Covrig, "Fair Play and Children's Concepts of Fairness," *Journal for a Just and Caring Education* 2 (July 1996), pp. 263-83.

19. Peter Arnold, *Sport, Ethics and Education* (London: Cassell, 1997).
20. Gary M. Smith, Report at the Cooperating School Districts conference, "For Home, School, Community and World," St. Louis, MO, July 8–10, 1999.
21. Wiley, *Comprehensive Character-Building Classroom*, p. 89.
22. Robert E. Slavin, *Cooperative Learning: Theory, Research and Practice* (Englewood Cliffs, N.J.: Prentice Hall, 1990); David W. Johnson, G. Maruyama, R. T. Johnson, D. Nelson and L. Skon, "Effects of Cooperative, Competitive and Individualistic Goal Structures on Achievement: A Meta-Analysis," *Psychological Bulletin* 89 (1981), pp. 47-62.
23. Philip Fitch Vincent, *Developing Character in Students* (North Carolina: New View, 1996), p. 78.
24. Lickona, *Educating for Character*, p. 187.
25. "The Child Development Project: A Brief Summary," p. 2.
26. Lickona, *Educating for Character*, p. 198.
27. Ibid., p. 232.

Chapter 13

1. John Graham, *It's Up to Us* (Langley, WA: Giraffe Project, 1999), pp. 3-4.
2. Michael Calandra, "Camden Middle School's Character Education Program," presentation at the Summer Institute in Character Education, Center for the 4th and 5th Rs, State University of New York College at Cortland, June 30, 1997.
3. Ruth Charney, *Teaching Children to Care: Management in the Responsive Classroom* (Greenfield, MA: Northeast Foundation for Children, 1992), p.14.
4. Kathy Winings, *Building Character through Service Learning*, International Educational Foundation, New York, unpublished.
5. Philip Fitch Vincent, *Developing Character in Students* (Lincoln: University of Nebraska Press, 1996), p. 134.
6. Graham, *It's Up to Us*, p. 15.
7. Vincent, *Developing Character in Students*, p. 136.
8. *At Home in Our Schools* (Oakland CA: Developmental Studies Center, 1994), p. 85.
9. "Schools of Character: Reclaiming America's Values for Tomorrow's Workplace," McGraw-Hill Companies and Character Education Partnership, 1998, p. 14.
10. Ibid., p. 19.
11. Winings, *Building Character through Service Learning*.
12. Kim Patrick Moore, "Designing Successful Service Learning Projects

for Urban Schools," *Urban Education* 34 (November 1999), pp. 480, 499.

13. Mary Prentice and Rudy M. Garcia, "Service Learning: The Next Generation in Education," *Community College Journal of Research & Practice* 24 (January 2000), p. 19.

14. Winings, *Building Character through Service Learning.*

15. Ibid.

16. Thomas Lickona, "Educating for Character: A Comprehensive Approach," in A. Molnar, ed., *The Construction of Children's Character* (Chicago: University of Chicago Press, 1997), p. 58.

17. Winings, *Building Character through Service Learning.*

18. *At Home in Our Schools*, pp. 91–93.

19. "1999 National Schools of Character: Best Practices and New Perspectives," McGraw-Hill Companies and Character Education Partnership, 1999, p. 17

20. Thomas Lickona, *Educating for Character* (New York: Bantam Books, 1991), p. 164

21. Barbara Lewis, *Kids With Courage: True Stories of Young People Making a Difference* (Minneapolis: Free Spirit Publishing, 1992), pp. 135-43.

22. John Sandlos, "The Storied Curriculum: Oral Narrative, Ethics, and Environmental Education," *Journal of Environmental Education* 30 (January 1998), pp. 5-10.

23. Loraine Keeney, "Teaching Values and Self-Esteem through the Environment," *Connect: The Newsletter of Practical Science and Math for K-8 Teachers* (Spring 1990).

24. Michael J. Caduto, "Ecological Education: A System Rooted in Diversity," *Journal of Environmental Education* 29 (Summer 1998), p.6.

Chapter 14

1. Margaret Mead and Ken Heyman, *Family* (New York: Macmillan, 1965), pp. 77-78.

2. *Marriage in America, A Report to the Nation*, Council on Families in America, March 1995, p. 4.

3. Brigitte Berger, "The Social Roots of Prosperity and Liberty," *Society* (March-April 1998), p. 43.

4. Ibid., p. 5.

5. Ibid., p. 44.

6. Mayor Bill Hardiman of Kitwood, Michigan, presentation at the Smart Marriages Conference sponsored by the Coalition for Marriage, Family and Couples Education, Washington, D.C., July 9, 1998.

7. Francis J. Schweigert, "Mending the Moralnet: Moral Education in Strengthening Personal and Family Networks," presentation, Annual Meeting of the Association for Moral Education, Dartmouth College,

Hanover, New Hampshire, November 20, 1998.

8. CBS *60 Minutes*, July 31, 1994.

9. Dom Elium and Jeanne Elium, *Raising a Son* (Hillsboro, OR: Beyond Words Publishing, 1992), p. 83.

10. Gabriel Moran, *Religious Education Development: Images for the Future* (Minneapolis: Winston Press, 1983), p. 169.

11. This notion is comparable to the Confucian idea of the Five Relations that should guide a moral person's life: between prince and minister, between father and son, between husband and wife, between elder and younger brothers, and between friends. See *Doctrine of the Mean* 20.8.

12. Marvin Berkowitz and John H. Grych, "Fostering Goodness: Teaching Parents to Facilitate Children's Moral Development," *Journal of Moral Education* 27 (September 1998), pp. 371-92; Linda Bakken and Charles Romig, "The Relationship of Perceived Family Dynamics to Adolescents' Principled Moral Reasoning," *Journal of Adolescent Research* 9 (October 1994), pp. 442-58.

13. B. Bauer, "Siblings Get Boost in Mental Knowledge," *Science News* 146 (September 10, 1994), pp. 65-67.

14. Barbara M. Stilwell, Matthew Galvin, and Stephen Mark Kopta, "Conceptualization of Conscience in Normal Children and Adolescents, Ages 5 to 17," *Journal of the American Academy of Child and Adolescent Psychiatry* 30/1 (January 1991), pp. 16-21.

15. Frank Pittman, *Grow Up! How Taking Responsibility Can Make You a Happy Adult* (New York: Golden Books, 1998), p. 233.

16. See Mohammadreza Hojat, "Satisfaction with Early Relationships with Parents and Psychosocial Attributes in Adulthood: Which Parent Contributes More?" *Journal of Genetic Psychology* 159 (June 1998), pp. 203-31; M. D. S. Ainsworth, "Attachment Across the Life Span," *Bulletin of the New York Academy of Medicine* 61 (1985), pp. 792-812.

17. N. L. Collins and S. J. Read, "Adult Attachment, Working Models, and Relationship Quality in Dating Couples," *Journal of Personality and Social Psychology* 58 (1990), pp. 644-63.

18. Mohammadreza Hojat, "Developmental Pathway to Violence: a Psychodynamic Paradigm," *Peace Psychology Review* 1/2 (1995), pp. 176-95; Mohammadreza Hojat, "Perception of Maternal Availability in Childhood and Selected Psychosocial Characteristics in Adulthood," *Genetic, Social and General Psychology Monographs* 122 (1996), pp. 425-50; G. Liotti, "Insecure Attachment and Agoraphobia," in C. M. Parkes, J. Stevenson Hinde and P. Marris, eds., *Attachment across the Life Cycle* (London: Tavistock/Routledge, 1991), pp. 216-33.

19. R. R. Kobak and A. Sceery, "Attachment in Late Adolescence: Working Models, Affect Regulation, and Representation of Self and Others," *Child Development* 59 (1988), pp. 136-46.

20. Harville Hendrix, *Keeping the Love You Find: A Guide for Singles* (New

York: Pocket Books, 1992), p. 23.

21. William W. Hartup, "Having Friends, Making Friends and Keeping Friends: Relationships as Educational Contexts," *ERIC Digest* (Educational Resources Information Center, University of Minnesota Center for Early Education and Development, 1992), p. 1.

22. This is a standard notion in Asian ethics. Thus Mencius 1.A.7: "Treat the aged in your own family in a manner befitting their venerable age, and extend this treatment to the aged of other families; treat your own young in a manner befitting their tender age and extend this to the young of other families."

23. Blaine J. Fowers, "Psychology and the Good Marriage," *American Behavioral Scientist* 41 (January 1998), p. 540.

24. James Q. Wilson, *The Moral Sense* (New York: Free Press, 1993), pp. 162-63.

Chapter 15

1. Mohammedreza Hojat, "Satisfaction with Early Relationships with Parents and Psychosocial Attributes in Adulthood," *Journal of Genetic Psychology* 159/2 (June 1998), pp. 203-204.

2. Jerome Kagan found that children's experiences become moralized through adults' emotional and behavioral responses when pleased or displeased. See Jerome Kagan, "Temporal Contributions to Social Behavior," *American Psychologist* 44 (1989), pp. 40-44.

3. Erik Erikson, *Childhood and Society* (1950); Erik Erikson, "The Human Life Cycle," International *Encyclopedia of the Social Sciences* (New York: Cromwell-Collier, 1968), pp. 286-92.

4. For a collection of Erikson's essays on the life cycle and early childhood, see Stephen Schlein, ed., *A Way of Looking at Things: Selected Papers of Erik Erikson from 1930 to 1980* (New York: Norton, 1987).

5. Marvin Berkowitz and John H. Grych, "Fostering Goodness: Teaching Parents to Facilitate Children's Moral Development," *Journal of Moral Education* (September 1998), p. 371.

6. James J. Garbarino, "Comparisons of the Constructs and Psychometric Properties of Selected Measure of Adult Attachment," *Measurement and Evaluation in Counseling and Development* 3 (1998), pp. 28-45.

7. R. Farber Kestenbaum and L.A. Sroufe, "Individual Differences in Empathy among Preschoolers: Relation to Attachment History, *New Directions for Child Development* 44 (1989), pp. 51-64.

8. M.H. van Uzendoorn, "Attachment, Emergent Morality and Aggression: Toward a Developmental Socio-emotional Model of Antisocial Behavior," *International Journal of Behavioral Development* 21 (April 1997), pp. 703-27.

9. J. Bowlby, *A Secure Base* (New York, Basic Books, 1988).

10. James Q. Wilson, *The Moral Sense* (New York: The Free Press, 1993), p.105.

11. Deirdre V. Lovechy, "Identity Development in Gifted Children: Moral Sensitivity," *Roper Review* 20 (December 1997), p. 93.

12. Mencius 7A45.

13. Children who are not strongly attached to a parent lag behind in the achievement of impulse control and control of bodily functions by at least six months. Selma H. Fraiberg, *The Magic Years* (New York: Simon & Schuster, 1959), p. 298.

14. Ibid., p. 282.

15. Barbara M. Stilwell, Matthew Galvin, Stephen Mark Kopta and Robert J. Padgett, "Moral Volition: The Fifth and Final Domain Leading to an Integrated Theory of Conscience Understanding," *Journal of the American Academy of Child Adolescent Psychiatry* 37 (February 1998), pp. 202-210; Stillwell, et al., "Moralization of Attachment: A Fourth Domain of Conscience Functioning," *Journal of the American Academy of Child Adolescent Psychiatry* 36 (August 1997), pp. 1140-47; Stillwell, et al., "Moral Valuation: A Third Domain of Conscience Functioning," *Journal of the American Academy of Child Adolescent Psychiatry* 35 (February 1996), pp. 230-39.

16. Prem S. Fry, "The Development of Personal Meaning and Wisdom in Adolescence: A Reexamination of Moderating and Consolidating Factors and Influences," in Paul T. P. Wong and Prem S. Fry, eds., *The Human Quest for Meaning: A Handbook of Psychological Research and Clinical Applications* (New Jersey: Lawrence Erlbaum, 1998).

17. William Goldfarb, "Psychological Privation in Infancy and Subsequent Adjustment," *American Journal of Orthopsychiatry* 15 (1945).

18. Fraiberg, *Magic Years*, p. 293.

19. For a classic study of this process, see Erik Erikson, *Young Man Luther* (New York: Norton, 1958).

20. M.B. Sperling and W.H. Berman, *Attachment in Adults: Clinical and Developmental Perspectives* (New York: Guilford Press, 1994).

21. For a discussion of adolescence and meaning making, see Sharon Parks, *The Critical Years: Young Adults and the Search for Meaning, Faith and Commitment* (San Francisco: Harper Collins, 1986).

22. See Erikson's essays on adolescence and identity in Schlein, *A Way of Looking at Things*.

23. "Korczak Ziolkowski's Family," www.crazyhorse.org

24. Stephen B. Oates, *Let the Trumpet Sound* (London: Search Press, 1982), p. 12.

Chapter 16

1.   V. H. Bedford, "Sibling Relationship Troubles and Well-Being in Middle and Old Age, *Family Relations* (October 1998), p. 370.
2.   Ibid., p. 369.
3.   See S. M. McHale and A. C. Crouter, "The Family Contexts of Children's Sibling Relationships," in G. Brody, ed., *Sibling Relationships: Their Causes and Consequences* (Norwood, NJ: Ablex, 1996), pp. 173-95.
4.   See W. Furman and D. Buhrmester, "The Contribution of Siblings and Peers to the Parenting Process," in M. Kostelnik, ed., *Child Nurturance: Vol. 2. Patterns of Supplementary Parenting* (New York: Plenum, 1982), pp. 69-100.
5.   Corinna Jenkins Tucker, Kimberly A. Updegraff, Susan M. McHale and Ann C. Crouter, "Older Siblings as Socializers of Younger Siblings' Empathy," *Journal of Early Adolescence* (May 1999), pp. 176-99.
6.   J. Dunn and E. Munn, "Siblings and the Development of Prosocial Behavior," *International Journal of Behavioral Development* 9 (1986), pp. 265-84.
7.   Benjamin Spock, *Baby and Child Care* (New York: Pocket Books, 1987), p. 411.
8.   Nancy Eisenberg and B. Murphy, "Parenting and Children's Moral Development," in M. H. Bornstein, ed., *Handbook of Parenting* (Mahwah, NJ: Lawrence Erlbaum, 1995), pp. 227-57.
9.   F. Klagsburn, *Mixed Feelings: Love, Hate, Rivalry, and Reconciliation among Brothers and Sisters* (New York: Bantam, 1992); P. G. Zukow, "Siblings as Effective Socializing Agents: Evidence from Central Mexico," in *Sibling Interactions Across Cultures: Theoretical and Methodological Issues* (New York: Springer-Verlag, 1989), pp. 79-105.
10. For a study on how older siblings function as agents in their younger sisters' and brothers' social cognitive development, see M. Azmitia and J. Hesser, "Why Siblings are Important Agents of Cognitive Development: A Comparison of Siblings and Peers," *Child Development* 64, pp. 430-44.
11. Victor G. Cirelli, "Sibling Relationships in Cross-Cultural Perspective," *Journal of Marriage & the Family* 56/1 (February 1994), pp. 7-21; T. S. Weisner, "Sibling Similarity and Difference in Different Cultures," in C. W. Nuckolls, ed., *Siblings in South Asia: Brothers and Sisters in Cultural Context* (New York: Guilford Press, 1993), pp. 1-18.
12. Jim Barrall, Sponsorship News, *Children International*, Autumn 1999, p. 3.
13. Corinna Jenkins Tucker, Kimberly A. Updegraff, Susan M. McHale, and Ann C. Crouter, "Older Siblings as Socializers of Younger Siblings' Empathy," *Journal of Early Adolescence* (May 1999), p. 187.
14. William W. Hartup, "Having Friends, Making Friends and Keeping Friends: Relationships as Educational Contexts," *ERIC Digest*, The Educational Resources Information Center, University of Minnesota's Center for Early Education and Development, 1992), p. 1.

15. Harville Hendrix, *Getting the Love You Want* (New York: Harper, 1988).
16. V. G. Cicirelli, *Sibling Relationships Across the Life Span* (New York: Plenum, 1995); J. G. Wilson, R. J. Calsyn and J. L. Orlofsky, "Impact of Sibling Relationships on Morale in the Elderly," *Journal of Gerontological Social Work* 22 (1994), pp. 157-70.
17. Frank S. Pittman, *Grow Up! How Taking Responsibility Can Make You a Happy Adult* (New York: Golden Books, 1998), p. 239.
18. E. M. Brody, *Women-in-the-Middle: Their Parent Care Years* (New York: Springer, 1990).
19. P. S. Avioli, "The Social Support Functions of Siblings in Later Life: A Theoretical Model," American Behavioral Scientist 33 (1989), pp. 45-58; Victor G. Cirelli, "Sibling Relationships throughout the Life Cycle," in L. L'Abate, ed., *Handbook of Family Psychology and Therapy*, Vol. 1 (Homewood, IL: Dorsey, 1985), pp. 177-214.

Chapter 17

1. Elizabeth McAlister, "Is Marriage Obsolete?" *Sojourners* 25/2 (March-April 1996), p. 18.
2. In discussing possible explanations for adultery, sociologist Andrew Greeley writes: "Clearly morality is important. The infidelity rate is only 10 percent for those who think that sex with someone other than a spouse is always wrong (80 percent of the married respondents). It rises to 70 percent for those who do not think it is wrong at all (1 percent of the married respondents)." *Society* 31 (May–June 1994), p. 13.
3. Lori H. Gordon, *Passage to Intimacy* (New York: Simon & Schuster, 1993), pp. 29-30.
4. W. Bradford Swift, "The Work of Oneness, Interview with Bo Lozoff," *Utne Reader*, November–December 1996, p. 54.
5. Robert Bellah, R. Madsen, W. M. Sullivan, A. Swidler and S. M. Tipton, *Habits of the Heart* (Los Angeles: University of California Press, 1985), p. 93.
6. Blaine J. Fowers, "Psychology and the Good Marriage," *American Behavioral Scientist* 41/4, (January 1998), pp. 516-42.
7. Harville Hendrix, *Getting the Love You Want* (New York: Harper, 1988).
8. Hara Estroff Marano, "Divorced? Don't Even Think of Remarrying Until You Read This," March 7, 2000, posted at http://archives.his.com/smartmarriages/index.html#start.
9. Erich Fromm, *The Art of Loving* (New York: Harper & Row, 1956), p. 46.
10. Swift, "The Work of Oneness," p. 54.
11. Donna Palladino Schultheiss and David L. Blustein, "Contributions of Family Relationship Factors to Identity Formation Process," *Journal of Counseling & Development* 73 (November 1994), pp. 159-67.

12. Gordon, *Passage to Intimacy*, p. 182.
13. Hendrix, *Getting the Love You Want*.
14. Carol Sorbet Cope, *Stranger Danger* (New York: Cader Books, 1997), p. 24.
15. Sheldon Harnick, lyrics, "Do You Love Me?" *Fiddler on the Roof*, Mirish Productions and Cartier Productions, released by United Artists, MGM/US Home Entertainment Group, 1971.

Chapter 18

1. Judith S. Wallerstein and Sandra Blakeslee, *The Good Marriage* (New York: Houghton Mifflin, 1995), pp. 232-33.
2. Ibid., pp. 232-33.
3. Fred Barnes, "The Family: A Reader's Digest Poll," *Reader's Digest* (July 1992), p. 50.
4. Brian Volck, "Welcoming a Stranger: A New View of Parenting," *America* 76/20 (1997), pp. 7-9.
5. S. A. Small and G. Eastman, "Rearing Adolescents in Contemporary Society: A Conceptual Framework for Understanding the Responsibilities of Parents," *Family Relations* 40 (October 1991), pp. 455-63.
6. On various ways parents can and do influence children's moral growth and identity, see William Damon, "The Moral Development of Children," *Scientific American* 28 (August 1999).
7. Robert Coles, *The Moral Intelligence of Children: How to Raise a Moral Child* (New York, Random House, 1997).
8. Farley and Betsy Jones, *Raising Children of Peace* (New York, 1997), p. 79.
9. Daniel Hart and Robert Atkins, "Family Influences on the Formation of Moral Identity in Adolescence: Longitudinal Studies," *Journal of Moral Education* 28/3 (September 1999), pp. 375-87.
10. According to Elizabeth Fox-Genovese, American parents spend 40 percent less time with their children than they did a few decades ago—from 30 hours a week to 17. See Elizabeth Fox-Genovese, *Feminism Is Not the Story of My Life* (New York: Doubleday), pp. 275.
11. Hillary Rodham Clinton, *It Takes a Village* (New York: Simon & Schuster, 1996), p. 8.
12. Small and Eastman, "Rearing Adolescents"; R. Rapoport, R. Rapoport and Z. Strelitz, *Fathers, Mothers and Society* (New York: Basic Books, 1977); S. B. Silverberg, "A Longitudinal Look at Parent Adolescent-Relations and Parents' Evaluations of Life and Self," in G. Naom, *Constructions and Constraints: The Adolescent and the Family*, Symposium conducted at the 10th biennial meeting of the International Society for the Study of Behavioral Development, Jyvaskyla, Finland, July 1989.
13. Small and Eastman, "Rearing Adolescents," pp. 9-10.
14. J. Belsky, "The Determinants of Parenting: A Process Model," *Child*

Development 55 (1984), pp. 83-96; S. Small, "Parental Self-Esteem and its Relationship to Childrearing Practices, Parent-Adolescent Interaction and Adolescent Behavior," *Journal of Marriage and the Family* 50 (1988), pp. 1063-72.

15. Mary Pipher, "Closing the Gap: Why We Need to Reconnect the Young and Old," *USA Weekend*, March 19-21, 1999, p. 50.
16. Ibid.
17. Erik H. Erikson, Joan M. Erikson and Helen Q. Kivnick, *Vital Involvement in Old Age: The Experience of Old Age in Our Time* (New York: Norton, 1986).
18. Ibid., p. 53.
19. Ibid., p. 306.

Chapter 19

1. James Q. Wilson, *The Moral Sense* (New York: Free Press, 1993), p. 158.
2. Brigitte Berger, "The Social Roots of Prosperity and Liberty," *Society* 35 (March–April 1998), p. 44.
3. Susan Clarke, National Center for Health Statistics, quoted by Mike McManus, website posting of the Coalition for Marriage, Family and Couples Education, March 13, 1999, smartmarriages@cmfce@smart-marriages.com.
4. Berger, "Social Roots of Prosperity and Liberty," p. 21.
5. John M. Gottman, *The Seven Principles for Making Marriage Work* (New York: Three Rivers Press, 1999), p. 4.
6. David Popenoe, "The Vanishing Father," *The Wilson Quarterly* (Spring 1996), pp. 12-13.
7. David Popenoe and Barbara Dafoe Whitehead, "The State of Our Unions, 1999," The National Marriage Project, Rutgers, The State University of New Jersey, 1999, p. 10.
8. *Newsweek*, January 20, 1997.
9. David Popenoe and Barbara Dafoe Whitehead, Overview of the Report "Should We Live Together? What Young Adults Need to Know about Cohabitation before Marriage," The National Marriage Project, Rutgers, The State University of New Jersey, January 1999.
10. Carroll Bogert, "Life with Mother," *Newsweek*, January 20, 1997, p. 42.
11. Popenoe and Whitehead, "The State of Our Unions, 1999," p. 30.
12. Bogert, "Life with Mother," p. 41.
13. Ibid., p. 43.
14. Steven Butler, "Japan's Baby Bust," *U.S. News & World Report*, October 5, 1998, p. 42.
15. U.S. Bureau of the Census, CPR Series P-23, No. 172, June 1989, 3-4, and Series P-20, No. 45, June 1990, 2, 9.
16. Popenoe and Whitehead, "The State of Our Unions, 1999," p. 29.
17. David Popenoe and Barbara Dafoe Whitehead, "The State of Our

Unions, 2000: Sex without Strings; Relationships without Rings," The National Marriage Project, Rutgers, the State University of New Jersey, June 2000.

18. Hillary Rodham Clinton, *It Takes a Village* (New York: Simon & Schuster, 1996), p. 50.
19. Gottman, *Seven Principles*, p. 5.
20. Robert Flewelling, et al., "Family Structure as a Predictor of Initial Substance Abuse and Sexual Intercourse in Early Adolescence," *Journal of Marriage and the Family* 52 (February 1990), pp. 17-81.
21. Joseph P. Shapiro, "Honor Thy Children," *U.S. News & World Report*, February 27, 1995, p. 39.
22. Deborah Dawson, "Family Structure and Children's Health and Well-Being: Data from the 1988 National Health Interview Survey on Child Health," *Journal of Marriage and the Family* 53 (August 1991), pp. 573-84.
23. Karl Zinsmeister, quoted by Glenn T. Stanton in "Twice As Strong: The Undeniable Advantages of Raising Children in a Two-Parent Family, a Research Report," Public Division of Focus on the Family, January 1995, pp. 6-7.
24. "Survey of Youth in Custody, 1987," U.S. Department of Justice, 1988, p. 1.
25. Partick Fagan, "The Real Root Causes of Violent Crime: the Breakdown of Marriage, Family, and Community," *Heritage Foundation Backgrounder*, March 17, 1995, p. 23.
26. David Courtwright, *Violent America* (Cambridge: Harvard University Press, 1996), p. 280.
27. David Blankenhorn, *Fatherless America* (New York: Basic Books, 1995), p. 31.
28. Beatrice and Jon Whiting, *Children of Six Cultures: A Psycho-Cultural Analysis* (Cambridge: Harvard University Press, 1975).
29. Norman Dennis, "Europe's Rise in Crime," *The World & I* 12 (October 1997), p. 28.
30. Blankenhorn, *Fatherless America*, p. 46.
31. Glenda Cooper and Jeremy Laurance, "Wealthier, Wiser, So Why Not Healthier?" *Independent*, April 15, 1997, p. 3.
32. Richard A. Panzer, "Latest Health Craze—Marriage?" *Free Teens Health News*, Free Teens USA, Westwood, NJ, 1997, p. 3.
33. Hara Estroff Marano, "Debunking the Marriage Myth: It Works for Women, Too," *New York Times*, August 4, 1998.
34. Linda J. Waite, Keynote address, second annual Smart Marriages Conference, Coalition for Marriage, Family and Couples Education, Washington, D.C., July 1998.
35. Les Parrott III and Leslie Parrott, *Questions Couples Ask* (Grand Rapids: Zondervan, 1996), p. 65.
36. Marano, "Debunking the Marriage Myth."
37. Neil Clark Warren, *The Triumphant Marriage* (Focus on the Family, 1995), p. 121.

38. Thomas J. Stanley and William D. Danko, *The Millionaire Next Door* (Atlanta: Longstreet, 1996).

39. Harville Hendrix, *Getting the Love You Want, A Guide for Couples* (New York: HarperCollins, 1988), p. 115.

40. Judith S. Wallerstein and Sandra Blakeslee, *The Good Marriage* (New York: Houghton Mifflin, 1995), p. 67.

41. Diane Medved, "Marriage as Liberation," *The World & I*, February 1991, p. 245.

42. Rodger Doyle, "Divorce American Style," *Scientific American* (March 1999).

Chapter 20

1. Carrie Abbott, "Parent Power," presentation at the annual conference of the National Abstinence Clearinghouse, Raleigh, North Carolina, October 23, 1999.

2. Kendall Hamilton and Pat Wingert, "Can Generation Xers—Many of Them the Children of Divorce—Make Their Own Marriages Last?" *Newsweek*, July 20, 1998.

3. Karen Peterson, "Schools to Teach Lessons of Marriage," *USA Today*, July 14, 1998.

4. "Partners: A Curriculum for Preserving Marriages," promotional literature, American Bar Association, Chicago, Illinois, 1998.

5. Diane Sollee, "Shifting Gears: An Optimistic View of the Future of Marriage," presentation at the Conference on Communitarian Pro-Family Policies, sponsored by the Communitarian Network, Washington, D.C., November 15, 1996.

6. Lynn Smith, "The School of Heart Knocks," *Los Angeles Times*, September 10, 1998, p. E1.

7. Kevin Hoffman, "Marry U.: College Program Prepares Students to Tie the Knot," Associated Press, January 14, 1999.

8. Michael J. McManus, *Marriage Savers: Helping Your Friends and Family Avoid Divorce* (Grand Rapids: Zondervan, 1995).

9. Jodie Morse, "Hitched in Home Room: Seeking to Curb Divorces, Schools Are Teaching the Facts of Married Life. Is It for Better or for Worse?" *Time*, June 21, 1999.

10. McManus, *Marriage Savers*.

11. Thomas Lickona and Judy Lickona, *Sex, Love and You* (South Bend, IN: Ave Maria Press, 1994), p. 101.

12. Josh McDowell, *Myths of Sex Education* (Nashville: Thomas Nelson, 1991), p. 262.

13. Erich Fromm, *The Art of Loving* (New York: Harper & Row, 1956), p. 26.

14. Charlene Kamper, *Connections: Relationships and Marriage, Teachers Manual* (Berkeley, CA: The Dibble Fund for Marital Enhancement, 1996), Lesson 12. The Partners course and others also have a pretend marriage component.

15. "He says... She says," *The California Educator* (November 1998), at www.smartmarriages.com/connections.html.
16. Josh McDowell and Paul Lewis, *Givers, Takers and Other Kinds of Lovers* (Wheaton, IL: Tyndale House, 1980).
17. Stephen G. Covey, *Principle-Centered Leadership* (New York: Simon and Schuster, 1992), pp. 178–79.
18. James Coughlin, *Facing Reality: A Handbook for Healthy Living, Parent/Teacher Guide* (Golf, IL: Project Reality, 1990), p. 18; Les Parrott, *Relationships Workbook: An Open and Honest Guide to Making Bad Relationships Better and Good Relationships Great* (Grand Rapids: Zondervan, 1998), p. 35.
19. Les and Leslie Parrott, *Saving Your Marriage before It Starts* (Grand Rapids: Zondervan, 1995), p. 20.
20. Lori H. Gordon, *Passage to Intimacy* (New York: Simon & Schuster, 1993), p. 47.
21. Florence Creighton, Virginia Scott and George Doub, *Family Wellness: Survival Skills for Healthy Families Workbook* (Santa Cruz, CA: Family Wellness Associates, 1994), p. 61.
22. Edward G. Ford and Steven L. Englund, *Permanent Love: Practical Steps to a Lasting Relationship* (Scottsdale, Arizona: Brandt Publishing, 1980), pp. 67–70.
23. Morse, "Hitched in Home Room."
24. David Olson, et al., *Building Relationships: Developing Skills for Life* (Minneapolis: Life Innovations, 1998).
25. "Partners: A Curriculum for Preserving Marriages."
26. Judd and Mary Landis, *Building a Successful Marriage* (Englewood Cliffs, NJ: Prentice Hall, 1958).
27. Frank Pittman, *Grow Up! How Taking Responsibility Can Make You a Happy Adult* (New York: Golden Books, 1998), p. 160.
28. Therese Mo Hannah, "EQ: Emotional-Social Intelligence," Department of Psychology, Siena College, Latham, New York, 1998.
29. Gordon, *Passage to Intimacy*, p. 40.
30. Connie J. Salts, et al., "Attitudes toward Marriage and Premarital Sexual Activity of College Freshmen," *Adolescence* (Winter 1994), p. 775.
31. Morse, "Hitched in Home Room."
32. From a discussion with Kay Reed, director of the Dibble Fund, at the annual conference of the Coalition for Marriage, Family and Couples Education, Washington, D.C., July 1999.
33. Maggie Gallagher, "The Age of Unwed Mothers: Is Teen Pregnancy the Problem?" press release, Institute for American Values, New York, September 22, 1999.
34. Maggie Gallagher, "Marriage Earlier and Better?" *The Washington Times National Weekly Edition*, October 4–10, 1999, p 30.
35. Peterson, "Schools to Teach Lessons of Marriage."
36. Kamper, *Connections*, p. 35.
37. M. Scott Peck, *The Road Less Traveled: A New Psychology of Love,*

Traditional Values and Spiritual Growth (New York: Simon & Schuster, 1993), pp. 119-20.

38. Gordon, *Passage to Intimacy*, p. 28.
39. Pittman, *Grow Up*, p. 159.
40. The Loving Well Project, *The Art of Loving Well: A Character Education Curriculum for Today's Teenagers* (Boston: Boston University, 1993).
41. Suzanne Fields, "Chaste Chase," *The Washington Times*, January 18, 2000; Amy A. Kass and Leon R. Kass, eds., *Wing to Wing, Oar to Oar: Readings on Courting and Marrying* (Notre Dame, IN: Notre Dame Press, 2000).
42. Les and Leslie Parrott, *Saving Your Marriage Before It Starts*, p. 31.
43. "Partners for Students: Teaching Teenagers the Relationship Skills that Maintain Marriage, Curriculum Manual for Teachers," American Bar Association, 1999, Unit 2.
44. Sara Eckel, "Love 101: Across the Country, a Fourth 'R' Has Been Added to Reading, 'Riting And 'Rithmetic: Relationships," *React for Teens*, February 8–14, 1999.
45. "Partners: A Curriculum for Preserving Marriages."
46. Carole M. Pistole, "Preventing Teenage Pregnancy: Contributions from Attachment Theory," *Journal of Mental Health Counseling* (April 1999), p. 15.
47. Parrott, *Relationships Workbook*, pp. 87, 105.
48. Terry Hargrave, presentation at the annual conference of the Coalition for Marriage, Family and Couples Education, Washington, D.C., July, 1998.
49. Ford and Englund, *Permanent Love*, p. 56.
50. Stephen G. Covey, *The Seven Habits of Highly Effective Families* (New York: Golden Books, 1997), p. 139.
51. Parrott, *Relationships Workbook*, p. 59.
52. The same is true for those youth who experience sexual attraction to their own gender.
53. Joshua Harris, *I Kissed Dating Goodbye* (Sisters, OR: Multnomah Publishers, 1997), pp. 32–34.
54. Terrance Olsen, et al., *A Sampler of AANCHOR*, Department of Family Science, Brigham Young University, Provo, Utah, p. 37.
55. Harris, *I Kissed Dating Goodbye*, p. 31–42; Valerie Richardson, "Growing Courtship Movement Focuses on Friendship," *Washington Times National Weekly Edition*, May 29-June 4, 2000, pp. 1, 23.
56. "Dating and Doing Good Deeds," *Washington Post*, July, 9, 1998.
57. Interview with Rajib Chandam, Brown University senior fraternity president. Cited in Richard A. Panzer, *Relationship Intelligence: Why Your RQ Is More Important to Your Success and Happiness than Your IQ* (Westwood, New Jersey: Center for Educational Media, 2000), p. 13.
58. Richardson, "Growing Courtship Movement," p. 23.
59. From remarks given at the *Business Week* Schools of Character awards dinner, New York, April 27, 1998.
60. Harville Hendrix, *Keeping the Love You Find: A Guide for Singles* (New

York: Pocket Books, 1992); Lori Gordon and Morris Gordon, *PAIRS for PEERS (Practical Exercises Enhancing Relationship Skills)* (Fort Lauderdale: PAIRS Foundation, 1997).

61. What Students Are Saying about PEERS," PAIRS for PEERS promotional literature.
62. Les & Leslie Parrott, *Saving Your Marriage Before It Starts*, pp. 114–124; Kamper, *Connections*, Lesson 7.
63. "Partners: A Curriculum for Preserving Marriages."
64. Coughlin, *Facing Reality*, p. 9.
65. "He says... She says."

Chapter 21

1. Thanks to Ellen Mininberg of Woodbridge, Connecticut, for this story.
2. "Adultery: New Furor Over an Old Sin," *Newsweek*, September 30, 1996, pp. 54-55.
3. Rona Subotnik and Gloria Harris, *Surviving Infidelity* (Holbrook, MA: Bob Adams, 1994), p. 118.
4. Catherine M. Wallace, *For Fidelity* (New York: Alfred A. Knopf, 1998), pp. 13-15.
5. Steven Wolin, "Resilient Marriages," presented at the annual conference of the Coalition for Marriage, Family and Couple Education, Washington, D.C., July 2, 1999.
6. www.couplesplace.com.
7. Wolin, "Resilient Marriages."
8. Gary Smalley, *Hidden Keys of a Loving, Lasting Marriage* (Grand Rapids: Zondervan, 1988).
9. Emily Nussbaum, "Inside the Love Lab," *Lingua Franca* 10 (March 2000), posted on www.smartmarriages.com.
10. Judith S. Wallerstein and Sandra Blakeslee, *The Good Marriage* (New York: Houghton Mifflin, 1995), p. 64.
11. Ibid., pp. 115-16.
12. Antoine de Saint-Exupery, *The Little Prince* (New York: Harcourt Brace, 1943).
13. Hugh Delehanty, "Bo Knows Love," *Utne Reader* (December 1996), p. 3.
14. Gary Smalley, *Hidden Keys of a Loving, Lasting Marriage* (Grand Rapids: Zondervan, 1988), pp. 243-44.
15. John M. Gottman, *The Seven Principles for Making Marriage Work* (New York: Three Rivers Press, 1999), pp. 27-34.
16. Blaine J. Fowers, "Psychology and the Good Marriage," *American Behavioral Scientist* (January 1998).
17. Ibid., p. 516.

Chapter 22

1. Diane Baumrind, "Effects of Authoritative Parental Control on Child Behavior," *Child Development* 37/4, p. 887-907.
2. Ross Campbell, *How to Really Love Your Child* (London: Victor, 1977), p. 81.
3. Theodor Reik, *For Mom*, compiled by Jennifer Habel (New York: Peter Pauper, 1992).
4. Steven Stosny, "Compassionate Parenting," presented at the Coalition for Marriage, Family and Couples Education annual conference, Washington, D.C., July 2, 1999.
5. M. Scott Peck, *The Road Less Traveled* (New York: Simon & Schuster, 1978), p. 24.
6. www.inspirationalstories.com.
7. Marvin Berkowitz, "The Complete Moral Person: Anatomy and Formation," in J. M. DuBois, ed., *Moral Issues in Psychology: Personalist Contributions to Selected Problems* (Landham, MD: University Press of America, 1997), pp. 11-42.
8. Joseph C. Pearce, *The Magical Child Matures* (New York: Dutton, 1985).
9. John H. Grych and Frank D. Fincham, "Marital Conflict and Children's Adjustment: A Cognitive-Contextual Framework," *Psychological Bulletin* 108 (1990), pp. 267-90.
10. Wendy Shalit, *A Return to Modesty: Discovering the Lost Virtue* (New York: The Free Press, 1999), pp. 195-210.
11. Laura Shapiro, "The Myth of Quality Time," *Newsweek*, May 12, 1997, p. 62.
12. Time/CNN Poll, 1993; "Talking with Teens: The YMCA Parent and Teen Survey Final Report," Global Strategy Group, New York, May 30, 2000, p. 3.
13. Florence Creighton, Virginia Scott and George Doub, *Family Wellness Survival Skills for Healthy Families Workbook* (Santa Cruz: Family Wellness Associates, 1994), p. 138.
14. Ibid., p. 134.
15. Joy Overbeck, "Sex Too Soon," *Parents* 69 (September 1994), p. 42.
16. Karen S. Peterson, "Reclaiming Family Time Is Group's Priority," *USA Today*, June 12, 2000.
17. A. C. Nielsen rating company figures for 1995 cited by Charlotte Kintslinger-Bruhn, "Turn Off that TV," *Daily Freeman*, April 28, 1997, p. 1.
18. American Psychological Association, "Violence and Youth: Psychology's Response," Vol. I: Summary Report of the American Psychological Association Commission on Violence and Youth (1993), cited in Bob Waliszewski and Jerry Melchisedek, *Bringing Out the Worst in Us: The Frightening Truth about Violence, the Media and Our Youth* (Colorado Springs, CO: Focus on the Family, 1996), p. 30.
19. Margit Feury, "Family Meals Heal," *Family Circle*, February 1, 1998, p. 57.

20. Michael Resnick, et al., "Protecting Adolescents from Harm: The National Longitudinal Study on Adolescent Health," *Journal of the American Medical Association* 278 (September 10, 1997).

21. Stephen R. Covey, *The Seven Habits of Highly Effective Families* (New York: Golden Books, 1997).

22. Stosny, "Compassionate Parenting."

23. Recounted in Jane Nelsen, *Positive Discipline* (New York: Ballantine Books, 1996).

24. David Elkind, *The Hurried Child* (Reading, MA: Addison-Wesley, 1981), pp. 26-27.

25. Edward Guest, "Only a Dad," *The Children's Book of Heroes*, ed. William J. Bennett (New York: Simon & Schuster, 1997), p. 20.

26. William J. Kilpatrick, *Why Johnny Can't Tell Right from Wrong* (New York: Simon & Schuster, 1992), p. 258.

27. John Rosemond, *A Family of Value* (Grand Rapids: Zondervan, 1995), p. 19.

28. www.inspirationalstories.com.

29. Rudyard Kipling, *Captains Courageous* (New York: Bantam Books, 1982, originally published by The Century Company, 1896).

Chapter 23

1. Catherine M. Wallace, *For Fidelity* (New York: Alfred A. Knopf, 1998), p. 58.

2. Rollo May, *Love and Will* (New York: Norton, 1969).

3. "Adultery: New Furor Over an Old Sin," *Newsweek*, September 30, 1996, p. 56.

4. Elisabeth Haich, *Sexual Energy and Yoga*. Cited in Gabrielle Brown, *The New Celibacy: A Journey to Love, Intimacy and Good Health in the New Age* (New York: McGraw-Hill, 1989), pp. 25–26.

5. Michael Ross, "The Sexual Revolution Is Continuing," in *Sexual Values: Opposing Viewpoints* (San Diego: Greenhaven Press, 1989), pp. 22–24.

6. Suzanne Fields, "Chaste Chase," *The Washington Times*, January 18, 2000.

7. For example, James Nelson, *Embodiment*. Cited by Philip Turner, "Sex and the Single Life," *First Things* 33 (May 1993), pp. 15-21.

8. Susan Jonas and Marilyn Nissenson, "Virgins: a Vanishing Species," *Cosmopolitan*, April 1994, p. 86.

9. Eberhard and Phyllis Kronhausen, *Sex Histories of American College Men* (New York: Ballantine Books, 1960), p. 20.

10. Judith A. Reisman, *Soft Porn Plays Hardball* (Lafayette, LA: Huntington House, 1991), pp. 69-81.

11. Max Werner, "In His Own Words: Hugh Hefner Remains in the Romantic Vanguard," *New York Post*, July 6, 1976, p. 25.

12. Robert T. Michael, et al., *Sex in America, a Definitive Survey* (Boston:

Little, Brown and Company, 1994), pp. 18-20.

13. Kim Painter, "Biography Re-examines Sex Researcher Kinsey," *USA Today*, October 20, 1997, p. 1D; Judith A. Reisman, *Kinsey: Crimes and Consequences* (Arlington, VA: Institute for Media Education, 1998).

14. Survey published in *USA Today*, 1985, cited by Reisman, *Soft Porn Plays Hardball*, p. 14.

15. Wallace, *For Fidelity*, p. 61.

16. Archibald D. Hart, *The Sexual Man: Masculinity without Guilt* (Dallas: Word, 1994), pp. 196-8.

17. Ibid., p. 125.

18. Mike McManus, "For Valentine's Day: Consider Courtship," *CMFCE Newsletter*, January 27, 2000, at www.smartmarriages.com.

19. Fields, "Chaste Chase."

20. From 46 percent in 1990-1995 to 52 percent in 1997. Cited in Stephanie Ventura, Sally Curtin and T. J. Matthews, "Teenage Births in the United States: National and State Trends, 1990-1996," *National Vital Statistics System* (Hyattsville, MD: National Center for Health Statistics, 1998).

21. From 39 percent in 1990 to 51 percent in 1997. "New Study Shows Higher Unwed Birthrates among Sexually Experienced Teens Despite Increased Condom Use," Consortium of State Physicians Resource Councils, press release, February 10, 1999, p. 2.

22. UCLA Higher Education Research Institute Survey, 1997. Cited in "Family News from Dr. James Dobson," *Focus on the Family*, September, 1999, p. 6.

23. Laurie Goodstein with Marjorie Connelly, "Teen-Age Poll Finds a Turn to the Traditional," *New York Times*, April 30, 1998.

24. Alan Guttmacher Institute, cited in George Gallup, *Growing Up Scared in America* (Gallup International Institute, 1995).

25. John Harlow, "Pop Princess Sets Her Heart on Celibacy," *London Sunday Times*, May 14, 2000.

26. Michael Resnick, et al. "Protecting Adolescents from Harm: The National Longitudinal Study on Adolescent Health," *Journal of the American Medical Association* 278 (September 10, 1997).

27. Harlow, "Pop Princess."

28. Jonas and Nissenson, "Virgins: a Vanishing Species," p. 86.

29. Phyllis Schafly, "Parents Are Starting to Win Victories," *Eagle Forum*, September 1, 1999.

30. Lynn Harris, "Casual Sex: Why Confident Women Are Saying No," *Glamour*, September 1997; J. J. Despain, "Virginity 2000," *Teen*, February, 1997, pp. 68–70; Suzanne Fields, "The New Love that Dares Not Speak Its Name: Abstinence," *Insight on the News*, May 20, 1996, p. 48; Cindy Waxer, "Boy Virgins," *Jump*, May 1999, pp. 90–94.

31. Maggie Kirn, "Teen Bride," *Harper's Bazaar*, February 1998; "Cut to the Chaste: The Idea of Virginity Stages a Comeback," *The New York Times*, June 20, 1994.

32. Fields, "Chaste Chase."

33. Dean E. Murphy, "A Time of Testing for Virginity," *Los Angeles Times*, July 15, 1999; Chris Mohrman, "Group Urges Japanese Youth to Abstain from Sex," Japan Economic Newswire, August 10, 1999.

34. Ruth Padawer, "Casual Sex Loses Its Appeal for Youth," *The Bergen Record*, December 8, 1999.

35. Rosalind Miles, "Current Affairs," *Prospect*, January 1996. Cited in Wendy Shalit, *A Return to Modesty: Discovering the Lost Virtue* (New York: The Free Press, 1999), pp. 212-13.

36. Padawer, "Casual Sex Loses Its Appeal."

37. Tara Roberts, "Am I the Last Virgin?" *Essence*, June 1994, p. 79.

38. Despain, "Virginity 2000."

39. Daniel Gray, "Is Marriage Worth the Wait?" *Project Reality News* (February 2000), p. 1.

40. Veronica Chambers and Theresa Smith, "Young, Hot and Celibate," *Essence*, July 1993, p. 55.

41. George Eager, *Love, Dating and Sex* (Valdosta, GA: Mailbox Club Books, 1989), pp. 153–54.

42. Neal Bernards, "A Sojourn through the Sexual Landscape of America," in *Sexual Values: Opposing Viewpoints*, p. 167.

43. A. T. Fleming, "Like a Virgin Again," *Vogue*, February 1995.

Chapter 24

1. Peter Marin, "A Revolution's Broken Promises," in *Perspectives on Marriage, A Reader*, ed. Kieran Scott and Michael Warren (New York: Oxford, 1993), p. 183.

2. Patricia Dalton, "Daughters of the Revolution," *Washington Post*, May 21, 2000.

3. Josh McDowell and Dick Day, *Why Wait: What You Need to Know about the Teen Sexuality Crisis* (San Bernardino, CA: Here's Life Publishing, 1987); Thomas Lickona, "The Neglected Heart," *American Educator* (Summer 1994), pp. 34-39.

4. Lickona, "The Neglected Heart," pp. 36–37.

5. Wanda Franz, "Sex and the American Teenager," *The World & I* (September 1989), p. 478.

6. D.L. Mosher and R.E. Anderson, *Journal of Research in Personality* 20 (1986), p. 77. Cited in Joe S. McIlhaney, *Sexuality and Sexually Transmitted Diseases* (Grand Rapids: Baker Book House, 1990), p. 62.

7. McIlhaney, *Sexuality and Sexually Transmitted Diseases*, p. 65.

8. Susan Cochran and Vickie Mays, *New England Journal of Medicine* (March 15, 1990), p. 774.

9. Jacqueline Jackson Kikuchi, speaking at the 1988 National Symposium on Child Victimization, Anaheim, California. Cited in Josh McDowell, *Myths of Sex Education* (Nashville: Thomas Nelson, 1991), p. 101.

10. Thomas and Judy Lickona, *Sex, Love & You* (South Bend, IN: Ave

Maria Press, 1994), p. 39.

11. Roper Starch Worldwide, *Teens Talk about Sex* (New York: Sexuality Information and Education Council of the United States, 1994); McDowell, *Myths of Sex Education*, p. 253.

12. Susan Browning Pogany, *SexSmart: 501 Reasons to Hold Off on Sex* (Minneapolis: Fairview Press, 1998), pp. 57-58.

13. William A. Galston, "Beyond the Murphy Brown Debate," paper presented at the Institute for American Values Family Policy Symposium, New York, December 10, 1993.

14. Anne Catherine Speckhard, "The Psycho-Social Aspects of Stress Following Abortion," thesis submitted to Graduate School of the University of Minnesota, May 1985.

15. E. Joanne Angelo, "The Negative Impact of Abortion on Women and Families," in Michael T. Mannion, ed., *Post-Abortion Aftermath* (Kansas City, MO: Sheed & Ward, 1994), p. 51.

16. Ann Landers, *Ann Landers Talks to Teenagers About Sex* (Englewood Cliffs, NJ: Prentice-Hall, 1963), p. 35.

17. McDowell and Day, *Why Wait*, pp. 268–69.

18. David Whitman, "Was It Good for Us?" *U.S. News & World Report*, May 19, 1997, p. 58.

19. McDowell, *Myths of Sex Education*, p. 254.

20. Veronica Chambers and Theresa Smith, "Young, Hot and Celibate," *Essence*, July, 1993, p. 54.

21. McDowell, *Myths of Sex Education*, p. 253.

22. Donald Orr, "Premature Sexual Activity as an Indicator of Psychosocial Risk," *Pediatrics* 87 (February 1991), pp. 141-147.

23. Ibid.

24. Center for Disease Control, "AIDS Cases in Racial/Ethnic Minorities, January 1986-June 1998, United States," 1999, www.cdc.gov/hiv/graphics/images/l238/l238.pdf; "Tracking the Hidden Epidemics: Trends in STD Epidemics in the United States," www.cdc.gov/nchstp/dstd/Stats_Trends/STD_Trends.pdf.

25. *Facts in Brief*, Alan Guttmacher Institute, September 1993.

26. H. Hunter Handsfield, et al., "Report of the Genital Herpes Prevention Consultants Meeting, May 5-6, 1998," Centers for Disease Control, July 30, 1998.

27. S. Samuels, "Epidemic among America's Young," *Medical Aspects of Human Sexuality* 23 (December 1989).

28. *OB/GYN News*, American Public Health Association, February 15, 1993.

29. Medical Institute for Sexual Health, *The National Guidelines for Sexuality and Character Education* (Austin, Texas: Medical Institute for Sexual Health, 1996), p. 5.

30. J. Anderson and M. Wilson, "Caring for Teenagers with Salpingitis," *Contemporary OB/GYN* (August 1990).

31. L. Westrom, "Incidence, Prevalence, and Trends of Acute Pelvic Inflammatory Disease and its Consequences in Industrialized Countries," *American Journal of Obstetrics and Gynecology* 138 (1991),

pp. 880-92.

32. J. J. Apuzzio and M. A. Pelosi, "The 'New' Salpingitis: Subtle Symptoms, Aggressive Management," *The Female Patient* 14 (November 1989).

33. M. S. McAfee, *OB/GYN Clinical Alert* (July 1988).

34. Thomas and Judy Lickona, *Sex, Love & You*, p. 39.

35. McDowell, *Myths of Sex Education*, p. 258.

36. J. J. Despain, "Virginity 2000," *Teen*, February 1997, pp. 68.

37. *Choosing the Best: A Values-Based Sex Education Curriculum, Leader's Guide* (Atlanta: Choosing the Best, 1993).

38. Ann Landers, *Daily News*, September 23, 1991, p. 20.

39. Jan E. Stets, "Cohabiting and Marital Aggression: The Role of Social Isolation," *Journal of Marriage and the Family* 53 (1991), pp. 669-80.

40. McDowell and Day, *Why Wait*, p. 283.

41. Ann Landers, *Daily News*, January 15, 1994.

42. Stacey Rinehart and Paula Rinehart, *Choices* (Colorado Springs: Navpress, 1982), p. 94.

43. McDowell, *Myths of Sex Education*, p. 255.

44. L.H. Buskel, et al., "Projected Extramarital Sexual Involvement in Unmarried College Students," *Journal of Marriage and the Family* 40 (1978), pp. 337-40.

45. McDowell, *Myths of Sex Education*, p. 263.

46. Controversy surrounds the question of what age, if any, may constitute sufficient maturity for sex before marriage. Board members of Sex Information and Education Council of the United States (SIECUS), a leading advocate of contraceptive promotion among teenagers, were sorely challenged to reach a consensus on this issue. They decided that those past early adolescence—ages 9–13 for girls and 11–15 for boys—were less liable for outright exploitation and more likely to handle sex responsibly, provided the couple assesses itself mature enough and uses protection. In any case, they assert, "Developmental age and readiness, as well as relationship context, are more important than chronological age." D. W. Haffner, ed., *Facing Facts: Sexual Health for America's Adolescents* (New York: Sexuality Information and Education Council of the United States, 1995), p. 18.

47. Maggie Gallagher, "The Age of Unwed Mothers: Is Teen Pregnancy the Problem?" press release, Institute for American Values, New York, September 22, 1999.

48. Whitman, "Was It Good for Us?" p. 57.

49. 1997 *U.S. News* poll. Cited in ʾbid., p. 59.

50. Haffner, *Facing Facts*, p. 17.

51. Gallagher, "The Age of Unwed Mothers."

52. Nell Bernstein, "Learning to Love," *Mother Jones*, January-February 1995, p. 44.

53. Whitman, "Was It Good for Us?" p. 58.

54. Ibid., p. 62.

55. Barbara Dafoe Whitehead, "Dan Quayle Was Right," *Atlantic Monthly*, April 1993.
56. Bernstein, "Learning to Love," pp. 43-44.
57. Whitman, "Was It Good for Us?" p. 62.
58. Debra Boyer and David Fine, "Sexual Abuse as a Factor in Adolescent Childbearing and Child Maltreatment," *Family Planning Perspectives* 24 (1992), pp. 4-19.
59. Mike A. Males, "Poverty, Rape, Adult/Teen Sex: Why 'Pregnancy Prevention' Programs Won't Work," *Phi Delta Kappan* (January 1994), pp. 407-10.
60. Jacqueline E. Darrock, et al., "Pregnancy Rates among U.S. Women and Their Partners," *Family Planning Perspectives* 31/3 (March-April 1999), p. 122-26.
61. Mike A. Males, "Infantile Arguments," *In These Times*, August 9, 1993.
62. Mike A. Males, *The Scapegoat Generation: America's War on Adolescents* (Monroe, ME: Common Courage Press, 1966).
63. Neal Bernards, "A Sojourn through the Sexual Landscape of America," in *Sexual Values: Opposing Viewpoints* (San Diego: Greenhaven Press, 1989), p. 167.

Chapter 25

1. This is to be distinguished from the idea of serial monogamy, or short-lived exclusive relationships.
2. Bernard I. Murstein and Todd Mercy, "Sex, Drugs, Relationships, Contraception, and Fears of Disease on a College Campus over 17 Years," *Adolescence* (Summer 1994), p. 303.
3. Robert T. Michael, et al., *Sex in America, a Definitive Survey* (Boston: Little, Brown and Company, 1994), p. 102.
4. Ibid., p. 125.
5. Ibid., p. 105.
6. Gabrielle Brown, *The New Celibacy: A Journey to Love, Intimacy and Good Health in the New Age* (New York: McGraw-Hill, 1989), p. 93.
7. Ibid., p. 2.
8. Peter Koestenbaum, *Existential Sexuality: Choosing to Love*. Cited in Ibid., p. 21.
9. Judith A. Reisman, *Kinsey: Crimes and Consequences* (Arlington, Virginia: Institute for Media Education, 1998); Tim Reid, "Kinsey Based Research on Child Abuser," *London Daily Telegraph*, August 9, 1998; Kim Painter, "Biography Re-examines Sex Researcher Kinsey," *USA Today*, October 20, 1997, p. 1D.
10. Lillian B. Rubin, *Erotic Wars: What Ever Happened to the Sexual Revolution?* (New York: Farar, Strauss & Giroux, 1990), p. 189.
11. "Voices of a Generation: Teenage Girls on Sex, School and Self," American Association of American Women, September 1999.
12. Jules Older, "Mother Nature's Dirty Trick," *Los Angeles Times*, March

12, 1988. Reprinted in *Sexual Values: Opposing Viewpoints* (San Diego, CA: Greenhaven Press, 1989), pp. 198–201.

13. Derek Freman, *Margaret Mead and Samoa: The Making and Unmaking of an Anthropological Myth* (Cambridge: Harvard University Press, 1983).

14. William Tucker, "Monogamy and its Discontents," *National Review*, October 4, 1993, p. 28.

15. J. D. Unwin, *Sex and Culture* (London: Oxford University Press, 1934). Cited in Josh McDowell and Dick Day, *Why Wait: What You Need to Know About the Teen Sexuality Crisis* (San Bernardino, CA: Here's Life Publishing, 1987), pp. 262-63.

16. Tucker, "Monogamy and its Discontents," p. 28.

17. George Gilder, *Men and Marriage* (Gretna, LA: Pelican, 1992), pp. 64–65.

18. Tucker, "Monogamy and its Discontents," p. 28.

19. Michael, et al., *Sex in America*; David Popenoe and Barbara Dafoe Whitehead, "Should We Live Together? What Young Adults Need to Know about Cohabitation Before Marriage," The National Marriage Project, Rutgers, The State University of New Jersey, January 1999.

20. Susan Jonas and Marilyn Nissenson, "Virgins: a Vanishing Species," *Cosmopolitan*, April 1994, p. 86.

21. Betsy Israel, "Going All the Way: Nineties Teens Still Want to Have Fun, but Fear Has Taken Its Toll on the Joy of Sex," *Playboy*, August 1994, p. 120.

22. Michael et al., *Sex in America*, p. 125. See also "The Redbook Survey on Female Sexuality," *Redbook* 145, September 1975.

23. Murstein and Mercy, "Sex, Drugs, Relationships," p. 303.

24. George Leonard, "Adventures in Monogamy," in *Sexual Values: Opposing Viewpoints*, p. 192.

25. Viktor Frankl, *The Unheard Cry for Meaning: Psychotherapy and Humanism* (New York: Simon & Schuster, 1978), p. 81.

26. Abraham Maslow, *Motivation and Personality* (1970). Cited in Brown, *The New Celibacy*, p. 22.

27. Wendy Shalit, *A Return to Modesty: Discovering the Lost Virtue* (New York: The Free Press, 1999), pp. 67-72, 122.

28. Daniel P. Moloney, "Eroticism Unbound," *First Things*, February 1999, pp. 13-15.

29. Shalit, *A Return to Modesty*, p. 37.

30. Paul Glanzrock, "In Praise of Guilt," *Psychology Today*, July-August 1994, p. 21.

31. Jonas and Nissenson, "Virgins: a Vanishing Species," p. 86.

32. Though the survey was not rigorously conducted, it used sample of 100,000 women. "Redbook Survey of Female Sexuality," *Redbook* 145, September 1975.

33. David M. Buss, et al., "Sex Differences in Jealousy: Evolution, Physiology, and Psychology," *Psychological Science* 3 (1992), pp. 251-55. See "Origins of Sexual Jealousy," at

http://www.junebug.com/flux/jealousy.

34. Jonas and Nissenson, "Virgins: a Vanishing Species," p. 86.
35. Sally Cline, *Women, Passion and Celibacy* (New York: Carol Southern Books, 1993), p. 169.
36. Simon Sebag Montefiore, "Love, Lies, and Fear in the Plague Years," *Psychology Today*, September-October 1992, p. 30.
37. Patricia Dalton, "Daughters of the Revolution," *Washington Post*, May 21, 2000.
38. David Buss, *The Evolution of Desire: Strategies of Human Mating* (New York: Basic Books, 1994).
39. Sarah E. Hinlicky, "Subversive Virginity," *First Things* October 1998, pp. 14–16.
40. Shalit, *A Return to Modesty*, p. 112.
41. Moloney, "Eroticism Unbound."
42. Hinlicky, "Subversive Virginity."
43. Remarks by teenage participants at the Summit on Abstinence, annual conference sponsored by the Medical Institute on Sexual Health, San Antonio, August 8, 1999.
44. Florence P. Creighton, George Doub and Virginia Morgan Scot, *Survival Skills for Healthy Families: Family Wellness Workbook* (Santa Cruz: Family Wellness Associates, 1998), p. 138.
45. Barbara Dafoe Whitehead, "Why Abstinence—Beyond Pregnancy and STDs," presentation at the Summit on Abstinence, annual conference sponsored by the Medical Institute on Sexual Health, San Antonio, August 8, 1999.
46. Nell Bernstein, "Learning to Love," *Mother Jones*, January-February 1995, pp. 44-45.
47. Mary Patricia Barth Fourqurean, "Chastity as Shared Strength: An Open Letter to Students," *America*, November 6, 1993, p. 10.

Chapter 26

1. Debra W. Haffner, ed., *Facing Facts: Sexual Health for America's Adolescents* (New York: Sexuality Information and Education Council of the United States, 1995), p. 21.
2. Susan Newcomer, "Is It O.K. for PPFA to Say 'No Way'?" Cited in Nancy Pearcey, "Teenage Sex: Why Saying No Is Not Enough," *The World & I* (February 1991).
3. Some programs aim to simply delay sexual activity until adulthood.
4. "Sexuality and Abstinence Education Policies in the U.S. Public School Districts," Fact Sheet, Alan Guttmacher Institute, December 14, 1999.
5. Medical Institute for Sexual Health, *Abstinence and "Safer Sex" Sexuality Education: A Comparison* (Austin, TX: Medical Institute for Sexual Health, 1998), pp. 10–11, 68.
6. Wirthlin Worldwide poll taken among diverse cultures and countries

shows strong global agreement about the family. 84 percent agree that marriage is defined as "one man and one woman." 78 percent affirm that families are the "fundamental unit of society." 86 percent of respondents outside the U.S. said that children should be raised by a married mother and father. Justin Torres, "Study: Support for Traditional Family is Global," CNS.com (November 4, 1999).

7.   Medical Institute for Sexual Health, *The National Guidelines for Sexuality and Character Education* (Austin, TX: Medical Institute for Sexual Health, 1996), pp. 52–53; Margaret Whitehead and Onalee McCraw, *Foundations for Family Life Education: A Guidebook for Professionals and Parents* (Arlington, VA: Educational Guidance Institute, 1991), p. 20.

8.   National Guidelines Task Force, *Guidelines for Comprehensive Sexuality Education, Kindergarten–12th Grade* (New York: Sexuality Information and Education Council of the United States, 1996) p. 22; Whitehead and McCraw, *Foundations for Family Life Education*, pp. 15–16.

9.   *Guidelines for Comprehensive Sexuality Education*, pp. 25, 40, 48.

10.   Susan Wilson and Catherine Sanderson, "The Sex Respect Curriculum: Is 'Just Say No' Effective?" *SIECUS Report*, New York, September-October, 1988.

11.   Haffner, *Facing Facts*, p. 21.

12.   Whitehead and McCraw, *Foundations for Family Life Education*, p. 21.

13.   *Guidelines for Comprehensive Sexuality Education*, pp. 5, 39–44; Whitehead and McCraw, *Foundations for Family Life Education*, p. 21.

14.   *Guidelines for Comprehensive Sexuality Education*, pp. 25, 40, 48.

15.   *Abstinence and "Safer Sex" Sexuality Education*, p. 7; Whitehead and McCraw, *Foundations for Family Life Education*, p. 13.

16.   *Guidelines for Comprehensive Sexuality Education*, pp. 5–36, 40.

17.   *National Guidelines for Sexuality and Character Education*, pp. 13, 42, 48, 51, 55–56, 66.

18.   *Guidelines for Comprehensive Sexuality Education*, p. 30.

19.   Thomas Lickona, "The Need for Character-Based Sex Education," Center for the 4th and 5th Rs, Cortland, New York, 1997, p. 2

20.   *Guidelines for Comprehensive Sexuality Education*, pp. 11–12, 35–37.

21.   Barbara Sprung, *Learning about Family Life* (New Brunswick, NJ: Rutgers University Press, 1992).

22.   *Guidelines for Comprehensive Sexuality Education*, p. 30.

23.   *National Guidelines for Sexuality and Character Education*, pp. 84–85.

24.   Ibid., pp. 13, 42, 48, 51, 55–56, 66.

25.   From 62 percent to 54 percent per 1,000 adolescents.

26.   "New Study Shows Higher Unwed Birthrates among Sexually Experienced Teens Despite Increased Condom Use," Consortium of State Physicians Resource Councils, press release, February 10, 1999, p. 2.

27.   Reynolds W. Archer, presentation delivered at "Prevention in Focus" conference, 1994. Cited in Glenda J. Jones, "Character-based Directive Abstinence Education: What the Experts Say," Midway

L.S.D. Health Education Advisory Council (August 1996).

28. A. Gruenseit, "Impact of HIV and Sexual Health Education on Sexual Behavior of Young People: A Review Update" (Geneva: UNAIDS, 1997). This study effectively reversed the 1993 UNAIDS study often cited to show the effectiveness of contraceptive-based programs.

29. Douglas Kirby, et al., "Reducing the Risk: Impact of a New Curriculum on Sexual Risk-Taking," *Family Planning Perspectives* 23/6 (November 1991), pp. 253–62.

30. Alberto Saracco, et al., "Man to Woman Sexual Transmission of HIV: Longitudinal Study of 343 Steady Partners of Infected Men," *Journal of Acquired Immuno Deficiency Syndromes* 6/5 (May 1993), pp. 497-506; I. DeVincenzi, "A Longitudinal Study of Human Immunodeficiency Virus Transmission by Heterosexual Partners," *The New England Journal of Medicine*, 331/6 (August 11, 1994), pp. 341–46; Mark Guimaraes, et al. for the Rio de Janiero Heterosexual Study Group, "HIV Infection among Female Partners of Seropositive Men in Brazil," *American Journal of Epidemiology* 142/5 (1995), pp. 538-47; M. A. Fischl, et al., "Heterosexual Transmission of HIV, Relationships of Sexual Practices to Seroconversion: Abstracts from the Third International Conference on AIDS," Washington, D.C., June 1-5, 1987, p. 178.

31. Kirby, et al., "Reducing the Risk," pp. 253–62.

32. Mark D. Hayward, et al., "Contraceptive Failure in the United States: Estimates from the 1982 National Survey of Family Growth," *Family Planning Perspectives* 18/5 (September-October 1986). For some groups of teenagers, the failure rate is one in three. Elise S. Jones, et al., "Contraceptive Failure Rates Based on the 1988 NSFG," *Family Planning Perspectives* 24/1 (January-February 1992), pp. 12-15.

33. Consortium of State Physician Resource Councils, p. 2.

34. W. Cates and K. M. Stone, "Family Planning and Sexually Transmitted Diseases, and Contraceptive Choice." Cited in *Family Planning Perspectives* 24/2 (March-April 1992), pp. 75-84; "Condoms Won't Prevent Transmission of Human Papillomavirus," *Family Planning News*, 22/12 (June 1992).

35. S. Samuels, "Epidemic among America's Young," Medical Aspects of Human Sexuality 23/12 (December 1989), p. 16; T. Eng and W. T. Butler, eds., *The Hidden Epidemic: Confronting Sexually Transmitted Diseases* (Washington, D.C.: National Academy Press, 1996), pp. 2–5; B. Binns, et al. "Screening for Chlamydia Trachomatis Infection in a Pregnancy Counseling Clinic," *American Journal of Obstetrics and Gynecology* 37, p. 1144-49; M. J. Bythe, et al., "Recurrent Genitourinary Chlamydial Infections in Sexually Active Female Adolescents," *Journal of Pediatrics* 37, pp. 133-37.

36. Susan Weller, "A Meta-Analysis of Condom Effectiveness in Reducing Sexually Transmitted HIV," *Social Science & Medicine*, 36/12 (June 1993), pp. 1635–44.

37. Debra W. Haffner, "Safe Sex and Teens," *SIECUS Report*,

September–October 1988.

38. "Study Cites AIDS Danger from Oral Sex," Associated Press, February 2, 2000.

39. Participant in conference sponsored by New Jersey Abstinence Coalition, September, 1999.

40. "Lost Children of Rockdale County," *Frontline*, PBS, October 19, 1999.

41. Peggy Brick, "Towards a Positive Approach to Adolescent Sexuality," *SIECUS Report*, May–July 1989.

42. This program is rare in that funding exists to evaluate it regularly. Cited in David Rowberry, "An Evaluation of the Washington, D.C. Best Friends Program," doctoral dissertation, University of Colorado, Boulder, 1995.

43. Pregnancies declined from 46 pregnancies to 12, according to Patricia Funderburk Ware, then director of the Office of Adolescent Pregnancy Program of the U.S. Department of Health and Human Services.

44. *National Guidelines for Sexuality and Character Education*, p. 12.

45. Michael Resnick, et al., "Protecting Adolescents from Harm: The National Longitudinal Study on Adolescent Health," *Journal of the American Medical Association* 278 (September 10, 1997).

46. Joseph P. Allen and Gabe Kuperminc, "Programmatic Prevention of Adolescent Problem Behaviors: The Role of Autonomy, Relatedness, and Volunteer Service in the Teen Outreach Program." Cited in Jay Mathews, "Teenage Girls Who Work as Volunteers Are Less Likely to Get Pregnant, Study Finds," *The Washington Post*, August 28, 1997, p. A22.

47. Douglas Kirby, "No Easy Answers: Research Findings on Programs to Reduce Teen Pregnancy," National Campaign to Prevent Teen Pregnancy, Washington, D.C., March 1996.

48. Amelia Kreitzer, "Evaluation of the Loving Well Curriculum," CSTEEP, Boston College, December, 1992.

49. Ronald S. Goldman, "Using Literature to Teach Sexuality Education," *FLEducator* (Winter 1993-1994), p. 9.

50. Rowberry, "An Evaluation of the Washington, D.C. Best Friends Program."

51. Only 4 percent of these students had begun sexual intercourse on average, as opposed to 20 percent of comparable students in other schools who did not use an abstinence-oriented course.

52. Marion Howard and Judith B. McCabe, "Helping Teenagers Postpone Sexual Involvement," *Family Planning Perspectives* 22/1 (January–February 1990), pp. 21-26.

53. Northwestern University in 1994–95 evaluated two Project Reality programs. One was "Choosing the Best," tested with 5,800 middle school students from 65 schools and the other was "Facing Reality," with 1070 high school students from 11 schools, all in Illinois.

54. "Abstinence Evaluation Report '94–95," Project Reality, Golf, Illinois, 1996. The 1995–96 evaluation of "Choosing the Best" found similar results with over 2,500 13-16-year-old students. Pro-abstinence atti-

tudes were maintained one year later, even among those at higher risk. There were fewer students who had lost their virginity during that year, according to estimates. It was also found that the number of non-virginal youth who had had sex in the three previous weeks declined by one-fourth compared to the year earlier. John T. Vessey, "Choosing the Best: Abstinence-Centered Curriculum Longitudinal Study, 1995–1996," Illinois Department of Public Aid, 1997.

55. "Abstinence Regarded Best for Control of Spread of AIDS," *All Africa News Agency*, April 9, 1999, in *Africa News Online*.

56. Marci McDonald, "How to Reduce Teen Pregnancy: Voluntary Community Service," *U.S. News & World Report*, December 29, 1997, pp. 48-50.

57. William J. Bennett, *Our Children and Our Country* (New York: Simon & Schuster, 1988), p. 91.

58. *National Guidelines for Sexuality and Character Education.*

59. Thomas Lickona, "The Need for Character-based Sex Education," copies of document given at the annual Institute of the Center for the 4th and 5th Rs, Cortland, New York, 1997, p. 2.

60. Jonathan D. Klein, "The National Longitudinal Study on Adolescent Health: Preliminary Results: Great Expectations," *Journal of the American Medical Association* 278 (September 10, 1997), pp. 864–865.

61. "Character-Based Sex Education in Public Schools: A Position Statement," The Character Education Partnership, Alexandria, Virginia, September 1996; Lickona, "The Need for Character-based Sex Education," pp. 2–5.

62. James Coughlin, *Facing Reality: A Handbook for Healthy Living, Parent/Teacher Guide* (Golf, Illinois: Project Reality, 1990), pp. 18, 30.

63. Simone de Beauvoir, *The Second Sex*, trans. H. M. Parshley (New York: Alfred A. Knopf, 1952), p. 400.

64. Havelock Ellis, "The Evolution of Modesty," *Studies in the Psychology of Sex* 1 (Philadelphia: F.A. Davis, 1910), pp. 8–10, 12–14; Kurt Reizler, "Comment on the Social Pathology of Shame," *American Journal of Sociology* 48 (January 1943), p. 461. Cited in Wendy Shalit, *A Return to Modesty: Discovering the Lost Virtue* (New York: The Free Press, 1999), p. 67.

65. Wendy Shalit, *A Return to Modesty*, p. 205.

66. Daniel P. Moloney, "Eroticism Unbound," *First Things* (February 1999), pp. 13-15.

67. Teen-Aid, *Me, My World, My Future, Teachers Edition* (Spokane: Teen Aid, 1993), p. xi.

68. S. Thompson, "Search for Tomorrow: On Feminism and the Reconstruction of Teen Romance." Cited in Stephanie Schamess, "The Search for Love: Unmarried Adolescent Mothers' Views of, and Relationships with, Men," *Adolescence* 28 (Summer 1993), p. 425.

69. Personal conversation, April 1998.

70. *National Guidelines for Sexuality and Character Education.*

71. Jerry Melson, "Sexual Choices: Should You Wait?" *Teen Magazine*,

November 1994, p. 24.

72. Dan Habib, "Sex Talk," *Mother Jones*, January–February 1995, p. 44.

73. Focus on the Family, *No Apologies: The Truth about Life, Love and Sex, Teacher's Guide* (Colorado Springs, CO: Focus on the Family, 1999), pp. 6.1–6.23.

74. Mike Long, *Everyone Is Not Doing It* (Durham, NC: M.L. Video Productions, 1997), video, part 2.

75. Focus on the Family, *No Apologies*, p. 5.25

76. Alan Guttmacher Institute, *Sex and America's Teenagers* (New York: Alan Guttmacher Institute, 1994).

77. Roper Starch Worldwide, "Teens Talk about Sex" (New York: Sexuality Information and Education Council of the United States, 1994).

78. Joy Overbeck, "Sex Too Soon," *Parents*, September 1994, p. 42.

79. The "designated driver" campaign may seem like an "abstinence plus" solution. But does the designated driver function like a condom? The designated driver is unquestionably sober and reliable and furthermore, able to take initiative to keep the drinking friends safe. However, the condom is not free to act on behalf of the partners and it is not nearly so reliable. It may fail to get used—or be used incorrectly—and even if it gets employed it will still predictably fail a portion of the time. It is more like a sleeping driver who may or may not be summoned by his drunken friends or even if alert, drives so poorly that there is still significant danger.

80. Nell Bernstein, "Learning to Love," *Mother Jones*, January–February 1995, p. 44.

81. Leslee Unruh, presentation at a conference sponsored by Project Reality, Connecticut, September 9, 1997, paraphrased.

82. Prior to the initiative, the county had about 60 pregnancies out of 1,000 girls aged 14–17. In the second and third years of the program, the rate more than halved to 25 out of 1,000 among participating students while rates for non-participants remained about the same, as reported in the *Journal of the American Medical Association*. Its credibility was questioned by Planned Parenthood, which claimed condom distribution and referrals to family planning clinics by a school nurse were responsible for the results. However, this nurse's activities were unknown to most students and her efforts bore no such fruits before or after the period in question. Cited in Medical Institute for Sexual Health, *Sexual Health Update*, Spring 1988, p. 2.

83. Overbeck, "Sex Too Soon."

84. B. C. Miller and K. A. Moore, "Adolescent Sexual Behavior, Pregnancy and Parenting: Research through the '80s," *Journal of Marriage and Family* 52 (November 1990), pp. 1025–44; G. L. Fox, "The Family's Influence on Adolescent Sexual Behavior," *Child Today* 8/3 (1979), pp. 21–36. Cited in Lawrence E. Kay, "Adolescent Sexual Intercourse," *Undergraduate Medicine* 97 (June 1995), p. 123. Resnick, et al., "National Longitudinal Study on Adolescent Health."

85. Teen-Aid, *Sexuality, Commitment & Family: Senior High School* (Spokane, WA: Teen Aid, 1990), p. 113.
86. Bernstein, "Learning to Love."
87. "Sexuality and Abstinence Education Policies in the U.S. Public School Districts," Fact Sheet, Alan Guttmacher Institute, December 14, 1999; Study by the Kaiser Family Foundation, December 1999.
88. Bernstein, "Learning to Love."
89. Sexuality and Abstinance Education Policies in the U,S. Public School Districts," Fact Sheet, Alan Guttmacher Intitute, December 14, 1999; study by the Keiser Family Foundation, December 1999.

Chapter 27

1. William J. Bennett, *The De-Valuing of America* (New York: Simon & Schuster, 1994), p. 94.
2. For a pessimistic view of the effectiveness of programs in the late '80s, see D. M. Gorman, "The Irrelevance of Evidence in the Development of School-Based Drug Prevention Policy, 1986–1996," *Evaluation Review* 22/1 (1998), pp. 118-46.
3. In an examination of 119 demonstration studies, Lipsey et al. found that only 9 percent of drug programs were based on a theory that considered causal issues. See M. W. Lipsey, S. Crosse, J. Dunkle, L. Pollard and G. Stobart, "Evaluation: The State of the Art and the Sorry State of Science," in D. S. Cordray, ed., *Utilizing Prior Research in Evaluation Planning*, New Directions for Testing and Measurement No. 27 (San Francisco: Jossey-Bass, 1985), pp. 7-28.
4. H. T. Chen, "Issues in Constructing Program Theory," in L. Bickman, ed., *Advances in Program Theory* (San Fransisco: Jossey-Bass, 1990), pp. 7-18.
5. Marvin W. Berkowitz, "Character Education as Prevention," in W. B. Hansen, S. M. Giles, M. D. Fearnow-Kenney, eds., *Increasing Drug Prevention Effectiveness: Readings for Educators* (Clemmons, NC: Tanglewood Research, in press); V. Battistich, E. Schaps, M. Watson and D. Solomon, "Prevention Effects of the Child Development Project: Early Findings from an Ongoing Multisite Demonstration Trial," *Journal of Adolescent Research* 11 (1996), pp. 12-35.
6. W. B. Hansen, L. A. Rose and J. G. Dryfoos, "Causal Factors, Interventions and Policy Considerations in School-Based Substance Abuse Prevention," U.S. Congress, Office of Technology Assessment, Washington, D.C., May 26, 1993; G. J. Botvin and E. M. Botvin, "School-Based and Community-Based Prevention Approaches," in J. Lowinson, P. Ruiz and R. Millman, eds., *Comprehensive Textbook of Substance Abuse* (Baltimore: Williams & Wilkins, 1992), pp. 910-27; C. L. Perry and S. H. Kelder, "Models for Effective Prevention," *Journal of Adolescent Health* 13 (1992), pp. 355-63; R.L. Bangert-Drowns, "The Effects of School-Based Substance Abuse Education—

A Meta-Analysis," *Journal of Drug Education* 18 (1988), pp. 243-64; W. H. Bruvold, "A Meta-Analysis of the California School-Based Risk Reduction Program," *Journal of Drug Education* 20 (1990), pp. 139-52; N. S. Tobler, "Drug Prevention Programs Can Work: Research Findings," *Journal of Addiction Disorders* 11 (1992); pp. 1-28.

7. "What Makes Drug-Free Schools Work?" *Education Digest,* October 1992, pp. 46-49.

8. Michael D. Resnick, Peter S. Bearman, Robert W. Blum, et al., "Protecting Adolescents From Harm: Findings From the National Longitudinal Study on Adolescent Health," *Journal of the American Medical Association* 278 (1997), pp. 823-32.

9. Neil Travis, "Wanted: Junkie Role Model," *New York Post,* October 8, 1997.

10. "Capriati Is Shown the Exit," *New York Post,* May 29, 1996.

11. Michael E. Holstein, William E. Cohen and Paul J. Steinbroner, *A Matter of Balance* (CNS Publications, 1995); Philip L. Rice, *Stress and Health: Principles and Practice of Coping and Wellness* (Monterey, CA: Brooks/Cole, 1987).

12. Peter L. Benson, *All Kids Are Our Kids* (San Francisco: Jossey-Bass, 1997), p. xiv.

13. J. D. Hawkins, R. F. Catalano and J. Y. Miller, "Risk and Protective Factors in Alcohol and Other Drug Problems in Adolescence and Early Adulthood: Implications for Substance Abuse Prevention," *Psychological Bulletin* 112 (1992), pp. 64-105.

14. Martin W. Berkowitz, et al., "Adolescent Moral Reasoning and Substance Use," unpublished manuscript.

15. L. Nucci, N. Guerra and J. Lee, "Adolescent Judgments of the Personal, Prudential, and Normative Aspects of Drug Usage," *Developmental Psychology* 27 (1991):pp. 841-848; Marvin W. Berkowitz, J. Kahn, G. Mulry and J. Piette, "Psychological and Philosophical Considerations of Prudence and Morality," in M. Killen and D. Hart, eds., *Morality in Everyday Life: Developmental Perspectives* (New York: Cambridge, 1995); J. K. Giese, "The Role of Personal Meaning and Multiple Risk and Protective Factors in Adolescent Alcohol Abuse," unpublished dissertation, Marquette University, 1998.

16. G. J. Botvin and T. A. Wills, "Personal and Social Skills Training: Cognitive-Behavioral Approaches to Substance Abuse Prevention," in C. Bell and R. J. Battjes, eds., *Prevention Research: Deterring Drug Abuse among Children and Adolescents*, NIDA Research Monograph 62 (Washington, DC: U.S. Government Printing Office, 1985), pp. 8-49.

17. L. N. Robins and T. R. Przybeck, "Age of Onset of Drug Use as a Factor in Drug and Other Disorders," in C. L. Jones and R. J. Battjes, eds., *Etiology of Drug Abuse: Implications for Prevention*, NIDA Research Monograph 56, DHHS Publication No. ADM 85-1335 (Washington, DC: U.S. Government Printing Office, 1985), pp. 178-192.

18. E. E. Werner and R. S. Smith, *Vulnerable but Invincible* (New York: McGraw-Hill, 1982).

19. Developmental Studies Center, "Helping Students Resist Drugs, Alcohol, and Tobacco (Oakland, CA: Developmental Studies Center, 1998). V. Battistich, E. Schaps, M. Watson, D. Solomon and C. Lewis, "Effects of the Child Development Project on Students' Drug Use and Other Problem Behaviors," *Journal of Primary Prevention*, in press.

20. Bridget Murray, "Programs Go Beyond 'Just Saying No': Innovative Programs Teach Children the Skills they Need to Resist Substance Abuse," *American Psychological Association Monitor* http://www.apa.org/monitor/sep97/curb.html.

21. Werner and Smith, *Vulnerable but Invincible*; "The Courage to Change: A Perspective on Alcohol, Tobacco, and Other Drugs," Catholic Charities USA, 1994, p. 7.

22. "Marijuana and Youth, 'The Fact Is...'" *Join Together*, 1966.

23. D. R. Black, N. S. Tobler, et al., "Peer Helping/Involvement: an Efficacious Way to Meet the Challenge of Reducing Alcohol, Tobacco and other Drug Use Among Youth?" *Journal of School Health* 68 (1998), pp. 87-94.

24. William J. Bennett, John J. DiIulio, Jr. and John P. Waters, *Body Count* (New York: Simon & Schuster, 1996), p. 61.

25. "The Relationship between Family Variables and Adolescent Substance Abuse: A Literature Review," *Adolescence* 29 (Summer 1994), p. 4; J. S. Brook, D. W. Brook, A. S. Gordon, M. Whiteman and P. Cohen, "The Psychosocial Etiology of Adolescent Drug Use: A Family Interactional Approach," *Genetic, Social, and General Psychology Monographs* 116 (1990); D. B. Kandel and K. Andrews, "Processes of Adolescent Socialization by Parents and Peers," *International Journal of the Addictions* 22 (1987), pp. 319-42.

26. Herting Eggert, "Preventing Teenage Drug Abuse," *Youth & Society* (June 1991), p. 491.

27. *Drugs and Our Youth*, International Educational Foundation, unpublished.

28. G. W. Peterson and G. K. Leigh, "The Family and Social Competence in Adolescence," in T. Gullotta, G. R. Adams and R. Montemayor, eds., *Advances in Adolescent Development: Social Competence* (Newbury Park, CA: Sage Publications, 1990), pp. 97-138; D. Rosenthal, T. Nelson and N. Drake, "Adolescent Substance Use and Abuse: a Family Context," in G. K. Leigh and G. W. Peterson, eds., *Adolescents in Families* (Cincinnati: South-Western, 1986), pp. 337-57.

29. A. R. Anderson and C. S. Henry, "Family Systems Characteristics and Parental Behaviors as Predictors of Adolescent Substance Abuse," *Adolescence* 29 (1994), pp. 405-20.

30. R. H. Coombs and J. Landsverk, "Parenting Styles and Substance Use During Childhood and Adolescence," *Journal of Marriage and the Family* 50 (1988), pp. 473-82; J. D. Hawkins, R. F. Catalano and J. Y. Miller, "Risk and Protective Factors in Alcohol and Other Drug

Problems in Adolescence and Early Adulthood: Implications for Substance Abuse Prevention," *Psychological Bulletin* 112 (1992), pp. 64-105.

31. "What Works, Schools without Drugs," U.S. Department of Education, 1992, p. 14.
32. G. M. Barnes, "Impact of the Family on Adolescent Drinking Patterns," in R. L. Collins, K. E. Leonard and J. S. Searles, eds., *Alcohol and the Family: Research and Clinical Perspectives* (New York: Guilford, 1990), pp. 137-62.
33. J. D. Hawkins, R. F. Catalano and J. Y. Miller, "Risk and Protective Factors in Alcohol and Other Drug Problems in Adolescence and Early Adulthood: Implications for Substance Abuse Prevention," *Psychological Bulletin* 112 (1992), pp. 64-105; G. M. Barnes and J. Welte, "Patterns and Predictors of Alcohol Use among 7th-12th Grade Students in New York State," *Journal of Studies on Alcohol* 47 (1986), pp. 53-62.
34. Black and Tobler, "Peer Helping/Involvement"; T. L. St. Pierre and M. M. Mark, "Involving Parents of High-Risk Youth in Drug Prevention: A Three-Year Longitudinal Study in Boys and Girls Clubs," *Journal of Early Adolescence* 17 (1997), pp. 21-51.
35. K. Johnson, M. Berbaum, D. Bryant and G. Bucholtz, "Evaluation of Creating Lasting Connections—A Program to Prevent Alcohol and other Drug Abuse among High Risk Youth: Final Evaluation Report," Louisville, KY: Urban Research Institute, 1995.
36. Black and Tobler, "Peer Helping/Involvement," reviewed assessments of 120 adolescent drug prevention school-based programs conducted in North America.
37. "What Makes Drug-Free Schools Work?" *Education Digest*, October 1992, pp. 46-49.
38. G. J. Botvin, E. Baker, E. M. Botvin, A.D. Filazzola and R. B. Millman, "Prevention of Alcohol Misuse through the Development of Personal and Social Competence: A Pilot Study," *Journal of Studies on Alcohol* 45 (1984), pp. 550-52.
39. Black and Tobler, "Peer Helping/Involvement."
40. K. A. Komro, C. L. Perry, S. Veblen-Moretenson and C. L. Williams, *Journal of School Health* 64/8 (1994), pp. 318-22.
41. "Changing Lives: Programs that Make a Difference for Youth at Risk," U.S. Department of Health and Human Services, CSAP, 1995.
42. "What Works, Schools without Drugs," U.S. Department of Education, 1992, p. 37.
43. National Assembly of State Arts Agencies, 1010 Vermont Avenue, Suite 920, Washington, DC 20005; 1995. (Available from the National Clearinghouse for Alcohol and Drug Information, P.O. Box 2345, Rockville, MD 20847; e-mail: info@health.org.)
44. Drug Abuse Prevention website: www.scsl.state.sc.us/sde/reports/echred4.htm. This site reviews programs in South Carolina schools that provide skills to enable stu-

dents to make anti-drug choices.

45. Center for Substance Abuse Prevention, "Prevention Works! A Case Study of Alternative Programs," National Clearinghouse for Alcohol and Drug Information, P.O. Box 2345, Rockville, MD 20847, e-mail: info@health.org.

46. Bridget Murray, "Programs Go Beyond 'Just Saying No.'"

47. Ibid.

48. R. Mathias, "Novelty Seekers and Drug Abusers Tap Same Brain Reward System, Animal Studies Show," *NIDA Notes,* July–August 1995, pp. 1-4.

Chapter 28

1. Gordon G. Vessels, *Character and Community Development: A School Planning and Teacher Training Handbook* (Westport, CT: Praeger, 1998), pp. 136-138.

2. Judith S. Wallerstein and Sandra Blakeslee, *The Good Marriage* (New York: Warner, 1996), p. 93.

3. In spite of his own usage of slaves, Jefferson's early drafts of the Declaration of Independence denounced slavery. Bruce Lancaster and J. H. Plumb, *The American Heritage Book of the Revolution* (New York: Dell, 1958) p. 147.

4. James Thomas Flexner, *Washington: The Indispensable Man* (New York: Little, Brown and Company, 1974) p. 386.

5. John Grafton, ed., *Abraham Lincoln, Great Speeches* (New York: Dover, 1991), p. 107.

6. Steven Stosny, *The Miracle of Empowered Love,* unpublished, 1997.

7. Peter Forsbrig, Columbine student, speaking on "Talking It Out" with John Donovan, *ABC News,* April 23, 1999.

8. Jonathan Dube, "High School Hell," *ABC News,* April 28, 1999.

9. *60 Minutes,* March 13, 2000.

10. Martin Luther King, Jr., *Strength to Love* (Philadelphia: Fortress, 1963), p. 49.

11. Kay Pranis, "Moral Education in Restorative Practices," conference of the Association for Moral Education, University of Minnesota, November 18-21, 1999.

12. Marian L. Vollmer, Ellen B. Drook, and Patricia J. Harnet, "Partnering Character Education and Conflict Resolution," *Kappa Delta Pi Record* (Spring 1999), pp. 122-25.

13. S. Dinwiddie, "The Saga of Sally, Sammy and the Red Pen: Facilitating Children's Social Problem Solving," *Young Children,* July 13-19, 1994.

14. F. Schmidt, A. Freidman, and J. Marvel, *Mediation for Kids: Kids in Dispute Settlement* (Miami Beach, FL: Grace Contrino Abrams Peace Education Foundation, 1992).

15. Howard Zehr and Harry Mika, "Fundamental Concepts of Restorative

Justice," Mennonite Central Committee publication, 1997.

16. Carol Tavris, "Anger Defused," *Perspectives on Marriage, A Reader*, Kieran Scott and Michael Warren, eds. (New York: Oxford University Press, 1993), p. 231.

17. Quoted in Harville Hendrix and Helen Hunt, *The Couples Companion: Meditations and Exercises for Getting the Love You Want* (New York: Pocket Books, 1994), p. 331.

18. Kay Pranis, "Victims in the Peacemaking Circle Process," *The Crime Victim Report* (September–October 1999), p. 63.

Index

About the Contributors

Tony Devine is the vice-president of the International Educational Foundation, an organization promoting holistic character education. Holder of a Masters in Education, in the late 1980s he developed and directed international exchange programs between the former Soviet Union and the United States. Mr. Devine gives presentations and training to educators, family experts and community leaders on current insights in character, marriage and family, and adolescent life skills education, and the interrelationships among these fields. His advocacy efforts have taken him throughout Europe and Asia, and he has been a featured speaker in national character education conferences in the United States.

Josephine Hauer has earned a Masters degree from Harvard University and is currently completing a doctoral dissertation at the University of Bridgeport. Her current research involves empirical evaluation of innovative character education practices on the moral development of Russian adolescents. Ms. Hauer co-founded a private elementary school in Connecticut and has been the Academic Dean of a high school specializing in moral education since 1997. She has taught English, Social Studies and Ethics for 9-12th grades. She frequently consults with both public and private schools on character-based program development, teacher training and curriculum infusion both locally and abroad.

June Saunders is the author of *Boundless as the Sea: A Guide to Family Love* (1997). She has presented papers on marriage, family and character issues at schools and conferences in America and overseas. She is a wife and mother of two sons and runs a women's support group on marriage and family matters. With her B.A. in English from the University of Iowa, where she was a member of the Writers Workshop, Ms. Saunders is particularly concerned with the moral impact of literature on young readers and advocates for an enriched literature program in schools and homes.

Dr. Joon Ho Seuk is the president of the International Educational Foundation. He holds a doctorate in public administration and oversees the organization of numerous international conferences for educational, family, community and cultural leaders in Russia, China and other countries. He has co-edited various textbooks on moral education, most notably *Family Ethics and Character Education*, published this year by the China Academy of Social Sciences, and he has directed the development of the widely used Russian character education texts, *First Peak* and *I in the World of People*. A native of Korea who lives in New York, Dr. Seuk has been working to integrate Eastern and Western values for the contemporary world.

John R. Williams is the editor of multimedia curricula on character-based abstinence, marriage and family education and has been a featured speaker at marriage and abstinence education seminars. He is co-author and editor of *Love, Life and Family*, a high school resource manual on sexuality and marriage education for teachers and administrators. With Cathy, his wife of 18 years, Mr. Williams provides couple mentoring. He holds degrees in education, sociology and history.

Dr. Andrew Wilson has a Ph.D. from Harvard University and teaches Moral Theology and Biblical Studies in upstate New York. His long-standing concern for inter-cultural ethics led him to produce *World Scripture: A Comparative Anthology of Sacred Texts* (1991), a widely used text that highlights the shared values and common ground among the world's religions. He wrote on the moral ideals of the family in *True Family Values* (1996) in addition to numerous other books and articles on ethics, education and culture.